# INDIA IN
# AFRICA
## AFRICA IN
# INDIA

# INDIA IN AFRICA

# AFRICA IN INDIA

Indian Ocean Cosmopolitanisms

EDITED BY

JOHN C. HAWLEY

*Indiana University Press*

BLOOMINGTON AND INDIANAPOLIS

This book is a publication of

Indiana University Press
601 North Morton Street
Bloomington, IN 47404-3797 USA

http://iupress.indiana.edu

| | |
|---|---|
| *Telephone orders* | 800-842-6796 |
| *Fax orders* | 812-855-7931 |
| *Orders by e-mail* | iuporder@indiana.edu |

The paper used in this publication meets
the minimum requirements of American
National Standard for Information
Sciences—Permanence of Paper for
Printed Library Materials,
ANSI Z39.48-1984.

Manufactured in the United States of America

Library of Congress Cataloging-in-Publication Data

India in Africa, Africa in India : Indian Ocean
cosmopolitanisms / edited by John C. Hawley.
    p. cm.
  Includes bibliographical references and index.
  ISBN-13: 978-0-253-35121-0 (cloth)
  ISBN-13: 978-0-253-21975-6 (pbk.)
    1. India—Relations—Africa.   2. Africa—
Relations—India.   I. Hawley, John C.
(John Charles), 1947–
  DS450.A35I66   2008
  303.48'26054—dc22        2007047747

1  2  3  4  5  13  12  11  10  09  08

To the memory of
MOHANDAS GANDHI,
PHASWANE MPE,
and
K. SELLO DUIKER

My opinion is that there are many things we could learn from India and other Asian countries, just as they have much to learn from us. . . . You know, it is thought by some that some Indians are of African descent. . . . I have a theory that the coastline of the Indian Ocean was once a cultural highway with constant migrations and exchange.

Kamĩtĩ, in Ngũgĩ wa Thiong'o's *Wizard of the Crow*

# CONTENTS

# ACKNOWLEDGMENTS

Pashington Obeng's article, "Religion and Empire: Belief and Identity among African Indians of Karnataka, South India," originally appeared in the *Journal of the American Academy of Religion* 71.1 (2003): 99–120. Permission from its publisher, Oxford University Press, to reprint is gratefully acknowledged.

Many thanks for the generous support of Don Dodson, associate provost at Santa Clara University, and the enthusiastic support of the book from Rebecca Tolen at Indiana University Press. Thanks, as well, to Lee Cassanelli, Howard Spodek, Ned Alpers, Jesse J. Benjamin, Shihan de Silva Jayasuriya, and Ned Bertz for early discussions of the book's topics.

# INDIA IN
# AFRICA
# AFRICA IN
# INDIA

# Introduction

*Unrecorded Lives*

John C. Hawley

When anthropology student (and later, novelist) Amitav Ghosh set out from Oxford to Egypt in 1980 to find a suitable subject for his research, he may not have suspected the impact the trip would have on his life. He succeeded in completing the required tome for his degree and then went on to write *In an Antique Land* (1992), an unusually constructed book that deals with themes of historical and cultural displacement, with alienation and something we might these days, under the influence of postcolonial theory, call "subaltern cosmopolitanism." Others might recognize the genre in which Ghosh is writing as one we have all tried our hand at, in one form or another: a record of discomfort in confronting the inconsistencies of another person's—the "other" person's—reality. The book is hardly recognizable as a novel; nor is it simply a historical investigation, since it blends an anthropological record with a travelogue, a diary, and speculations. "Within the parameters of history," Ghosh told one interviewer, "I have tried to capture a story, a narrative, without attempting to write a historical novel. You may say, as a writer, I have ventured on a technical innovation" (Dhawan 1999: 24). In *India in Africa, Africa in India* we

1

are attempting a parallel "innovation": using what we know of the past to inform our understanding of the present Indian Ocean world; examining today's imaginative interpretations of India by Africans and Africa by Indians to speculate on how, historically, these regions understood each other.

Ghosh gathered evidence relating to a Jewish merchant operating in the twelfth century in Aden, and he was seeking to document, more remarkably, the merchant's barely recoverable Indian slave. In the process, Ghosh learns as much about the interpretation his visit gets from the Africans he meets as he does about the merchant Ben Yiju's reception in India and the role of the slave "Bomma" in the world of Indian Ocean commerce seven hundred or so years ago—for Ghosh was as much an object of fascination to the Egyptians as they were to him. There has been a coming and going for centuries, sometimes enforced, sometimes enthusiastically entered into, and one might have thought that this would have made for greater understanding among the various parties. But exactly the opposite was the case when the young doctoral student sat across from the aged imam in the Egyptian village and was told by him to stop doing the strange things that the villagers had heard were done by Hindus. Did his people bury their dead, or cremate them, he was asked. Was he circumcised? Did they worship cows? Is there military service for all in India, as there is in Egypt? Why did they not "purify" (i.e., infibulate or circumcise) their women? In fact, the imam and his villagers seemed to encourage him to remain apart from them, making sure that the young interloper did not enjoy the sense of community that they created during Ramadan. As Ghosh puts it, "to belong to that immense community was a privilege they had to re-earn every year, and the effort made them doubly conscious of the value of its boundaries" (A. Ghosh 1992: 76).

These defensive lines in the sand brought Amitav Ghosh to the depressing conclusion that Indians and Africans were now "delegates from two superseded civilizations." He had been constantly objectified by the Muslims in the villages, constantly made to feel ridiculous for the "reprehensible" practices that the Egyptians had been told were typical of the Hindus. He tried for months to be allowed to visit this crusty old religious leader, and when they finally sit down together, he records that both Indians and Africans, with such a long history of cooperation and exchange on various levels, now built walls of intolerance against each other, as though they were competitors for scraps at the table:

> [W]e understood each other perfectly. We were both traveling . . . in the West. . . . [I]t seemed to me that the Imam and I had participated in our own final defeat, in the dissolution of the centuries of dialogue that had

linked us. . . . We had acknowledged that it was no longer possible to speak, as Ben Yiju or his Slave, or any one of the thousands of travelers who had crossed the Indian Ocean in the Middle Ages might have done: of things that were right, or good, or willed by God; it would have been merely absurd for either of us to use those words, for they belonged to a dismantled rung on the ascending ladder of Development. (A. Ghosh 1992: 236–37)

"Traveling in the West" is a stunning description of the apparently complete domination of world commerce and cultural motifs by the United States and its economic partners, and the impact this continues to have on the peoples on the periphery.[1] Partha Chatterjee argues elsewhere that, whereas "most countries in Asia have become deeply entangled with the global economy in the last ten or fifteen years [including India] . . . nearly half of the countries of Africa seem to have lost their connections with international trade. Thus, one thing is clear: globalization is not some great carnival of capital, technology, and goods where we are all free to walk away with what we want" (Chatterjee 2004: 85–86). The imam and the young Ghosh were well aware of the impact this has had on relations among the "lesser" players on the world stage, despite their own prominence in former centuries.[2]

Some Indians reading Ghosh's account of Egyptians scrutinizing the young writer might wince, recalling that barely eight years before his uncomfortable trip Uganda had expelled its Indian citizens with breathtaking speed and, some have argued, with national relief. The role of the Indian merchant in Uganda and elsewhere in Africa had been a contentious issue since the time of British occupation, and even if several generations had followed that earlier time of arguable manipulation of one group against another, scapegoating Indians served Idi Amin's strategies for self-preservation. For those who lived through it, the memories are sharp, lasting—and conflicted. As Jameela Siddiqi (n.d.) puts it, "the vast majority of Asians never thought of Uganda as home. But when ousted heartlessly [in August 1972]—and inhumanly—many cried bitter tears of fury for the 'homeland' from which they were being forcibly evicted. It took an expulsion to make Uganda feel like home." A student at Makerere University at the time, Siddiqi recalls that "the vast majority of educated, and reasonable-minded Black Ugandans were actually very supportive of Amin's decision. . . . The only Black Ugandans who were genuinely upset at the Asian expulsion were the very poor ones, many of whom were employed in Asian businesses and homes." In Nairobi, meanwhile, according to Trevor Grundy (2002), "the mood among Kenya's much larger and even more powerful Indian community was of good-humored incredulity"—but that humor soon changed when they saw that Ugandan Indians were being forced to leave with less than fifty pounds sterling and two suitcases of possessions per family.

If we were to shift our focus now, and in our imaginations see thousands of Africans in the Middle Ages and later who made the journey to Pakistan, India, and Sri Lanka, we would find a history as troubled—though not as well known—as that of the Indians in Africa. It would be multi-layered, still controversial in interpretation, richly variegated across geographical borders, of individuals and communities either assimilated into local Indian cultures, or standing apart as defiantly African ( for their history, see, in this volume, Singh, Obeng, Oka and Kusimba, and McLeod; elsewhere, see Basu 1998, 2005; Chauhan 1995; Chaudhuri 1985, 1990; Risso 1995, Catlin-Jairazbhoy and Alpers 2004, and Robbins and McLeod 2006). In some contexts these Indians of African heritage are called Habshis (*habashi* designating people of Abyssinian heritage in Arabic/Persian dictionaries); more frequently they are referred to as Sidis, possibly from a northern African term of respect, an honorific term specially coined to designate respected descendants of loyal defenders of Muslim rulers in India, or an association with black sainthood (Basu 2005: 5).[3] They came in several shifts and for varying purposes, many in the 1100s, with the largest numbers arriving in the 1600s. Some were slaves; others, merchants. Over time, some groups ruled specific areas. Nowadays there are about 30,000 in Gujarat, Andhra Pradesh, Karnataka, and Kerala. Their social position in India is the subject of several of this volume's essays (see, especially, Oka/Kusimba, Obeng, and McLeod).

The position of Sidis in Indian society is complex: among the Sidis themselves there is a mix of pride in their African musical heritage, in their particular form of Islam, and in their special gifts of emotional expression (Basu 1998: 119–35), countered by a suspicion by some of them that they are, in fact, seen by fellow citizens as non-Indian (Caitlin-Jairazbhoy 2004: xii). Among other Indians, they are sometimes looked down upon as low caste (Basu 2005: 5); they are, some argue, neglected by the government (Caitlin-Jairazbhoy 2004: xiii–iv), yet in some districts they have been accorded status as a Scheduled Tribe (Chowdhury 2005: 1).

The history of relations between communities surrounding the Indian Ocean remains something of a "hidden transcript" in our world, though the historical record of these encounters has drawn lively academic interest in recent years.[4] Joseph Harris noted in 1971 that there were comparatively fewer studies of African Indians than there were of Indian Africans, perhaps because, as Amy Catlin-Jairazbhoy and Edward Alpers surmise, "the slave trade from East Africa to India did not become the kind of grand enterprise that developed from West Africa to the Americas" (Caitlin-Jairazbhoy and Alpers 2004: 13). Careful records were not kept.

Many of the slaves converted to Islam and adopted new names. Today, though, "an explosion of interest (relatively speaking) in African Indians" can be explained by the increasing communalization in India that "has put the Sidis themselves on alert, making at least a few of them more self-conscious of their identity as African Indians and others of the inherent tension between being both African and Indian" (17).

In any case, Alpers has demonstrated that all parts of the Western Indian Ocean were connected at least as long as the first century (Alpers 2004: 27), and archaeological evidence suggests that contacts go back as far as the Harappa Civilization (2600–1760 BC). In the Persian Gulf and Arabia, most Africans were enslaved (Alpers 1997); during the era of Muslim domination in India, Africans played a significant role as military slaves (Alpers 2004: 31),[5] and the Portuguese, English, and French later used African slaves as both servants and soldiers in India (2004: 34). And the movement was not simply one-way, from Africa to India: Alpers notes that a group of African Christians near Mombasa were known as "Bombay Africans" (35).

Entering into this revitalized conversation, the contributors to our volume confirm that the exchange between Africa and India has been well established over centuries. But they also demonstrate that it remains vibrant today. Several of the essayists offer specific examples in support of the recent book by Sugata Bose which, in focusing on the period between 1830 and 1970, contends that the Indian Ocean continues to be a "system or arena" (Bose 2006: 13–14).[6] Bose suggests that it always retained a vibrant symbiotic relationship with the colonizer that allowed it to function with a continuing internal consistency and independence (31), as it continues to do. "The peoples of the Indian Ocean," he writes, "made their own history, albeit not without having to contend with economic exploitation and political oppression, and the oceanic space supplied a key venue for articulating different universalisms from the one to which Europe claimed monopoly" (273).[7]

In this volume we present the facts of these encounters between India and Africa over the centuries: we present them as a history of displacement, of re-rootedness in a new place, of cultural challenge and cross-fertilization. In the process of this exposition of the relevant history, two larger questions regarding other such migrations run as an undercurrent throughout the book. First among them is the issue of how one defines oneself or one's nation against the backdrop of a new geography; second is the question of how this long history of interchange between India and Africa might still inform contemporary discussions of globalization. Taken together, these questions suggest that the Indian Ocean world offers a philosophical challenge to the hegemony of Western modernity.

### The Need to Claim One's (African or Indian) Home

Consider Amitava Kumar's recent collection *Away* (2004), subtitled *The Indian Writer as an Expatriate.* The book demonstrates that one's origins are today increasingly imaginary and garbled. Giorgio Agamben notes that "the birth-nation link has no longer been capable of performing its legitimating function inside the nation-state, and the two terms have begun to show themselves to be irreparably loosened from each other" (Agamben 1998: 131–32). As evidence, consider the musings in the fiction of Abdulrazak Gurnah and M. G. Vassanji. Responding to a reporter's question about why he wrote *The Gunny Sack* about his native land of Tanzania, Canadian writer Moyez Vassanji remarks:

> I think all people should have a sense of themselves, a sense of where they come from, and it just happens that people in East Africa—I think Indians as well as Africans and especially in Tanzania—don't have a sense, a historical sense, of where they come from. . . . [I]f you just compare it with what goes on in the West, where everything is recorded, you can see that *our lives have not been recorded* (Nasta 2004: 70; emphasis added)[8]

Asked a similar question about why *he* writes stories, Zanzibar novelist Abdulrazak Gurnah notes that his writing "began from a sense of being loose or adrift," and his memory itself becomes his subject:

> You don't always remember accurately and you begin to recall things you didn't even know you remembered. Sometimes such gaps are filled in so convincingly that they become something "real." . . . At first it might seem like this is a bit of a lie; in reality what you are doing is reconstructing yourself in the light of things that you remember. (Nasta 2004: 353)

With such artists trying to "re-construct" something that may never have existed for these individuals (stories told to them, bits and shards of personal experience), our essayists attempt to imagine an Indian Ocean culture—partially localized in Africa and India, but existing, as well, wherever contemporary Indians and Africans now live. In what ways is conversation between and among Indians and Africans still ongoing, and how constructive is it?

Does the concept of India speak to Africans, and the concept of Africa speak to Indians?[9] If essays here by Campbell and Obeng examine an arguably successful assimilation of Africans into Indian society (though the writers may disagree about the depth of that acceptance), those by Nair and Govinden underscore the subterranean tensions that ground the Indian reception in Africa. May Joseph elsewhere writes movingly of the "performance" of citizenship that such migrants often feel is required of them even if their families have lived in the adopted country for several generations.[10] Can (and should) pan-Indianism find common cause in pan-Africanism?[11] Many of the essays in this collection deal with literature and the creative arts, the world of the imagination, the world that expands beyond national boundaries and finds a home in unlikely places—"Indian" dance, however that may be conceived, in Senegal; "African" music in India, and thereby in the Indian diaspora in Africa and beyond. Writing in 1997, Brian Larkin notes that, "for over thirty years Indian films, their stars and fashions, music and stories have been a dominant part of everyday popular culture in northern Nigeria" (406). Such cultural exchange is elaborated upon in Gwenda Vander Steene's article in our collection and suggests that Africans and Indians continue to fascinate each other, fully independent of what may be going on in Europe or America.

### The Lure of the Global

Aihwa Ong describes a "flexible citizenship" in the twenty-first-century interchange among mainly well-educated and financially privileged international travelers, but this class's glorification of hybridity is criticized by others as self-serving (e.g., Revathi Krishnaswamy 1995: Meenakshi Mukherjee 1971; Tim Brennan 2001). As Bishnupriya Ghosh writes, "the endless troping of mobility, hybridity, travel, nomadism, and flexibility in postcolonial critical theory, despite all claims of resistance to oppressive political and economic regimes, finally serves to flatten structural antagonisms and make light of abiding cultural differences" (B. Ghosh 2004: 20). A discussion of cosmopolitanism without the inflection of status shows that it shares a family resemblance to the concept of alternative modernities so that, in contrast to the *jouissance* in slipping the yoke of one's national bonds, Samir Dayal can offer Amitav Ghosh's *In an Antique Land* as proof that "cosmopolitanism is not to be claimed as exclusively the fruit of Western expansionism."[12] The larger world is indeed increasingly "flat," in Thomas Friedman's sense, but the Indian Ocean world exemplifies the smaller "worlds" that have for many centuries shared a sophisticated knowledge of other cultures as daily factors in their lives.

The present collection of essays supports Dayal's thesis. As Kwame Anthony Appiah argues, "Thoroughgoing ignorance about the ways of others is largely a privilege of the powerful. The well-traveled polyglot is as likely to be among the worst off as among the best off—as likely to be found in a shantytown as at the Sorbonne. So cosmopolitanism shouldn't be seen as some exalted attainment: it begins with the simple idea that in the human community, as in national communities, we need to develop habits of coexistence: conversation in its older meaning, of living together, association"

(2007: xviii–xix). Janet Abu-Lughod provides a useful summary of the countervailing history that supports a less Eurocentric (and now, U.S.-centered) understanding of that term.[13] In light of the long history of commerce that she describes, *India in Africa, Africa in India* floats the notion of a globalization from below (from the global south, in one imaginary; from subalterns, in another). Such revisualization, still inevitably caught up in the historical ramifications of the terms upon which it must rely, prompts a series of interrelated questions that various of our essayists here address: how, for example, was the general sense of an expanding cultural and mercantile exchange experienced differently in Indian Ocean trade of earlier centuries compared to that of today's global market?

If we seek to de-link cosmopolitanism from "the Modern" in this volume's essays, it is because we follow Wai Chee Dimock's notion of "deep time," the idea that "the continuum of historical life does not grant the privilege of autonomy to any spatial locale . . . [and neither does it] grant the privilege of autonomy to any temporal segment" (Dimock 2006: 4). Following Fernand Braudel and the *Annales* school, Dimock argues that scale enlargement, viewed as an alternative to standard national histories, "changes our very sense of the connectedness among human beings. . . . [so that] the subnational and the transnational come together here in a loop, intertwined in a way that speaks as much to local circumstances as it does to global circuits" (5, 23). The essays in this volume, therefore, consider a cosmopolitanism that has been long established between India and Africa, that is not tied to high social class, and that precedes the concept of the nation-state.

### Social Science and the Humanities in Conversation

Michael Pearson asks his readers to see "the seas and shores of the Indian Ocean as being a discrete unit that can be investigated like a state, or a city, or a ruler" (1998: 8), and draws a conclusion that may surprise many: namely, that "the mere presence of Europeans in other parts of the world did not ipso facto 'make a difference'" (9). Which leads to a question central to our volume: what of the presence of Africans in India, or Indians in Africa—to what extent did they (and do they) make a "difference"?

This returns us to our earlier question about the impact of geography on one's sense of origin. In this volume's first substantive essay, Gwyn Campbell discusses the anthropological and sociological ramifications of slave trading and other forces that brought Africans to India in the first place. Campbell's argument echoes the anthropological perspective advocated by Aradhana Sharma and Akhil Gupta, who note that "cultural struggles determine what a state means to its people, how it is instantiated in their daily lives, and where its boundaries are drawn" (2006: 11). But in Devarakshanam (Betty) Govinden's very personal essay that follows Campbell's, the state seems hardly relevant: Govinden instead recuperates a whole generation's history by discussing her family's roots in South Africa, echoing some of the perceptions touched upon in Amitav Ghosh's *In an Antique Land*. What value did the state have in her family's life and sense of itself as African? Seeking some middle ground between the two essays, Savita Nair next explores local and under-explored levels of contact between individuals, broadly grouped as Asian, European, and African, as an alternative to formal activities at the Colonial Office and India Office. Looking at Kenyan court cases from 1918 to 1920, Nair shows that Kenyan Indians' subordinate position was complicated by Britain's imperial and administrative control over Indians in India. Due to British Indian ascendancy, British administrative control of Indians in East Africa was becoming less clear—most of all, to the Indian expatriate community. This was all doubly infuriating, since Indians had been in East Africa longer than Europeans, as accepted plainly in Churchill's defense of Indian claims to rights. The economic definition and implications of being "middlemen" may have been apparent, but Indian self-referential understanding of social place and worth was far from "middle" and far from apparent. These first three essays focus principally on the legal constraints in the lives of Indians and Africans.

Almost directly as a response to these constraints, Anjali Gera Roy, Gwenda Vander Steene, and Dana Rush demonstrate how the arts offer a more democratic access to the control of "India," in its various incarnations, by today's Africans. The section concludes by discussing "the space between," the various island communities of the Indian Ocean, here represented by Mauritius, east of Madagascar, and Sri Lanka. Thangam Ravindranathan offers a fascinating analysis of the dilemma of an uprootedness and tenuous nationality that continues for generations, roughly paralleling Amitav Ghosh's recent novel about the Sundarbans, *The Hungry Tide* (2004), and the "restrained melancholy" of a "dismembered posthumous journey" that dominates Ravindranathan's haunting historical recuperation of the doubly sited Benares. These essays chart the impact on one's psyche of being away from home.

Our book's second geographical section deals with the African diaspora in the Indian Ocean world. Rahul C. Oka and Chapurukha M. Kusimba discuss the role commerce played in this traffic. Once the Africans had arrived in India, by whatever means, acculturation became the leading issue for their community. The next two essays deal with aspects of that accommodation: Pashington Obeng notes the place of religion in their history and in our own times, and John McLeod looks at contemporary influences of marriage practices among the Sidi. As a parallel to the earlier section on the arts, Jaspal Singh concludes the section by discussing the continuing fascination that "Africa" elicits from contemporary movie-goers as it is imagined by Indians not of African descent.

Elsewhere Malcolm Waters describes globalization as being the "direct consequence of the expansion of European culture across the planet via settlement, colonization and cultural mimesis" (Waters 1995: 3). But how European is the global system today—or, for that matter, in earlier ages when the Indian Ocean world did rather well for itself without European dominance? In this volume we turn to the Indian Ocean world as an intriguing sphere of mutual exchange on economic and cultural levels that continues to run parallel to the current dominance of the West: in a word, we are looking at alternate universalisms, analogous to the discourse communities that hold together Latin American cultures, Eastern European, Western Asian, Southeast Asian histories—"global" histories defined by preoccupations other than those of the West.

When Gandhi arrived in South Africa he says that he expressed a desire to study the conditions of Indians there, and that his first step was to call a meeting of all the Indians in Pretoria and "to present to them a picture of their condition in the Transvaal" (Kumar 2004: 113). He had been greeted by white South Africans as a "coolie barrister" and saw that he was to be treated much the same as the black South Africans were treated. After a while, he says, he "made an intimate study of the hard condition of the Indian settlers, not only by reading and hearing about it, but by personal experience. [He] saw that South Africa was no country for a self-respecting Indian, and [his] mind became more and more occupied with the question as to how this state of things might be improved" (117). The speech in Pretoria, as he recalls it, was the first public speech of his life (113) and may, perhaps, serve as a fitting reminder that the ramifications of the interchange between India and Africa have extended, and continue to extend, far beyond the common shores of the Indian Ocean. The book is dedicated to his memory, and also to that of Phaswane Mpe and K. Sello Duiker, whose short lives embodied "the hard condition" of many in today's Indian Ocean world.

### Notes

1. Michael Peter Smith and Luis Eduardo Guarnizo argue that those who might resist the globalizing juggernaut are complicit in its inequities: "the enduring asymmetries of domination, inequality, racism, sexism, class conflict, and uneven development in which transnational practices are embedded and which they sometimes even perpetuate" (2002: 6).

2. Scholars such as Paulin Hountondji (1997) make the case for a pre-colonial African epistemology, and for Africa as an independent source of knowledge. We acknowledge, of course, with Philip D. Curtin, that even those who consciously set out to avoid their own ethnocentric biases cannot help but stumble and fall (Curtin 1984: x). See also George 2003: 196.

3. There is little agreement among scholars on the spelling of the term, with most opting either for *Sidi* or *Siddi*, but not to be confused with the Hindi *Siddhi*. In the present volume, we have generally chosen the shorter spelling unless we are quoting or using someone's formal name. See note 1 in chapter 11 by Jaspal Singh in this volume.

4. James C. Scott elsewhere advocates "the analysis of the hidden transcripts of [both] the powerful and the subordinate [because such an analysis] offers us one path to a social science that uncovers contradictions and possibilities, that looks well beneath the placid surface that the public accommodation to the existing distribution of power, wealth, and status often presents" (Scott 1990:15).

5. See Shihan de Silva Jayasuriya and Richard Pankhurst (2003) for more on this history of Africans in India and for the implications of point of origin in the distinction among the terms *habshi, sidi,* and *kaffir.*

6. Seeking to temper the arguments of historians such as Andre Wink, K. N. Chaudhuri, Ashin Dasgupta, and Kenneth McPherson, Bose contends that their work "has hampered the development of a historical method that would unsettle the discredited, yet entrenched, notions of a West versus rest and other accompanying dichotomies" (2006: 21).

7. For the history of the region, see Chaudhuri (1990), Chittick and Rotberg (1975), Ward and White (1972); of the Sidis, see Rashidi (1993), Chauhan (1995), Indrani Chatterjee (2006); of Indians in East Africa, see Mangat (1969); for economics and trade issues, see Risso (1995), Clarence-Smith (1989), Chaudhuri (1985); for politics, see Bhargava (1990), Mukherjee and Subramanian (1998), Rumyantsev (1988), Rais (1987), Misra (1978), Allen (1966).

8. Vassanji strikes a resonant chord here, in the context of this volume's recurring interest (starting with our discussion of Ghosh) in the subaltern in history. As Gyanendra Pandey wisely notes, "In the critique of historiography, as in that of politics, one may begin with a question about perspective: whose standpoint does the historian adopt, whom does s/he speak for? . . . Whose voice *can* we recover (or represent)?" (Pandey 2006: 50).

9. For all the dreams of Bandung, plenty of xenophobic stereotypes war against optimism: in Siddiqi's opinion, for example, Indians in Uganda "managed their own community affairs from a largely moralistic Indian standpoint," standing apart from a full Africanization of their identities; and, in fact, "Black African servants were often the only (rather limited) link that Asians had to African culture" (Siddiqi n.d.).

10. "I recall my own efforts at expressively staging citizenship in those early years of independence, my enthusiastic attempts to demonstrate that I was, indeed, a good Tanzanian socialist: marching along with my peers, emulating the best *ngoma* dancers by shaking my hips just so, beefing up my Swahili so that I would be among the handful of Asians accepted into the local Swahili medium secondary schools, singing Swahili songs with the right accent (Asians were constantly mocked for their poor pronunciation of Swahili), trading my skill in drawing frogs and butterflies for help from green-thumbed comrades with my *shamba*, or vegetable garden, so that I would not fail the year" (Joseph 1999: 2).

11. The history of Indians and Africans living together in the Caribbean is beyond the scope of this book but surely would make an appropriate companion volume. Consider, for example, Brinda Mehta's study (2004). For examples of works on Pan-Africanism see Ronald Segal's work (1995), Emmanuel Chukwudi Eze's reader (1997), and Fred Hord's edited volume (Hord and Lee 1994).

12. James Ferguson argues that "the anthropologist's evenhanded assessment of 'modernities' . . . by pluralizing without ranking the different relations to 'modernity' of different world regions, runs the risk of deemphasizing or overlooking the socioeconomic inequalities and questions of global rank that loom so large in African understandings of the modern. In this way, a well-meaning anthropological urge to treat modernity as a cultural formation whose different versions may be understood as both coeval and of equal value ends up looking like an evasion of the demands of those who instead see modernity as a privileged and desired socioeconomic condition that is actively contrasted with their own radically unequal way of life" (Ferguson 2006:33).

13. "In the thirteenth century and considerably before as well, the Asian sea trade that traversed the Arabian Sea, the Indian Ocean, and the South China Sea was subdivided into three interlocking circuits, each within the shared 'control' of a set of political and economic actors who were largely, although certainly not exclusively, in charge of exchanges with adjacent zones. . . . The westernmost circuit was largely inhabited by Muslims, with ship owners, major merchants, and their resident factors being drawn from the ports of the Arabian Peninsula or the more interior capitals of Baghdad and Cairo . . . Muslim merchant ships exiting the Gulf made stops along the northwestern coast of India (usually of Gujarat) before proceeding to the Malabar Coast farther south . . . [where] they conducted their business through sizable resident 'colonies' of Muslim merchants. Some of these merchants originally came from the Middle East but had settled, married, and generally assimilated to their new home; others, however, were indigenous to the region but, through the prolonged contacts of trade, had converted and adopted Muslim culture and language" (Abu-Lughod 1989: 251).

## Works Cited

Abu-Lughod, Janet L. 1989. *Before European Hegemony: The World System A.D. 1250–1350*. New York: Oxford University Press.

Agamben, Giorgio. 1998. *Homo Sacer: Sovereign Power and Bare Life*. Stanford: Stanford University Press.

Allen, Philip M. 1966. "Self-Determination in the Western Indian Ocean." *International Conciliation* (Carnegie Endowment for International Peace) 560 (November).

Alpers, Edward A. 1997. "The African Diaspora in the Northwestern Indian Ocean: Reconsideration of an Old Problem, New Directions for Research." *Comparative Studies of South Asia, Africa and the Middle East* 17.2: 62–81.

———. 2004. "African in India and the Wider Context of the Indian Ocean." In Catlin-Jairazbhoy and Alpers, *Sidis and Scholars*, 27–41.

Appiah, Kwame Anthony. 2007. *Cosmopolitanism: Ethics in a World of Strangers*. New York: W. W. Norton.

Basu, Helene. 1998. "Hierarchy and Emotion: Love, Joy and Sorrow in a Cult of Black Saints in Gujarat, India." In Werbner and Basu, *Embodying Charisma*, 117–39.

———. 2005. "Africans in India." *Frontline* (India) 22.18 (27 August–9 September). www.hinduonnet.com/fline/f12218/f1221800.htm, accessed 8 May 2007.

Bhargava, M. L. 1990. *Indian Ocean Strategies through the Ages.* New Delhi: Reliance.

Bose, Sugata. 2006. *A Hundred Horizons: The Indian Ocean in the Age of Global Empire.* Cambridge, Mass.: Harvard University Press.

Brennan, Timothy. 2001. "Cuts of Language: The East/West of the North/South." *Public Culture* 13.1: 39–64.

Catlin-Jairazbhoy, Amy, and Edward Alpers, eds. 2004. *Sidis and Scholars: Essays on African Indians.* Trenton, N.J.: Red Sea Press.

Chatterjee, Indrani. 2006. "Renewed and Connected Histories: Slavery and the Historiography of South Asia." In *Slavery and South Asian History,* ed. Indrani Chatterjee and Richard Eaton, 17–43. Bloomington: Indiana University Press.

Chatterjee, Indrani, and Richard Eaton, eds. 2006. *Slavery and South Asian History.* Bloomington: Indiana UP.

Chatterjee, Partha. 2004. *The Politics of the Governed: Reflections on Popular Politics in Most of the World.* New York: Columbia University Press.

Chaudhuri, K. N. 1985. *Trade and Civilization in the Indian Ocean: An Economic History from the Rise of Islam to 1750.* Cambridge: Cambridge University Press.

———. 1990. *Asia before Europe: Economy and Civilization of the Indian Ocean from the Rise of Islam to 1750.* Cambridge: Cambridge University Press.

Chauhan, R. R. S. 1995. *Africans in India: From Slavery to Royalty.* New Delhi: Asian Publication Services.

Chittick, H. Neville, and Robert I. Rotberg, eds. 1975. *East Africa and the Orient: Cultural Syntheses in Pre-Colonial Times.* New York: Africana.

Chowdhury, Fatima. 2005. "India's African Past." *Boloji.com,* 20 November. www.boloji.com/wfs4/wfs492.htm, accessed May 8, 2007.

Clarence-Smith, William Gervase, ed. 1989. *The Economics of the Indian Ocean Slave Trade in the Nineteenth Century.* London: Frank Cass.

Curtin, Philip D. 1984. *Cross-Cultural Trade in World History.* Cambridge: Cambridge University Press.

Dhawan, R. K., ed. 1999. *The Novels of Amitav Ghosh.* New Delhi: Prestige.

Dimock, Wai Chee. 2006. *Through Other Continents: American Literature across Deep Time.* Princeton: Princeton University Press.

Eze, Emmanuel Chukwudi, ed. 1997. *Postcolonial African Philosophy: A Critical Reader.* Cambridge, Mass.: Blackwell.

Ferguson, James. 2006. *Global Shadows: Africa in the Neoliberal World Order.* Durham, N.C.: Duke University Press.

George, Olakunle. 2003. *Relocating Agency: Modernity and African Letters.* Albany: State University of New York Press.

Ghosh, Amitav. 1992. *In an Antique Land.* London: Granta.

———. 2004. *The Hungry Tide.* London: HarperCollins.

Ghosh, Bishnupriya. 2004. *When Borne Across: Literary Cosmopolitics in the Contemporary Indian Novel.* New Brunswick, N.J.: Rutgers University Press.

Grundy, Trevor. 2002. "If Only the Queen Had Asked Him to Tea." *Daily Telegraph* (London), 2 August 2002. http://ismaili.net/timeline/2002/20020802dt.html, accessed 10 December 2006.

Harris, Joseph. 1971. *The African Presence in Asia: Consequences of the East African Slave Trade.* Evanston, Ill.: Northwestern University Press.

Hord, Fred Lee (Mzee Lasana Okpara), and Jonathan Scott Lee, eds. 1995. *I Am Because We Are: Readings in Black Philosophy.* Amherst: University of Massachusetts Press.

Hountondji, Paulin, ed. 1997. *Endogenous Knowledge: Research Trails.* Dakar, Senegal: Codesria.

Jayasuriya, Shihan de Silva, and Richard Pankhurst, eds. 2003. *The African Diaspora in the Indian Ocean.* Trenton, NJ: Africa World Press.

Joseph, May. 1999. *Nomadic Identities: The Performance of Citizenship.* Minneapolis: University of Minnesota Press.

Krishnaswamy, Revathi. 1995. "Mythologies of Migrancy: Postcolonialism, Postmodernism, and the Politics of (Dis)Location." *Ariel* 26.1: 125–46.

Kumar, Amitava, ed. 2004. *Away: The Indian Writer as an Expatriate.* New York: Routledge.

Larkin, Brian. 1997. "Indian Films and Nigerian Lovers: Media and the Creation of Parallel Modernities." *Africa* 67.3: 406–40.

Mangat, J. S. 1969. *A History of the Asians in East Africa, c. 1886 to 1945.* Oxford: Oxford University Press.

Mehta, Brinda J. 2004. *Diasporic Dis(Locations): Indo-Caribbean Women Writers Negotiate the "Kala Pani."* Kingston, Jamaica: University of West Indies Press.

Misra, K. P. 1978. "Indian Ocean Politics: An Asian-African Perspective." *Occasional Papers / Reprints Series in Contemporary Asian Studies* 1.13. College Park: School of Law, University of Maryland.

Mukherjee, Meenakshi. 1971. "The Anxiety of Indian Englishness." *Economic and Political Weekly of India,* 27 November, 2607–11.

Mukherjee, Rudrangshu, and Lakshmi Subramanian, eds. 1998. *Politics and Trade in the Indian Ocean Worlds.* Delhi: Oxford University Press.

Nasta, Susheila, ed. 2004. *Writing across Worlds: Contemporary Writers Talk.* London: Routledge.

Pandey, Gyanendra. 2006. *Routine Violence: Nations, Fragments, Histories.* Stanford, Calif.: Stanford University Press.

Pearson, Michael N. 1998. *Port Cities and Intruders: The Swahili Coast, India, and Portugal in the Early Modern Era.* Baltimore: Johns Hopkins University Press, 1998.

Rais, Rasul B. 1987. *The Indian Ocean and the Superpowers: Economic, Political and Strategic Perspectives.* Totowa, N.J.: Barnes and Noble.

Rashidi, Runoko. 1993. *The Global African Community: The African Presence in Asia, Australia, and the South Pacific.* Washington, D.C.: Institute for Independent Education.

Risso, Patricia. 1995. *Merchants and Faith: Muslim Commerce and Culture in the Indian Ocean.* Boulder, Colo.: Westview.

Robbins, Kenneth X., and John McLeod, eds. 2006. *African Elites in India: Habshi Amarat.* Usmanpura, Ahmedabad, India: Mapin.

Rumyantsev, Yevgeni. 1988. *Indian Ocean and Asian Security.* New Delhi: Allied.

Scott, James C. 1990. *Domination and the Arts of Resistance: Hidden Transcripts.* New Haven, Conn.: Yale University Press.

Segal, Ronald. 1995. *The Black Diaspora: Five Centuries of the Black Experience outside Africa.* New York: Farrar, Straus and Giroux.

Sharma, Aradhana, and Akhil Gupta. 2006. *The Anthropology of the State: A Reader.* Malden, Mass.: Blackwell.

Siddiqi, Jameela. N.d. "Uganda: A Personal Viewpoint on the Expulsion, 30 Years Ago." *Information for Social Change*, no. 15. www.libr.org/ISC/articles/15-Siddiqi-1.html, accessed 12 November 2006.

Smith, Michael Peter, and Luis Eduardo Guarnizo, eds. 2002. *Transnationalism from Below*. New Brunswick, N.J.: Transaction.

Ward, W. E. F., and L. W. White. 1971. *East Africa: A Century of Change, 1870–1970*. New York: Africana.

Waters, Malcolm. 1995. *Globalization*. London: Routledge.

Werbner, Pnina, and Helene Basu, eds. 1998. *Embodying Charisma: Modernity, Locality and the Performance of Emotion in Sufi Cults*. London: Routledge.

# 1

# Slave Trades and the Indian Ocean World

Gwyn Campbell

## Background

The British in mid-nineteenth-century India were possibly the first to identify and characterize people there of "African" descent as a distinct ethnic category (Mamphilly 2001), largely as a result of grouping "Prize Negroes" from captured slaving ships in localities such as Aden, where 2,200 were landed between 1865 and 1870 (Ewald 2000), Cape Town, the Seychelles, Mauritius, Surat, and Bombay, in the 1830s to 1875 (Shroff 2002). Most "Prize Negroes" landed in India were taken by local elites as domestic servants, although some served in the British military or police force (Shroff 2002). A proportion settled in and around Bombay, where in 1864 more than half the reported 2,000-strong African community was engaged in "maritime" activities, largely as sailors, coal trimmers, firemen, or dock workers (Ewald 2000). Many Makrani males of African descent also worked as stokers and firemen aboard European steamers ("Baluchistan" 1911). Such maritime workers were termed "Seedies" by the British (Ewald 2000). Other "Prize Negroes" in India migrated to Hyderabad, where in 1863 the nizam established an African

Cavalry Guard for which he recruited Africans locally and in Arabia (Harris 1971: 102–3).

However, academic "essentialists," more than the British authorities in India, have proved the major force in molding an "African" identity for Asians of African descent. Their campaign dates from the 1970s when Joseph E. Harris, a prominent African American scholar, published *The African Presence in Asia: Consequences of the East African Slave Trade* (1971) and *Global Dimensions of the African Diaspora* (1993). Possibly provoked by Edward Blyden's comment that "The countless caravans and dhowloads of Negroes who have been imported into Asia have not produced, so far as we know, any great historical results" (quoted in Kilson and Rotberg 1976: 4), academic essentialists have taken up Harris's challenge to identify the "African" heritage in Asia (Prashad 2000; Wilson 1997; Alpers 1997, 2000; Rashidi 1998; Obeng 2000). They assert that Africans "in exile" retain innately "African" attributes, reflected in their physiognomy (Negroid features, black skin color, even gait) and culture (music, dance, religion). They were affected only marginally by their Indian Ocean world (IOW) environments in which they remained alien, quintessentially "African," in body and culture, able to interact on the deepest levels only with other "Africans." Whether consciously or not, they formed an integral part of the African Diaspora and possessed unalterably closer links with, for example, African Americans than with "Asian" members of local IOW societies in which they and their families lived and had lived for generations (see Walker 2006).

As indicated by the title of Harris's 1971 book, the African presence in the IOW was, like that of the African American Diaspora, a consequence of the slave trade. It is assumed that Africa's historical role in international trade was as an exporter of slaves and raw materials, such as gold and ivory, in return for European manufactures. This inequitable exchange led, even prior to the "Scramble for Africa," to a "proto-colonial" system that established the basis for the "underdevelopment" of Africa and the formation of African Asian communities in exile (Sutton 1972: 11; Harris 1971; Biermann and Campbell 1989: 19–20) that, like exile Jewish, African American, and Armenian groupings, formed a "victim" diaspora, as opposed to trade, labor, imperial, and cultural diasporas (Basu 2002). Graham Irwin described a victim diaspora as "the enforced expatriation over many centuries of millions of Africans from their homeland" (Irwin 1977: ix). Unlike free migration, the traffic in slaves was one-directional, and "in the countries to which they were taken they constituted for centuries the most oppressed and exploited element in society" (ix; see also Kilson and Rotberg 1976: 1–10). UNESCO has recently backed the essentialist position by deciding, at least initially, to focus exclusively on the history and experience of Black Africans in the extension of its Slave Route Project to the Indian Ocean world (Iye 2006).

Scholars, including Pashington Obeng and John McLeod in this volume, have identified a number of "African" groups in the IOW, notably in the Middle East and South Asia, researched their histories, and recorded their speech and cultural traditions. Initially, their emphasis was upon African slaves turned heroes, and, as in the Atlantic paradigm, the highlight fell upon males. Thus most conventional accounts of Africans in India concerned slave soldiers who rose to positions of great political power in the Deccan states of the Bahmani (from 1347 to 1538) and Bijapur (1580–1627), or under Nizam Shahi (1589–1626) (Ali 1987: 27; Hardy 1999; Hunwick 1978: 31–32). Some even transformed themselves into rulers, as in the Dehi sultanate (c.1399–1440) and Bengal (1486–93) (Hunwick 1978: 32). More spectacularly, the Sidis of Janjira, an island forty-five miles south of Bombay, from 1618 established a naval presence and degree of political independence that endured well into the nineteenth century (Harris 1993: 327–31; Ali 1996: ch. 8).

Attention has also focused on communities in the IOW with identifiably "African" physiognomic and cultural traits. Some have been identified in historical literature. For example, an estimated one third of Bahrein's "African" pearl divers in 1831 and Kuwait's "African" population in the early 1900s were non-slaves, while in early twentieth-century Oman there were about 10,000 "Bayasirah" probably of ex-African-slave descent on the maternal side (Sheriff 2005; Clarence-Smith 2005). Again, in the 1872 Indian census, 15 percent of Janjira's registered population of 1,700 were Sidis (Harris 1971: 80–82).

Geographical place names revealed other groups of African slave descent. Hence the 1898 "Blacks' Quarter," *Manbar-i Sīyāhān* ("Blacks' pulpit"), and *Pusht-i Shahr* ("Behind the city") areas of Bandar 'Abbās (in Iran), which in the nineteenth century took approximately 25 percent of African slave imports (Mirzai 2002: 234). *Zanjiabad* ("village built by Africans"), Deh-Zanjian ("village of Africans") indicate other originally African settlements in Iran, as does *Gala-Zanjian* ("castle of Africans") in Baluchistan (Harris 1971: 77; Mirzai 2002: 240). Similarly, Kaniz (Persian for "slave girl"), a small town near Anand, in northern Gujarat, was once a major slave barracoon (Bhattacharya 1970: 579). The localities of *Siddipet* ("African market") and *Habshi Guda* ("African village") indicate the presence of early African communities in Hyderabad (Harris 1971: 114), while Africans recruited into the Nizam of Hyderabad's African Cavalry Guard lived in the *Siddi Risala* ("African Regiment") quarters; some of their descendants, two thousand strong in the early 1970s, still live there (Harris 1971: 103, 111, 124). Likewise, *Kapiri Gama* ("Kaffir village") in Puttalama,

Sri Lanka, still houses a genetically African-Sinhalese community (De Silva Jayasuriya 2002).

Ethnic names may also indicate African descent, notably "Sidi" in India (Vijayakumar et al. 1987: 98), and "Kaffir" in Sri Lanka (De Silva Jayasuriya 2002). The Sidi, possibly the most visible "African" grouping in contemporary India, are concentrated in Gujarat (especially in the Gir forest villages of Jambar, Sirwan, Moruka, and Akolbadi in the Junagadh district) (Bhattacharya 1970: 579), with smaller communities in Maharashtra, Karnataka (Western Ghat forests of North Kanara), Andhra Pradesh, Kerala, and Diu (Basu 2002; Ali 1996: 223; Vijayakumar 1987: 98; Prashad 2000: 195; K. Cooper 1999; Obeng 2000). Estimates of the Sidi population vary considerably, most falling within the range of 14,000 to 30,000.[1]

### The Indian Ocean World Slave Trade

The essentialist and conventional Western view is that the IOW slave trade was a mirror image, albeit on a smaller scale, of the Atlantic slave trade in which from c.1500 to 1860 some 10–12 million slaves, mostly West African adult males, were shipped to New World mines and plantations, where they constituted the basis of a "slave mode of production." They were a clearly visible Black chattel class of hereditary slave status, uncivilized "outsiders," deprived of civil rights. Violence was a universal and pervasive feature of master-slave relations. Slave owners controlled the slave's productive and reproductive capacities and could legally punish, sell, or transfer a slave and separate a slave mother from her children or male companion (Davis 1970, esp. 300–15 and ch. 15; Patterson 1982; Meillassoux 1991: 74–75).

The IOW slave trade similarly reflected the export of notably East Africans to perform unskilled labor as soldiers, miners, and field workers. In some regions, such as nineteenth-century Zanzibar, Pemba, and Madagascar, they underpinned "slave modes of production" (Manning 1993, ch. 6; Davis 1970: 9–40; Lovejoy 1983: 8–11; Sheriff 1987: 247). Slaves were chattels, and violence was a universal characteristic of their treatment by slave owners who, in the IOW, comprised both Europeans and Muslims. In the IOW, as in the Atlantic world, African slaves and their descendants formed distinct communities imbued with African cultural traits (Harris 1971; Alpers 1997: 62–63; Bhattacharya 1970; Ali 1996; Akyeampong 2000.

However, non-essentialist studies of IOW slavery signal significant divergences from the Atlantic model. They reveal complex trans-IOW slave trades that started well before the Common Era, remained vigorous into the twentieth century, and in some areas are still maintained. In all of these trades, sources, markets, routes, and slave functions varied considerably.

Overall, Black Africans probably formed a minority of slaves traded. Moreover, slaves in the IOW were heavily affected by forces of assimilation and integration that had major repercussions for the identity of slaves and their descendants and thus on the viability of the concept of an African Diaspora. This is most apparent in Islamic communities that dominated vast swathes of the IOW. Recent scholarship has steadily undermined the conventional Western assumption that there existed a specifically "Islamic" form of slavery. Rather, there emerged different schools of legal interpretation, within which individual scholars could differ significantly on the niceties of Islamic law, while the application of the *sharia* outside the Middle East was tempered by local customs. However, all were characterized by considerable assimilation of slaves into local society (Reid 1983: 13–14; Warren 2004; Sheriff 2005; Clarence-Smith 2005; Eno 2005).

### The Origin of Slaves

The IOW slave trade started at least 4,000 years ago, was multidirectional, involved overland and maritime routes, changed over time, and involved many different ethnic groups. In the IOW, "slave" cannot be equated with "African" (Schottenhammer 2004; Wink 1996: 30–31; Goody 1980: 18).

### Eastern IOW

In the eastern IOW, African slaves, imported chiefly via the Middle East and Southeast Asia, were a rare luxury. By the second century CE, demand may have developed in China for skilled African sailors and Alexandrian slave jugglers (Van Leur 1955: 99). From the fourth century a regular market existed there for *K'un-lun* ("Black") slaves (Worden and Ward 1998: 850), but *"K'un-lun"* could refer specifically to inhabitants of Pemba, in East Africa, and any dark-skinned person from Africa, Papua New Guinea and Melanesia (Filesi 1972: 21; Irwin 1977: 169–72). By the late ninth century, east African slaves were certainly highly esteemed in China as divers to caulk boat seams with oakum, because of their strength and ability to keep their eyes open underwater (Duyvendak 1949: 24; Filesi 1972: 22; Irwin 1977: 171; Hermann 1954: 313). They were also imported as sailors, who possibly helped man the great Chinese navies of the twelfth to early fifteenth centuries (Lo 1955: 500). However, few were employed inland, as is demonstrated by the excitement surrounding the arrival in 976 of a Negro slave accompanying an Arab envoy to the imperial Tang court (Filesi 1972: 4–5; Wallenstein 1998: 177).

From the tenth century, there were increased references to African slaves. In the 1400s, Malagasy and east African slaves were imported into Aceh (Indonesia) by Bengali traders and into Melaka (via the Maldives) by

Banten merchants, and from there some were transshipped to China (Hunwick 1978: 31; Vérin 1999; Worden and Ward 1998: 850). It was à la mode for elite households in Mongol times (1260–1368) to possess Negro manservants (Irwin 1977: 169), and the Javanese court in 1382 presented a tribute of 101 Negroes to the emperor (168). African slave imports to the East increased after 1500, due to demand from Europeans, notably Portuguese settlements in Macao and Japan, and VOC (*Vereenigde Oost-Indische Compagnie*—Dutch East India Company) forts in Indonesia. Large merchant cities arose, the populations of which were largely composed of slaves and other bondspeople; in 1694 there were some 25,000 slaves of multiple origins in Batavia alone (Van Goor 1998: 196; Chakravarti 1997: 81, 85).

However, African slaves in the East were always a strict minority. China and other centralized states obtained most of their slaves from the military operations associated with state and empire building (Coedès 1966: 60). Most slaves came from decentralized hill "tribes" and "maritime" communities within the region who were easier to locate than Africans, were cheaper to transport, and suffered fewer losses en route; for instance, in 1684 only 108 of the 278 Malagasy slaves on one ship survived the voyage to Batavia (Arasaratnam 1995: 200). Indonesians were shipped to markets across Southeast Asia and to Cape Town, Indochinese and Koreans were exported to China, and in the nineteenth century, Chinese slaves were sent to Singapore and San Francisco (Campbell 2004, 2005a).

### The Western IOW

#### South Asia

Arab merchants in the third century CE possibly shipped the first African slaves to India, to the Sopara, Kalyan, Chaul, and Pal forts in Konkan (Ricks 1998a: 70, 1998b: 833; Vérin 1999; Kidwai 1990; Trimingham 1964: 2–3; Shirodkar 1985: 28). With the commercial expansion of Islam, demand for African slaves increased, and from the tenth century significant numbers of Berbers, Ethiopians, and sub-Saharan Africans—eyewitnesses from Ibn-Batuta (1342–49) to Tomé Pires (1512–15) emphasize "Abyssinians" (Reinaud 1848: cdxvii; Pires 1944: 51)—were shipped to South Asia. Michel Boivin claims that the majority of slaves in Sind (present-day Pakistan) were Sidi, of east African origin (Boivin 2000), although Salim Kidwai argues that while African slaves predominated in Bengal and South India, Turks and Slavs comprised the majority of slave imports into medieval South Asia (Kidwai 1990: 80–81, 86–88).

The Portuguese settlements of Goa, Dui, Daman, and Sri Lanka augmented Indian demand for African slaves, notably from the Mozambique coast (Machado 2004; Alpers 1997: 75). Portuguese and Indian traders initially shared this trade, but it became progressively concentrated in the hands of Indians (Haight 1942: 22–23). Dutch and British posts in Sri Lanka subsequently imported Malagasy and east African slaves directly and indirectly, via Cape Town, Bombay, and Goa.[2] All the while, the traditional African slave import trade via Zebid, Aden, and the Persian Gulf continued to grow (Machado 2004; Lewis 1990: 12–13; Brunschwig 1999). The literature focuses on imported African slaves, but most slaves in South Asia were probably of local origin (Kidwai 1990: 86–88; Miller 2004), while Indian slaves were also shipped to Macao, Japan, Indonesia, Mauritius, and Cape Town (Campbell 2004; Sheriff 2005; Worden 2005; Machado 2004; Arasaratnam 1995: 200).

### Middle East

African slaves were more numerous in the western than in the eastern IOW, but even there they constituted a majority only in specific regions and time periods. The Middle East constituted probably the earliest and certainly the greatest overall IOW market for African slaves (Lewis 1990: 13). It imported slaves from Nubia from pharaonic times (Ewald 1998b: 2: 651; Straus 1998: 1: 282) and from Ethiopia, Sudan, and Somalia by the early centuries CE (Harris 1971: 3, 11; Hirth 1909–10: 49; Huntingford 1980: 23–24, 28; Duyvendak 1949: 8). Aksum's commercial expansion led by the seventh century to considerable slave exports from its southern frontiers, to Egypt via the Nile and to Arabia and the Persian Gulf via Zeila and Zebid/Zabid—the major Yemeni slave market (Fernyhough 1986: 105–6; Brunschwig 1999; Ewald 1998a: 2: 653). Arab and Persian traders and raiders also obtained slaves directly from Somalia (Duyvendak 1949: 13; J. Allen 1993: 26). From the rise of Islam in the seventh century, when it became illegal for Muslims to enslave co-religionists, slave imports increased, and by the ninth century the Middle East had become a significant and durable market for African slaves.[3] Some of these originated from subtropical East and West Africa (Trimingham 1964: 2–3), but recent scholarship has undermined traditional assumptions (Morton 1998: 1: 265; J. Allen 1993: 66, 73–74) that a major revolt in late ninth-century Iraq by the Zanj (purportedly from East Africa) indicated a vast traffic in east African slaves: the uprising embraced large numbers of "free" men, Persians as well as Bedouin and "Marsh" Arabs, while most African slave rebels originated from northeast Africa (Fisher 1989: 382; Hunwick 1978: 34).

African slave imports increased from the tenth to thirteenth centuries, at the height of Islamic commercial expansion. Many accompanied African Muslim pilgrims to Mecca and Medina (Lewis 1990: 18). Also, the advancing Islamic trading frontier created a durable slave export trade from East Africa as far south as Sofala (Hunwick 1978: 31; Vérin 1999) and in the process helped to found the economic basis for the Swahili civilization (Nurse and Spear 1985: 3; see also Morton 1998: 1: 265). Only at this time did the proportion of African slaves probably equal or at times surpass slaves of Georgian (Circassian) and Central Asian origin in the Middle East (Hunwick 1978: 23–24).

African slave exports dipped in the fourteenth century, but grew again from the late fifteenth century. Most traveled via Ethiopia and the Nile Valley, but some were also shipped from East Africa and Madagascar. Cairo, the African Red Sea ports of Zeila and Berbera, and the Arabian markets of Zebid and Aden served as major redistribution points (Pires 1944: 1: 14; Badger 1863: 81, 86; Grandidier and Grandidier 1908: 4.1: 324, 1928: 4.4: 298, 302–3). From 1500 to 1800, annual African slave imports into the Muslim world increased from possibly 8,000 to between 10,000 and 12,000, half of which passed through Cairo (Aksan 1998: 1: 285). Slave exports from the east African coast grew dramatically in the nineteenth century when, according to Ralph Austen, some 800,000 east Africans were exported to the Middle East, 300,000 across the Red Sea and Gulf of Aden, and the rest from the Swahili coast (Austen 1989). In the early twentieth century the Middle East also imported slaves from the Makran coast of Iran, some from western India, and a few from Indonesia and China (Sheriff 2005; Miers 2005; Klein 2005).

### Africa

Conventional literature emphasizes Africa as a source of slaves for external markets. However, Africa also proved a market for non-African slaves. For example, from 1658 to 1807, the Cape imported slaves from Bengal, Coromandel, Malabar, Kerala, Cochin, Sri Lanka, Java, Sulawesi, Macassar, Bali, Timor, Ternate, Macao, Madagascar, and the Mascarenes, and probably from Banda and Iran (Worden 2005: 31–35).

Moreover, probably the majority of enslaved Africans were retained in Africa, albeit often far from their region of origin. For instance, from the mid-eighteenth century considerable numbers of East Africans were shipped to Zanzibar, Pemba, Somalia, Madagascar, and the Mascarenes, and some to Cape Town, while significant numbers of Malagasy slaves were sent to Réunion and Mauritius, and some to the Swahili coast and the Cape (see, e.g., Sheriff 2005; F. Cooper 1997; Campbell 2005b: ch. 9; Worden 1985; R. Allen 1999; Manning 1993; Lovejoy 1983). Abdul Sheriff argues that the relocation of the Omani ruling elite to Zanzibar in 1832 reflected the greater economic importance by then of East Africa to the Persian Gulf and consequently of Swahili coast plantation slavery (Sheriff

2005; Mirzai 2005; see also Sheriff 1987). Similarly, the "African" islands (Comoros, Madagascar, Mascarenes) established a vigorous nineteenth-century demand for slaves—some 700,000 of whom originated from East Africa, notably from highland Mozambique and Tanzania (Campbell 2005b: ch. 9). In sum, throughout the history of IOW slavery, from 2,000 BCE to the present day, it is unlikely that African slaves predominated except within African, the western Indian Ocean islands, and, during certain periods, the Middle East (Campbell 2004, 2005a).

### Gender Profiles, Functions, and the Issue of Violence

Slavery studies have focused overwhelmingly on male slaves. This largely reflects scholarly emphasis on the Atlantic system in which predominantly male slaves were shipped to the Americas. By contrast, most slaves traded in the IOW were female, notably girls and young women who generally commanded higher prices than male and older female slaves. The exceptions were eunuchs ("males made female"), who were universally highly prized, and boys in China—where patriarchal ideology restricted the supply of boy slaves, whose prices were often four to five times that of girl slaves (Miers 2005; Watson 1980c: 235).

In what forms part of a wider "orientalist" debate over the supposedly non-progressive nature of African and Asian economies (see, e.g., Eaton 1993; Frank 1998) there is also considerable debate over the productive capacity of slaves in the IOW. Clearly, however, IOW slaves were employed in tasks the range and responsibilities of which were far wider than those encompassed by the Atlantic model of predominantly mine and plantation labor. Slaves performed possibly the bulk of agricultural work in Africa and India (Patnaik 1990: 2–4, 26), but there as elsewhere in the IOW, peasant slave owners generally worked alongside their slaves in predominantly subsistence production (Goody 1980: 36; Boomgaard 2004; Klein 1993: 9). Slaves also labored in mines, craftwork, porterage, fishing, commerce, and textile production (chiefly female) (Goody 1980: 21, 32). Some received shelter, food, and clothing from their owners; others were given land from which they were expected to obtain the resources to sustain themselves. Yet others were rented out or left free to seek livelihoods (Warren 2004; Reid 1983: 11).

However, in the IOW probably only a minority of slaves were directly involved in full-time productive or commercial activities. Rather, most were acquired as symbols of conspicuous consumption, to reflect the power and wealth of their owners (Boomgaard 2004; see also Patnaik 1990: 2–4, 26; Reid 1983: 13; Goody 1980: 36–37; Klein 1993: 8–13). Children and young women, the majority of slaves traded in the IOW, were predominantly absorbed by wealthy households where females, employed chiefly in domestic and sexual services and in entertainment (Miller 2004; Goody1980: 20–21), enjoyed a lifestyle and a respect often superior to that of both male slaves and female peasants (Goody 1980: 21, 32; Miller: 2004). There are instances of concubines in the Middle East sending for family members to join them—albeit as non-slaves (Miers 2005). Similarly, most male slaves worked in sectors of indirect economic impact, such as domestic service, stewardship, bureaucratic service, soldiering, and diplomacy. In some cases, the costs of maintaining such "status" slaves exceeded the benefits accruing from their services and in exceptional circumstances bankrupted the owner (Boomgaard 2004).

Conventional literature also assumes that violence was universally employed to extract labor from slaves. In the IOW, harsh working conditions existed in some places at certain times and could provoke revolt, suicide, and attempts to curtail reproduction; low birth rates, characteristic of the Mauritian slave plantations, may have marked even milder slave regimes, as in the Gulf (Sheriff 2005; Boomgaard 2004; Alpers 2004). However, violence was a consistent feature of slavery only on the relatively few European-managed plantations where economies of scale made higher levels of coercion profitable. It was comparatively rarely used on "status" slaves—the majority—while even ordinary slaves represented a capital asset the value of which was worth maintaining or even enhancing. Indeed, maximum slave productivity could be achieved only through acknowledging the essential humanity of slaves (Klein 1993: 11–12; Meillassoux 1991: 9–10).

### Freedom versus Slavery: The IOW Context

As indicated above, the concept of "slavery" in the IOW often differed markedly with New World slavery. Fundamental to the Western tradition is the contrast between enslavement and freedom: whereas a "free" individual enjoyed basic rights of citizenship, choice of occupation and lifestyle, and security of person and property, the slave was a chattel of hereditary status, permanently segregated and alienated from non-slaves.

Thus the slave-free dichotomy that characterized New World slave societies was premised on the notion of the absence or possession of liberty. However, there was little concept of individual liberty in IOW societies that rather embraced individuals in social hierarchies wherein each person had an allotted status that carried with it a multiplicity of rights and obligations, and where statuses were fluid and often overlapped. For example, in late eighteenth- and early nineteenth-century Sulu, *banyaga* slaves married, owned property, and performed wide-ranging functions, on the same terms as non-slaves.[4] Overlapping statuses renders it difficult to forge hard and fast distinctions between types of servitude, or to contrast "slave" with "free" for, as Anthony Reid underlines, the concept of personal freedom can only be pitched against that of slavery when all other forms of servitude are subsumed into a clearly defined category of "slaves" (Reid 1983: 21).

The meaning of IOW systems of slavery becomes clearer if Western notions of a division of society into free and slave, of individual liberty, and of slaves as property are replaced by a vision of society as a hierarchy of dependency in which "slaves" constituted one of a number of servile groups that performed both productive and nominally unproductive services. It was a reciprocal system in which obligation implied servitude to an individual with superior status, to a kin group, or to the crown, in return for protection (Goody 1980). The highest status fell generally in acephelous societies to a group of elders and in centralized societies to the sovereign who theoretically "owned" all of inferior status. This was possibly most visible with corvée labor imposed on subjects who in most IOW countries were considered crown "property." In this sense, it could be argued, corvée fits the concept of "property" performing "compulsory labor" used by some authors as a defining characteristic of slavery (see Watson 1980b: 7).

Moreover, in the world-view of pre-industrial societies, there was no division between the temporal and the spiritual; the supernatural could bless or curse human activities and so required respect and appeasement from mortals. Thus, in most communities, the living and the dead were incorporated into a giant hierarchy of overlapping statuses, each with associated rights and obligations, in which the concept of bondage transcended temporal life. Kings were considered to be imbued with sacred power but were in turn governed by the ancestors or gods. In Islam, for example, all Muslims were "slaves" of Allah (see, e.g., Reid 1983: 4; Campbell 1992).

### Slavery as a Form of Social Security

Europeans often characterized slavery in the IOW as "mild" compared to New World slavery. The British even described types of slavery in nineteenth-century India as a form of poor relief, saving destitute people from starvation. Judged by Western concepts of slavery and individual liberty, such notions appear curious if not absurd. Historians have sought to explain them in part by European ignorance of what constituted slavery, and in part by the desire by officials to conceal aspects of the slave trade in which they colluded (Klein 2005; Delaye 200442; Chatterjee 2005; Campbell 2005a, Introduction).

Possibly more important in explaining such attitudes, which were sometimes shared by indigenous authorities, were pre-industrial patterns of human and natural disasters—an ever-present threat in the IOW. Monsoons and cyclones frequently brought flooding to major rice-producing areas from China to India and Madagascar. In addition, Southeast and East Asia formed a center of volcanism that could wreak both immediate local destruction and, through cloud-veil-induced lower temperatures, years of depressed agricultural productivity that affected vast areas of the globe. Volcanism could sharply reduce precipitation, ruin harvests, and induce famine. For instance, seven major sulfur-rich volcanic eruptions in the period 1638–43 contributed to the five worst years of continuous drought in China (1637–41) and to the collapse of the Ming dynasty in 1644 (Atwell 2001: 31–32, 34–35, 42, 62–64; McNeill 1976: 266). Again, the "El-Niño–Southern Oscillation" (ENSO) effect, produced every seven to ten years by changes in the pressure gradient across the Pacific Ocean, often provokes severe droughts throughout the IOW. Moreover, it tends to be followed in consecutive years by "La Niña," a cold ENSO that causes unusually heavy rain in affected regions (Atwell 2001: 39–40). When a strong ENSO effect coincided with sulfur-rich volcanism, as in 1641, the effect could be catastrophic (Gudmundson 2002).

The famine and disease which frequently accompanied natural disasters could independently have catastrophic consequences. A notable example was the Black Death or bubonic plague (*Pasteurella pestis*). Eurocentric historiography has focused on the devastation wrought in Europe by the Black Death, but its impact was greater in Asia. The plague first erupted in epidemic form in China in 1331, spreading along the main commercial caravan routes of Asia before reaching the Crimea and Europe in 1346. An estimated 90 per cent of those infected died. While it killed probably one third of Europeans in 1346–50, it halved the population of China (to 65 million) and Egypt (to an estimated 2 million). The impact was probably as devastating in centers of population in India and the Middle East (McNeill 1976: 144–49; Ponting 1991: 228–29; Chaudhuri 1992: 381–82).

This forms the backdrop against which IOW systems of servile labor should be considered. In hard years, densely populated monocrop regions, such as Makassar in Indonesia and areas of South India, exported the destitute as slaves (Boomgaard 2004). In China, desperate parents sold prepubescent daughters to anyone who could feed or clothe them (Warren 1994: 80). The trade in children, outright, as redeemable "pawns," or for adoption, was frequently a measure of last resort during disastrous times, taken because it might ensure survival for both remaining kin members and the enslaved child. Indeed, in China and India, the sale of young girls for "adoption" was commonly viewed as a charitable system. Usually very little money was involved, and parents trusted that the adoptive family would care for the girl and find her a suitable spouse (see, e.g., Jaschok and Miers 1994: 11, 18).

In this context, debt bondage, which most people entered voluntarily as a credit-securing strategy, often overlapped with slavery. Debt bondage embraced a vast range of people in the IOW, from farmers mortgaging future harvests and potential grooms borrowing a bride price to small traders living off credit from larger merchants, the ubiquitous rural gambler of Southeast and East Asia, and opium addicts in nineteenth-century China (Boomgaard 2004; Delaye 2004; Schottenhammer 2004; see also Watson 1980c: 228–36). During catastrophes, people often entered debt bondage or slavery in return for subsistence as a survival strategy, either voluntarily, as was the case of many *dvija* caste members in India from about 500 BCE, or propelled by their kin group (Klein 1993: 11; Patnaik 1990: 25–26). Those subject to debt bondage could outnumber slaves; they formed possibly the most numerous social category in Majapahit, in Java, and up to 50 percent of the total population in central Thailand in the eighteenth and nineteenth centuries. Debt-bondage servitude was generally taken as paying off interest on the loan that debtors had contracted, to which was added the cost of their lodging, food, and clothing. Consequently the debt usually increased, and servitude could become permanent, even hereditary, at which point there was little to distinguish debt bondage from slavery (Kim 2004; Reid 1983: 12; for debt bondage from another angle, see Miller 2004).

Here, concepts of "slave" and "free" are of limited analytical utility. For most of the IOW population, security, food, and shelter, rather than an abstract concept of liberty, were the primary aims. Indeed, "liberty" in the sense of individual freedom from inherited status and responsibilities would have effectively destroyed the web of obligations that offered protection from human-made and natural dangers (Boomgaard 2004; Miers 2005; Salman 2005). This helps explain the remarkable absence of group-consciousness and of revolt among IOW slaves who generally sought to integrate into the slave-holding society that provided them with basic sustenance and sometimes the chance for an enhanced lifestyle. It also explains why some slaves who were presented with the opportunity to gain "freedom" through manumission or redemption preferred to retain their slave status (see, e.g., Campbell 1988).

### An African-Asian Diaspora?

Most scholars of Africa and the African American Diaspora hold that Asians of African descent form part of the African Diaspora. This is an implicit assumption of several of the contributors to this volume who speak of "African Asians" and "African Indians" as the counterparts in Asia of "African

Americans." However, rarely do they examine if Asians of African descent meet the generally agreed criteria for that diaspora, summarized as follows:[5]

a) Displacement from an original homeland to two or more peripheral or foreign regions.
b) Non-assimilation resulting in the formation of a "relatively stable community in exile" (Wilson 1997: 118) characterized by alienation and insulation from the dominant society.
c) The development of a diasporic "consciousness" comprising continued awareness and memory (real or imagined) of a common homeland and its heritage and the injustice of their removal from it, with conscious efforts to maintain links with, and contribute to the betterment of life in, the homeland and a desire to ultimately return to resettle the homeland.

### Displacement

African slaves exported to IOW markets certainly underwent dislocation and suffering. Malagasy slaves destined for the Mascarenes commonly believed that they would be eaten by whites (Griffiths 1840: 26; Ellis 1870: 4),[6] while it was commented in 1788 that Mozambican slaves preferred suicide to being exported (Rea 1976: 117–118). Slave mortality was high. In addition to suicides, slaves often had no immunity to local diseases, although the reverse was true for Madagascar, a more isolated disease-free environment than mainland Africa, to which in the nineteenth century African slaves brought diseases such as cholera (Lewis 1990: 10; for Madagascar see Campbell 1991). For instance, approximately 25 percent of African male slaves imported into Sri Lanka in 1817 died within the first year (De Silva Jayasuriya 2002). In some regions, such as Imperial Madagascar (c. 1790–1895), slaves, as low status "foreigners," were also the most suspect in witchcraft cases, consequently suffering high mortality. Some female slaves decided the prospects for their children were so dire that they practiced abortion and infanticide (Hunwick 1978: 22; Lovejoy comment in "Slavery and Gender" n.d.).

However, evidence for a specifically "African" victim diaspora is difficult to maintain in the IOW where "slave" was not synonymous with "African," let alone "Black African," and where, as importantly, Africans played a central role in enslaving and selling their own kind, from warrior kings taking captives in military campaigns to Swahili trader slave-raiders to parents selling their own children in times of extreme dearth. It made little sense for slaves to cultivate an attachment to "Africa" and "Africans" if the latter were responsible for their enslavement and "enforced exile."

## Non-Assimilation: The Slave as "Outsider"

Essentialist scholars argue that Asians of African descent constituted a cohesive community of Africans "in exile." Rejected by the locally dominant group and thus alienated from it, they were "socially dead" "outsiders."

Where strong, hierarchical, and centralized societies enslaved members of relatively weak, egalitarian, and decentralized communities, the term "outsider" might be applicable—as in Indian Hindu societies that forced "tribals" into the *shudra* slave outcaste (see, e.g., Patnaik 1990: 3), lowland Southeast Asian and Indochinese peoples who raided "barbaric" mountain groups, and "piratical" Sulu who enslaved members of coastal communities in the Indonesian Archipelago and South China Seas (Boomgaard 2004; Warren 2004; Delaye 2004; Turton 2004; Salman 2005). Slavers generally dispatched the newly enslaved to distant regions in order to reduce the possibility of escape or of kin finding them. Again, most new slaves in the Middle East were "outsiders" because the *sharia* stipulated that the only legitimate targets of enslavement were non-Muslims opposed to Islam—which by the ninth century meant anyone living in non-Muslim lands (Sheriff 2005; Miers 2005; Klein 2005).

Some authors argue that increased demand for slaves promoted a marked differentiation between non-slaves and the enslaved that ensured for the latter a permanent status as "outsiders." Igor Kopytoff and Suzanne Miers stress that large complex societies were more likely to institutionalize inter-generational slave status and slave stigma than simpler decentralized polities (Kopytoff and Miers 1977: 42). James Watson contends that societies where this became entrenched in rigid law codes were characterized by "closed" slavery systems wherein the enslaved formed a hereditary category, legally excluded from the dominant slave-holding society in which they lived and worked (Watson 1980b). Thus in India, and South China, among the Nyiuba of Tibet, as in Imperial Madagascar, the outsider status of ex-slaves was institutionalized in structures that, in theory at least, ensured them a permanent and hereditary "out-caste" status. The essence of this was not occupation but a ritual distinction between "purity" and "pollution" that was maintained into the post-abolition era (Eno 2005: 83–93; Evers 1995: 157–88; Watson 1980b: 10, 1980c: 237–38, 246–47; Harris 1971: 116–17, esp. n. 4). In Madagascar, slaves were termed *"mainty"* ("black") and *"maloto"* ("impure") as opposed to the *"fotsy"* ("white" and "pure") non-slave (Campbell 2005c; see also Evers 1996). In both India and Madagascar, ritually impure tasks were conferred on members of the slave caste, with whom much social contact, including sexual relations, was taboo for non-slaves (Patnaik

1990: 4; Klein 1993: 14). Characteristically, it is asserted, slaves in such "closed" systems were treated worse than non-slaves, and coercion was applied to all aspects of their work (Kopytoff and Miers 1977: 14–16, 51; Klein 1993: 4–5, 11; Reid 1983: 12). Caste slavery of this sort, suggests Suzanne Miers, should be included in the category of "collective slavery" (Miers 2005).

Again, in China, not only slaves, but all females, were "outsiders" because they were excluded from the patriarchal structure of ownership, power, and religion. The Chinese form of marriage could be viewed as institutionalized servitude for wives, while daughters, concubines, and secondary wives were considered and treated as expendable "outsiders" who could be sold when times were bad. Certainly, as elsewhere in the IOW, the slave trade in China was predominantly in young females (Watson 1980c: 227–28; Jaschok and Miers 1994: 10).

Sometimes, however, it was difficult to classify the enslaved as "outsiders." First, not only were many enslaved within their home societies as a result of indebtedness, but slave raiding and kidnapping were often conducted against neighbors of the same linguistic and cultural community. This was evident in the Philippines, Indonesia, Madagascar, and even in Arabia and the Persian Gulf region into the twentieth century (see, e.g., Sheriff 2005; Salman 2005), while Europeans and frequently neighboring peoples were unable to differentiate between slaves and owners in some African communities (Klein 1993: 13; Kopytoff and Miers 1977: 5).

Moreover, slaves in the IOW rarely formed a cohesive social group or slave class. Those exported to IOW markets were usually shipped in small groups, supplementary to other commodities, and were dispersed throughout a wide variety of both indigenous and European slave-owning contexts, from the Middle East and Persian Gulf to South Asia, the Indian Ocean islands, Southeast Asia, and the Far East (Hunwick 1978: 31; Vérin 1999; Van Goor 1998: 196; Chakravarti 1997: 81, 85; Boomgaard 2004; De Silva Jayasuriya 2002; Bhargava 1990: 30). In addition, while the enslaved comprised between 20 and 30 percent of the population of many IOW societies (rising to 50 percent and over in Indonesian ports), they performed a large variety of functions, and as on the few European plantations which, exceptionally in the IOW, possessed large concentrated slave populations, they were in most cases of many different ethnic and cultural origins and statuses (Boomgaard 2004; Kim 2004; Kopytoff and Miers 1977: 60–61; Reid 1983: 12, 29; Campbell 1988: 474–75; R. Allen forthcoming).

Again, the "outsider" status of slaves was undermined by the often open disregard in the IOW for social barriers separating the enslaved and slave owners who generally developed close working relations with their slaves. Non-elite farmers and craftsmen often labored alongside their slaves. Most slaves, however, were employed in non-agricultural pursuits, many in elite households where some, notably child and young female slaves, had intimate relations with their owners forbidden to non-kinsmen. Terms for slaves were frequently cognates of those used for "children," "foster children," or "nephews" and "nieces" (Schottenhammer 2004; Kim 2004; Klein 1993: 8; Reid 1983: 9). In most African societies, it was considered "unseemly" to sell second-generation slaves as they possessed local kinship ties, sometimes with non-slave lineage groups (Kopytoff and Miers 1977: 35). In societies with slave castes, rules governing relations between slaves and non-slaves were sometimes openly ignored. Thus some female slave owners in Imperial Madagascar broke caste rules with impunity and took male slaves as their sexual partners (Poirier 1942–43: 100, n. 1), while in Korea it was not exceptional for daughters or wives of slave owners to sleep with male slaves (Kim 2004).

Indeed, forms of slavery and the relationship of the "slave" to the "free" populations in the IOW were everywhere more complex than the essentialist view permits. The many terms Europeans translated as "slave" from languages indigenous to the IOW have a range of meanings that changed according to time and locality. They thus reflected not one but a number of different servile statuses, most of which enjoyed some rights and property (Boomgaard 2004; Worden 2005). In wet-rice economies, for example, owners were often expected to provide their male slaves with a bride, whereas peasants were frequently incapable of raising a bride price or became indebted in doing so (Reid 1983: 8–9). Even in Korea and China, where the most extreme systems of hereditary slavery were practiced, slaves possessed a legal status and rights. They were immune from state corvées, and their marriages were in general respected. Such rights, it could be argued, meant that they were not true outsiders, as they had entered into the dominant society's system of reciprocity (Schottenhammer 2004; Kim 2004; see also Salman 2005).

Moreover, although IOW societies were hierarchically ordered, they rarely demonstrated a rigid and permanent dichotomy between superior and servile populations. They were characterized by considerable social mobility in which individuals of servile status could sometimes accede to a non-servile status, and vice versa. In the Middle East and Muslim India there are a number of documented examples of slaves acceding to positions of great political power and wealth. In Egypt and India, some individual slaves transformed themselves into rulers (Harris 1971: 39–40; Goody 1980: 29; Hunwick 1978: 27, 29–32; Hardy 1999; Bosworth 1999; Pellat 1999c; Ayalon 1999; Kidwai 1990: 92; Petry 1998; Chauhan 1995). In exceptional times, such as nineteenth-century Madagascar, there even occurred complete reversals of hierarchy that permitted of slave status to enjoy better standards of living than those of nominally 'free' peasant status (Campbell 2005b: chs. 5, 9).

### Assimilation and Integration

There also existed strong forces promoting the integration of slaves into the dominant society in many IOW regions where, in contrast to the Atlantic system, most slaves were subject to forces promoting assimilation into local society rather than separation and alienation from it (Campbell 2004: vii–xxxii). In large part, this stemmed from Islamic influence which by the fourteenth century dominated much of the region, from East Africa to Indonesia. The *sharia* taught that manumission of slave converts was meritorious, slaves could redeem themselves, and children resulting from the sexual union of slave masters and concubines inherited a non-slave status, as did a concubine mother upon the death of her owner. The rate of manumission could theoretically be high; whereas a rich Muslim was legally restricted to four wives, the number of concubines he might possess was unlimited (see Sheriff 2005; Clarence-Smith 2005; Brunschwig 1999; Lewis 1990). Manumission, relatively common where close owner-slave relationships existed, was accorded more readily to domestic slaves than to those employed in activities and areas that separated them from the slave-owning household. Thus under most Islamic slave regimes, the number of manumitted slaves was considerable.

Because wealthy and powerful Muslims had more concubines than others, significant numbers of their progeny by slave women became part of the local elite. Many of Mecca's *Qurayshī* elite were the progeny of Arab males and African concubines, and the three greatest early Arab poets, "Antara bin Shaddād al-Kalbī, Khafāf bin Nudba al-Sulakhī, and Sulayk bin al-Sulaka were known as the "Crows of the Arabs" because they possessed Black mothers (Hassad, Mufuta, and Mutunda) (Ross 1994: 18–19). Similarly, Atā ibn Abī Rabāh, born in Saudi Arabia of Nubian parents, became a celebrated Muslim teacher and jurist at Mecca in the early eighth century (Irwin 1977: 66), while a century later Abū Al-Djāhiz, of probably Ethiopian slave origin, achieved fame and influence in Basra and Baghdad as author of sociological commentaries, theology, and politico-religious polemics (Pellat 1999a). Again, some Muslim monarchs had African mothers who were publicly revered (Irwin 1977: 54, 58).

Assimilation also marked non-Muslim societies. Children of slaves in Dutch Sri Lanka were freed upon conversion to, and marriage in, the Dutch Reformed Church, while their parents could not be sold and were freed upon the death of their master (De Silva Jayasuriya 2002). Slaves employed by British families in Bombay in the late eighteenth century were usually freed by testament will following the death of their owner (Chakravarti 1997: 83), while in Imperial Madagascar manumission was considered meritorious for *zazahova*, or Merina enslaved chiefly for indebtedness (Poirier 1942–43: 122–24; Campbell 1994).

Again, genetic studies reveal considerable gene flow between "Africans," notably African women, and other local groups (see, e.g., Ramana, Su, Lin, et al. 2001; L. Singh, Ramana, Wang, and Chakraborty 2000; Jenkins, Hewitt, Krause, Campbell, and Goldman 1996; "Slavery and Gender" n.d.). While some of this reflected sexual violence by male slave owners toward their female slaves, this was not always, or even generally, the case. In rare instances, as Sheriff notes for Bahrein, "free" women married slave men (Sheriff 2005). In Muslim societies and European territories in the IOW, slave soldiers were usually freed after a period of service, married local women, and were assimilated (Lewis 1990: 10, 15; Basu 2002). High-status Sidi of Janjira intermarried with the Ismaili Tyabji, who in the nineteenth century emerged as leading entrepreneurs and bankers (Basu 2002); in Hyderabad, the nizam encouraged his African soldiers to marry Arab girls (Harris 1971: 112), many Sidi Hindus of Karnataka married local Hindus (Ali 1996: 225–26), and in the Makran and Gujarat some African males formed liaisons with local members of low castes and with "tribals" (Alpers comment in "Slavery and Gender" n.d.). Under British-administered Ceylon in the early nineteenth century, the rate of intermarriage of "Kaffir" soldiers (from Africa, notably Mozambique and Madagascar) with Sri Lankan women was so high that the African-Sinhalese community sharply declined; continued intermarriage threatens its very existence (De Silva Jayasuriya 2002).

### Acculturation

Acculturation, notably the adoption of the slave-owners' language, religion, and general culture, played an essential part in slave assimilation. As noted, possibly the majority of enslaved Africans in the IOW, in contrast to the Americas, were employed in sensitive positions—within the household, court, administration, or commerce. For most owners, it was vital that slaves understood orders. Child slaves and young concubines, in particular, rapidly learned the local language and customs. Given the multiethnic origin and generally diffuse distribution of IOW slaves, many young slaves and almost all second-generation slaves largely shed their cultural origins and became monoglot speakers of the host community's language. That so many slaves in Southeast Asia had similar linguistic and cultural backgrounds to their masters facilitated the process there (Reid 1983: 13, 25–26), as did language classes in slave reception camps in China and Imperial Madagascar (Delaye 2004; Campbell 1981: 224).

In consequence, Asians of African slave descent have largely shed their cultural and linguistic origins (Harris 1971: 99–100, 111–12; Mirzai 2002: 241; Chauhan 1995: 261–63; De Silva Jayasuriya 2002; Bhattacharya 1970: 579–80; Ali 1996; Drewal 2002). For instance, there currently exist only some 500 speakers of Sri Lankan Portuguese Creole, the "mother tongue" of the African-Sinhalese community (De Silva Jayasuriya 2002). Vestiges of all other singular "African" languages, such as Makhuwa in Madagascar, are fast disappearing (Alpers 2000: 93–94). That Swahili is still current in Muscat (93–94) and spoken by members of some Asian communities of African descent in other coastal areas of the Middle East reflects more its role as a lingua franca in the western Indian Ocean than as an "African" language.[7]

Similarly, acceptance of the dominant ideology was a pre-requisite for slaves employed in sensitive posts in the royal household, army, and administration. Equally crucial was the conversion of imported child brides and concubines to local belief and value systems, in order that these might in turn be transmitted to their children, whose position was secured if as offspring of the owner they became integrated into the slave owner's lineage (Kopytoff and Miers 1977: 28–29; Watson 1980c: 249; Schottenhammer 2004; Kim 2004; Sheriff 2005). Today, most Asians of African descent adhere to local religious beliefs, from Islam, Hinduism, and Christianity to ancestor worship (Harris 1971: 99–100, 111–12; Mirzai 2002: 241; Chauhan 1995: 261, 263; De Silva Jayasuriya 2002; Bhattacharya 1970: 579–80; Ali 1996: 224; Drewal 2002).

Such adaptation reflects integrationist impulses among the enslaved, whose chief aim was less to rebel than to secure a niche within the dominant society, improve that position over time, and, if granted non-slave status, assume a new, local ethnicity. Individual slaves therefore sought to forge linkages not with other slaves but with slaveholders who alone could ameliorate their conditions and station. One reflection of this was the tendency of some enslaved Africans to alter their names in order to blend in better with the local community. For example, many Sidi Christians in Goa adopted Portuguese names to hide their origins (Ali 1996: 226).

Again, many Muslim communities of African descent constructed their own mosques (Harris 1971: 122; Mirzai 2002: 235). More strikingly, some individuals of African slave descent carved for themselves a powerful role within local religious systems (see, e.g., Ghatwai 2000). In nineteenth-century Madagascar, some slaves gained a powerful "religious" influence—a temporary one within the early Christian church and a more enduring one as ancestral mediums (Campbell 2005c). Again, Sidi mediums of Bava Gor gained ritual power over former slave owner devotees of the saints and thereby an honorific place in local history and society (Basu 2002; Alpers 1997: 74). Thus cults in South Asia centered around male and female saints (Bava Gor, Mai Goma, Sidi Mubarak Nobi, Bava Habash, Mai Mishra) have cemented for their Sidi practitioners a local rather than African identity (Basu 2002), as have the *Nobān* and *Gwāti/ Damal* healing ceremonies of southern Iran and Baluchistan, respectively, and the essentially female-dominated *Zār* spirit possession/healing cult of probably Ethiopian origin practiced in the Middle East–Persian Gulf–Baluchistan regions (Hunwick 1978: 37; see also Nelson 1974: 555–56). Certainly integration often took a few generations, and many groups retained a servile status, but it has occurred almost throughout the IOW.

### Diasporic Consciousness

Lovejoy posits that "a diaspora by its nature cannot exist without a homeland" (Lovejoy 2001: 9).[8] However, Asians of African descent show remarkably little consciousness of an African homeland. Indeed, the concept of "Africa" as a geographical entity is a twentieth-century phenomenon and still fragile. African migrants in the IOW represented widely varying ethnicities and cultures located variously in West, North, Central, and East Africa and the islands (Trimingham 1964: 2–3; Hunwick 1978: 31; Vérin 1999; Alpers 2000: 85). Conventional assumptions that names for peoples of African descent are indications of precise origins (e.g. Zanj / Sidi = Swahili Coast and hinterland; Habshi = Ethiopia; "K'un-lun = African) are incorrect, as these terms were applied by the "host" communities and tend to be generic. For example, "Zanj" indicated someone from the "uninhabitable" regions of sub-Saharan Africa, and "Ethiopian," any dark-skinned person, African or Asian (Lewis 1976: 37; Ross 1994: 12–13; Irwin 1977). On Mauritius, the term "Mozambique" subsumed at least thirteen different southeastern African ethnicities (Alpers 1999: 1–2). The IOW possessed few New World–style concentrations of slaves. In Imperial Madagascar and on the plantation islands (Mauritius and Réunion from the mid-eighteenth century and Zanzibar and Pemba from the 1830s) African slaves formed a significant group, with common living and working conditions that provided the potential for the emergence of a slave "consciousness." Even there, however, no natural identification with "Africa" as a place of origin or sense of common "African" (or "slave") identity emerged (see, e.g., Teelock 1999: 3–8).[9] Ethnic and cultural differences militated strongly against the development of any pan-African slave consciousness, as did an internal slave hierarchy in which those of local origin were often considered superior to imported slaves. New arrivals often raised the status of resident slaves, as did recaptured fugitive slaves, whose inferior status was often visibly clarified through branding or tattoos (Campbell 2005c; see also Reid 1983: 12). Another sign of superior slave status was avoidance of ritually degrading activities (Schottenhammer 2004; Klein 1993: 7; Chauhan 1995).

Indeed, save in places of recent and concentrated African settlement, such as Hyderabad, few Asians of African descent today have any clear idea of their African origins, and most deny any African identity (Harris 1971: 111–12; Bhattacharya 1970). The forces of integration are clearly at work. For instance, in c. 1900 over 50 percent of the population of Qatar's two main cities of Doha and Wakra were "African," both slave and manumitted. Slavery was abolished there only in 1952, but groups of "African" descent can be identified by their physiognomy and with few exceptions are socially stigmatized and suffer from poor living and working conditions. Local Arabs assert that these "Africans" form the fifth and lowest "tribe" according to purity of descent. Nevertheless, they are Muslim, speak Arabic, and claim an Arab identity—to the point of denying an African heritage, having been integrated into the ranks of noble tribes, as soldiers (male) and concubines (female), and thus to lie second in tribal ranking. They assert an Arab identity, stressing as proof not only their profound knowledge of Arabic and Arab culture but also their code of honor and contributions to Arab history and Arabic literature (Montigny 2002: 214–17, 223). In like vein, "Kaffirs" stress their Sri Lankan rather than African identity (De Silva Jayasuriya 2002). Indeed, despite pressure from academic researchers in the form of a constant barrage of questions as to their African identity, Asians of African descent, from the Middle East and Persian Gulf to India and Madagascar, almost always deny any identity with Africa and, by contrast, affirm their local identity.[10]

Some scholars highlight African influences in the songs and dances of Asians of African descent as evidence of an African identity (Alpers 1997: 67–68, 73; 2000: 90–91; Basu 2002; Drewal 2002; Fernandes 2003; De Silva Jayasuriya 2002; Bhattacharya 1970: 579, 581–82; Harris 1971: 112; Mirzai 2002: 241–45). However, these activities occur in local cultural contexts in which the local language predominates and the actors involved overwhelmingly claim a local identity (Montigny 2002: 221–22). Of the music of "African" inspiration played by people of African or part African descent in Qatar, Anie Montigny comments: "It is above all for its liberty of expression that music is taken up, and Blacks do not search through it to return to their roots, nor to contest their social condition. Rather, they emphasize its arabicized character, taken as a proof of their Arab roots" (Montigny 2002: 223–24).

The literature has tended to concentrate on the role of elite male slaves, but the same was true of elite female slaves, such as the *kayna* (pl. *kaynāt / kiyīn*), female slave singers of African or mixed African-Asian descent in Muslim countries. These singers could earn renown and fortune and, through their compositions of Arabic poetry, which indicated no sense of "African" identity, helped shape and enrich the Arabic language and literature, notably of modernist (*muhdath*) Islamic poetry (Montigny 2002: 221; Lewis 1990: 13; Pellat 1999b).

Sidi musicians and dancers similarly demonstrate little consciousness of being "African" or of any common inter-Sidi cause beyond the purely local or (in Gujarat, Karnataka, and Andhra Pradesh) regional level (Prashad 2000: 195; Cooper 1999; Obeng 2000).[11] Pashington Obeng, who contends that Sidis in general exhibit an African diasporic consciousness, produces evidence only of class or caste consciousness that incorporates Sidis and "non-African" Indian groups based on a communality of economic interests (Obeng 2000). Shanti Ali affirms that the Sidi Hindus of Karnataka claim to be part of the local caste hierarchy (Ali 1996: 225–26), while some Sidis at the January 2006 Goa Conference considered themselves integrated into the local caste system above the Dalits (untouchables) and claimed that individual Sidis could move, by virtue of wealth, into non-Sidi strata of Indian society.[12] Again, Sunni Sidis claim a direct descent from Mohammed and insist that they be called "Muslim Sidis" (Ali 1996: 226).

Edward Alpers considers that a major reason for the negation of an African identity is the lack of Western-educated elites to articulate the notion of African origins, the struggle of those with African ancestry, and the way in which African traditions have been transformed in the Asian world (Alpers 2000: 84–85). However, as indicated above, some people of African slave descent did become highly educated, cultivated, and literate figures, and others became politically powerful. Nevertheless, they without exception expressed a local rather than "African" identity. Historically, those at the top of the slave hierarchy, and any other slaves who could afford to do so, became slaveholders—surely the most manifest sign of the lack of a diasporic consciousness (Schottenhammer 2004; Klein 1993: 7; Chauhan 1995: 112–17). They displayed a marked disinterest in Africa and Africans, rather displaying total commitment to the values and well-being of the slave-owning society of which they had become an integral part (Cole and Altorki 2000).

### Return to the Homeland

Lovejoy also posits that to qualify as a diaspora, its members must demonstrate "the quest to re-attain" the homeland (qtd. in Lovejoy 2001; see also Lovejoy 1997). However, Asians of African descent show even less inclination to "return" to an imagined homeland than they do to claiming an "African" identity. The only known example of Africans in Asia returning to the "homeland" in order to promote its development was the result of Western pressure. From 1874, Church Mission Society missionaries to India sent freed African slaves from a special asylum at Nasik, a hundred miles from Bombay, to establish a mission at Freretown in Mombasa, the activities of which continued to the 1930s (Akyeampong 2000: 197; Basu 2002). Otherwise, attempted returns were sporadic, generally the result of escape bids by freshly captured young adult male slaves, such as certain Malagasy shipped to the Mascarenes (Alpers 2004; Mampilly 2001). Such attempts in no way represented an African diasporic consciousness. The few ex-slaves in the IOW offered passage to their region of origin generally found re-integration difficult (see, e.g., Warren 2004). When offered passage back to Africa, many African or African-Asian slaves in Asia refused (see, e.g., Miers 2005). Indeed, for many present-day Asians of African descent, Africa is seen as an undeveloped region whose populations they might wish to proselytize, but with whom they do not wish to identify (Montigny 2002: 223–34).

Thus Asians of African descent clearly fail to qualify as a diaspora according to conventionally accepted criteria. Acknowledging this, Alpers proffers a more flexible definition of diaspora as "a loosely coherent adaptive constellation of responses to dwelling-in-displacement. . . . Diaspora cultures . . . mediate, in a lived-tension, the experiences of separation and entanglement, of living here and remembering/ desiring another place" (James Clifford qtd. in Alpers 2003: 22). However, such a definition renders meaningless the concept of diaspora, as it could apply equally to the sense of displacement and nostalgia experienced by the many millions who have been impelled to migrate long distances since the development of the international economy in the nineteenth century.

### Identity and Empowerment: The Future for Asians of African Descent

The issue of identity for Asians of African descent is not purely academic. As the 2006 Goa conference demonstrated, a major focus of current concern is the empowerment of groups, such as the Sidi in India, of identifiably African descent who suffer from social, economic, and political disadvantages. There exist two conflicting views concerning their empowerment. Essentialists consider it vital that these groups claim empowerment through asserting their identity as members of a global African victim diaspora. As Harris stated in his address to the Goa Conference: "Given the legacy of the slave trade, enslavement and subsequent disadvantage, Africans and peoples of African descent must assume a more visible and assertive role in the movement for human and economic justice. This could well be the great challenge of the 21st century" (Harris 2006).

Essentialist scholars insist on the African identity of such groups, irrespective of the group's own self-perception. In India, particularly, the government has taken note of this essentialist interest and started to accord Sidis special consideration. Believing that their "African" origins made Sidis genetically gifted for sports, the Indian government Sports Authority in 1987 established a special program to recruit and train Sidis for international competitions. The strategy has failed due to poor Sidi motivation, according to government spokespeople (Drewal 2002; Cooper 1999). The government has also funded musical events in which Sidis adopt "African" clothes, as when Gujarati Sidi *goma* dancers were called upon to sport peacock feathers during a visit from Nelson Mandela. Bollywood has subsequently portrayed them in the same costumes to embellish films (Shroff 2002; see also Fernandes 2003), as have some African Diaspora scholars who consider that international recognition of such "African" troupes will bring Sidis greater status and revenue (see, e.g., Catlin-Jairazbhoy 2006).

The approach of essentialist scholars is disquieting for two main reasons. First, as indicated above, it is historically misleading to apply the Atlantic model of slavery to the IOW. This has an important resonance for the debate over empowerment of Asian communities of African descent because history shapes the identity of individuals and groups and informs their actions and policies. The history of Africans in Asia is overwhelmingly one of integration, in which they have shed their African identity and adopted a local Asian identity. The existence in some groups of some "African" cultural traits in no way alters this fundamental historical reality.

The argument that Asians of African descent should identify themselves as members of an African victim diaspora is not only historically misleading, but it also raises concern about how best to empower such communities. Are their interests best served by molding for them an identity as "Africans," as a foreign community in Asia, or through recognizing their claims to a local identity and promoting the already strong forces of integration? While many scholars might look askance at the Indian government's recent classification of Sidis as a "Scheduled Tribe" (Rahul Singh), pressure upon political authorities to recognize such communities as an integral part of a local society composed of a mosaic of peoples of different origins appears to offer the best path to both empowerment and community relations.

## Conclusion

A major debate exists between essentialist African Diaspora scholars and other scholars of the Indian Ocean world (IOW) over the issue of Asians of African descent. Essentialists, applying the Atlantic model to IOW slavery, argue that Asians of African descent constitute part of an African victim diaspora. By contrast, other scholars underscore the historical complexity of the IOW and the inapplicability of either an essentialist or an Atlantic model. In the IOW, people of African descent demonstrated an overwhelming tendency to integrate into local society and claim for themselves a local identity. Indeed, members of present-day communities in Asia of recognizably African descent have no consciousness of an African homeland, overwhelmingly affirm a local rather than African identity, and demonstrate no interest in "returning" to Africa. Thus the criteria for an African Diaspora do not exist. At the same time, slaves in the IOW were neither uniquely nor predominantly African. Studies that focus only on Black African slaves are historically unbalanced and serve to obscure the history of slaves of other origins, notably females who formed probably the majority of IOW slaves.

Such observations raise major questions as to the best means of social and economic empowerment for present-day low-status groups of Asians of African descent. Essentialists contend that their bid for empowerment should be based on claims to be members of an African victim diaspora, a position reinforced by the exclusively "African" focus of the UNESCO Slave Route Project's first forays into the IOW. The counter-argument is that the essentialist view is historically misleading, and that forcing a foreign "African" identity upon such groups seriously risks weakening integrationist impulses, accentuating inter-community friction, and undermining the bid of lower-status Asians of African descent for social, economic, and political empowerment.

### Notes

I gratefully acknowledge comment by Rustom Bharucha on earlier drafts of this paper.

    1. Helene Basu's estimates are considerably larger. See Basu 2002.

    2. The Dutch landed the first cargo of 41 Malagasy slaves at Colombo in 1693 (Armstrong 2000; Hunwick 1978: 31; Boomgaard 2004: 83–96; De Silva Jayasuriya 2002).

    3. Some scholars consider that Islam per se greatly stimulated the slave trade. However, more important was the demand for menial labor that accompanied the concomitant growth in IOW global economy—as occurred again with the rapid expansion of the international economy in the nineteenth century (Campbell 2004: in-

troduction, 2005a: introduction; Chaudhuri 1985); Wink 1996, 1997); Eaton 1993: 1–36; Brunschvig 1999).

4. However, a slave's property upon the death of the slave passed to his or her master (Warren 2004).

5. See, e.g., the chapter by Pashington Obeng in this volume; Okpewho, Davies, and Mazrui 1999; Akyeampong 2000: 184–86; Hine and McLeod 1999; Thompson 2000; see also the introduction to Matsuoka and Sorenson 2001; Basu 2002.

6. See also Miller 2004; for comparative material see Piersen 1977.

7. Numbers of sea-faring and coastal Arabs also speak Swahili (Mirzai 2002: 237–38).

8. Lovejoy follows William Safran: see Akyeampong 2000: 184–85.

9. Alpers asserts that there was such a consciousness but can find no evidence of it (1999: esp. 18).

10. For Iran, see Mirzai 2002: 241; for India, see Basu 2002; Mampilly 2001; for Sri Lanka, see F. Cooper 1997.

11. Personal communication with Rustom Bharucha, February 2006.

12. Sidi testimonials at the TADIA conference on "The Siddis of India and the African Diasporas in Asia," Goa, India, 9–20 January 2006.

### Works Cited

Adas, Michael, ed. 1993. *Islamic and European Expansion. The Forging of a Global Order.* Philadelphia: Temple University Press.

Aksan, Virginia H. 1998. "Ottoman Egypt." In Finkelman and Miller, *Macmillan Encyclopedia of World Slavery,* 1: 285.

Akyeampong, Emmanuel. 2000. "Africans in the Diaspora: The Diaspora and Africa." *African Affairs* 99.395: 183–216.

Ali, Shanti Sadiq. 1987. *India and Africa through the Ages.* New Delhi: National Book Trust.

——. 1996. *The African Dispersal in the Deccan from Medieval to Modern Times.* Hyderabad: Orient Longman.

Allen, James de Vere. 1993. *Swahili Origins: Swahili Culture and the Shungwaya Phenomenon.* London: James Currey.

Allen, Richard B. 1999. *Slaves, Freedmen and Indentured Laborers in Colonial Mauritius.* New York: Cambridge University Press.

——. Forthcoming. "A Traffic Repugnant to Humanity: Children, the Mascarene Slave Trade and British Abolitionism." In Gwyn Campbell, Suzanne Miers and Joseph C. Miller, *Children in Slavery around the World.*

Alpers, Edward A. 1997. "The African Diaspora in the Northwestern Indian Ocean: Reconsideration of an Old Problem, New Directions for Research." *Comparative Studies of South Asia, Africa and the Middle East* 17.2: 62–81.

——. 1999. "Becoming "Mozambique": Diaspora and Identity in Mauritius." Paper presented at the Harriet Tubman Seminar, Department of History, York University, Toronto, 15 November.

——. 2000. "Recollecting Africa: Diasporic Memory in the Indian Ocean World." *African Studies Review* 1.43: 83–99.

——. 2003. "The African Diaspora in the Indian Ocean: A Comparative Perspective." In *The African Diaspora in the Indian Ocean, ed.* Shihan de S. Jayasuriya and Richard Pankhurst, 19–53. Trenton, N.J.: Africa World Press.

———. 2004. "Flight to Freedom: Escape from Slavery among Bonded Africans in the Indian Ocean World, c. 1750–1962." In Campbell (ed.), *Structure of Slavery*, 51–68.

Arasaratnam, S. 1995. "Slave Trade in the Indian Ocean in the Seventeenth Century." In *Mariners, Merchants and Oceans: Studies in Maritime History*, ed. K. S. Mathew, 195–208. New Delhi: Manohar.

Armstrong, James C. 2000. "Ceylon and the Slave Trade during the Dutch East India Company Period." Paper presented at the conference on Slave Systems in Asia and the Indian Ocean: Their Structure and Change in the Nineteenth and Twentieth Centuries, Université d'Avignon, Avignon, France, 18–20 May.

Atwell, William S. 2001. "Volcanism and Short-Term Climatic Change in East Asian and World History, c.1200–1699." *Journal of World History* 12.1 (2001): 31–64.

Austen, Ralph. 1989. "The 19th Century Islamic Slave Trade from East Africa (Swahili and Red Sea Coasts): A Tentative Census." In *The Economics of the Indian Ocean Slave Trade*, ed. William Gervase Clarence-Smith, 21–44. London: Frank Cass.

Ayalon, D. 1999. "Mamlūk." *Encyclopaedia of Islam*. CD-ROM ed. v.1.0.

Badger, George Perry. 1863. "Notes" to Lodovico di Varthema, *Travels in Egypt, Syria, Arabia Deserta and Arabia Felix, in Persia, India and Ethiopia AD 1503 to 1508*, trans. J. W. Jones. London: Hakluyt Society.

"Baluchistan." 1911. Encyclopaedia Britannica. http://82.1911encyclopedia.org/B/BA/BALUCHISTAN.htm, accessed February 2006.

Basu, Helene. 2002. "Indian Siddi—African Diaspora: A Query." Paper presented at the Conference on Cultural Exchange and Transformation in the Indian Ocean World, University of California at Los Angeles, 5–6 April.

Bhargava, M. L. 1990. *Indian Ocean Strategies through the Ages*. New Delhi: Reliance.

Bhattacharya, D. K. 1970. "Indians of African Origin." *Cahiers d'Etudes Africaines* 10.40: 579.

Biermann, Werner, and John Campbell. 1989. "The Wheels of Commerce: The Indian Ocean and the East African Coast during the Period of Portuguese Hegemony, c.1500–1600." In *Transition and Continuity of Identity in East Africa and Beyond—In Memoriam David Miller*, ed. Elisabeth Linnebuhr, 19–53. Bayreuth, Germany: Bayreuth University.

Boivin, Michel. 2000. "La Condition servile dans le Sindh colonial—remarques préliminaires." Paper presented at the conference on Slave Systems in Asia and the Indian Ocean: Their Structure and Change in the Nineteenth and Twentieth Centuries," Université d'Avignon, Avignon, France, 18–20 May.

Boomgaard, Peter. 2004. "Human Capital, Slavery and Low Rates of Economic and Population Growth in Indonesia, 1600–1910." In Campbell, *Structure of Slavery*, 83–96.

Bosworth, C. E. 1999. "Ghulām, Persia." *Encyclopaedia of Islam*. CD-ROM ed. v.1.0.

Brunschwig, R. 1999. "Abd." *Encyclopaedia of Islam*. CD-ROM ed. v.1.0.

Campbell, Gwyn. 1981. "Madagascar and the Slave Trade, 1810–1895. *Journal of African History* 22.2: 203–27.

———. 1988. "Slavery and Fanompoana: The Structure of Forced Labor in Imerina (Madagascar), 1790–1861." *Journal of African History* 29.3: 463–86.

———. 1991. "The State and Pre-colonial Demographic History: The Case of Nineteenth Century Madagascar." *Journal of African History*, 31.3: 415–45.

———. 1992. "Crisis of Faith and Colonial Conquest: The Impact of Famine and Disease in Late Nineteenth-Century Madagascar." *Cahiers d'Études Africaines* 32.127: 409–53.

———. 1994. "The History of Nineteenth Century Madagascar: 'Le royaume' or 'l'empire'?" *Omaly sy Anio* 33–36: 331–79.

———. 1996. "The Origins and Demography of Slaves in Nineteenth Century Madagascar: A Chapter in the History of the African Ancestry of the Malagasy." In *Fanandevozana ou esclavage*, ed. François Rajaison, 5–38. Antananarivo, Madagascar: Musée d'Art et d'Archéologie de l'Université d'Antananarivo.

———. 2000. "Madagascar and the Slave Trade in the South West Indian Ocean." In *Globalization and the South West Indian Ocean*, ed. Sandra J. T. Evers and Vinesh Y. Hookoomsing, 91–109. Leiden, Netherlands: International Institute for Asian Studies; Réduit, Mauritius: and University of Mauritius.

———, ed. 2004. *The Structure of Slavery in Indian Ocean Africa and Asia*. London: Routledge, 2004.

———, ed. 2005a. *Abolition and Its Aftermath in Indian Ocean Africa and Asia*. London: Routledge.

———, 2005b. *An Economic History of Imperial Madagascar, 1750–1895: The Rise and Fall of an Island Empire*. Cambridge: Cambridge University Press.

———. 2005c. "Unfree Labor and the Significance of Abolition in Madagascar, c. 1825–97." In Campbell, *Abolition and Its Aftermath*, 66–82.

Campbell, Gwyn, Suzanne Miers, and Joseph C. Miller, eds. Forthcoming. *Children in Slavery around the World*.

Catlin-Jairazbhoy, Amy. 2006. "From Africa to India: Siddi Music in the Indian Ocean Diaspora." 74-minute film presented at the TADIA conference on "The Siddis of India and the African Diaspora in Asia," Goa, India, 10–20 January.

Chakravarti, Sudesha. 1997. "The Dutch East India Company and Slave Trade in Seventeenth Century India: An Outline by Pieter van Dam, an Advocate of the Company." *Journal of the Asiatic Society* 39.2.

Chatterjee, Indrani. 2005. "Abolition by Denial: The South Asian Example." In Campbell, *Abolition and Its Aftermath*, 15–68.

Chaudhuri, K. N. 1985. *Trade and Civilization in the Indian Ocean: An Economic History from the Rise of Islam to 1750*. Cambridge: Cambridge University Press.

———. 1992. *Asia before Europe: Economy and Civilization of the Indian Ocean from the Rise of Islam to 1750*. Cambridge: Cambridge University Press, 1992.

Chauhan, R. R. S. 1995. *Africans in India: From Slavery to Royalty*. New Delhi: Asian Publication Service.

Clarence-Smith, William Gervase. 2005. "Islam and the Abolition of the Slave Trade and Slavery in the Indian Ocean." In Campbell, *Abolition and Its Aftermath*, 137–49.

Coedès, G. 1966. *The Making of South East Asia*. Berkeley: University of California Press.

Cole, Donald P., and Soraya Altorki. 2000. "Family in Changing Saudi Arabia (I): Substantive Development, circa 1955–1975." http://ist-socrates.berkely.edu/~mescha/famabtracts/altorki%20and%20cole.html, accessed August 2005.

Cooper, Frederick. 1997. *Plantation Slavery on the East Coast of Africa*. Portsmouth, NH: Heinemann.

Cooper, Kenneth J. 1999. "Within South Asia, a Little Touch of Africa." 12 April. www.maxpages.com/apu/Articles_from_Members, accessed August 2005.

Davis, David Brion. 1970. *The Problem of Slavery in Western Culture*. Harmondsworth, UK: Penguin.

De Silva Jayasuriya, Shihan. 2002. "The Ceylon *Kaffirs: A Creole Community in an Indian Ocean Island.*" Paper presented at the Conference on Cultural Exchange and Transformation in the Indian Ocean World, University of California at Los Angeles, 5–6 April.

Delaye, Karine. 2004. "Slavery and Colonial Representations in Indochina from the Second Half of the Nineteenth to the Early Twentieth Centuries." In Campbell, *Structure of Slavery,* 129–42.

Drewal, Henry John. 2002. "Aliens and Homelands: Identity, Agency and the Arts among the Siddis of Northern Karnataka." Paper presented to the International Conference on Cultural Exchange and Transformation in the Indian Ocean World, University of California at Los Angeles, April 5–6.

Duyvendak, J. J. L. 1949. *China's Discovery of Africa.* London: A. Probsthain.

Eaton, Richard M. 1993. "Islamic History as Global History." In *Islamic and European Expansion: The Forging of a Global Order, ed.* Michael Adas, 1–36. Philadelphia: Temple University Press.

Ellis, William. 1870. *The Martyr Church.* London: John Snow.

Eno, Omar A. 2005. "The Abolition of Slavery and Its Impact on the Benadir Coast." In Campbell, *Abolition and Its Aftermath,* 83–93.

Evers, Sandra. 1995. "Stigmatization as a Self-Perpetuating Process." In *Cultures of Madagascar: Ebb and Flow of Influences,* ed. Sandra Evers and Marc Spindler, 157–88. Leiden, Netherlands: International Institute for Asian Studies.

———. 1996. "Solidarity and Antagonism in Migrant Societies on the Southern Highlands." In *Fanandevozana ou Esclavage,* ed. François Rajaison, 565–71. Antananarivo: Université d'Antananarivo.

Evers, Sandra J. T., and Vinesh Y. Hookoomsing, eds. 2000. *Globalization and the South West Indian Ocean.* Leiden, Netherlands: International Institute for Asian Studies; Réduit, Mauritius: University of Mauritius.

Ewald, Janet J. 1998a. "Ethiopia." In Finkelman and Miller, *Macmillan Encyclopedia of World Slavery,* 2: 653.

———. 1998b. "Upper Nile Region." In Finkelman and Miller, *Macmillan Encyclopedia of World Slavery,* 2: 651.

———. 2000. "Slaves and Seedies in British Ports and Vessels, 1840–1900." Paper presented at the Conference on Slave Systems in Asia and the Indian Ocean: Their Structure and Change in the Nineteenth and Twentieth Centuries," Université d'Avignon, Avignon, France, 18–20 May.

Fernandes, Naresh. 2003. "Redemption Songs." *Outlook Traveler,* May.

Fernyhough, Timothy Derek. 1986. "Serfs, Slaves and Shefta: Modes of Production in Southern Ethiopia from the Late Nineteenth Century to 1941." Ph.D. diss., University of Illinois at Urbana-Champaign, 1986.

Filesi, Teobaldi. 1972. *China and Africa in the Middle Ages.* Trans. David L. Morison. London: Frank Cass.

Finkelman, Paul, and Joseph C. Miller, eds. 1998. *Macmillan Encyclopedia of World Slavery.* 2 vols. New York: Macmillan Reference.

Fisher, Humphrey. 1989. "The Western and Central Sudan and East Africa." In *The Cambridge History of Islam,* ed. P. M. Holt, Ann K. S. Lambton, and Bernard Lewis, 2A: 382. Cambridge: Cambridge University Press.

Frank, Andre Gunder. 1998. *Reorient: Global Economy in the Asian Age.* Berkeley: University of California Press.

Ghatwai, Milind. 2000. "Shrine Where Crime Suspects Face Unusual Test." *Indian Express*, 5 October. www.indianexpress.com/ie/daily/20001005/ina05039.html, accessed August 2005.

Goody, Jack. 1980. "Slavery in Time and Space." In Watson, *Asian and African Systems of Slavery*, 16–42.

Grandidier, Alfred, and Guillaum Grandidier. 1908. *Histoire Physique, Naturelle et Politique de Madagascar*. Vol. 4.1. Paris: Imprimerie Nationale.

———. 1928. *Histoire Physique, Naturelle et Politique de Madagascar*. Vol. 4.4. Paris: Imprimerie Nationale.

Griffiths, David. 1840. *Hanes Madagascar*. Machynlleth, UK: Richard Jones.

Gudmundson, Candace. 2002. "El Niño and Climate Prediction." *Reports to the Nation on Our Changing Planet*. www.atmos.washington.edu/gcg/RTN/rtnt.html, accessed 8 March 2007.

Guillot, Claude, Denys Lombard, and Roderich Ptak, eds. 1998. *From the Mediterranean to the China Sea*. Wiesbaden, Germany: Harrassowitz Verlag.

Haight, Mabel V. Jackson. 1942. *European Powers and South-East Africa (1796–1856)*. London: Routledge & Kegan Paul.

Hardy, P. 1999. "Ghulām. India." *Encyclopaedia of Islam*. CD-ROM ed. v.1.0.

Harris, Joseph E. 1971. *The African Presence in Asia: Consequences of the East African Slave Trade*. Evanston, Ill.: Northwestern University Press.

———. 1993. *Global Dimensions of the African Diaspora*. 2nd ed. Washington, D.C.: Howard University Press. (Orig. pub. 1979.)

———. 2006. "The Global African Diaspora: A Challenge for the 21[st] Century." Address presented in absentia to the TADIA conference on "The Siddis of India and the African Diasporas in Asia." Goa, India, 9–20 January.

Hermann, Paul. 1954. *Conquest by Man: The Saga of Early Exploration and Discovery*. New York: Harper.

Hine, Darlene Clark, and Jacqueline McLeod, eds. 1999. *Crossing Boundaries: A Comparative History of Black People in Diaspora*. Bloomington: Indiana University Press.

Hirth, Friedrich. 1909–10. "Early Chinese Notices of East African Territories." *Journal of the American Oriental Society* 30: 46–57.

Huntingford, G. W. B., trans. and ed. 1980. *The Periplus of the Erythraean Sea circa* AD 95–130. London: Hakluyt Society.

Hunwick, J. O. 1978. "Black Africans in the Islamic World: An Under-Studied Dimension of the Black Diaspora." *Tarikh* 5.4: 20–40.

Irwin, Graham W. 1977. *Africans Abroad*. New York: Columbia University Press.

Iye, Ali Moussa. 2006. Speech at the TADIA conference on "The Siddis of India and the African Diaspora in Asia." Goa, India, 10–20 January.

Jaschok, Maria, and Suzanne Miers, eds. 1994. *Women and Chinese Patriarchy: Submission, Servitude and Escape*. London: Zed Books.

Jenkins, T., R. Hewitt, A. Krause, G. Campbell, and A. Goldman. 1996. "ß-Globin Haplotype Analysis Suggests That a Major Source of Malagasy Ancestry Is Derived from Bantu-Speaking Negroids." *American Society of Human Genetics* 58: 1303–8.

Kidwai, Salim. 1990. "Sultans, Eunuchs and Domestics: New Forms of Bondage in Medieval India." In Patnaik and Dinwaney, *Chains of Servitude*, 76–96.

Kilson, Martin L., and Robert I. Rotberg, eds. 1976. *The African Diaspora. Interpretative Essays*. Intro. George Shepperson. Cambridge, Mass: Harvard University Press.

Kim, Bok Rae. 2004. "*Nobi*: A Korean System of Slavery." In Campbell, *Structure of Slavery*, 155–68.

Klein, Martin. 1993. "Introduction: Modern European Expansion and Traditional Servitude in Africa and Asia." In *Breaking the Chains: Slavery, Bondage and Emancipation in Modern Africa and Asia*, ed. Martin Klein. Madison: University of Wisconsin Press.

———. 2005. "The Emancipation of Slaves in the Indian Ocean." In Campbell, *Abolition and its Aftermath*, 198–218.

Kopytoff, Igor, and Suzanne Miers. 1977. "African 'Slavery' as an Institution of Marginality." In *Slavery in Africa: Historical and Anthropological Perspectives*, ed. Suzanne Miers and Igor Kopytoff. Madison: University of Wisconsin Press.

Lewis, Bernard. 1976. "The African Diaspora and the Civilization of Islam." In Kilson and Rotberg, *African Diaspora*.

———. 1990. *Race and Slavery in the Middle East: An Historical Enquiry*. New York: Oxford University Press.

Linnebuhr, Elisabeth, ed. 1989. *Transition and Continuity of Identity in East Africa and Beyond: In Memoriam David Miller*. Bayreuth, Germany: Bayreuth University.

Lo, Jung-Pang. 1955. "The Emergence of China as a Sea Power during the Late Sung and Early Yüang Periods." *Far Eastern Quarterly* 14.4: 489–503.

Lovejoy, Paul E. 1983. *Transformations in Slavery*. Cambridge: Cambridge University Press.

———. 1997. "The African Diaspora: Revisionist Interpretations of Ethnicity, Culture and Religion under Slavery." *Studies in the World History of Slavery, Abolition and Emancipation* 2.1. http://www2.h<->net.msu.edu/~slavery/essays/esy-9701love.html, accessed August 2005; currently available at http://web.archive.org/web/20010606194224/www2.h<->net.msu.edu/~slavery/essays/esy9701love.html, accessed 24 September 2007.

———, ed. 2001. "Research on Slavery and Abolition: Significance and Trends." *African Diaspora Newsletter* 4: 7–9. www.yorku.ca/nhp/newsletter/news4_aug2001. PDF, accessed 24 September 2007.

Machado, Pedro. 2004. "A Forgotten Corner of the Indian Ocean: Gujarati Merchants, Portuguese India and the Mozambique Slave Trade, c.1730–1830." In Campbell, *Structure of Slavery*, 17–32.

Mampilly, Zachariah Cherian. 2001. "The African Diaspora of the Indian Sub-continent." *The-southasian.com*, issue 14, September. www.the-south-asian.com/Sept2001/Indo-African_diaspora3.htm, accessed August 2005.

Manning, Patrick. 1993. *Slavery and African Life: Occidental, Oriental, and African Slave Trades*. Cambridge: Cambridge University Press.

Matsuoka, Atsuko, and John Sorenson. 2001. *Ghosts and Shadows: Construction of Identity and Community in an African Diaspora*. Toronto: University of Toronto Press.

McNeill, William H. 1976. *Plagues and Peoples*. New York: Anchor Books.

Meillassoux, Claude. 1991. *The Anthropology of Slavery: The Womb of Iron and Gold*. Chicago: University of Chicago Press; London: Athlone Press.

Miers, Suzanne. 2005. "Slavery and the Slave Trade in Saudi Arabia and the Arab States on the Persian Gulf, 1921–63." In Campbell, *Abolition and Its Aftermath*, 120–36.

Miller, Joseph C. 2004. "A Theme in Variations: A Historical Schema of Slaving in the Atlantic and Indian Ocean Regions." In Campbell, *Structure of Slavery*, 169–94.

Mirzai, Behnaz A. 2002. "African Presence in Iran: Identity and Its Reconstruction in the 19th and 20th centuries." *Revue française d'histoire d'outre-mer* 89, nos. 336–37: 229–46.

———. 2005. "The 1848 Abolitionist *Farmān*: A Step towards Ending the Slave Trade in Iran." In Campbell, *Abolition and Its Aftermath*, 94–102.

Montigny, Anie. 2002. "L'Afrique oubliée des noirs du Qatar." *Journal des Africanistes* 72.2: 214–47.

Morton, Fred. 1998. "East Africa: Swahili Region." In Finkelman and Miller, *Macmillan Encyclopedia of World Slavery* 1: 265.

Nelson, Cynthia. 1974. "Public and Private Politics: Women in the Middle Eastern World." *American Anthropologist* 1.3: 555–56.

Nurse, Derek, and Thomas Spear. 1985. *The Swahili: Reconstructing the History and Language of an African Society, 800–1500*, 551–63. Philadelphia: University of Philadelphia Press.

Obeng, Pashington. 2000. "Survival Strategies: African Indians of Karnataka, South India." *inSpire* 4.4. www.ptsem.edu/read/inspire/4.4/feature3/survival1.htm, accessed August 2005; currently available at http://ptsem.edu/Publications/inspire2/4.4/index.htm, accessed 14 July 2007.

Okpewho, Isidore, Carole Boyce Davies, and Ali A. Mazrui, eds. 1999. *The African Diaspora: African Origins and New World Identities*. Bloomington: Indiana University Press.

Patnaik, Utsa. 1990. Introduction to Patnaik and Dingwaney, *Chains of Servitude*, 2–26.

Patnaik, Utsa, and Manjari Dinwaney, eds. 1990. *Chains of Servitude: Bondage and Slavery in India*. Hyderabad, India: Sangam.

Patterson, Orlando. 1982. *Slavery and Social Death*. Cambridge, Mass.: Harvard University Press.

Pellat, Ch. 1999a. "Al-Djāhiz." *Encyclopaedia of Islam*. CD-ROM ed. v.1.0.

———. 1999b. "Kayna." *Encyclopaedia of Islam*. CD-ROM ed. v.1.0.

———. 1999c. "Khāsī." *Encyclopaedia of Islam*. CD-ROM ed. v.1.0.

Petry, Carl F. 1998. "Medieval Egypt." In Finkelman and Miller, *Macmillan Encyclopedia of World Slavery*. 1: 283–84.

Piersen, William D. 1977. "White Cannibals, Black Martyrs: Fear, Depression, and Religious Faith as Causes of Suicide among New Slaves." *Journal of Negro History* 62.2: 147–59.

Pires, Tomé. 1944. *Suma Oriental* in *The Suma Oriental of Tomé Pires and The Book of Francisco Rodrigues*. Trans. Armando Z. Cortesão. Vol. 1. London: Hakluyt Society.

Poirier, Ch. 1942–1943. "Un 'Menabe' au coeur de la fort de l'Est." *Bulletin de l'Acadmie Malgache* 25: 25.

Ponting, Clive. 1991. *A Green History of the World*. New York: Penguin.

Prashad, Vijay. 2000. "Afro-Dalits of the Earth Unite!" *African Studies Review* 43.1: 189–201.

Rajaison, François, ed. 1996. *Fanandevozana ou esclavage*. Antananarivo: Musée d'Art et d'Archéologie de l'Université d'Antananarivo.

Ramana, Gutala Venkata, Bing Su, Li Jin, et al. 2001. "Y-Chromosome SNP Haplotypes Suggest Evidence of Gene Flow among Caste, Tribe, and the Migrant Siddi Populations of Andhra Pradesh, South India." *European Journal of Human Genetics*, 9.9: 695–700.

Rashidi, Runoko. 1998. "The African Presence in India: An Historical Overview." *History Notes*. www.mumia.org/wwwboard/messages/1221.html, accessed August 2005.

Rea, William Francis. 1976. *The Economics of the Zambezi Mission, 1580–1759.* Roma: Institutum Historicum S.I.

Reid, Anthony. 1983. "Introduction: Slavery and Bondage in Southeast Asian History." In *Slavery, Bondage and Dependency in Southeast Asia*, ed. Anthony Reid, 1–43. St. Lucia: University of Queensland Press.

Reinaud, M. 1848. Introduction to Aboulféda, *Géographie*. Trans. M. Reinaud. Vol. 1. Paris: Imprimerie Nationale.

Ricks, Thomas M. 1998a. "Persia." In Finkelman and Miller, *Macmillan Encyclopedia of World Slavery* 1: 70.

——. 1999b. "Slave Trade: Islamic World." In Finkelman and Miller, *Macmillan Encyclopedia of World Slavery* 2: 833.

Ross, Eric S. 1994. "Africa in Islam: What the Afrocentric Perspective Can Contribute to the Study of Islam." *International Journal of Islamic and Arabic Studies* 11.2: 1–36.

Salman, Michael. 2005. "The Meaning of Slavery: The Genealogy of 'An Insult to the American Government and to the Filipino People.'" In Campbell, *Abolition and Its Aftermath*, 180–97.

Schottenhammer, Angela. 2004. "Slaves and Forms of Slavery in Late Imperial China (Seventeenth to Early Twentieth Centuries)." In Campbell, *Structure of Slavery*, 143–54.

Sheriff, Abdul. 1987. *Slaves, Spices, and Ivory Zanzibar: Integration of an East African Commercial.* Athens: Ohio University Press.

——. 2005. "The Slave Trade and Its Fallout in the Persian Gulf." In Campbell, *Abolition and Its Aftermath*, 103–19.

Shirodkar, P. P. 1985. "Slavery in Coastal India." *Purabhilekh-Puratatva* 3.1: 27–44.

Shroff, Beheroze. 2002. "Siddis and Parsis—A Film Maker's Notes." Paper presented at the Conference on Cultural Exchange and Transformation in the Indian Ocean World, UCLA, 5–6 April.

Singh, L., G. V. Ramana, N. Wang, R. Chakraborty. 2000. "Short Tandem Repeat-Based Y-Chromosome Haplotype Data Reveals a High Level of Admixture in the Migrant Population, the Siddis, with Local Indian Populations." Abstract, American Society of Human Genetics. www.faseb.org/genetics/ashg00/f1194.htm, accessed August 2005.

Singh, Rahul. "Letter From Mumbai." *Gulf News.* www.gulf-news.com/archives/17032000/friday/fri8.htm, accessed August 2005.

"Slavery and Gender in the Indian Ocean." N.d. African Diaspora Forum Topic, Harriet Tubman Resource Centre on the African Diaspora, York University. www.yorku.ca/nhp/forum/fold/forum05.asp, accessed August 2005.

Straus, Jean A. 1998. "Greco-Roman Egypt." In Finkelman and Miller, *Macmillan Encyclopedia of World Slavery*, 1: 282.

Sutton, J. E. G. 1972. *Early Trade in Eastern Africa*. Historical Association of Tanzania Paper no. 11. Dar es Salaam, Tanzania: East African Publishing House.

Teelock, Vijaya. 1999. "The Influence of Slavery in the Formation of Creole Identity." *Comparative Studies of South Asia, Africa and the Middle East* 19.2: 3–8.

Thompson, Vincent B. 2000. *Africans of the Diaspora: The Evolution of African Consciousness and Leadership in the Americas.* Trenton, N.J.: Africa World Press.

Trimingham, J. Spencer. 1964. *Islam in East Africa.* Oxford, UK: Clarendon Press.

Turton, Andrew. 2004. "Violent Capture of People for Exchange on Karen-Thai Borders in the 1830s." In Campbell, *Structure of Slavery,* 69–82.

Van Goor, Jurrien. 1998. "A Hybrid State: The Dutch Economic and Political Network in Asia." In *From the Mediterranean to the China Sea,* ed. Claude Guillot, Denys Lombard, and Roderich Ptak. Wiesbaden, Germany: Harrassowitz Verlag.

Van Leur, J. C. 1955. *Indonesian Trade and Society: Essays in Asian Social and Economic History.* The Hague, Netherlands: W. Van Hoeve.

Vérin, P. 1999. "Madagascar." *Encyclopaedia of Islam.* CD-ROM ed. v.1.0.

Vijayakumar, M., et al., 1987. "Genetic Studies among the Siddis of Karnataka, India: A Migrant Population from Africa." *Zeitschrift fur Morphologie und Anthropologie* 77.2: 98.

Walker, Sheila. 2006. "Scattered Africa: Faces and Voices of the African Diaspora." 55-minute film shown at the TADIA conference on "The Siddis of India and the African Diaspora in Asia," Goa, India, 10–20 January.

Wallenstein, Peter. 1998. "Cheng Ho." In Finkelman and Miller, *Macmillan Encyclopedia of World Slavery,* 1: 177.

Warren, James Francis. 1994. "Chinese Prostitution in Singapore: Recruitment and Brothel Organization." in *Women and Chinese Patriarchy: Submission, Servitude and Escape,* ed. Maria Jaschok and Suzanne Miers. London: Zed Books.

———. 2004. "The Structure of Slavery in the Sulu Zone in the Late Eighteenth and Nineteenth Centuries." In Campbell, *Structure of Slavery,* 111–28.

Watson, James L., ed. 1980a. *Asian and African Systems of Slavery.* Berkeley: University of California Press.

———. 1980b. "Introduction: Slavery as an Institution, Open and Closed Systems." In Watson, *Asian and African Systems of Slavery,* 1–15.

———. 1980c. "Transactions in People: The Chinese Market in Slaves, Servants, and Heirs." In Watson, *Asian and African Systems of Slavery,* 223–50.

Wilson, Carlton. 1997. "Conceptualizing the African Diaspora." *Comparative Studies of South Asia, Africa and the Middle East* 17.2: 118–22.

Wink, André. 1996–97. *Al-Hind: The Making of the Indo-Islamic World.* 2 vols. Leiden, Netherlands: Brill.

Worden, Nigel. 1985. *Slavery in Dutch South Africa.* Cambridge: Cambridge University Press.

———. 2005. "Indian Ocean Slavery." In Campbell, *Abolition and Its Aftermath,* 29–50.

Worden, Nigel, and Kerry Ward. 1998. "Slave Trade: Southeast Asia." In Finkelman and Miller, *Macmillan Encyclopedia of World Slavery.* 2: 850.

# PART 1

# INDIA IN AFRICA

# 2

# The Indentured Experience

*Indian Women in Colonial Natal*

Devarakshanam Govinden

"Writing history" is an important reclamatory project for marginalized groups and has become more and more important in South Africa in this post-apartheid period. This is not done, I believe, to find "identity" or "roots" in some kind of simplistic way. One engages in it, even if the outcome is tentative and uncertain. We are aware, before we begin, that our attempts at reconstructing and reconstituting the past will be flawed, incomplete, and even imagined. Stuart Hall argues that we should think of identity as a "'production,' which is never complete, always in process, and always constituted within, not outside, representation. This view problematizes the very authority and authenticity to which the term 'cultural identity' lays claim" (Hall 1996: 110). Hall asks whether, when Fanon called for "profound research," it was not a *production* of identity, a re-telling of the past, rather than a rediscovery of identity, an archaeological exercise (111). This is similar in many ways to the self-construction in autobiography. Pratibha Parmar connects identity, historical memory, and representation when she says, "All aspects of our . . . representation are organically informed by and shaped through our historical memories and the raw cultural signs and processes of our subjectivities" (Parmar 1990: 101). Indeed, "writing history" may reveal how we may mythologize our history.

In this essay I consider aspects of the general indentured experience of Indians in colonial Natal, with particular reference to the experiences of Indian women. I attempt to write this slice of history, albeit a slender narrative, from the vantage point of my grandmother's experiences as a paradigm case to reflect something of the life and times into which she was born, as a possible background against which questions of identity in South Africa may be explored today. Homi Bhabha, recalling Franz Fanon, notes that "remembering is never a quiet act of introspection or retrospection. It is a painful re-membering, a putting together of the dismembered past to make sense of the trauma of the present" (Bhabha 1994: 63).[1]


### In Memory of Her: Asseerwadhum Manikkam

The larger workings of imperialism and capitalism were to determine where I would be born: Kearsney, Natal, South Africa. Kearsney is a few miles inland from the eastern seaboard town of Stanger, which, like Durban, is along the Indian Ocean shoreline. It is one of the rural areas where the early tea and sugar plantations were established by Indian indentured laborers.

I remember very well the day my grandmother died—13 January 1948, my fourth birthday. She arrived at our home early. She made a delicate rope of little white flowers as a braid for my hair and had tea with my parents and me. She said a special prayer for me and left. Later that day she died suddenly. I remember the family coming together that afternoon. Everyone was deeply shocked. Ever since that day my birthday was always remembered (though never celebrated) together with the passing away of my grandmother. Yearly visits to her grave at the Stanger cemetery on my birthday became the family custom, and the recounting of the incidents of the day she died a family ritual. I remember her name so well, because it appears in bold print on her tombstone: *ASSEERWADHUM MANIK-KAM*. Ironically, I now feel the strongest connection with her, transforming what had undertones of a negative memory into a celebratory one.

Many years before, at the turn of the twentieth century, my grandmother, a young girl of eight, came with her mother and father, three sisters, and three brothers from Bezwada, Andhra Pradesh, India, where she was born in 1896, a year before Queen Victoria's Diamond Jubilee. Being immigrants of Andhra or Telegu background, they were described as "Pravasandras" in the nomenclature of the time (Prabhakaran 1991:4). My grandmother's youngest brother had actually been born on the ship. Not much is known of my great-grandmother's life in India, or of the circumstances of their coming to South Africa. The family had left their mother country to make a living as indentured immigrants in a strange land. Although my great-grandfather had been a magistrate in the district where he lived in India, he had to adjust to the difficult demands of manual labor in the tea fields in Kearsney, in colonial Natal.

### From Slavery to Servitude: The Indentured Experience

What kind of world was my grandmother born into? The world of the mid-nineteenth century was entering a new phase in history. Slavery had been abolished, but other forms of labor had to be found to maintain the infrastructure of trade and expansion for the European nations, especially Britain. P. S. Joshi argues that indentured labor was a new form of slavery and was inaugurated in India from 1830:

> The system of indentured labor had a history of its own. It was unique in that it was an invention of the British brain to substitute it for forced labor and slavery. The indentured 'coolies' were half-slaves, bound over body and soul by a hundred and one inhuman regulations. (Joshi 1942: 44)

Savita Nair, in her chapter in this book, makes the important point that the "rhetoric of utility underpins the metanarrative of race and empire." In 1857 the East India Company was abolished, and the Indian sub-continent came under the direct rule of the British Crown. The pattern of indentured labor had already been established in the movement of Indians to Mauritius in 1833, to British Guinea in 1838, and to Trinidad and Jamaica around the same time (Joshi 1942: 41). Indians also went to work in the tea plantations in Assam and Bhutan (1860), Ceylon (1870s), Fiji (1879), and Burma (1880s). It is estimated that by 1870 a million Indians had gone overseas to work on indenture contracts, with Indians forming one of the largest labor diasporas of the nineteenth century (Kahn 1995: 143). The trend certainly extended Britain's "sphere of influence" and marked its expansionist, assertive, and self-conscious approach to empire (Boehmer 1998: xv). While there was free movement of white colonial settlers in the colonial world at this time, indentured laborers were moved from "one boundedness and bondedness to another" (van der Veer 1997: 91). It was this "experiment" in social engineering that took half a million Indians from India to the Caribbean (referred to here as East Indians) as indentured laborers in the decades after Britain's abolition of slavery. It is also important to remember that a global pattern developed whereby indigenous peoples were alienated from their land and were also excluded, through the large scale of indentured labor, from the commercial developments taking place around them (Kahn 1995: 144).

It was at this time that colonial eyes were being turned to the East Coast of Natal in South Africa, where the soil was fertile and the prospects seemed promising for sugar farming. The movement of labor was directly linked to the nineteenth-century expansion of colonialism in these parts of the world, with this period being seen as the time of classical colonialism. Wherever white British migrants settled they required labor, and colonized subjects in the colonies such as India, as Bhana and Brain record, became the logical transportable "commodity" (Bhana and Brain 1990:15).

And so began the "wandering across terrain and time," as Takaki writes of Asians generally (see Takaki 1993: 2), and the emergence of the diasporic experience for South Asians. Boehmer has written that "it is often forgotten that millions of people, both colonized and colonizing, who were identified with or unconcerned about colonization, formed part of the British Empire, in the sense of responding to it, having to deal with it, and in many millions of cases surviving through it" (Boehmer 1998: xviii).

The arrival of Indians in Natal was not the first encounter that Indians had had with Africa. Joshi points out that Indians were connected to Africa from the first century AD. There was trade in cotton cloth, grain, oil, sugar, and ghee with western India, and in the tenth century in glass beads and porcelain. According to reports, Vasco da Gama, on his way to India, found Indians in East Africa (Joshi 1942: 41).

Indians had first come to South Africa as slaves imported by the Dutch East India Company; and half of the early Cape slaves in the seventeenth and early eighteenth centuries were from Bengal and South India. Uma Dhupelia-Mesthrie also draws attention to the fact that, although the "main marker" of the history of Indians in South Africa was the arrival of indentured laborers, many Indian slaves had come from India—mainly from Bengal and the Coromandel and Malabar coasts—and the Indonesian islands in the seventeenth century and formed part of the 40,000 slave population in the south-western Cape (Dhupelia-Mesthrie 2000: 10).

The Indian settlers of 1860 were coming to a region that had seen a turbulent history since the early nineteenth century. From the early 1800s, with the growing consolidation of Zulu influence under Shaka, there was both settlement (*Mfecane*) and flight (*Difaqane*) of Nguni clans across the region. The Voortrekkers, moving into the interior from the Cape, came into Natal in the late 1830s, and the Battle of Blood River between Boers and Zulus took place in 1838. The British annexed Natal as a British colony in 1843, bringing with them a capitalist system that demanded capital and labor, putting heavy strains on the traditional homestead system that had given Africans a sense of stability. The impoverishment of the African peasantry further transformed the face of South Africa (see Bhana and Brain 1990: 17). During the 1880s, when Indian indentured laborers were coming in large numbers to Natal, there was further massive movement of Africans in South Africa, and with the emergence of wage labor through gold mining, many of them, impoverished through the changes that engulfed them, moved to the mining centers.

It is often popularly stated (even by historians, such as Shireen Munsamy in her book *Sunrise to Sunset*) that Indians came to work on the sugar cane fields because the "Africans were lazy," but this perception has been contested. Keletso E. Atkins questions these stereotypes in well-documented research on the subject and gives an important alternative view:

> Natal Africans were themselves experiencing an unprecedented socioeconomic crisis; and both private and governmental agencies had already invested time and energy designed to mould blacks into a European ideal of what workers ought to be like. From the beginning, however, the results of their efforts were discouraging. Finally, the European recognized that only by a complete immersion in Western culture—that is, only after a prolonged process of acculturation—would the pre-industrial African worker be transformed into a model based on the Protestant capitalist work ethic, itself a contested area in nineteenth-century Europe. (Atkins 1993:2)

African men were being thrown into a wage economy, and the emergence of colonial capitalism at this time in the development of South Africa led to their increasing proletarization during the rest of the century. This was a time of major changes on many fronts, amounting to an "upheaval" of considerable magnitude. Cheryl Walker, historian of note, points out that there were

> massive changes in the economic, political and social life, from precapitalist to capitalist relations of production, from African political independence to subjugation, from rural to urban forms of social and spatial organization, and from white co-existence with indigenous societies (and Indian settlers) to white supremacy within a new, racially structured state. (Walker 1990: 1)

Agnes Sam, a South African Indian writer now living in the United Kingdom, also gives a corrective view on the subject that the arrival of Indian indentured laborers in Natal was due solely to the African workers being considered unsuitable for labor on the sugar plantations:

> Illiterate Indian peasants were introduced into a political situation of which they were wholly ignorant. Transporting people from India to work on the plantations effectively frustrated the Zulus' attempt to bring about the failure

of the sugar cane economy. Yet, from another perspective, the introduction of Indentured laborers from India is testament to the victory of Africans who refused to labor for the plantation owners in Natal. (Sam 1989: 10)

In the economy of the overarching liberation struggle we should remember that "people generated forms of resistance that were dissonant, alternative and polyvalent" (Sitas 2004: 19). Throughout the history of struggle in South Africa we see how social identities oppositional to apartheid constantly converged and diverged. For example, the neighborhood of Gandhi's Phoenix Settlement, a suburb of Durban, would later show that a strategic essentialism was necessary against the undermining of Indian and African identities by the dominant powers. There was a common history of discrimination and oppression shared among Indians, Africans, and Coloureds, and within that there were different experiences. Relations, of course, between the Indian and African were not always cordial and co-operative and show in ensuing decades the usual tensions common in a colonial society. There was resentment against the Indian business group in particular, who were seen as a threat to African attempts at entrepreneurship. Gandhi for his part during his sojourn was trying to unite disparate Indian communities, divided by competing allegiances to India and to South Africa, exhibiting class and entrepreneurial divisions, and divisions of language and religion and narrow sectarianisms. He was also fighting untouchability among Indians (see Parekh 1999).[2] To this very day there is a long and simmering disquiet about the way this history is understood and related, with the theme of African and Indian relations itself being a persistent one throughout the past century and a half.

In any event, in the nineteenth century the history of indentured Indians is arguably linked to the advent of the steamship as the sole means of travel between India and South Africa. The first "batch" of Indians, a total of 341 laborers, mainly from Madras, came to Natal in the SS *Truro* on 16 November 1860. A few years later (in 1870), apart from the indentured Indians, there came "Passenger Indians"—entrepreneurs, mainly from Bombay and other parts of the west coast of India. They formed an independent, privileged group and set up businesses of all kinds among the new immigrants. By 1866 a total of 6,445 indentured immigrants had arrived in South Africa. Immigration was temporarily halted in 1871 to deal with complaints about the treatment of Indians in Natal and then resumed in 1874. By 1911, a total of 152,184 indentured migrants from India had arrived in Natal, and an estimated 30,000 Passenger Indians (Bhana and Brain 1990: 15, 36).

All indentured laborers endured abject working conditions. Although they constantly claimed their British subjecthood, they were treated as second-class citizens and hardly in the same category as British settlers in Canada and Australia. Indians were imported as "Coolies," a term that had a derogatory connotation at the time. They always fought the perception that "India was going to South Africa as a serf" (Joshi 1942: 43). For this reason Indians in South Africa always felt constrained to emphasize the heritage of an "ancient" civilization and culture, especially when they were subjected to inhuman laws of segregation. For example, in 1946, Yusuf Dadoo, a renowned activist in the history of the liberation struggle in South Africa, in response to the iniquitous Ghetto Act, wrote: "It must not be forgotten that the Indian people are sons and daughters of a country with a proud and cultured heritage. Their ancient motherland is the bearer of a tradition of civilization as old as any in the world" (Dadoo 1991: 75).

Indentured workers came in accordance with an agreement (*girmit*) or contract concerning their stay, and they were referred to as *girmityas*. They worked for sugar farmers in Natal—farmers who were mainly English. A near-feudal system of labor operated, with the indentured workers being recruited to work for a particular employer and being bound by contract to live on the estate of the employer for a stipulated period of time. This is seen by many historians as not unlike slavery, which was, as defined by Takaki, a "system of bonded black labor" (Takaki 1993: 7). The laborers were offered a monthly wage of ten shillings. In the decade that my grandmother arrived there was a particularly "virulent anti-Indianism" (Desai 1996: 4) among whites in the province. It was also the time after the Anglo-Boer War (1899–1902) when, as Rob Turrell points out, there was "an explosive climate of ideological race purity" (Turrell 1998: 19).

Recruiting Indian women was not the principal part of the scheme for indentured labor in Natal since the need was for male workers to come to the sugar plantations. Although Indian women made up only 29 percent of the total number of Indians who came to South Africa, they nevertheless played an important part in the development of the country, and their presence in the colony had implications for the rest of the inhabitants, as I argue below.

By the end of the nineteenth century and over the decade into the twentieth, when my grandmother actually arrived in South Africa, peace between Boers and Britons had been signed in 1902, and British hegemony was consolidated over all South Africa. There were greater restrictions on movement of Indians to other parts of South Africa, and the segregation of Indians from the rest of the population groups began in earnest. The place to which she and her family were taken immediately on their arrival was Kearsney, six miles north of Stanger or Kwadukuza, which was developing into an important town in the North Coast sugar belt. Kearsney had a large concentration of indentured workers (it was to the larger towns such as Durban that the Passenger Indians mainly went), and was divided into two areas, Old Factory and New Factory. Kearsney was controlled by Sir John Liege Hulett, a sugar baron, who was prime minister of Natal in 1903. The Hulett dynasty continued in successive decades under Jack Neville Hulett, Ted, Hulett and G. N. Hulett, who were to dominate my family story for many years to come, with family members of successive generations being in their employ.

## Women in Colonial India

What was the nature of the colonial home that my grandmother was leaving? It is necessary to ask this question, as the background of life in India is often omitted in considering the history of indentured labor. India was declared part of the British Empire in 1858, two years before the Indian indentured scheme to South Africa got under way, and it is clear that the British Crown readily assumed that it could do as it pleased with its subjects. The scientific theories of race that had originated in the late eighteenth century were very much the order of the day by the mid-nineteenth century, as Jenny Sharpe has pointed out (Sharpe 1993: 5). It seems to me that this ideological background is not unconnected to the indentured schemes that were promoted at this time.

Politically, British rule was firmly entrenched in India. The War of Independence in 1857 had been lost, and there was no hope of withdrawal of the British. India was to continue to be under the British until 1947. For women the entrenched traditional patriarchal society did not seem to slacken under the new dispensation. The classic examples of the status and plight of Indian women are reflected in the paradigmatic practices of *sati*, of child marriages and polygamy. The British government did not unequivocally condemn these aspects of Indian society. For example, although practices such as *sati*, common in North India, were condemned during the time of the British Raj, there was no immediate attempt to legalize widow marriage. *Sati* was also a class issue, mainly performed by upper-class Brahmin women who seemed to have been immobilized by very tight societal control. Ironically, it seems that "lower-class" women had more scope to negotiate social transgressions of all sorts.

Sunder Rajan argues cogently for a more critical interpretation of *sati* in the context of "continuities and discontinuities" of the colonial period in India, with its interplay of ideology and politics (Sunder Rajan 1991: 40). Protests against the discriminatory practices, both direct and tacit, under British rule were hardly heard. Further, colonialist history tended to denounce practices such as *sati* as being backward, and yet it condoned and ignored the oppression of women in Victorian England. Sharpe argues that the confinement and "absolute devotion" expected of Victorian women may be seen as a form of "self-immolation"; yet "unlike the Victorian woman, the Hindu widow is positioned as an object in colonial discourse and a victim to be saved" (Sharpe 1993: 14).

It was also not uncommon for Indian women to be abandoned by their husbands or widowed early. Many who chose to come to work in South Africa, then, were leaving situations that were becoming untenable for them, both at a personal and social level. I wonder sometimes about my own great-grandmother and her family. With what tales of the new land flowing with milk and honey were they regaled by the *kanganis*, who were paid to entice prospective laborers to the new land? Even though they were not specifically recruited, as pointed out earlier, Sam notes that women in particular "fell easy prey to the *kanganis* if they were escaping a domestic or legal situation, or even if they were simply looking for work" (Sam 1989: 3).

What is worth exploring is the kind of life many of the indentured laborers, such as my great-grandmother, had been subjected to in India. We need more scholarship on the histories of peasant groups in India, of differentiation among the peasantry (see, for example, Damodaran 1992), especially in those places from which indentured labor was mainly drawn. Although developed in India, scholarship in South Africa on this aspect of indentured experience has been absent, and the time for a new "subaltern" project of historical analysis—a more "rounded history"—here in South Africa as in India is long overdue. Such scholarship will take in a more critical analysis of colonialist and nationalist interpretations of history of the period. This was a time when, in the main, the colonials defended themselves against possible moral condemnation of colonialism by posing as the saviors of barbaric groups (see Sharpe 1993).

### Treated as Chattels

The sea journey from India to South Africa was not in the same category as that of the Middle Passage of the slave-trade days, but it was hardly a journey made in comfort and safety. Women, in particular, were subjected to all kinds of ordeals and abuse on the ships. Jo Beall records that, apart from those who came in families, many Indian women who came to Natal were abandoned wives and widows or destitute prostitutes. The women, like the male travelers, were subjected to diseases such as cholera, typhoid and dysentery, and venereal disease but were also victims of sexual assault.

On arrival in South Africa, the newcomers had a difficult time. Family life among Indians was affected by the sparse and poor living conditions.

The disparity in social spaces reflected the inequalities of the social hierarchy. Life in small, crowded barracks-styled apartments for the new immigrants did not afford much privacy, and this was compounded by inadequate ablution and medical facilities. On the other hand, the white employers lived in large, manor-like country estates. Fatima Meer draws attention to the fact that "life on the Coolie lines, or barracks, was grim, highly controlled and not conducive to developing free and spontaneous associations" (Meer 1990: 5). Hassakhan (1990: 9), writing of the situation in Trinidad, has pointed out that with the plantation system being generally one of rigid control, separation, and social and geographical isolation, it did not augur well for relations between Indians and Africans.

Women received rations and had to supplement their income with work on plantations (Beall 1990: 157). The worst hit were single women, who were treated as chattels. Sam records aspects of the discrimination that the women endured: "The regulations governing the payment of indentured laborers provided a clue: there was a proviso that 'females and children under ten years of age' were to be paid half the adult male ration" (Sam 1989: 5). There were poor standards of health in the settlements, and diseases such as colds, fever, and dysentery were quite common. I often heard my parents speak about the scourge of "TB," with sufferers being ostracized. In 1904, when my grandmother arrived in Natal, tuberculosis accounted for 27 percent of deaths among Indians. The incidence of infant mortality was also high.

At the time when my grandmother arrived, market gardening and farming were an important source of income. As many of the Indians earned ex-indentured status when their contracts ended, they were able to move into the free labor market and become self-employed in a range of occupations, becoming in the process successful traders, hawkers, and farmers. Although there was greater diversification in the rest of Natal, the coastal area where my grandmother lived still concentrated predominantly on the cultivation of coffee, tea, and sugar.

Indian women worked very hard. My grandmother worked from the time she arrived until her marriage in the Hulett's tea plantations in Kearsney, near Stanger. Beall reports that "the most intensive use of women's labor on plantations was made by tea estates in the Stanger district on the North Coast" (Beall 1990: 153). Young women were seen to be particularly suited for this job since they were considered to have small, deft fingers, as Munsamy points out (Munsamy 1997: 29). My grandmother worked for a shilling a month. When she moved to work in the nearby mill, her work included scaling and packing the tea that was brought in by ox wagon from the outlying fields. The bags were hoisted up to the second floor of the mill, where they were spread out to dry. My grandmother's job involved turning the leaves on the shelves lined with hessian and then packing them for transportation by train to Durban via Stanger; ships then took this cargo to India. In India the leaves were processed, blended with "Ceylon Tea," and exported to different parts of the world. My grandmother was thus a small participant in a larger capitalist enterprise for the "mother country," Great Britain.

Women like my grandmother contributed to the growth of the colony, not only in terms of capital accumulation, by virtue of their role as forced laborers, but later as independent peasants, petty traders and merchants (Beall 1982: 175). Although women's economic participation was solicited, they were not given economic recognition. In spite of their contributions, Indian women were subjected to the social ills of a rampantly patriarchal society. They were victims of rape; some took to prostitution due to their social and economic circumstances. The earlier commissions set up to look into the plight of Indian women did not make much difference to their lives: the Coolie Commission of 1872 reported on the incidence of prostitution and its link with desperate socioeconomic conditions, and the Wragg Commission of 1885 saw all Indian women in general as being wantonly and naturally promiscuous.

Educational opportunities for Indian women were scarce. Like numerous child workers around her, my grandmother received no formal education. Indian, Coloured, and African groups as a whole were neglected in the sphere of education, and the most severely disadvantaged were the women and girls in these groups. The lack of educational opportunities must be seen as one of the reasons why Indian women's output in writing in English was minimal at this time. The conservative attitudes of Indian families regarding the education of girls exacerbated the situation.

Missionary effort was responsible for at least some educational opportunities being opened up for Indian boys and girls in the years when the indentured laborers first arrived. In 1869 Rev. Ralph Stott had commenced a boys' day school. An Indian schoolteacher, John Thomas, opened a school in 1883 and, with the help of the Anglican Church, established 9 of the 21 schools for Indians in Natal. By 1886 this number had increased to 14. In the same year St. Aidan's Mission schools were established by Dr. Lancelot Parker Booth, an English medical missionary. In 1889 the first school in the colony for Indian girls was opened. By the turn of the century, through the efforts of Dr. Booth, there were 62 Indian girls in mission schools (and 1,251 Indian boys) in Natal. (Jo Beall notes that there was a very small number of Indian girls attending school: there were 400 Indian female children in the schools compared to 8,000 white girls, at the time when my grandmother arrived in South Africa). I feel a personal link to this history as well, as my parish church is St. Aidan's in Durban, part of St. Aidan's Mission, and now in its 125th year, with the pioneering work of Dr. Booth being frequently recalled and celebrated.

It is worth noting that the rise of the white private schools in Natal for English boys and girls, developed by the churches during these decades of economic growth, may be linked to the successful sugar industry. All the established private schools in Natal—and the majority were for girls—were developed in the decades after the first indentured Indian laborers arrived: Hilton, 1872; St. Anne's Diocesan College, 1877; Girls' Collegiate, 1878; Durban Girls' College, 1877; Michaelhouse, 1896; St. John's Diocesan School for Girls, 1897; Wykeham Collegiate, 1905; St. Mary's Diocesan School for Girls, 1919 (Randall 1982: 77). Many Indian and African women who continued in their proletarianized state in colonial Natal, before and after my grandmother arrived, were undoubtedly part of the unacknowledged props that supported this social and cultural infrastructure for the dominant class.

### A New Restricted Homeland

My grandfather, Manikkam Munisamy, was born in 1891, and as a seven-year-old boy, he came, with his mother and younger brother, from Ussoor in Vellore, Tamil Nadu, to South Africa on 28 March 1898 in the SS *Congella*. I find it worth noting that in his case his mother, who was a daughter-in-law in a large family in India, did not come with her husband. My grandfather arrived from India in the same decade as Gandhi. Gandhi was born in 1869, nine years after the first settlers arrived in Durban, and spent the period from 1893 to 1913 in South Africa. Like my grandmother, my grandfather worked in the tea fields in Kearsney. My grandparents married around 1909, when my grandmother would have been barely thirteen years old. In time my grandfather rose to the rank of "sirdar" or supervisor (a status that Indian women seem not to have enjoyed) in Huletts Estate.

My grandmother and her family had come as Christians from India, and my grandfather's family as Hindu (he converted to Christianity here in South Africa), and they were to be described as "Christian pioneers" in Kearsney. Together my grandparents set up a proud family home in Kearsney. Their eldest daughter, Mercy Karunnama, was born on 29 November 1914 (the first native-born South African Indian in the family), the year when indentured labor was officially terminated, and the time when many colonials from around the British Empire were fighting for the "mother country." The second daughter, Sampoornam, died at the age of two, during a great flu epidemic. Of all the homes of my growing-up days, my grandparents' homestead is the one I most clearly remember, with its large and spreading tamarind tree, curry leaf and navel-orange trees, and sprawling mango and banana plantations.

In fact, my grandmother's entire life was spent in Kearsney. She raised her seven children—my mother, aunts, and uncles—who naturally thought of South Africa as "the land of their birth," with questions of "home," identity, and history obviously taking on different meanings for her and her children, in contrast presumably to her own mother. By all accounts she certainly did not contemplate leaving South Africa. Regarding the majority of immigrants, Fatima Meer states: "For many, no matter how deplorable the condition, there was no return to India, for their manner of leaving was such as to constitute an irreconcilable breach" (Meer 1969: 12). Or, perhaps, as with the fictional Mrs. Tulsi in V. S. Naipaul's *A House for Mr. Biswas*, living away from India was to constitute an "interlude," as Michael Gorra suggests (Gorra 1997: 69), but an "interlude" that for so many immigrants was gradually to become permanent.

The ideal of "the family" (reflecting both Victorian and Indian values) certainly held sway in my grandparents' household, and Indian women were as much the preservers of their "race" through the values of motherhood, tradition, and stability as were their colonial counterparts, as Catherine Nash points out in her discussion of women in the context of colonial and postcolonial geographies (Nash 1994: 237). My grandparents' home became, as I realize now, that private recuperative space in a society based on power relations (see Blunt and Rose 1994a). This situation had its obvious merits in a racially alienating world, but it also meant that it would have been extremely difficult for my grandmother to be aware of, let alone challenge, the patriarchal order into which her life was inexorably embedded and inscribed. For Sam, Indian women played an absolutely essential role in the family's general survival in a new country.[3] Indian women, like my grandmother, contributed mainly to the development and cohesion of family and community life. This is all the more remarkable, considering the young age at which she married and set up a household and her lack of formal education.

My grandmother did all this (and continued to do so for almost half a century more, right up to 1948, the year in which she died), as she was setting down new roots in a new land and contributing to its development, while there was a sustained and vicious campaign for the repatriation, and failing that, segregation, of Indians. Periodically from 1885 there were various anti-Indian laws that ensured segregation, discrimination against Indian trading and land rights, restrictions on movement, and withdrawal of political rights. The threat of repatriation hung over Indians as a sword of Damocles into the middle of the twentieth century (consider the case of Uganda under Idi Amin). However, only a few Indian immigrants returned to India, and by 1911 my grandmother was among the 152,184 Indians who had decided to make South Africa their permanent home.

### Inspired by Heroines

Both my maternal grandparents came to Natal during the phase of growing resistance to the inequities of the indentured system. They were to witness during their lifetime the institution of the Union of South Africa, the growing impact of the Natal Indian Congress, the rise of the African National Congress, and the consolidation of the apartheid stranglehold. Gandhi's own role is pivotal in this history; he led two Passive Resistance campaigns in the first decade of the century. A third gained momentum in 1946 when the Indian Land Act was passed by the Smuts Government, which imposed segregation on Indians and gave them a "loaded franchise" (Russell 1988: 71). In her interview with Diana Russell, Meer points out: "This 1946 Passive Resistance Campaign was very important because it marked the beginning of international concern over racism in South Africa. It coincided with the independence of India—which gave India an important position in the United Nations" (71).

My grandmother's inclination to eulogize Indian women well known for their struggle against injustices must say something about her own longings for a brave new world. Two exemplary women, Sarojini Naidu and Pandita Rama Bai, were much revered by my grandmother and, in turn, by my mother and father. The representation as "mothers of the nation" in the discourse of nation and nationalism in India perhaps gave my grandparents and parents, like so many other Indians in South Africa, a sense of belonging to a wider family. At the same time it is worth noting that Rama Bai and Naidu, part of a larger history of anti-colonial feminist struggle in India, were admired by both Indian men and women, as in my family, who still continued to live in, and accept, a traditionally sexist society and imperialist world.

My earliest memory of Sarojini Naidu as a personality of importance is of a sepia-colored photograph of her, mounted on the coarse white-washed wall of my grandparents' sitting room. (I was to discover gradually that this was a familiar sight, as was the photograph of Gandhi, in many an Indian home of the period). There were many references to Naidu in the family conversations, and she acquired a legendary status for me when I was growing up. It is only now, however, that I am beginning to appreciate the full stature and greatness of these two women.

Sarojini Naidu (1879–1949) was considered the most prominent woman in the mass movement for independence in India (Paranjape 1996: vii). She first came to South Africa in 1924, as part of an official African tour from India. For the four months that she was here, she protested strongly on behalf of the Indian government against the discriminatory measures endured by Indians in South Africa, and she formed the South African Indian Congress, in direct protest to new restrictions on Indian land and trading rights (Meer 1969: 43). In a speech to the South African Congress in April 1924, Naidu stated categorically that there was no place for "colour bar" in Africa. In 1925 she was elected president of the Indian National Congress and was president of the South African Indian Congress at the same time, thereby becoming an eminent figure in South African politics during this period. Her vision for the liberation of the wider continent marked her approach to her work among Indians. Her efforts, along with those of Vijayalakshmi Pandit and South African leaders such as Yusuf Dadoo, were largely responsible for putting South Africa eventually on the United Nations agenda—in the same month that my grandmother died.

Pandita Rama Bai Saraswati (1858–1922), of Brahmin ancestry, was born two years before the first indentured settlers arrived in Natal. She has been acclaimed as "the greatest woman produced by modern India and one of the greatest Indians in all history . . . the one to lay the foundations for a movement for women's liberation in India" (Tharu and Lalitha 1991: 243). I realize now that the fact that she converted from Hinduism to Christianity would have added to her appeal for my grandparents and parents. At Pandita Rama Bai's memorial service in 1922, Sarojini Naidu described her as "the greatest Christian saint among the Hindus" (Naravane 1996: 82).

It is ironic from the vantage point of the end of twentieth century, that the other "heroine" for Indian indentured laborers was Queen Victoria. I grew up in a family where deference to the British Crown was accepted as indisputable. I see vividly, in the photographs of my grandmother, her gold sovereign brooch with the depiction of Queen Victoria on it, although when the queen died my grandmother was still a little girl. In spite of the treatment that Indians received at the hand of the British Crown, and the resistance that the very persons they adulated (such as Sarojini Naidu) presented to it, my grandmother and her family were also ardent royalists, and spoke of the royal family (the succeeding Edwardian British royal household) with great affection. Clearly, there was an ambiguous relationship between Indians and their colonial masters. Indians in South Africa saw themselves as a proud part of the British Empire, even if they were treated as its step-children. Savita Nair observes that "identities such as 'colonial subject' versus 'citizen of empire' haunted the discursive landscape" (and it is worth pondering how Gandhi exploited this division to fight the discriminatory practices of British colonial governments against its "own people").

Thus, the grand design of the British Crown proceeded inexorably, affecting the lives of those who lived in the little rural outpost in Kearsney, Natal. Queen Victoria was represented by colonial women who supported and maintained the super-structure of colonialism at "home" and in the far-flung parts of the empire. Elleke Boehmer points out that at the time of Queen Victoria's Diamond Jubilee, in 1897 (a year after my grandmother was born), "the entire course of the British nineteenth century . . . seemed to have unfolded in accordance with a uniquely ordained pattern" (Boehmer 1995: 29). My grandmother would have surely believed this—that there existed a divinely "ordained pattern"—for Queen Victoria, for her (my grandmother's) own private life, and for the affairs of "men."

### A New Pattern of Racial and Cultural Complexity

We have to reflect on how British political appropriation of the colony and subsequent apartheid policies resulted in cultural appropriation as well, as generally occurs in such contexts (see Takaki 1993: 1). The introduction of Indian indentured labor was to change the racial composition of Natal and introduce a new pattern of racial diversity in South Africa. Both the indigenous and indentured peoples were seen as foreigners and outsiders and were systematically "othered." But it is important to remember that when my grandmother left her home country to settle in this strange land, she was hardly moving out of a "pure" home country to a "contaminated" diasporic location, as Grewal and Kaplan point out about all Indians who left as indentured laborers (see Grewal & Kaplan 1994: 16). It is also worth stressing that the sense of a single political and cultural identity—a nationalistic identity—was hardly present at the time when my grandmother left India (Kaviraj 1993: 3, 5, 8; Grewal and Kaplan 1994: 7, 8; Rushdie 1991: 17). At the same time, if the immigrants were transporting a homeland culture and ethos that seemed, in part, homogenized, this was largely due to colonial manipulations already in India. This commodifying tendency, which persists to this day, facilitated complicity with racial ghettoizing under colonialism and apartheid in South Africa, where individual identity was predicated on racial difference.

Migration, then, through indentured schemes, and later "voluntary" movement, was to have a significant impact on the character of the Empire. A "deep disorder" resulted, which persists to this very day, altering the character of the contemporary world (Naipaul 1969: 32). The general effects of migration and uprooting and the consequences of the peculiar practice of apartheid in South Africa resulted in considerable measure in the naturalizing, and "solidifying" of ethnic identity among Indians in South Africa, by the creation of "imagined communities." V. S. Naipaul, in *India—A Million Mutinies Now* (1991), points out that it is the very dislocation from "home," when one is on foreign soil, which creates an exclusive identity (1991: 7). Sonya Domergue, a French academic specializing in Asian literature, is among those who support this contention (1998: 7).

Predictably, therefore, the early indentured settlers, in the process of cultural transplantation, created "little Indias" here (whether this meant, among other things, building temples or mosques, observing religious festivals, setting up shops for saris or Indian musical instruments, or nurturing plants required for typical Indian cuisine). This did not entail replicating the mother country but, as with settlers everywhere, reworking and re-creating it in a new context. Rushdie argues that a "sense of loss" through separation from the "homeland" results in all sorts of constructions of it, that emigrants "create fictions, not actual cities or villages, but invisible ones, imaginary homelands, Indias of the mind" (Rushdie 1991: 10). In an insular new world it is difficult to realize this, and ethnic identity is embraced, even naturalized (Naipaul 1981: 45–46). There has always been this tension between embracing difference and resisting being perceived as different.

Something of this complexity is evident in my grandmother's own life. Indian Christians formed a small percentage of the Indian population in the early years of settlement and continue to do so. Originally my grandparents belonged to the Telegu Baptist Church, started by the first Indian Baptist minister in South Africa, the Reverend John Rangiah, in Kearsney in 1908. The Apostolic Faith Mission (AFM) to which my grandparents later became affiliated was part of an important wave of Pentecostalism, which had its roots in African spirituality in the United States. The AFM was founded in South Africa in 1908, and a branch was initiated in Kearsney in my grandparents' home in the 1930s. Dean Charles Reddy, a local pastor who has done research in this field, notes that the "Pentecostal Movement made its greatest gains in the laboring class of the Indian community rather than among the traders and others from the Passenger class" (Reddy 1992: 47). In South Africa it was organized along separate racial lines, and I only discovered in later years that this was not a solely "Indian" church but that it had strong Afrikaner and African membership.

My grandmother was literate in Telegu—reading the Telegu Bible at family prayers and instructing her children in the ways of the world with confidence. She learned Tamil, the language of my grandfather, and together with him also developed competence in conversing in Zulu as the community in which they interacted expanded culturally. My grandparents' linguistic heterogeneity was adeptly transmitted to my mother and her brothers and sisters. The little girl who worked in the tea plantations grew into a woman of stature, running a household that became the center for family and friends, missionaries and community leaders. She was clearly mediating a complex subjectivity that cut across racial, cultural, religious, and linguistic affiliations; and my grandmother was merely one of many, many "permutations" of "Indian identity." Savita Nair rightly argues in her chapter, drawing from Van den Berge, that the idea of a uniform "community" exists as an "external characterization."

My parents were resolutely taught by the white missionaries that religious syncretism was a cardinal sin. Still, I imagine that my grandmother was yearning for a Christianity in an "eastern cup," but the missionaries around her and her family would have been oblivious to this need. My parents would often talk about Sardu Sundar Singh, referred to as "the Saint Paul of India" (Parker and Parker 1922), and of his resolute preservation of his Indian identity even when he became a Christian. The church would not have emphasized questions of culture and identity. As a devout Christian woman, my grandmother was to accept unquestioningly the teachings of the missionaries of this period that she and her family were being saved from superstition and "idol worship," and what her "proper place'" was to be in the larger scheme of things as a Christian woman. And while there were very cordial relationships with families of other faiths (mainly Hindu in Kearsney) in the neighborhood, friendships that endure to this day, there was a complex mix of contact and separation between "self" and what was perceived to be "other." While many Indian cultural practices were preserved, a continual process of sieving and sifting out "true" Christian identity was also taking place.

What is clear is that more critical reflection is required on the construction of the "Indian woman" in the context of the dominant ideologies of patriarchy, colonialism, and capitalism in colonial Natal of the late nineteenth century and early twentieth century. What were the ways in which Indian women like my grandmother were being constructed and culturally determined and what were their self-representations? And what were the differences among them? How did they, as they moved from one diasporic location to another, spell out the "fragments of a broken geography," to use Meena Alexander's ringing phrase (Alexander 1993: 2)?

### Conclusion

Of course, the challenge now, as postcolonial academics have argued, is to assert a suppressed cultural identity yet avoid a narrow ethnocentricity; to straddle the line between authenticity and "a cult of authenticity" (Brydon 1991). Against this background of reflecting our oppressor's invention of us and of inventing ourselves, we have to consider the question of identity among Indians in South Africa since the advent of the new democracy, and what it is to be "South African." Apartheid's exclusivist ethnic and racial divisions, institutionalized as "cultural diversity," still linger in different guises in the "new South Africa" and not least among persons of Indian descent. The need to move from *filiation* to *affiliation*, in Edward Said's sense of the words, remains an imperative in the quest for racial harmony and community.

Even if my grandmother was oblivious to the fact that she was part of, to use Gorra's phrase, "an experiment in human engineering" (Gorra 1997:67), and some of her colonial contemporaries little understood these questions of identity and difference, certainly her offspring now grapple with the incessant "existential" question: "How do we live in the world" (Rushdie 1991: 18). Or as Fanon would have asked: "How can the human world live its difference; how can a human being live Other-wise" (Bhabha, 1994: 64).[4] The question calls to mind, for me, the following poem written in South Africa:

> I love thee my land Afrique!
> I love the sea, that rolls on its coast
> Love the rivers that flow through its veins
> Love its every bird, every flower,
> Each mountain, hill, rock, grain of dust
> I love all of these and share with these
> My love, my Africa, my land. (Meer 1969: 230)

It may still surprise some to learn that this poem was written in the nineteenth century—in Urdu. I feel instinctively that when my grandmother came to see me on my fourth birthday and then died on that very day, at the age of fifty-two (six months after independence was gained in the land of her birth, and seventeen days before Mahatma Gandhi's own death), my own "pilgrim life," as Pandita Rama Bai would have said, had begun.

**Notes**

1. An earlier version of this essay appeared in my doctoral study ("Sister Outsiders: The Representation of Identity and Difference in Selected Writings by South African Indian Women"; Ph.D., University of Natal, 2000), to be published by Unisa Press.

2. When tourist groups now go on *The Inanda Heritage Route* in "hermetically sealed" coach tours it would be illuminating if they stopped to appreciate the way complex and complementary relationships developed across the neighborhood fences of the early decades of the twentieth century in South Africa. The move toward more uniform forms of resistance, exemplified in the Defiance Campaigns of the 1950s and the Mass Democratic Movement of the 1980s and early 1990s, was to come later. When one thinks today of "geographies of resistance" in the historical and political

landscape of South Africa, the best known being Soweto, the Phoenix area as a whole, and the Phoenix Settlement in particular, are important landmarks.

3. "Indian women were essential to the process of adaptation. They confronted new school systems for their children; struggled to maintain the old religion in a new country; faced prohibitions about marriage that further restricted the limited number of suitors from the same religious background, the language group or caste; they experienced indentured labor; discriminatory laws; a poll tax and imprisonment when they could not pay; isolation from their families in India; and even the unwanted attentions of European men" (Sam 1989: 10; see also Beall 1982: 183).

4. Ironically, as Zoe Wicomb points out: "One of the less predictable phenomena to develop out of the scramble for Africa is the current scramble for alterity. . . . Otherness then comes to acquire a peculiar valency within metropolitan culture, peculiar, that is, from the point of view of the native who can only be baffled by her new symbolic status" (Wicomb 2001: 161).

## Works Cited

Alexander, Meena. 1993. *Fault Lines: A Memoir.* New Delhi: Penguin Books.

Atkins, Keletso E. 1993. *The Moon Is Dead! Give Us Our Money! The Cultural Origins of an African Work Ethic, Natal, South Africa, 1843–1900.* Portsmouth, N.H.: Heinemann.

Beall, Josephine. 1982. "Class, Race and Gender: The Political Economy of Women in Colonial Natal." Master's diss., University of Natal, Durban.

Beall, Jo. 1990. "Women under Indentured Labour in Colonial Natal, 1860–1911." In Walker, *Women and Gender,* 146–67.

Bhabha, Homi K. 1994. *The Location of Culture.* London: Routledge.

Bhana, Surendra, and Joy B. Brain. 1990. *Setting Down Roots: Indian Migrants in South Africa 1860–1911.* Johannesburg, South Africa: Witswatersrand University Press.

Blunt, Alison and Gillian Rose. 1994a. "Introduction: Women's Colonial and Postcolonial Geographies." In Blunt and Rose, *Writing Women and Space,* 1–25.

———, eds. 1994b. *Writing Women and Space: Colonial and Postcolonial Geographies.* New York: Guilford Press.

Boehmer, Elleke. 1995. *Colonial and Postcolonial Literature: Migrant Metaphors.* Oxford: Oxford University Press.

———, ed. 1998. *Empire Writing: An Anthology of Colonial Literature, 1870–1918.* Oxford: Oxford University Press.

Brydon, Diana. 1991. "The White Inuit Speaks: Contamination as Literary Strategy." In *Past the Last Post: Theorizing Post-Colonialism and Post-Modernism,* ed. Ian Adam and Helen Tiffin, 191–204. Hemel Hempstead, UK: Harvester Wheatsheaf/Simon and Shuster.

Dadoo, Yusuf. 1991. "The Indian People in South Africa: Facts about the Ghetto Act." Pamphlet published in 1946. Reprinted in *Dr. Yusuf Mohammed Dadoo— His Speeches, Articles and Correspondences with Mahatma Gandhi, 1939–1983,* ed. Fatima Meer and comp. E. S. Reddy, 74–84. Durban, South Africa: Madiba.

Damodaran, Vinita. 1992. *Broken Promises: Popular Protest, Indian Nationalism, and the Congress Party in Bihar, 1935–1946.* Delhi: Oxford University Press.

Desai, Ashwin. 1996. *Arise Ye Coolies: Apartheid and the Indian, 1960–1995*. Johannesburg, South Africa: Impact African.

Dhupelia-Mesthrie, Uma. 2000. *From Canefields to Freedom: A Chronicle of Indian South African Life*. Cape Town, South Africa: Kwela Books.

Domergue, Sonya. 1998. "The Mistress of Spices: Falling through a Hole in the Earth." Paper presented at the Institute for Commonwealth and American Studies and English Language (ICASEL) International Conference on "The Writers of the Indian Diaspora," Mysore, India, 5–9 January.

Gorra, Michael. 1997. *After Empire: Scott, Naipaul, Rushdie*. Chicago: University of Chicago Press.

Grewal, Inderpal, and Caren Kaplan, eds. 1994. *Scattered Hegemonies: Postmodernity and Transnational Feminist Practices*. Minneapolis: University of Minnesota Press.

Hall, Stuart. 1996. "Cultural Identity and Diaspora." In *Contemporary Postcolonial Theory: A Reader*, ed. Padmini Mongia, 110–21. London: Arnold.

Hassakhan, Maurits. 1990. "Settlement and Integration of Indian Contract-Immigrants in a Plantation Economy: The Case of Surinam." Paper presented at the UNESCO Conference on Interactions of the African, Chinese and Indian Diasporas with Their New Socio-cultural Environment. Trinidad and Tobago, 28 May–1 June.

Joshi, P. S. 1942. *The Tyranny of Colour: A Study of the Indian Problem in South Africa*. Durban, South Africa.

Kahn, Joel S. 1995. *Culture, Multiculture, Postculture*. London: Sage.

Kaviraj, Sudipta. 1993. "The Imaginary Institution of India." In *Subaltern Studies: Writings on South Asian History and Society*, ed. Partha Chatterjee and Gyanendra Pandey, vol. 7: 2–39. Delhi: Oxford University Press.

Meer, Fatima. 1969. *Portrait of Indian South Africans*. Durban, South Africa: Aron House.

———. 1990. "Indian South Africans: Their Shared Experience, Self-identity and Cross-cultural Relations in a Racist Society." Paper presented at the UNESCO Conference on Interactions of the African, Chinese and Indian Diasporas with Their New Socio-cultural Environment. Trinidad and Tobago, 28 May–1 June.

Munsamy, Shireen Sarojini. 1997. *Sunrise to Sunset: A History of the Contributions of Indentured and Free Indians to the Economy of Natal, 1960–1910*. Durban, South Africa: Afro-Indus.

Naipaul, V. S. 1969. *The Mimic Men*. Harmondsworth, UK: Penguin.

———. 1981. *An Area of Darkness: An Experience of India*. New York: Vintage.

———. 1991. *India: A Million Mutinies Now*. India: Minerva.

Naravane, Vishwanath. S. 1996. *Sarojini Naidu: Her Life, Work and Poetry*. New Delhi: Orient Longman. (Orig. pub. 1980.)

Nash, Catherine. 1994. "Remapping the Body/Land: New Cartographies of Identity, Gender, and Landscape in Ireland." In Blunt and Rose, *Writing Women and Space*, 227–50.

Paranjape, Makarand, ed. 1996. *Sarojini Naidu: Selected Letters, 1890s to 1940s*. New Delhi: Kali for Women.

Parekh, Bhiku. 1999. *Colonialism, Tradition, and Reform: An Analysis of Gandhi's Political Discourse*. Rev. ed. New Delhi: Sage.

Parker, Arthur, and Mrs. Parker, trans. 1922. *At the Master's Feet*, by Sardhu Sundar Singh. New York: Fleming H. Revell.

Parmar, Pratibha. 1990. "Black Feminism: The Politics of Articu-lation." In *Identity: Community, Culture, Difference*, ed. Jonathan Rutherford, 101–26. London: Lawrence and Wishart.

Prabhakaran, Varijakshi. 1991. "The Telugu Language and Its Influence on the Cultural Lives of the Hindu 'Pravasandras' in South Africa." D.Litt., University of Durban–Westville.

Randall, Peter. 1982. *Little England on the Veld: The English Private School System in South Africa*. Johannesburg, South Africa: Ravan Press.

Reddy, Dean C. 1992. "The Apostolic Faith Mission of South Africa with Special Reference to Its Rise and Development in the Indian Community." Master's diss., University of Durban–Westville, South Africa.

Rushdie, Salman. 1991. *Imaginary Homelands: Essays and Criticism, 1981–1991*. London: Granta Books.

Russell, Diana E. H. 1988. "Fatima Meer: South African Community Leader and Fighter against Apartheid." *Sage* 5.2: 69–73.

Sam, Agnes. 1989. *Jesus Is Indian*. London: Heinemann.

Sharpe, Jenny. 1993. *Allegories of Empire: The Figure of Woman in Colonial Text*. Minneapolis: University of Minnesota Press.

Sitas, Ari. 2004. *Voices That Reason: Theoretical Parables*. Pretoria, South Africa: Unisa Press.

Sunder Rajan, Rajeswari. 1991. *Real and Imagined Women: Gender, Culture, and Post-colonialism*, London: Routledge.

Takaki, Ronald. 1993. *A Different Mirror: A History of Multicultural America*. Back Bay Books. Boston: Little, Brown.

Tharu, Susie, and K. Lalita, eds. 1991. *Women Writing in India: 600 B.C. to the Present*. Vol. 2: *The Twentieth Century*. Delhi: Oxford University Press.

Tharu, Susie, and K. Lalita, eds. 1991. *Women Writing in India: 600 B.C. to the Present*. Vol. 1: *600 B.C. to the Early Twentieth Century*. New York: Feminist Press at the City University of New York.

Turrell, Rob. 1998. Review of *Liberating the Family? Gender and British Slave Emancipation in the Rural Western Cape, South Africa, 1823–1853*. *Sunday Independent*, 23 August, p. 19.

Walker, Cheryl, ed. 1990. *Women and Gender in Southern Africa to 1945*. Cape Town, South Africa: David Philip.

Wicomb, Zoe. 2001. "Five Afrikaner Texts and the Rehabilitation of Whiteness." In *Culture in the New South Africa: After Apartheid*, ed. Robert Kriger and Abebe Zegeye, 2: 160–81. Kwela Books: Cape Town.

van der Veer, Peter. 1997. "'The Enigma of Arrival': Hybridity and Authenticity in the Global Space." In *Debating Cultural Hybridity: Multi-cultural Identities and the Politics of Anti-racism*, ed. Pnina Werbner and Tariq Modood, 90–105. London: Zed Books.

# 3

## Shops and Stations

*Rethinking Power and Privilege in British/Indian East Africa*

Savita Nair

It is not as imported labour that I advocate the
introduction of the Indians [into East Africa],
but as colonist and settler.

—Frederick D. Lugard, 1893

When Frederick Lugard, captain in the British East Africa Company, goes
from England to East Africa in 1889 to explore and establish the company's claim to East Africa, he recommends that "the Indian" be used in
multi-tiered, somewhat contradictory, ways. Eventually, Indians are imported as indentured laborers to build the Uganda Railway—the practical
and symbolic heart of imperial power—and Indians indeed are recruited
to settle and help develop these newly established British lands. Among
the many tiers of Lugard's proposals is the assertion that the British development of East Africa was good for Africans and good for the British. It is
in this particular instance that Lugard endorses the use of Indians: "If the
laziness of the [African] natives should make it impossible for us to reap
advantage, we must find means to do so in spite of them" (Lugard 1893:
497). Among other things, Lugard heralds the Indian laborers as "more ci-
vilised settlers" and as potential examples for the "extremely imitative" African. Most significantly, he argues that Indians be imported as colonists
and settlers and "not as imported coolie labour," and that Indians give a
much-needed impetus to trade. Though appalling today for its racism and

self-interest, his reasoning had logic at that time. Lugard speculates that if the Indians brought commercial gains to East Africa for the British, then it would be an automatic success for the African as well. He defends this position by citing the successful, centuries-long history of Indian traders along the coasts of Africa (488–89).

Just over a decade later, in 1908, Winston Churchill praises and defends the Indian community in East Africa by stating:

> The Indian was here long before the first British Official. He may point to *many generations of useful industry* of the Coast and inland as the white settlers, especially the most recently arrived contingents from South Africa . . . can count years of residence. Is it possible for any Government, with a scrap of respect for honest *dealing between man and man*, to embark on a policy of deliberately squeezing out the native of India from regions in which he has established himself under every security of public faith. (Churchill 1908: 34; emphases mine)

Parallel to Churchill, Lugard, and the imperial government, Indians justify their East African presence on precedence, utility, and rights when facing imperial uncertainties. The historical record indicates that if Indians had civic equality, Kenya would have, in effect, functioned as an Indian colony. Thus, the position of Indians in colonial Kenya has unique features when compared to other British colonies with a history of Indian indenture, although scholarship tends to belie this fact. The question of how to negotiate the role of British Indian subjects in other British colonies looms large especially when the population in Kenya is not primarily an indentured or post-indentured one.

As a historian of modern South Asia, my aim is to explore local and under-explored levels of contact between individuals, most broadly grouped as Asian, European, and African, by examining a small sample of colonial East African court records from 1918 to 1920. Of the dozens I examined, a handful stand out as revealing and representing defiance, insecurity, marginalization, and perceived superiority among the various players. The Court of Kenya was established in Mombasa in 1902, was moved to Nairobi in 1905, and was known as the Supreme Court, and later as the High Court (*IFLA/FAIFE* 2006); Muslim personal law and customary laws were applied. Like in India, the colonial Kenyan court had parallel legal systems in place. The shining "jewel" in the British Crown may have been losing its luster by the early part of the twentieth century with the rise of Indian nationalist movements swaying from more-to-less moderate, but the institutional and policy development of British India would be spliced and implanted into British East Africa, such as the Indian Penal Code and acts of Evidence and Contract (White 1990: 65; Mangat 1969: 63).[1]

By 1919, indentured labor in East Africa had been phased out for a decade, with only remnants of those who had remained behind (Gregory 1972: 77–78).[2] It is important to keep in mind that Indians in East Africa not only originated from different Indian regions (Gujarat and Punjab, primarily, and less so from Goa) than their counterparts in South Africa, but also that the socioeconomic classes of Indians varied. Kenya's Indian population included those who became merchants and professionals and who grew into commercial livelihoods from agricultural backgrounds. Thus, out of a heterogeneous community of interests and desires came heterodox reactions to and by colonial authority. Evidence suggests that the Nairobi Magistrate's office also was far from streamlined or consistent, and serves to emphasize that claims by Indians were far from uniform. The cases selected give insight into activities that had not been collected under the auspices of any larger association intended to reflect the goals or priorities of the Indian "community" (Van den Berghe 1975).[3] Rather, they are perceived injustices between individuals first, and individuals as members of communities second—yet significantly. Community membership, thus, becomes deployed in strategic ways.

Immigration from western India into East Africa was sizable and encouraged informally by Indian employers and British agents. In a general climate where power was up for grabs and who controlled what was continually contested, East Africa in the late teens and 1920s represents a hotbed of struggle, segregation, and dissatisfaction. The 1921 Census of the British East Africa Protectorate (Kenya) shows that there were approximately 2.5 million Africans, 25,000 Indians, 10,000 Arabs, and 9,600 Europeans. The Goan population, listed as a separate category, was approximately 2,400. Kenya and German East Africa (Tanganyika), a British territory after World War I, witnessed growing hostility toward Indians based on economic rivalries, resulting in demands for immigration restrictions. Indian settlement went on with great fervor. Market towns, "the bazaars," exploded across the East African landscape, especially with railway construction making way for commercial access to interior lands and local populations. The growth of market towns, prompted by Indian merchants, progressed until the first decade of the twentieth century, and then these towns began to witness conflicts among European powers over East African territories as well as between Europeans and Indians over treatment and rights. New cosmopolitan centers with a variety of imported goods began to serve local, colonial, and immigrant desires. Situated within the market town—on the streets, in the shops, and around the railway stations of colonial Kenya—Indians and Africans and Britishers shopped, traveled, and lived. And they fought, disagreed, and got angry. And, sometimes, these exchanges became the subject and substance of court records.

## Stations, Streets, and Shops: 1918–1919

Cases brought before the court and statements of grievance shed light on the nature of tensions and strategies of interactions between the diverse racial constituents of colonial East Africa. The activities of large-scale associations that claimed to represent their constituencies must be considered alongside the actions of individuals in their daily activities. Daily life and conflicts, nonetheless, make manifest broader political issues of the day. The simple fact that these cases arose due to acts that "offended against Government policy" and then were recorded for archives marks the institutionalization of complex racial and class-based practices. The National Archives of Kenya has served as a repository for those things that offended.

The first case is a 1919 criminal case involving a British assistant stationmaster of the Nairobi Railway Station, Mr. Jones, and his alleged inappropriate execution of railway policy concerning the reservation of seats in the waiting area reserved for European passengers.[4] The charge and the findings both contradict *commonly understood* notions of power and privilege in East African power politics: the plaintiff was Indian, and the defendant, British. The plaintiff was Rahim Currim, a manager in the firm of Allidina Visram. Currim's position in the prestigious, long-standing, and successful firm of Allidina Visram, one of the earliest and pioneering Indian traders of East Africa, factors into the favorable decision (Visram 1990). In fact, Allidina Visram had served as the first president of the Indian Association in Nairobi in 1906 (Gregory 1972: 81). In his affidavit, Currim states that he was seated along with some other gentlemen on a bench on the platform when the accused "came over from behind and pushed the bench and threw them down on the platform." Currim explains how he later wrote through his advocate to Mr. Jones asking for an explanation and an apology for his conduct but received no reply. Currim evokes his relationship to the Visram firm again and again. Clearly, it seems to matter.

In his defense Jones maintains that he saw Indians occupying all the seats reserved for Europeans and spoke to them three times without success before he tipped up the bench from the back. Jones's testimony alleges that his action caused the Indians to "get up" and "not to fall." In the letter to Jones, Currim's advocate points out that the stationmaster's actions could have ended in far more serious consequences had his client not restrained in counteracting the assault. The letter implies that Rahim Currim could have retaliated justifiably. With no more evidence than both parties' testimonies, the court's ruling identifies the assistant manager's action as "guilty of a technical assault."

In a second case, the litigation narrative tells a different story when the racial dynamic switches to an Indian defending himself against "the Crown." The Crown is acting on behalf of an African plaintiff. The outcome here invokes the class position of the Indian defendant. In the case of "The Crown versus Jadavji Jagjivan Parekh" and its subsequent application for revision, the point of conflict occurs when Parekh arrived at the Nairobi Railway Station in order to send a letter.[5] Parekh claims to have been assaulted by a "native askari,"[6] Kamau, who had prevented him from entering the station. Kamau contends that 1) the defendant did not have a platform ticket and, therefore, was not allowed to enter the platform, and 2) that he did not assault the defendant while stopping him from entering the platform. The judgment by C. M. Barton in favor of the Crown states that:

> [Relying] on the evidence of the European constable who states that he saw the Indian, Jadavji, trying to push past the askari; if this were so, the askari would have been justified in pushing him back; I do not believe the askari slapped Jadavji on the face, the askari denies that he did this and I do not consider it to be likely that he did. I acquit the askari; I convict the Indian, Jadavji, of the offence of assaulting a public servant in the execution of his duty Section 353 I.P.C.

In the end Parekh is released on his own bond in the sum of Rs. 50 since, in the magistrate's consideration, the assault was not serious and since the police had procrastinated one month before applying to the court for a summons. In the High Court order of 7 July that refused revision of the 25 June judgment, there is agreement that the askari was exercising his duties as a public servant by verifying that the applicant was indeed an authorized person, and that the askari, according to his own testimony, is aware that Indians were permitted to enter the station in order to send a letter. The order reaffirmed the court's ruling on the side of the askari, who, it is believed, would not have attempted to prevent the defendant from entering the station if there *had been* a letter to be mailed.

The fact that Parekh would have been allowed into the station if he had a letter for posting is complicated by the fact that Parekh was a successful merchant in Nairobi. From the testimony and the court's account, it is clear that his commercial status is as relevant as his racial standing. During his cross-examination at the original court hearing, the *askari* Kamau states:

> I did not hit accused in the face; I have been on duty at the Railway Station many times; Natives and Asiatics may not go through the European place without a pass; I asked all Asiatics and Natives for a pass if I saw them wanting to pass through the European entrance; they can get a pass from the Indian clerks; there is a small window where passes are purchased; better class

> Indians are allowed to purchase passes at the European place. I did not see a letter with accused. *I do not know if accused is a leading Indian merchant in Nairobi;* people wanting to post a letter in the train always show them at the entrance; if a person shows a Barua[7] and says that he wants to post it I would let him pass. [Emphasis mine]

Kamau's statement indicating his own uncertainty about Parekh's class membership encodes several conditions about plural East Africa: 1) the diversity among the Indian community is great enough that those in the upper economic echelons stood out and, therefore, are in a position to receive certain privileges; 2) privileges received are still tempered by the judgment of the authority—in this case, the African railway guard at the service of British authority; 3) the breadth of the privilege approaches, but is not commensurate with, those of Europeans; and 4) these privileges certainly exist above those of "natives" in ordinary circumstances except when that "native" is a public servant executing duties on behalf of the British East African Protectorate.

In the original case, Parekh states to the court, "I am a Bania by caste, there are 4 castes, Bania is the 2nd. I consider myself one of the leading merchants in the Bazaar. I was dressed like I am now; I had no tie or collar on." What provokes these specific comments and the intended purpose of the defendant's statement are absent from the court record. His self-referential description and use of indigenous, community-specific terms implies an understood set of collective priorities in a growing colonial market system.[8] Furthermore, it seems to be aimed to highlight many features: his status in Nairobi society within the bazaar, his value as a "citizen in the empire" within the protectorate, and his social location vis-à-vis the native askari. Evidence of the latter arises even further in Parekh's sworn account of his interactions with the askari and of his emotional state during these events:

> I knew that there was no necessity to buy a pass when I only wanted to post a letter. I showed the letter to the askari. I did not show it to the European Constable but I had it in my hand when I spoke to him. I did not show the letter to the European Constable because he did not ask me why I wanted to go to the platform; if he had asked me I would have shown it to him; I was also under the impression that the European Constable might have seen the letter; this is why I did not show it to him. I was not annoyed at the askari not allowing me to pass; I was not annoyed and I did not try and push past him. I was puzzled and was in confusion but I was not angry.

Parekh's assertion about his knowledge of station protocol regarding mailing letters in combination with his expression of "annoyance" rather than "anger" degrades the position of the African askari. The comments suggest layers of seemingly understood propriety. Implicit in Parekh's comment seems to be the query: "Who is this native to presume that I, a leading Indian merchant, would not know the procedures for pass requirements and posting letters." In the constable's sworn testimony, he reiterates the policy. He states, "a person wanting to post a letter is allowed to pass without a platform ticket. An Asiatic intending to post a letter is not stopped even if he has not a platform ticket. Indians may buy platform tickets at the 1st or 3rd class booking offices." Referring to the askari's lower occupational position, racial status, and making of false assumptions, the defendant questions the character and authority of the askari. Characterizations such as annoyance, puzzlement, and confusion deflect responsibility, inscribe blame, and shift hierarchies.

Juxtaposed to Parekh's case where descriptions of the askari's attitude and demeanor are causes for alarm and defense is the following case of defiance and "bad manners." In this 1918 case in Fort Hall the Indian is also the accused, but the charge is based solely on acts of insubordination and not on any physical improprieties. An Indian merchant is accused of not selling goods to a district commissioner and his accompanying Africans. This case is more complicated, however, because multiple events create the causes for adjudicating Criminal Case No. 66, and several related cases. According to the accused, shopkeeper Hamchand Keshavji, on 1 June 1918 around 8:00 A.M., he noticed that several people had gathered in front of a shop, Walli Hassum's & Co. He comes to learn that the district commissioner, Mr. Lawford, had "entered Gulam Hussain's bedroom, had taken off the blanket from Hashan [sic] and had assaulted Maganbhai, Jamal Hirji & Sons' book-keeper." According to Keshavji's testimony, it is then decided by Gulam Hussain and Maganbhai that they would close their shops, and that Hussain would go to Nairobi to report the altercation to higher authorities. The area shopkeepers then decide to close their own shops "as a protest against the conduct of Mr. Lawford, the District Commissioner in charge of the District." Later that morning, when Mr. Lawford arrives at Keshavji's shop and instructs his accompanying African natives "to demand" rice, Keshavji refuses to sell any and explains upon inquiry that he was waiting to hear a reply from the provincial commissioner, Nyeri, or the chief secretary about the earlier incident at Gulam Hussain's. Mr. Lawford then warns Keshavji that because he was not selling goods, there would be a Rs. 5000 fine and a six-month sentencing. Later that afternoon, Keshavji receives a summons to attend court in three days. In his defense, Keshavji maintains, "there was no genuine attempt to purchase food stuff required by the native. At the time the request was made my shop was closed under justifiable circumstances." Keshavji justified his actions based on a freedom to protest and to withhold services until a more legitimate and higher authority intervened.

Lawford's accusations against Keshavji for not selling goods are followed by additional complaints against Kassam Ebrahim. Ebrahim, the accused, is "charged with intentional insult to provoke a breach of the peace, Section 504." Lawford recounts that as he and his assistant passed Wali Hassum's shop, he noticed the accused, Ebrahim, and another Indian approximately 15–20 yards away. Lawford states:

> they both looked at me and the other Indian got up and went into the shop leaving the accused sitting on the verandah washing his face or mouth; I passed by within a few yards and noticing that *he took no notice of my official position.* I walked my horse across the small bridge which divided the roads from the shop and went close to him. I said to him, "Who are you." He did not answer but remained sitting down washing his face. I said to him *"Do you know that I am the District Commissioner here."* He then stood up and said in English, "Alright I don't care." Either immediately before he said this or immediately afterwards he spat in my direction. I have not exact recollection of my saying anything else but immediately afterwards he deliberately spat directly towards me, his spittal or water I am not sure which missing my horses feet by the barest margin. *I was very much upset and blindly furious at being treated like this* and it was with the greatest difficulty that I refrained from getting off my horse and giving accused the thrashing his insolence deserved. [Emphases mine]

Lawford's perceived affront is based on the "loss of politeness in this man [Ebrahim]" and also based on his belief that "the Indians were against me." Although Lawford's own testimony does not mention what exactly he wanted the accused to do and how exactly he expects the accused to act, Ebrahim states that Lawford had said, "It is the custom here in Fort Hall that when I pass by everybody should salute me." To this Ebrahim states that he had replied, "I do not know you so how could I salute you." Ebrahim then remarks that Lawford commanded Ebrahim to salute him. Ebrahim testified that his response to Lawford was: "Why should I salute you, I am not your servant." Later in the testimony, Ebrahim concedes that he was "unaware of regulation compelling [him] to salute any European who orders [him] to do so." In the final judgment, Ebrahim is sentenced to one month's imprisonment for insulting a district commissioner. While aspects of Ebrahim's actions provide powerful evidence for "everyday forms of resistance" (Scott 1985),[9] I seek to highlight how the place of Indians in colonial East Africa further complicates stories of empire when sites of colonial contest are themselves marked many times over by various forms of "subjects" and power brokers.

The proceedings in the previous case against shopkeeper Hamchand Keshavji are used in the case against Gulam Hussain, manager of Walli

Hassum's shop. Gulam Hussains's refusal to sell rice to Lawford's assistant, Juma bid Mohammad, serves as grounds for prosecuting him along similar lines to those against Keshavji. The judgment states that the court was satisfied that "the accused refused to sell a rupee's worth of rice to one Juma bin Mohammed and thereby committed a breach of the Martial Law regulated dated 5th June 1917." The magistrate clarifies that a grievance against Mr. Lawford does not provide legitimate grounds for excusing the accused's actions. Since the accused's grievances against Mr. Lawford are personal, the magistrate concludes that it is even more important that the accused "be careful to obey the Martial Law Regulations which affect the Public, especially in view of the notice circulated by Mr. Lawford in which he warned all shopkeepers in the Indian Bazaar to open their stores and continue peaceful trading." Hussain is convicted because his actions are considered to be "in direct defiance of the authority of the Government representative." In Hussain's sentencing, the magistrate opts for a "severe punishment" of Rs. 1,500 and two months of "rigorous imprisonment" and invokes the moral character of Hussain's employer, the shop owner himself, as if to disseminate the responsibility as well as guilt across racial and political lines:

> Taking all the considerations into consideration I intend to give this accused a severe punishment; it is admitted that Walli Hassum's shop of which accused is the manager is one of the principal shops in Fort Hall and *I am convinced that no one would more strongly condemn accused's action than Wali Hassum himself who is one of the most respectable Indian traders in the country.* [Emphasis mine][10]

In Magistrate Barton's words rest the representation of Indians as good citizens of British East Africa who themselves would be expected to uphold the British government's punitive actions against any criminal, an uncivil subject. Such evidence as this allows me to speculate that officials like Barton rope in Indians to create a civil society in East Africa like the one that had been established in British India. For British and Indians alike, the expectations placed upon Indians in East Africa reflect a long legacy of colonial and civil society in British India. Transplanted to British East Africa are models of administration and rule first established in British India.

Whereas earlier we see accommodations being made toward the African askari who was viewed and treated almost as a ward of the court, Indians are held to a different standard. The British themselves seem to place East Africa Indians in a precariously liminal category between colonized and colonizer, including codes and acts that reflect British *Indian* paramountcy. Placements and priorities were apt to change without compulsory reason when it best suited the interests of British rule and control. Their need for an orderly, civil, and compliant East African society came first.

### Unlikely Protesters in a Civil Society

As early as 1906, leading Indian professionals and merchants began formulating collective opposition to discriminatory policies. A. M. Jeevanjee, then-president of the Indian Association, called a meeting in Mombasa about the European campaign to reserve the agriculturally and climatically desirable Kenya highlands solely for European occupation. The East African Indian National Congress, formed in Mombasa in 1914, was modeled on the Indian National Congress, formed in Bombay in 1885. The highlands issue was not settled until 1923, when a decision was upheld to keep the highlands for European use and temporarily reserve lowlands for Asian agricultural use (Gregory 1972: 242–49). The move for exclusive European occupation of the Kenya highlands became emblematic of the many factors that disrupted Indian understandings of their own role, identity, and privilege in East Africa. Situated between the years following World War I and preceding the 1923 Kenya Highlands White Paper, these cases based on daily social exchanges are both representative of and offer alternate interpretations to historically documented and popularly understood political and societal concerns of the Indian community-at-large. Details of those interactions bring individual variation to questions of position and place of Indians in early British East African society. While court cases *may* reflect more public, large-scale, and better-documented grievances of the Indian collective, the point is to focus on the local language of power negotiations and see how they reflect broader imperial contestations, how the courts both encode and give meaning to colonial social hierarchies.

Unlike the British who see the Indian "middleman" as serving a colonially stipulated need, Indian merchants in the early twentieth century perceive their presence in East Africa in less utilitarian and more cosmopolitan ways. Elsewhere I have examined contributions by and awareness about overseas Indian nationalists that have been missing from accounts of Indian independence through an analysis of vernacular and English-language newspapers published in the former Bombay presidency, areas of modern-day Maharashtra and Gujarat (Nair 2001). At its crux, the evidence reveals that a heightened sense of Indian nationalism by 1915 was pervasive not only in India but throughout many Indian overseas communities. Claims of equality, rights, and privilege are being made on behalf of Indians in South and East Africa, the West Indies, and Fiji, for instance, on the grounds of *being* Indian—asserted by the emerging nation. Indian East African nationalist activities provide substantial evidence to their dual yet contradictory positions as freedom fighter for India and neo-colonizer in Kenya. Although Indian nationalism is defined by the nation, and the nation had its exclusions, the sense of Indian nationalist identity in Kenya is evident in the court testimonies. Kenyan Indians' activities may not have produced any flamboyant and charismatic personalities, like South Africa's Gandhi, or any sudden and dramatic political methods or measures like *satyagraha*.[11] Nevertheless, East Africa's internal conflicts and resolutions are manifest in Indian newspapers and in the imaginations of government officials and communities from which migrants originated. Thus, I have argued, such manifestations created extra fodder for the body of Indian nationalism. Only because Gandhi's life and works have become inextricably linked with the history of Indian nationalism, his beginnings in South Africa, and therefore South Africa itself, have played a part in official and common historical understandings of British India. What has been missing and necessary is a greater understanding about the colonies in which other Indians resided. Overseas Indians from middle-class, skilled and semi-skilled, literate populations were also involved in expanding the possibilities for imagining India and remapping identities. And remap they did.

Negotiating between a British Indian civil society and an Indian cultural home in East Africa mirrors how Indians straddled political realms of rights and privileges. Theirs was a dubious status, and the status varied based on British East African, East Africa Indian, or British Indian points of view and interests. The vagaries of Indians as economic leaders in East Africa, as natives of a highly "civil" British Indian society (from which British East Africa would take cues), as racially superior to their African counterparts (both from their own and British perspectives), and finally as nationalists who fought for what they saw as overdue entitlements are all reflected in the shifts in judgment from court case to court case.

Before concluding, I want to remark on two statements made twelve years apart by two British officials. Viewed together, they divulge the overt distrust and suspicion of the Indian presence in East Africa. More importantly, the statements indicate the changing nature of who is the object of distrust and suspicion. Indian business and service were the support systems on which much of the British colonial project in East Africa rested, and it is clear that the British were unsure about how to deal with Indians in East Africa.

In 1912, several years after Indians were excluded from owning land in the fertile White Highlands, but well before the 1923 White Paper reserved those lands for exclusive appropriation by white British, Lord

Cranworth commented that Indians were draining resources from British East Africa and "there is hardly a crime among natives which is not directly traceable to the Indian" (Kimenyi 1988: 60). For Cranworth, Indians posed a threat to British sovereignty in the East Africa territories. Subsequently, in 1924, the Machakos district commissioner, Campbell, reflected his concern over the British policy of African paramountcy and commented that Indians were dishonest and cheating Africans in trade: "I should say that Indians have contributed more to the ruination of the youth of the country and stagnation in trade than any other factor" (60). The commissioner's declaration in 1924 points the finger at Indians for the African condition. Clearly, African trading interests served as a flimsy guise covering true British political initiatives and priorities. The pursuit of African interests seems to be less about a concern about Africans themselves and more a British motivation to quell an Indian rise to economic or political power. One half century later, President Idi Amin evoked the exact same line of argument. Unlike the British who had a use for the skilled Indian population and had to contend with pressures from rising British Indian nationalism and, therefore, pressures from London as well, Idi Amin did not have a use for the Indians and did not have to answer to anyone else. Amin fulfilled his mission through the 1972 Asian expulsion from Uganda.

### Conclusion

All the cases discussed occurred in the period between World War I and the 1923 White Paper; which subordinated Indian claims to those of African interests. Equal rights were desired as commerce flourished. The period witnessed almost complete dominance of Indian commercial enterprise although Indian business advantage was reduced only through government intervention in the 1930s. The influence of the community's prosperity did not necessarily and consistently transfer over into individual and indiscrete privileges. Although Indians were becoming a powerful force, as far as they were an ethnic group with economic significance and with demands for a political voice, Indians also had to be "formally subordinate to the purposes of the imperial power" (Kimenyi 1988: 134). Most significantly, however, their subordinate position was complicated by Britain's imperial and administrative control over Indians in India. Due to British Indian ascendancy, British administrative control over Indians in East Africa was becoming less clear—most of all, they were blurred by the Indian expatriate community. Indians had been in East Africa longer than Europeans, as accepted plainly in Churchill's earlier quote defending Indian claims to rights, and Indian merchants and government servants fulfilled a valuable economic role for the colony and for the empire. The economic definition and implications of being "middlemen" may have been apparent, but Indian self-referential understanding of social place and worth was far from "middle" and far from apparent.

This essay has explored how Gujarati Indian migrants settled easily yet uneasily into the shifting landscape of colonial Kenya. Race relations and negotiations over space that occurred on a daily basis in towns and cities all over East Africa represent how institutional relationships filtered down to personal interactions and commercial transactions. Contests over space, resources, nationality, and economic entitlements continue to mark post-independence East Africa, first with the "Asian expulsion" and later with the government-initiated repatriation of overseas "Asian" families. The processes by which people overseas have come to see themselves as part of multiple communities, nationalized and diasporic, is made evident by Gujarati Indians in East Africa who were there *not* as part of or descendant from an indentured labor pool, but rather who arrived in Kenya as traders, merchants, professionals, educators, and artisans. Through "circular migrations" (Markovits 2000; Nair 2001) and the peculiarities of trade, nationalism, and regionalism, Gujaratis in East Africa made places unfixed. By border crossings of all sorts, migrants have made spaces come alive through commerce, practice, imagination, and social life. Diaspora takes on new light in this context because many of the movements of people overseas that constitute diaspora demographically do not constitute it culturally because the homeland is never actually left behind but rather is extended and attached to regions of social life that extend over space without alienation or stark separation; and because the homeland is not an imagined place of origin but rather a living land of family life. These aspects of "globalization" are often discussed with a presentist bias starting in the early 1990s. The period of the early twentieth century, in which these so-called alienations came into being, shows how the life histories of migrants escape the confines of diaspora mentalities while at the same time give rise to them through efforts to adjust migrating identities to a nationalized world.

Just as Govinden's material elsewhere in this collection deals with her family's respect and affection for the British Crown vis-à-vis resistance against policy and treatment, colonial East Africa refashioned Indian/British/African power dynamics. The ambiguity between Indians and British and the systematic "othering" articulated in Govinden's Natal case, however, was less pronounced in Kenya. Again, perhaps due to the non-indentured nature of its then-population and pre-colonial history of migration and trade on the coasts, Indians were confronted with discrepancies in their roles as merchants and entrepreneurs on one hand and as relegated civil servants and "Asiatics" on the other; identities such as "colonial subject" versus "citizen of empire" haunted the discursive landscape.

The evidence presented here privileges individual actions rather than collective movements of Indians and analyzes how interactions were acted out, narrated, arbitrated, interpreted, and penalized. While I agree with Anjali Gera Roy, who, elsewhere in this volume, has recognized the longevity of India's dynamic cultures and stressed the historical reality that relations between Indians and Africans have been brokered by other parties, I argue that it is precisely the challenge to being *brokered* that must be understood in early twentieth-century colonial Kenya. Further, my evidence has as its premise that Indian appeals for equality were based in part on a legacy of late nineteenth-century British/Indian ideas about subjecthood, democratic rights, and freedoms, but also on inherited ideas about Indian/British racial equality and civilizational parity. In other words, aspects of Indian self-perception were founded on the notion that they had as much *right* to the lands as British colonists—rights based on community contributions that were tangible and appeared self-evident in addition to a less overt yet profound notion of "civilizational worth"—part of a trajectory of Indian nationalism and Indo-centrism overseas. If one supports Roy's suggestions, for instance, "civilizational worth" is encapsulated by the following: Indians imagined themselves as the inheritors of the *arya* indigenous core. Such "lineage" implicitly underscored court testimonies. My essay also supports, at least in part, Jameela Siddiqi's comment in this volume's introduction by John C. Hawley: "Indians had managed their own community affairs from a largely moralistic Indian standpoint." Such moralistic high ground, coupled with a civilizational high ground, undergirded Indian accountability and demands. Not only did Indians strive to reside in the desirable Kenya White Highlands, but the historical record verifies a desire to administer Kenya as India's possession on the grounds that it was "pre-eminently an Indian colony and best adapted to Indian life and civilization" and, according to one suggestion, should be administered under the India Office, not the Colonial Office (Gregory 1972: 193, 197). Expectations of entitlements prevailed, though they were not fulfilled in terms of residential desegregation or political control.

Two features need to be understood to explain community making and hierarchies for Indians in colonial Kenya: 1) Indians constituted much of government service, small business, and other professional and industrial sectors; and 2) India was central in British imperial politics. Thus, Indians existed in a liminal category between being colonizer and being colonized while they composed the economic hub of British/African/Indian society. The question that drives this study is: how did middle-class Indians negotiate the race and power politics of early twentieth-century East Africa—and secondarily the formation of a particular sort of community. Court cases serve as moments of contact and contestation and present glimpses into local and personal exchanges that illuminate how we study collective identity formation. To this extent, court cases allow us to peek into enunciations of identity, thus crystallizing them.

Standard stories place Indians in the middle of a three-tiered colonial system. This picture is not useful for scholars and students as it denies non-European theoretical reflections and, more problematic, remains historically inaccurate. Methodologically, the present study includes migrants as social actors in mobility and provides contexts for colleagues of African history to continue a dialogue. Questioning the static view of Indians as simply "in the middle" and challenging such a narrative not only erase fragmentation but also perpetuate isolationist explanations and apologist history writing. Finally, a volume like this that brings together scholars from across the world, across the disciplines, and across geographic areas of expertise is one step toward collaborations and conversations among those who reflect cosmopolitanisms, with global interests in such intellectual pursuits. Like the subjects of our various scholarly inquiries, we too have to locate and unravel the ties that bind.

### Notes

1. Because of uncertainty about how, or even *if*, these cases were publicly received, a future project includes an examination of *The African Standard* (a limited English-language newspaper; Kenya's oldest, established in Mombasa in 1901; founded by prominent Indian merchant and political leader A. M. Jeevanjee). While the few writings about Jeevanjee have been of scholarly use, he has come to represent the "Indian community" in ways that are historically limiting; thus, there are many gaps to be filled (Patel: 1997; Patel and Mulla 2002). Similarly, in her chapter in this book, Devarakshanam Govinden works to close absences in history writing, particularly about women in colonial Natal. Just as indentured laborers in South Africa evoked their subject position, Indians in 1919 colonial Kenya further exerted their less liminal non-indentured status.

2. Independent migration from India to East Africa preceded, accompanied, and followed the exportation of over 34,000 Indian indentured laborers between 1895 and 1901, primarily used for the construction of the Uganda Railway. Only roughly 2,500 Africans were used during the years of intense railway building. Approximately 20 percent of the Indian laborers remained in East Africa after the expiration of their contracts; others repatriated to India.

3. At the time of the court cases, all British territories of East Africa (Kenya, Tanganyika, Uganda, and Zanzibar) had a population that included over 54,400 Indians. Although Indians clearly outnumbered Europeans and their numbers kept increasing

with immigration activity double that of the Europeans, Indians were still negotiating their role in this burgeoning colonial economy.

4. All references from Criminal Case No. 149, Nairobi 1919, and its Revision, Case 20, 1919.

5. All references from High Court of the East Africa Protectorate, Criminal Revision No. 20 of 1919; Original Judgment in Criminal Case No. 546 of 1919, Nairobi.

6. *Askari*: African guard.

7. *Barua*: letter.

8. The ability of caste delineations to arise in a court of law and to prove a high position in Indian social hierarchy suggests that the particular term "Bania" had meaning far beyond parochial and internal usages.

9. Here I borrow from James C. Scott (1985) and also refer to the writings by the Subaltern Studies collective of scholars on South Asia, whose work also seeks to complicate relationships between "colonizer" and "colonized."

10. All references from Criminal Case No. 66, Fort Hall, 1918.

11. It should be noted that A. M. Jeevanjee, in the first two decades of the twentieth century, and Makhan Singh, in the 1930s, are becoming increasingly well known among scholars. The term *satyagraha* refers to Gandhi's philosophy of practicing non-violent forms of resistance. The notion of *satyagraha* is generally defined as "truth" or "soul" (*satya*) and "force" or "determination" (*agraha*).

**Works Cited**

Churchill, W. S. 1908. *My African Journey*. London: Hodder and Stoughton.

Gregory, Robert. 1972. *India and East Africa: A History of Race Relations within the British Empire, 1890–1939*. Oxford: Clarendon Press.

IFLA/FAIFE World Report: Libraries and Intellectual Freedom: Kenya. 27 January 2006. www.ifla.org/faife/report/kenya.htm, accessed 11 March 2007.

Kimenyi, Mwangi. 1988. "Asians in the Economy." *Finance*, August.

Lugard, Frederick D. 1893. *The Rise of Our East African Empire: Early Efforts in Nyasaland and Uganda*. London: W. Blackwood.

Mangat, J. S. 1969. *A History of the Asians in East Africa c. 1886 to 1945*. Oxford: Clarendon Press.

Markovits, Claude. 2000. *The Global World of Indian Merchants, 1750–1947: Traders of Sind from Bukhara to Panama*. Cambridge, Cambridge University Press.

Nair, Savita. 2001. "Moving Life Histories: Gujarat, East Africa, and the Indian Diaspora, 1880–2000." Ph.D. diss., University of Pennsylvania.

Patel, Zarina. 1997. *Challenge to Colonialism: The Struggle of Alibhai Mulla Jeevanjee for Equal Rights in Kenya*. Nairobi, Kenya: Publishers Distribution Services.

Patel, Zarina, and Alibhai Mulla. 2002. *Jeevanjee*. Nairobi, Kenya: East African Educational.

Scott, James C. 1985. *Weapons of the Weak: Everyday Forms of Peasant Resistance*. New Haven, Conn.: Yale University Press.

Van den Berghe, Pierre L. 1975. "Asian Africans before and after Independence." *Kroniek van Afrika* 3.6: 197–205.

Visram, M. G. 1990. *Allidina Visram: The Trailblazer*. Mombasa, Kenya : MG Visram.

White, Luise. 1990. *The Comforts of Home: Prostitution in Colonial Nairobi*. Chicago: University of Chicago Press.

*Court Cases*

*Kenya National Archives Microfilm and Microform collection.* Maxwell Graduate School of Citizenship and Public Affairs, Program of Eastern African Studies, Syracuse University.
Criminal Case No. 149, Resident Magistrate's Court at Nairobi, 1919.
Criminal Revision No. 20, High Court of the East Africa Protectorate, 1919; original judgment in Criminal Caste 546, Nairobi, 1919.
Criminal Case No. 546/18, Resident Magistrate's Court, Nairobi, 1919.
Criminal Case No. 66, Fort Hall, 1918.

# 4

## Bhangra Remixes

Anjali Gera Roy

It is to insist that in black popular culture,
strictly speaking, ethnographically
speaking, there are no pure forms at all.

—Stuart Hall, "What Is This 'Black' in Black Popular Culture?"

I don't go with the people who say you
shouldn't tamper with Indian music. I want to
know who makes up the law about how
music should sound?

—Bally Sagoo, quoted in "Remixing Identities" by Shirin Housee and Mukhtar Dar

In the 1960s, the Punjabi farmer overcame his suspicion of hybrids to make India's Green Revolution happen. Three decades later, the Punjabi artist, probably the farmer's son, synthesized Afro-Caribbean rhythms with dhol beats to make Bhangra the most "happening" music in the world.[1] An anxious *siapa* about Bhangra's contamination by alien cultural sounds can be heard in response to the call of celebratory *tappas* of Bhangra revival.[2] Bhangra's participation in South Asian diasporic and national identity politics problematizes issues of purity and authenticity, cultural imperialism and resistance, and the production, distribution, and marketing of cultural products. Much has been said about Bhangra's reinventing itself by mixing with the sounds of the "black" diaspora (Baumann: 1990). But not much has been said about why the black and the brown did not mix for the entire century of the Punjabi migration to Africa.[3] This essay examines the new Bhangra hybrids to show that it is the "diaspora space" that enables the black brown sonic contact, but it does so through accentuating rather than dissolving cultural difference in the performance of new Punjabi/Indian/Asian ethnicities.[4] As Devarakshanam Govinden points out elsewhere in this collection, because Indian diasporic experience is nuanced by language, class, sect, caste, and gender, studies of particular diasporas would be more rewarding than totalizing perspectives on an "Indian" experience. In this essay, therefore, I have narrated a specific tale—of Punjabi migration, contact, and mixing—but embedded it in the framing narrative of the Indian pollution complex as an example of diasporicity (Hesse 2000).

An essentialist logic projecting indigenous cultures as unitary and pure underlies *globophobes'* fear of the contamination of autochthonous cultures by "corruptive" alien forces. Post-colonial celebrations of hybridity, similarly, are conveniently amnesiac to pre-colonial hybrid zones that produced India's composite, dynamic cultures. Indian history records more moments of cultural contact rather than those of insulation. Pre-colonial contact zones, though fewer compared to post-colonial, testify to the fruitful fertilization of Indian cultures through cross-cultural exchanges. The current outcry against the contamination of "Indian" culture following India's satellite invasion, therefore, appears greatly out of proportion. Compelling evidence of selective hybridization through which Indian cultures have constantly reinvented themselves refutes the idea of a pure, autochthonous essence, which is often invoked to oppose contemporary global cultural influences. However, their strong eclecticism has always coexisted with a deep-seated pollution complex embedded in the notion of ritual cleanliness. Brahminical Hinduism, in particular, has displayed an obsessive fear of contamination through physical contact with the stranger who is dubbed *mlechcha* (unclean). The ambivalence in the resistance to invading cultures was resolved here by banishing the "stranger" from sacred spaces while incorporating "strange" concepts. India has subsequently co-opted several invading cultures through this selective approach, rejuvenating itself without sacrificing its indigenous knowledge base.

The most recent example of an Indian culture reinventing itself is the Bhangra revival of the 1980s. Though several overlapping factors have led to the Bhangra resurgence, its mixing with the sounds of the black African diaspora such as reggae, rap, and hip-hop largely accounts for its newfound popularity among global youth. Rediscovered by Br-Asian Bhangra practitioners, Bhangra imploded back home to India across many continents and seems poised to conquer even more, based on its growing visibility in the United States, Canada, and, even Australia. This coincided with the emergence of the remix, a postmodern genre with a global youthful following. Contemporary Bhangra mutants mix pure Bhangra forms with other musical sounds, the main musical influence being "black." Though Bhangra remixes are believed to have ushered in the remix era in Indian music,

Bhangra presents as many samples of remixes as collaborative fusions with black beats. It will be instructive to investigate why a Punjabi harvest ritual chose to mix with African-derived black diasporic sounds, where and how this unique mixing occurred, and the implications of both forms of "remixing" for the formation of post-colonial cultural identities. Post-colonial "hybridity talk" often converges on Bhangra hybrids in engaging with the contamination issue. Framing Bhangra hybrids against the notion of ritual pollution practiced by several Indian ethnic groups might provide us with another perspective on hybridity because pollution taboos on intermixing, interdining, and intermarrying, evolved during the middle Vedic period, continued to govern Indian diasporic groups' cross-cultural exchanges.[5]

There has not been much documentation of Indian-African intermixing during the first two waves of Indian migrations to Africa. It is possible that the strong pollution complex and boundary fetish prevented Indian migrants from intermingling freely with their African hosts. Descendants of pioneers who have contributed to Harjinder Singh Kanwal's project on Punjabi Heritage in East Africa by sharing their reminiscences remain silent on their forefathers' private life while hailing their role in African public life. Though some of them might have settled eventually in Africa, they appear to have viewed their sojourn in Africa as a temporary visit compelled by economic constraints and continued the practice of returning home to marry till the second generation that might have facilitated cultural continuity. Most pioneers are reported to have been married when they set sail for Africa, but they were accompanied by male relatives and friends while wives and children were left behind. It is only with the second generation that wives came to accompany their spouses to Africa. Hansraj Aggarwal reports:

> He [Munshi Ram] never brought his wife over, but all his sons came. The wives never came over in those early days. That was the general system of Indians. We Aggarwals married other Aggarwals but the men here would get their wives in India and leave them there, to raise the children. Munshi Ram got married to an Aggarwal girl and they had three sons: W'aliati Ram, Puranchand and Lekraj who was my father. All three came to Kenya but Waliati Ram only came to look, for being the eldest he was running the family business back in India. Puranchand lived here until 1954 and then he returned to India with all of his sons. When my father grew up he was married in India to a girl named Durgadevi. But by then things were different and ladies were coming to Kenya. She came and stayed here and had eight children five sons and three daughters. (Kanwal n.d.)

But there are only three references to intermarriage between Sikhs and African women in the interviews and letters collected by Kanwal other than the rumor about Kala Singha's Masai wife.[6] The documents do not address the coping strategies adopted by notoriously hypermasculine Sikh men unnaturally forced into all-male habitation to deal with the absence of the feminine.

Shashi Tharoor's account of his visit to a Punjabi home in Kenya fills us in on the contemporary relations between Indians and Africans. Asked if Kenya reminded him of Paradise, Tharoo muses:

> I couldn't help wondering, as I devoured a delicious Punjabi lunch on his [Mr. Shankardass's] porch with three generations of his Kenya-born family, whether the garden was an oasis as well, isolating the Asians from the Africans amongst whom they prospered. Indians abroad are often an insular people, focusing on their own community, customs and (as I could savour it) cuisine. Did Mr. Shankardass' heaven have room for African angels too? (Tharoor 2004)

His worries, Tharoor reports, were put to rest later in the day when he not only found Indians mixing with Africans to prove "We're all Kenyans here" but also met an Indian who had adopted an African child. However, none of the "ordinary men and women in Africa" to whom Nikki talks in the episode entitled "Africa Today" (4–8 July) of a BBC Asian Network chat called "In Drive with Nikki" care to mention any African friends in their reminiscences.[7]

Against Gilroy (1987), who reintroduced race as a category in black cultural politics, Hall has announced the end of the "innocent notion of the essential black subject," which he sees as now being "crossed and recrossed by the categories of class, of gender and ethnicity" (1996b: 444). With the end of the era of "the innocent notion of the essential black subject," diverse groups with "different histories, traditions and ethnic identities," who shared "the common experience of racism and marginalization," have borrowed it as a cultural construct (443). But Gilroy's "reluctance to work with a notion of Black that includes Asian politics" is understandable given the circumstantial nature of Asian identification with blackness (2000: 9). "The unifying notion of an open blackness" in favor of "more particularistic conceptions of cultural difference" was bound to be discarded because other than the "commonality" of racial subordination in the UK, people of Indian descent have differentiated themselves from the *hubshi*, the Arabic-derived Hindi term for the African people.[8] Savita Nair's essay in this volume very effectively captures the class, caste, and racial dimensions of the Indian African contact in her account of the Gujarati *bania*'s sense of affront at being evicted from the station by the African boy. I have no quarrel with John Hutnyk's suggestion that as a "strategic essentialism" the signifier black can unify the marginalized Afro-American, Afro-Caribbean, or Asian groups against white racism. But I am more inclined to agree with Hall that the new phase in black cultural politics can accommodate "the politics of ethnicity predicated on difference and diversity" (Hall 1996a). Even at the risk of repeating the epidermalism of old miscegenation discourses from which post-colonial hybridity distances itself, I am forced to fall back on the semiotics of color in employing a color coding of brown and black to distinguish between Indian and African cultural difference. I wish to fore-ground the ambivalence underlying the Indian adoption of a black identity, which undergirds the Indian expression of solidarity with African others.[9]

The integration of blackness is a problematic liaison because blackness, like whiteness, is constructed as an otherness in the Indian imaginary. While the extended colonial encounter went a long way to make the white stranger familiar, intercourse with the black stranger occurred only on ancient trade and travel routes in pre-colonial India.[10] Besides, Indian African relations, whether in the pre-colonial, colonial, or post-colonial encounter, have always been brokered through a third party either through the Arab merchant, the colonial administration, or American popular culture. Most important, brown meeting with black inevitably occurs against the background of a caste color elision in Indo-Aryan racism.[11] The shock of the light-skinned Aryan's first encounter with the dark-skinned Dravidian sets the tone for all future conversations between black and brown in the Indian cultural space.

Derogatory references to "the black skin" or "*krishnam vacham*" (RgV. IX.41.1, Sam.V. I.49.1, II.242 in Hunter 1987: 114) such as those about *dasyus* (hosts) springing "*from a black womb*" (RgV. II.20.6 in Muir 1972, I.174), "the slave bands of *black descent*" or "*the vile Dasyan color*" (RgV. II.20.7 and II.12.4 in Hunter 1987: 115), and "*the impious varNa*" (RgV. II.12.4 in Muir 1972, I.43, II. 284, 323) abound in the *Rigveda*. Phrases such as "the ancient singer praises the god who 'destroyed the Dasyans and protected *the Aryan color*'" (RgV. III.34.9 in Hunter 1987: 114) confirm brahminism's obsession with color coding and horror of miscegenation (RgV. IX.41.1, Sam.V. I.49.1, II.242 in Hunter 1987: 114).

In ancient India, pollution-related taboos effectively policed the invading Aryan's ambivalent fascination for the indigene. This desire for the dark-skinned indigene was sublimated in the eroticization of the dusky *dasyu* woman. Indian literature and folklore frequently thematize the fatal attraction of the light-skinned Aryan male for the dark-skinned Dravidian or *dasyu* female.[12] The ambivalent relation between the Aryan and the *dasyu* frames Indian African relations with the transference of the desire for the dark-skinned *dasyu* on the black African.

Though India's truly indigenous core is believed to have been derived from the same stock as the African, Indians' contacts with Africans intensified only after colonialism.[13] Indian migrations to Africa, the UK, and the West Indies, where they were forced to rub shoulders with black Africans, were the direct fallout of the British Empire. Although the distinction between the Aryan (*arya*) and the non-Aryan (*anarya*) in vedic literature was defined as much by conduct as by color, relations with all invaders and indigenes, both black and white, indigenes or migrants, continued to be governed by ancient pollution rituals and strictures against intermixing, interdining, and intermarrying. Though black and brown laborers were yoked together in the empire's service, resulting in the public expressions of solidarity between Indians and Africans in Kenya, and Indian nationalism first received a kick start in South Africa with Gandhi's *Satyagraha*, Indian settlements in Africa did not permit blackness to penetrate inner courtyards. Racial segregation, the logic of colonial domination, complemented the Indian pollution complex in discouraging black-brown mixing. M.G. Vassanji's *The Gunny Sack* (1999) documents Gujarati settlers' desire to cross the racial divide without transgressing Asian segregation strictures. But sanctions against intermarrying, despite strong evidence of cohabitation in Vassanji's Africa, continue to be in force among Gujarati migrants to the United States as portrayed in Mira Nair's *Mississippi Masala* (1991). I argue that the trace of this may be detected even in the black-brown brotherhood of oppressed minorities recently forged in the diaspora in the United Kingdom. While the Indian *dukawallah* might adopt black anti-racist politics as a strategic move against white racism, pollution taboos would take much longer to overcome.[14]

Gilroy mentions that "the spaces in which cultural consumption takes place provide locations in which racial politics can be erased" (1987: 211). He cites youth culture as "a space in which the struggle between nationalism, ethnic absolutism and their foes is already being played out" (1993b). Youth subcultures appear to be carnivalesque grounds on which ancient pollution taboos on interdining and intermixing, if not intermarrying, might be successfully flouted. The new diaspora space in Britain enables free intermingling and intercultural borrowing from which Bhangra hybrids are born. Sukhbir, the Kenya-born Bhangra artist, when asked why he used Punjabi lyrics, displayed true bewilderment. He claimed that Punjabi was so widely spoken in the Kenyan neighborhood in which he grew up that his Gujarati friends too spoke Punjabi. If one is to believe Apache Indian, this applies not only to his Gujarati and Bengali friends but also black friends in England.[15] "He [Priest] said to me [Apache], 'I've got Punjabi friends, I hear this language and I understand all the time—why shouldn't I be a part of it?' It wasn't just a gimmicky thing, you know, he grew up with the language. So I said, 'Why don't you sing it?' And he sang it—why not?" (Apache Indian 2002).

In response to his South Asian detractors who ask, "Why does he try to be so kaalaa?" Apache points out that the Birmingham in which he grew up was dominated by immigrants from India and Jamaica, and the two communities quite naturally picked things up from each other. The unique Apache Indian Maxi Priest Bhangra reggae fusion with the Punjabi rapping in Jamaican patois and the Jamaican addressing the crowd in Punjabi ("*tussi tappo /haan ucchii bolo,*" "come on leap, speak louder") could occur only in such immigrant fringes. The second generation Br-Asian hybridization of Bhangra may, therefore, be viewed as the first boundary-crossing act that blazes the trail for other border crossings.

Apart from the unavoidable evidence of mixing at the level of everyday lives, the black-brown alliance is also underwritten by a racial and class solidarity. The lead singer of the East London group Cobra is of the opinion that Britain's racial politics of exclusion encourages the visible minorities to present a united front: "Asians were lost, they weren't accepted by whites, so they drifted into black culture, dressing like black, talking like them, and listening to Reggae" (Sharma 1996: 35). Asian African solidarity, forged by the political ascription of the label "black" on all non-white ethnic groups in Britain, was further cemented by Br-Asian Bhangra's working-class origins.

But Br-Asian Bhangra's integration of black features, as Rupa Huq demonstrates, is also an attempt to appropriate BlackKool in the construction of AsianKool (1996: 63). Unlike Asianness, which carries connotations of "squareness" in white Britain, blackness has come to signify hip, smart, street savviness that is "cool" among youth of all colors. British Asian youth needed to inscribe their subjectivities not only in opposition to white culture but also to traditional Indian culture in which the black mixing came in quite handy. Bhangra doubles as a generational resistance song with second-generation Indians rebelling against the parental generation's essentialist self-definition by crossing over.

Finally, Bhangra's *boliyaan* origins have far more in common with black call-and-response poetics than with Western pop. Bhangra is essentially a drumbeat played with or without vocal or visual accompaniment. Bhangra's minimalist formulaic lyrics are set in the *boliyaan* format, which literally means "call." A Bhangra performance normally begins with the lead singer making a formulaic call to which the audience is required to respond. The lead singer starts his act with the formula: "*Barein Barsi khatan gaya si*" (I was away a dozen years to earn a living). "*Ki khat ke lehanda?*" (What did I bring home?). The audience responds with a single word, an everyday item—for instance, a *sota* (a wooden bat for pounding clothes clean). The singer improvises the lyrics on the spot in response to the audience's reply, taking into account the situational context. The rules of composition demand that the last word of the couplet rhyme with the sound of the audience's response word. The following couplet would be composed to the above response: *"Babule ne var dhoodya mere gut de parande naalon chota"* (My father found me a groom shorter than the *paranda* in my braid). Bhangra artists, whether at home or in the diaspora, draw on this shared formulaic stock when composing their lyrics. Hutnyk contends that the participatory character that Gilroy associates with Black Atlantic music is not patented by Africa. Anyone who has attended a Bhangra performance, traditional or modern, will vouch that "the antiphonal, the communicative, the storyteller role of the musician that dissolves the distance between performer and audience" Gilroy celebrates are not "exclusively African pleasures" (Hutnyk 2000).

Bhangra's hybridization with black music takes place in border zones where diasporic Indian subjectivities construct themselves in relation to a forbidden blackness. Br-Asian Bhangra artists hybridize it with black sounds to close the race, color, class, and generation gap as they participate in the identity politics of multicultural, multiethnic Britain. Yet the deep-seated Indian pollution complex forbids or restricts contact with the black otherness, despite the expression of solidarity with black others in anti-racist politics. The Asian's ambivalent desire for the black other results in an oscillatory seesaw between separation and identification. Black is adopted as a strategic essentialism to challenge white racism until the advantage of speaking from a particularized location makes Asian ethnicities trace a separate route signified by the preference for an increasingly specific ethnic tag—Br-Asian, Brit-Indian, or Brit-Punjabi:

> But Bhangra has given them their music and made them feel that they do have an identity. No matter if they are Gujaratis, Punjabis or whatever—Bhangra is Asian music for Asians. (The lead singer of the East London group Cobra quoted in Sharma 1996: 35)

> Among younger Punjabis in particular, the newly vibrant "bhangra scene" was valued not only because it re-invented a traditional genre, but also because it made the Punjabi, and indeed south Asian, presence in Britain visible and audible for the first time. (Baumann 1990: 88)

Though other contenders claim to have pioneered the Bhangra reggae fusion, Apache Indian, aka Steve Kapur, the Birmingham-based Br-Asian Bhangra artist, is the most visible signifier of brown-black sonic collaboration today.[16] Apache Indian's mixing of Bhangra with reggae in a West Indian patois punctuated with Punjabi phrases proved to be truly trailblazing in its boundary-crossing character. Ashwani Sharma sums it up, "His innovative cross-cultural call and response, with a linguistic authenticity and humor in Punjabi, as well as Jamaican English, captured a particular experience of being British Asian—at once at home in the urban sounds of the African diaspora, as well Asian and white Britain" (2002: 2).

Apache Indian's intercaste marriage of Punjabi with patois transgresses the arranged marriage norms celebrated by his protagonist, which forbid marriage outside caste or community. The emblematic status of "Arranged Marriage" in sonic hybridity is significant because the arranged marriage practice dates back to the Indo Aryan fear of miscegenation, one of the reasons for the elaborate strictures devised to prevent marriage with "lower" castes. Apache Indian's protagonist in "Arranged Marriage" transfers Black Atlantic nostalgia to the Punjabi town of Jallandar in a reaffirmation of the Indian practice of arranged marriages.

> The time has come mon fe Apache
> Fe find one gal and to get marry
> But listen when me talk tell everybody
> Me wan me arranged marriage from me mum and daddy
> Chorus
> Me wan gal from Jullunder City
> Me wan gal say a soorni curi
> Me wan gal mon to look after me
> Me wan gal that say she love me

It apotheosizes all things Punjabi symbolized by the Punjabi bride: beautiful like a princess, dressed in the traditional Punjabi costume, and, like a dutiful wife, able to cook him his favorite Punjabi meal.

> Me wan gal fe me Don Rani
> Me wan gal dress up in a sari
> Me wan gal say soorni logthi
> Me wan gal sweet like jelebee
> Me wan gal from Jullunder City
> Me wan gal say a soorni curi
> Me wan gal mon to look after me
> Me wan gal to mek me roti

Intoned in a deep-throated West Indian patois, Apache Indian's debut album could pass for a reggae act but for the interspersed Punjabi phrases, the *dhol* beats, and the haunting Indian melody in the background. Though his albums are often sold as reggae, Apache Indian created a truly hybrid musical genre for which a new name had to be coined—ragamuffin.

> The Boomshackalak it a the brand new style
> Wicked say it wicked Jah Jah no say it wild
> Raggamuffin style fe the discipline child
> Dip and go down ca it well versatile

You fe move fe your waist, move fe your back
Wine and go down do the shack-a-lak-a-lak
Get in a the groove ca you are the top notch
Bubble and a wine gal right pon the spot

Apache Indian's music, like his own mixed identity, foregrounds the problems of belonging, authenticity, and subjectivity, problematizing postcolonial identities. Winning the "best newcomer award" in both the reggae and Asian categories in 1991, Apache Indian continues to elude all attempts at classification, as the "best male newcomer," British Reggae Industry Awards 1992; winner of the Vaisakhi Award Vaisakhi Celebration Award 1993; "best rapper/rap track/best live act," Independent Asian Music Poll Awards 1994, among others. Apache Indian's first album was recorded in Jamaica. He co-presented *Reggae Sound System* with *Ragga Star Patra* for MTV from Jamaica. His collaborations defy national, linguistic, and generic boundaries:

> I have worked with top names such as Yami Bolo, Luciano, Frankie Paul, Brian and Tony Gold, Anthony Redrose, Maxi Priest, Shaggy and Sly and Robbie. I have also worked with Wrexk 'N' Effect, Teddy Riley and Tim Dog. I am in a unique position to be able to collaborate with Reggae, Hip-hop, Asian and Mainstream artists. I have also had the privilege to work with great artists such as Boy George, Asha Bhosley, A.R. Rahman and Malkit Singh. (Apache Indian 2001a)

As Back and Nayak put it:

> Apache's music is a crossroads, a meeting place where the languages and rhythms of the Caribbean, North America and India intermingle in the context of Europe. Apache himself was raised in the multi-ethnic area of Handsworth, Birmingham, born of Hindu Punjabi parents. He performs and expresses himself through snatches of Jamaican patois, Punjabi and a culturally diverse vernacular English. This language is part of a wider urban experience and symbolizes the dynamic culture of Birmingham. (1993: 141–43)

Bally Sagoo, better known for his remixes of old Bollywood hits today, could claim to have begun the Bhangra revolution in the UK along with Apache Indian. The music of Bally Sagoo, who started out as a Bhangra artist but switched over to deejaying, steers the Bhangra debate around issues of mixing and remixing, originality and plagiarism, voice and technology. Bally Sagoo's remixes of Bhangra and Bollywood hits have spawned a new musical category dubbed 'Bally Sagoo music' in India. Like Apache Indian, Bally Sagoo straddling a multiple musical heritage, is a purist's nightmare. "Dil Cheez" broke all records by being the first Indian-language song to enter mainstream charts, and "Tum bin Jiya" made number 21 in the UK. In 2000, Bally won multiple awards for his *Bolly-wood Flashback II* including the prestigious EMMA (Ethnic Multicultural Media Awards) for the best British production. He takes the credit for mainstreaming Bhangra: "Today we have not only Punjabis and Indians but also *gore* and *kale* dancing to it" (2003).

Bally Sagoo believes in remixing as the key to preserving tradition: "Remix is obviously something that is going to be there for a long time, both good and bad." The remix was born out of the deejay culture led by West Indian immigrants that Houston Baker Jr. celebrates as the return of the "voice" (1992: 54). And the sounds that Sagoo mixes with Bhangra are once again black:

> Mix it with hip hop, rap and reggae because that's the style of music that a lot of people listen to. And probably even more can hear it if it is collaborated with Asian stuff. There's different type of people. Some like hip hop, some like house, some like reggae. We kind of play with, experiment with different style of music. That's what has made me so successful! (Bally Sagoo 2003)

The success of "Star Crazy 2" a decade later illustrates that Bally Sagoo's multiple agendas, to cross over as well as to go back to roots, lead him to remix as often as recompose. Going by the number of Punjabi folk singers Bally has brought global recognition, Bally seems to be able to feel the pulse of the global youth as he fuses the ethnic folk sounds of the Punjab with bass-heavy reggae-tinged grooves.

Apache Indian and Bally Sagoo represent the two poles of the British Afro Bhangra fusion with folksingers providing the third angle. While Apache creates original compositions collaborating with black artists or mixing black styles, Bally largely remixes or creates new scores of well-known Bhangra songs. If Birmingham's street culture engendered Apache Indian, it also produced "the most popular Asian DJ" who took it to the West End's Asian underground. Malkit Singh, a folk artist from Jallandar now based in Birmingham, who actively collaborates with both on original albums as well as remixes, may be cited as the example of a hybridized Punjabi folk. Malkit Singh's celebrated collaborations with the two Br-Asians could be used to illustrate the difference between the two Br-Asian Bhangra acts. While Malkit Singh was already known on the Punjabi Bhangra scene in Britain since the early 1980s, he turned into an international celebrity after Bally Sagoo's remixing of his "Gur nalon ishq mitha" a decade later. Malkit Singh and Apache Indian set off a different kind of *jugalbandi* in "The Independent Girl," with Singh doing the pure Punjabi and Apache playing the West Indian. Apache's strategy to make Punjabi hip was to have unadulterated Punjabi share space with creolized Jamaican with neither interfering with the other. In the process of hybridizing the folk genre, however, both Br-Asian artists have not only globalized the harvest ritual but also made folk artists internationally known. They have created a diaspora space in which Punjabi folk meets folk-derived African popular tunes.

My contention is that Bhangra fuses with Afro rhythms in the real British diaspora space but also in the sending areas courtesy its return through the virtual American popular cultural space. What is American popular culture? Paul Gilroy points out that American popular culture is composed of the musical legacy of the descendants of slaves from Africa and the West Indies (1993b: 208). Neil Lazarus, in his analysis of Afropop's indigenization of American popular culture, argues that the black core that modern African music co-opts is essentially Africa's own contribution to the shaping of American popular culture (1999: 198). Richard Pells has turned this argument around to refute the American cultural imperialism thesis (2002: B7). He establishes American popular culture as a space constituted by immigrants contributing their unique talents to the vast melting pot. Pells argues that this space, rather than promoting any nationalist agenda, acts as a hub where the world's cultural diversity is stored and disseminated. American popular culture, disseminated through transnational media networks, has undoubtedly become the meeting ground of cultures not even remotely connected. The popular cultural space initiates a conversation between black and brown unshackled for the first time by essentialist self-definitions. I agree that the space of popular culture proves to be emancipatory here to the extent that it enables a dialogue between the black and brown cultures. Borrowing from the black core of American popular culture that was also the bedrock of British black culture leads to a meeting of two orally oriented cultures in the Afro Bhangra fusion in Britain. Bhangra, reggae, rap, and hip-hop are all diasporic voices whose roots go back to the rich oral cultures of Africa and India. The global diffusion of American popular culture also sets off an unheard of duet between two orally oriented cultures.

While establishing that the common orality of black and brown traditions strikes a chord in a far removed oral culture, I argue that the collaborative moment of black brown fusion accentuates cultural difference rather than similarity. The ambivalence marking the Indian integration of black musical traditions is in sharp contrast to the eclectic absorption of Indian iconography in West African Vodun art and thought of which Dana Rush speaks elsewhere in this volume. While the shared orality of the African and the Indian holds immense dialogic scope, their embeddedness in specific local traditions hammers home the difference between the drum and the *dhol*. While Punjabi and black cultures share a vibrant orality and a celebratory corporeality, black corporeality is differently inflected from the wheatish. Bodily difference, not merely the sharp spectroscopic contrast of black against brown, makes the mingling of black and brown bodies on the dance floor dangerously significant. In spite of the elision between physical vitality, virility, and labor in the inscription of both black and Punjabi male bodies, Punjabi free labor has been spared the reification of black slave labor. Similarly, though the Punjabi harvest ritual has shades of African mating dances, Indian cultural Puritanism straitjackets Punjabi sexuality. Notwithstanding the similarity between the *dhol* and the drum rhythms, the celebratory narratives of the black-brown sonic encounter simplify the complex undercurrents audible backstage.

While racial barriers might be crossed in the "dancing" public sphere, the purity of sacred spaces is protected from alien encroachments. While brown bodies might freely w(rap) with black and white on the dance floor, the self's hidden spaces remain impermeable. The segregated space is gendered by permitting male bodies to collaborate in Bhangra dance and music to perform hybridity while the female body becomes the site for the play of the politics of pollution. Despite the declaration of black-brown brotherhood voiced through the sonic collaborations and patois, the hybrid Bhangra cordons off a secret space locked in Punjabi language and the Punjabi female's veiled body to protect it from the stranger's profane gaze, including the urban Indian's.

The cross-cultural encounter—auditory and visual—clicks by its articulation of cultural shock rather than cultural meeting through the violent yoking of Punjabi folk with black pop, of Punjabi lyrics with English, the *dhol* with drums and synthesizers. Though the music, sound, and movement might still offer avenues for dialogue, the Punjabi lyrics and the veiled female body resist penetration. Bhangra albums construct these segregated spaces by alternating between Punjabi and English, *dhol* and drum, and dance floor and home/village setting. In each case, the displacement of the item from its original home, while enhancing its appeal, drums aloud its foreignness and untranslatability. More than the audio clip, the music video's visual imagery violently and sharply silhouettes corporeal difference. The audio replicates the shocking juxtaposition of the veiled Punjabi female and semi-clad black bodies in the unexpected glide from Punjabi to English lyrics and the alternation of black and brown beats. The visual and vocal arrangement suggests that cross-cultural contact can occur only in the in-between space of hyphenated identities, while certain cultural spaces must remain locked in language and in the body.

I have demonstrated elsewhere how Bhangra's lyrics are coded multiply to include as well as exclude.[17] The subordination of lyrical content to the sound and music smoothes Bhangra's crossover. But the punctuation of Punjabi lyrics with English phrases or sentences in the remixes seems to accentuate the difference between the two by calling attention to the intrinsic foreignness of languages. The Punjabi lyrics lock in a space from which the outsider is effectively excluded. For instance, Gurdas Mann's voice, lyrics, and music are transcoded in the rap remix of his song "apna Panjab hove" as foreign "roots," which the non-Punjabi is at a loss to decode. Maxi Priest's knowledge of Punjabi, for the same reason, enables him to enter the intimate linguistic zone in the collaborative album with Apache Indian. Apache's patois in "The Independent Girl" must not be mistaken for a transliteration of Malkit Singh's formulaic paean to female beauty. Apache undoubtedly creates a space for the folk artist, allows him to speak, and takes great care not to trespass into his personal space. But Apache's hybrid patois accents the foreignness of pure Punjabi in Jamaica.

The gap between Punjabi and English booms cultural incommensurability, which must be respected even as one is invited to enter the Punjabi space through the repeatable loop. Nonsense syllables are extremely effective as loops that even non-Punjabi speakers might repeat. However, the play on traditional formulae is the prerogative of the Punjabi speaker alone. The knowledge of the rules and regulations governing speaking in a Bhangra performance distinguishes the Punjabi speaker, the wheatish, from the non-Punjabi, white, black, or brown. In the process, the hybrid sonic space of the music cassette and video can be seen to articulate three distinct identity spaces—Br-Black, Br-Asian, and Punjabi—enabling cultural contact at the borderlines while protecting cultural interiority.

The music video replays the ancient Indian strategy of selective hybridization without violating pollution taboos. The Bhangra music video performs pollution taboos visually. While the presence of *goras* and *kaalas* might be cited as the Bhangra artist's ultimate dream of Bhangra's mainstreaming, it also recalls the pre-colonial fantasy of the sensual dark-skinned *dasyu* in the Indian/Punjabi male imaginary.[18] It is interesting to see how the woman's body becomes the site for inscribing cultural difference. Most Bhangra videos replay the Aryan desire for the dark-skinned *dasyu* in the image of semi-clad black female dancers performing sinuous Bhangra movements. While the Indian woman is apotheosized through the heavy drapes, the black woman is eroticized through the undraping of body parts. The black woman's body becomes the site of Punjabi/Indian desires in the Bhangra video.[19] The Punjabi male gaze undresses it for the play of untrammeled sexual fantasies forbidden by Punjabi/Indian Puritanism. The Punjabi woman, on the other hand, is racialized by being draped in traditional outfit and locked in a private space.

This may be illustrated by the Kenya-born Dubai-based artist Sukhbir's "Punjabi munde," hailed as a new style mixing Bhangra with ragga. The camera glides over Indian musical exotica, the *tabla* and the *tumbi*, before picking out the Punjabi boys, *munde*, accompanying Sukhbir. But the girls, *kudiyaan*, caught in close-up are a *gori* and a *kaali* who athletically join in the Bhangra in sports bra and shorts as the camera navel-gazes on bared midriffs. This is true even of Bhangra albums featuring female artists. The new version of Bally Sagoo's new find, Gunjan's "dil naiyyon lagda," has a halter-necked Gunjan floating in a sea of multihued bodies in a nightclub. As the camera follows her faraway gaze to dissolve into the ethnic narrative of separation in the home space, the outsider is virtually shut out.

What I am try to show is that though the carnivalesque space of the dance floor enables brown bodies to freely mingle with black, they must return to the sanctified exclusivity of the ethnic quarters. The music video captures this in its iconography. Apache Indian's "pyar pyar bhangra flava" would do as well as any other. The mellifluous Hindi melody punctuating Apache's Bhangra reggae act shocks through its being displaced from its original context just as the veiled Indian fantasy appears grossly over-dressed after the generous display of black bodies in motion. Apache Indian's hybrid figure crosses over with consummate ease from the uninhibited, gyrating black bodies to the shy, shrinking Indian woman. Apache inhabits both spaces without letting either cross into the other. The violent juxtaposition of the wildly "breaking" (break dancing) black bodies against the gentle swaying of the veiled woman heightens the cultural gap that neither Apache nor the video attempt to bridge. While the brown woman is shielded from the black male's gaze, the black woman's body is undressed for the brown man's pleasure.

Despite the utopian images of cross-cultural sonic fusions and positive hybridity talk, the spatial organization of the music video, the preferred format of contemporary Bhangra, segregates. The music video's visual grammar enacts the logic of "decontextualized commodities" that Appadurai (1996) observes in the present global condition, with the difference that here the folk artist is decontextualized and commodified. Malkit Singh is the native displaced from the mustard field to the beach in the album *The Independent Woman*, who is not allowed to step out of his frame. Dressed in traditional *lungi kurta*, singing in rustic Punjabi, and performing old Bhangra moves, Malkit Singh's appeal is doubly enhanced by the mode of racialization, the strategy conventionally employed in marketing black music. The music video, as the truly pornographic visual text, follows the gaze of the watcher to fix the folk artist in the space of the object. The diasporic artist, in his attempt to identify with the folk artist, becomes implicated in the exoticization of the "decontextualized object." Apache's valorization of ethnicity in Malkit Singh's music archaizes it and ghettoizes it in a pure space. The folk artist and his music become the signifiers of the "endangered authenticity" that the diasporic artist sees as his burden to preserve. Singh becomes 'the non-duped', the site of authenticity and true knowledge. In this context, Singh's Punjabi lyrics signify the silencing but also the untranslatability of the other. Similarly, though "the diaspora space" enables the folk artist to speak, his speech may be mediated only through the diasporic interpreter. The folk artist's own desire to hybridize with other musical traditions is subordinated to the Western or diasporic longing for the "authentic" voices of the non-West.

The Br-Asian youth's amalgamation of black musical traditions seems to replay the ambivalence of the ancient Aryan desire for the forbidden black stranger. Hybrid Bhangra draws on blackness in the reinvention of Asian youthful subjectivities transferring the desire for the dusky *dasyu* woman on the black woman's body. The desire for blackness here grows sublimated into an untrammeled sexual fantasy that liberates the diasporic Punjabi self to break free of prescriptive cultural taboos imposed by the parental generation. In the desire for the black body, the Punjabi self articulates the longing to break free of essentialist identity ascriptions of the home space, the seat of pollution taboos. These taboos might be transgressed on the dance floor in performing new Asian/Indian/Punjabi ethnicities. But Bhangra's hybridity ethic unfortunately constitutes itself in relation to an anterior purity constructed through idealized images of the Punjabi woman, the folk artist, and the home village. Post-colonial hybridity is insensitive to the reinvention of "pure" forms through selective hybridization. Bhangra has been extremely eclectic in its borrowings, which range from the Ukrainian to the Jamaican. The celebration of diasporic hybridity is myopic to the experimentation of folk artists such as Malkit Singh, who confesses to a reggae weakness, or *desi* Bhangra stars such as Daler Mehndi, who integrates black beats in his music. The authenticity cult not only archaizes and underplays the folk genre's syncretism but also exercises control by privileging only the music that may be fitted into the traditional mode.

Going by the number of Bhangra remixes circulating globally, one might begin to wonder if any unmixed Bhangra still exists. Reinvented as new Asian dance music, Bhangra transmutes as a new genre welding "reggae and rap styles with traditional Indian instruments and vocals" (Solaar 1994: 37). As Solaar puts it, paraphrasing the words of "Arranged Marriage," Bhangra artists "talk de Indian wit de patois." Bhangra's hybridization of traditional Bhangra sounds with reggae, rap, or hip-hop epitomizes the neither/nor, both/either diasporic Asian/Indian/Punjabi subjectivity.

Br-Asian Bhangra artists' collaborative ventures involving black musicians hint at a different black-brown unison than the remixed rap, reggae, or techno versions of well-known Bhangra songs. But black diasporic beats, in both forms of remixes, provide hyphenated diasporic and homeland identities with a bridge they could straddle, sidestepping both an essentialist whiteness or a unitary Indian self-inscription.

This in-process diasporic subjectivity constructed in relation to other ethnic minorities fits in extremely well with contemporary multicultural Britain's politics. The diasporic artist, straddling multiple identity spaces, glides smoothly across British, black, Indian, and Punjabi spaces without an attempt at synthesis. The patois of Bhangra reggae or rap articulates this hybridized identity space in original compositions as well as remixes. According to Ashwani Sharma, "British Asian music is at the heart of a cultural globalization where greater levels of interaction and hybridity create new forms of artistic expression, while at the same time the music provides a particular history of racial and social change" (2002:2).

Accounts that provide a glimpse into the lives of the first globopolitans have begun to appear only recently.[20] Sikh migration to Africa truly belongs to the narrative of the British Empire when two groups of Sikhs—soldiers and skilled and semi-skilled craftsmen—were recruited to serve the army or to construct the railways in various parts of Africa. However, the mobility of Sikh pioneers who belonged largely to the lower castes of masons, blacksmiths, and carpenters inscribes a difference in the narrative of elite migrations.[21] Contemporary British youth subculture proves to be the carnivalesque diaspora space in which Indian youth transgress parental taboos and marry Punjabi dhol beats with African-derived rhythms to reinvent Bhangra, the Punjabi harvest ritual. The Indian and African diasporas in Britain initiate a sonic conversation which the "native" Punjabi artist is invited to join to produce a truly global beat. Since Bhangra artists and their "black" collaborators have a distinct working-class/caste location, Bhangra's transmutation into global dance music has been cited as an example of "low" globalization. I argue that the space of popular culture creates a new contact zone enabling the orally oriented African and Indian cultures to converse. But I hold that the cultural dialogue occurs through the accentuation rather than subsumption of cultural difference.

What happens to pure Bhangra and pure Punjabi in the process? Punjabi ambivalence to the hybrid varieties of wheat is replicated in the reception of Bhangra hybrids at home. The adoption of hybrid seeds, which maximized the yield of food grains, accounts for the state's unparalleled prosperity as well the much-touted "Green Revolution." While Punjab cashes in on the increased yield of the hybrid by feeding the rest of the country, it prefers indigenous or *desi* varieties for home consumption.

While Punjab exports hybrid Bhangra, the homegrown Pammi Bai up-stages the Apache Indian–Malkit Singh duo in the road shows held in Punjabi villages. The answer lies in a Punjabi joke. When the Bhakra Nangal hydroelectric project was being launched at the peak of India's re-construction program, one peasant was heard asking another, "If the dam is going to produce electricity from the water, the wheatfields irrigated from the river water will be denuded of their power. Whoever will con-sume that wheat sans power?" The global village is. *Chak de re!*

### Notes

1. Though Bhangra simultaneously performs youthful, black, Asian, Indian, and Punjabi identities today in its different contexts, one must remember that it has a spe-cific Punjabi location. Because Bhangra glides between Punjabi, Indian, and Asian identity spaces depending upon its performance contexts, this chapter borrows the terminology currently used in analyzing Bhangra texts.

2. *Siapa* refers to the ritual wailing by female relatives and friends in a house of mourning. *Tappa*, a couplet composition commonly used in Bhangra texts, has happy associations.

3. Zarina Patel (n.d.) traces the history of the East African name for Sikhs Kalas-inghas to an individual named Sardar Kala Singh, who arrived in Kenya in 1896. She reports that Sikhs, mostly of the Ramgarhia sect, were artisans and free laborers who came to build the Uganda railways for British colonialists. Kenya's grand old Sikh, Narain Singh Bhari (known as Mistriji or Bhaia ji, who was originally from Amritsar, migrated to East Africa from Lahore in 1898 and worked as a carpenter at the Makupa Railway Bridge. Shashi Tharoor (2004) places the migration even earlier. "Indian la-bour had built forts in Kenya as early as the 16th Century; Indian masons and carpen-ters had practised their craft in even larger numbers from 1820, and over 31,000 con-tract labourers from Punjab and Gujarat had built the famous Mombasa railroad, 2,500 of them perishing in the process. The city of Nairobi (like 43 other railway towns along the line) was erected by Indian hands."

4. The term "diaspora space" draws on the work of Avtar Brah, who advances it as "a point of confluence of economic, political, cultural and psychic processes . . . where multiple subject positions are juxtaposed, contested, proclaimed or disavowed" (Brah 1996: 208). Though the color black, the symbol of racial alterity in white dis-course, is inscribed with multiple meanings and has been adopted in Asian ascrip-tions and self-descriptions, I use the color coding of brown to distinguish Indian sub-continental difference from black African. I separate Punjabi difference by employing the color wheatish, which is a transliteration of the Hindi *gehuan*. Sanjay Sharma in-vents the term "Asian dance music" to signify Bhangra as well as other dance music from the subcontinent.

5. The notion of ritual pollution may be found in Hinduism, Buddhism, and Jainism. Though Bhangra is often appropriated exclusively in Sikh diasporic forma-tions, traditional Bhangra was split between Hindu, Sikh, and Sufi forms in undi-vided Punjab. The notion of ritual purity, though defined differently from Hinduism, is equally crucial in the definition of the Amritdhari Sikh. Several of the contributors to Sikh Heritage in East Africa testify to their preservation of rituals even in African homes (Kanwal n.d.).

6. Hansraj Aggarwal of Nairobi, the grandson of Munshiram, Kala Singh's partner in Munshiram & Co., says of Kala Singh: "it's not true that he had a Masai wife. He was not that sort: he came from a good family and had a wife back home in India." Only Mohinder Singh Chadha of Nairobi from Kericho mentions an uncle Lakha "who never married" but "kept a Nandi woman as a wife for a year or so but they didn't have any children." Apart from Gulab Singh's wife from the Wakamba tribe mentioned by Hawks in a document reproduced by Kanwal, Nauranga (Rangi) Singh of Meru testifies to the melting pot through Sikh African marriages including those of Amar Singh to a Meru woman (after losing his first wife) and of Nooran Singh to a Sikh-Meru wife and half-caste children such as Anu Wanja Singh of Lare (Nauranga's wife), whose father Kirparam Singh married a Meru woman called Wanja. See Kanwal n.d.

7. See BBC Asian Network (n.d.). A family I interviewed on 25 December 2006 in Bangalore who had lived for extended periods in different parts of Africa including Kenya and Zimbabwe from the 1970s to the 1990s before migrating to the United States informed me that social mixing between Indians and Africans was restricted to the workplace or on formal occasions and did not extend to the home. However, their daughter, who went to school in Africa, has many close African friends with whom she continues to keep in touch.

8. One of Naipaul's short stories, "One Out of Many" (1971), rather than the novels, breaks the silence on Indian black mixing. The young Indian manservant who accompanies an Indian diplomat to the United States finds a cold reception except from black women, including a black shopgirl and a cleaning woman. Naipaul panders to the American stereotype of the sexually liberated black woman who is made to stalk, not the white man, but the Indian. He captures in *hubshi* the hillbilly's swing between fascination and repulsion for the black women he encounters.

> A few days later I had my adventure. The *hubshi* woman came in, moving among my employer's ornaments like a bull, I was greatly provoked. The smell was too much, so was the size of her armpits. I fell. She dragged me down on the couch, on the saffron spread, which was one of my employer's nicest pieces of Punjabi folk-weaving. I saw the moment helplessly, as one of dishonour. I saw her as Kali, goddess of death and destruction, coal black, with a red tongue, and white eyeballs and many powerful arms. (1971: 33)

One has to turn to Kipling's "A Sahib's War" (1999), for the Sikh Umr Singh's view of the *hubshi*: "Kurban Sahib appointed me to the command (what a command for me!) of certain woolly ones—*Hubshis*—whose touch and shadow are pollution."

9. Zarina Patel (n.d.) mentions a number of Sikhs who expressed solidarity with Africans in the public sphere: Gujjar Singh, who had been president of the Workers' Society of Kenya in the 1930s; Makhan Singh, one of Kenya's most committed intellectuals, who made the first call for *uhuru* in 1950; Chanan Singh, who defended Kenya's freedom fighters and was parliamentary secretary to Prime Minister Jomo Kenyatta; and Jaswant Singh Bharaj, who made guns for the Mau Mau. This is in spite of the fact that Kipling's Sikh in "A Sahib's War" clearly distinguishes himself from Africans. "I am a—trooper of the Gurgaon Rissala (cavalry regiment), the One Hundred and Forty-first Punjab Cavalry. Do not herd me with these black Kaffirs. I am a Sikh—a trooper of the State" (1999: 87). The uneasy silence on blackness in brown discourses is an indication of the contentious history of these relations.

10. The famous Greek historian Diodorus Siculus refers to Osiris's visit to India in the first century BCE, and Apollonius of Tyana maintains that Ethiopians are colonists sent from India. Indian history, remarkably taciturn on this matter, records no other interaction except the visit of a Moorish traveler, Ibn Batuta. From 1333 to 1342, Ibn Battuta stayed at Delhi, where Sultan Muhammad bin Tughluq gave him a position as judge, and then he traveled through central India and along the Malabar coast to the Maldives. An old quarter in the Muslim city of Hyderabad, *Habshigunda*, is a monument to the Nizam's resettlement of his African slaves. The black Siddis, a tribal Sufi community with East African origins, are living proof of a flourishing black slave trade in India in the thirteenth century.

11. Though the Aryan invasion theory has been challenged as another orientalist construct to fissure Indian society, linguistic difference between Indo Aryan and Dravidian languages strongly suggests Aryan Dravidian difference.

12. This tradition appears to be carried over in the popular Indian imagination represented by Bollywood. The North Indian male and the South Indian female lead have always enjoyed a mysterious chemistry in commercial Hindi cinema beginning with the unbeatable Raj Kapoor–Vijayantimala screen pair continued by Dharmendra–Hema Malini, Amitabh Bacchhan–Rekha, Anil Kapur–Sridevi hit screen couples.

13. The Indus Valley civilization is believed to be Dravidian, whose descendants retreated to the South after the Aryan invasion.

14. Punjabi migrants to Africa, mainly Sikhs, were skilled artisans rather than *dukawallas*.

15. Rampton's (1998) research on code switching among British adolescents confirms that Panjabi has entered the British vocabulary.

16. Apache Indian acknowledges reggae as one of his main inspirations: "I have always told people that I just love the sound of Reggae music. Ever since I heard the sounds of Bob Marley, Dennis Brown, Burning Spear, Black Uhuru, Culture, Super Cat Nicodemus and many many more. . . . I have known that this is something that I have to be apart of. It is not about just loving the music" (2001b).

17. Though songs like "Chok There" and "Arranged Marriage" became such hits, South Asian languages were treated more or less like cacophonic gibberish in the West. Apache claims, however, that he was able to experiment with the language in that way because he wasn't targeting a huge mainstream audience in the first place (Gera 2004).

18. The pornographic music video format sexualizes the female body. When Sukhbir performed the same song live in Chandigarh, though the accompanying dancers sported Western outfits, their non-sexualized dance movements were in keeping with the setting (*Sukhbir Live, Etc Channel Punjabi*, 13 July 2003).

19. The polarization of black/ Indian in Bhangra albums not featuring black artists/dancers is replicated in other polarities such as urban/rural, Indian/Western, Punjabi/non-Punjabi through the semiotics of dress and appearance. The music video's voyeuristic format unclads not only the black, *kaali*, or white, *gori*, but also the brown urban/expatriate woman. Compare, for instance, two songs, "Sohniye, tu saadi ki lagdi" and "Naag saambh lai" from Jazzy B's new release *Roop tera*.

20. Harjinder Singh Kanwal's project on Punjabi Heritage in East Africa includes valuable interviews, photographs, and letters submitted by descendants of Sikh pioneers, which are largely concerned, however, with citing examples of Sikh industry and resourcefulness (Kanwal n.d.).

21. Two of the earliest migrants—Kapur Singh, the first Indian inspector general of police in Africa, who was posted there in 1895, and Kala Singh, who arrived in

1897—were *jat* Sikhs. Karen Blixen's *Out of Africa* contains one of the first literary references to Pooran Singh, the Fundee, "which means an artisan of all work, carpenter, saddler and cabinet-maker as well as blacksmith; he constructed and built more than one wagon for the farm, all on his own. But he liked the work of the forge best, and it was a very fine, proud sight, to watch him tiring a wheel" (Blixen 1988: 333–35; 392–94).

## Works Cited

Apache Indian. 2001a. "Boomshackalak." 28 April. www.karmasound.com/artists/apache/music.htm, accessed 26 December 2005.

——. 2001b. "The Best of Apache Indian." 28 April. www.karmasound.com/artists/apache/pressreleases/bestof.htm, accessed 26 December 2005.

——. 2002. "Interview August 2002." MyBindi_com.htm, accessed 26 December 2005.

Appadurai, Arjun. 1996. *Modernity at Large: The Cultural Dimensions of Modernity.* Delhi: Oxford University Press.

Back, Les, and Anoop Nayak. 1993. *Invisible Europeans? Black People in the "New Europe."* Handsworth, Birmingham, UK: All Faiths for One Race.

Baker, Houston, Jr. 1992. "Hybridity, the Rap Race and Pedagogy for the 1990s." In *Postmodernism: A Reader,* ed. Patricia Waugh. London: Edward Arnold.

Baumann, G. 1990. "The Re-Invention of Bhangra: Social Change and Aesthetic Shifts in a Punjabi Music in Britain." *World of Music* 32.2: 81–95.

BBC Asian Network. 2005. "Africa Today." 4–8 July. http://www.bbc.co.uk/asiannetwork/africaweek/africatoday.shtml, accessed 8 December 2005.

Blixen, Karen. 1988. *Out of Africa.* London: Penguin.

Brah, A. 1996. *Cartographies of Diaspora: Contesting Identities.* London: Routledge.

Gera, Anjali. 2004. "*Punjabiyaan di shaan wakhri*: Ethnic Returns." *New Quest,* July–December.

Gilroy, Paul. 1987. *There Ain't No Black in the Union Jack.* London: Routledge.

——. 1993a. "Between Afro-centrism and Euro-centrism: Youth Culture and the Problem of Hybridity." *Young: Nordic Journal of Youth Research* 1.2: 2–12.

——. 1993b. *The Black Atlantic: Modernity and Double Consciousness.* London: Routledge.

——. 2000. *Against Race: Imagining Political Culture beyond the Color Line.* Cambridge, Mass.: Harvard University Press. Quoted in John Hutnyk, *Critique of Exotica: Music, Politics and the Culture Industry* (London: Pluto Press, 2000).

Hall, Stuart. 1996a. "Culture Identity and Diaspora." In *Contemporary Postcolonial Theory: A Reader,* ed. Padmini Mongia, 110–21. New Delhi: Oxford University Press.

——. 1996b. "New Ethnicities." In Morley and Chan, *Critical Dialogues in Culture Studies,* 441–49.

——. 1996c. "What Is This 'Black' in Black Popular Culture?" In Morley and Chan, *Critical Dialogues in Culture Studies,* 465–75.

Hesse, B. 2000. "Diasporicity: Black Britain's Post-colonial Formations." In *Un/settled Multiculturalisms: Diasporas, Entanglements, Transruptions,* ed. Barnor Hesse, 96–120. London: Zed Books.

Housee, Shirin, and Mukhtar Dar. 1999. "Remixing Identities: 'Off' the Turn-Table." Shirin Housee and Mukhtar Dar talk to Bally Sagoo and Radical Sista. In Sharma, Hutnyk, and Sharma, *Disorienting Rhythms,* 81–104.

Hunter, W. W. 1987. *Landmarks in Indian Anthropology.* New Delhi: Cosmo.

Huq, Rupa. 1996. "Asian Kool? Bhangra and Beyond." In Sharma, Hutnyk, and Sharma, *Disorienting Rhythms,* 61–80.

Hutnyk, John. 2000. "Adorno at Womad: South Asian Crossovers and the Limits of Hybridity Talk," 19–27. *Critique of Exotica: Music, Politics and the Culture Industry.* London: Pluto Press.

Kanwal, Harjinder Singh. N.d. "Punjabi Heritage in East Africa: Kenya Becomes a Republic." Sikh Heritage in East Africa. www.sikh-heritage.co.uk/heritage/sikhhert%20EAfrica/sikhsEAfricapart5.htm, accessed 26 December 2005.

Kipling, Rudyard. 1999. "A Sahib's War." *War Stories and Poems.* Ed. Andrew Rutherford. Oxford: Oxford University Press. 87–104.

Lazarus, Neil. 1999. *Nationalism and Cultural Practice in the Postcolonial World.* Cambridge: Cambridge University Press.

*Mississippi Masala.* 1991. Dir. Mira Nair. SCS Films.

Morley, David, and Kuan-Hsing Chan. 1996. *Critical Dialogues in Culture Studies.* London: Routledge.

Muir, J. 1972. "Mythical and Legendary Accounts of the Origin of Caste." Part I. *Original Sanskrit Texts on the Origin and History of the People of India, Their Religion and Institutions.* Delhi: Oriental.

Naipaul, V. S. 1971. "One out of Many." *In a Free State.* London: Picador.

Patel, Zarina. N.d. "Arrival of Kenya's Sikhs." Sikh Heritage in East Africa, part 3. www.sikh-heritage.co.uk/frame.htm, accessed 20 July 2007.

Pells, Richard. 2002. "American Culture Goes Global, or Does It?" *Chronicle of Higher Education,* 12 April 2002. http://chronicle.com/weekly/v48/l31b00701.htm, accessed 15 July 2007.

Rampton, Ben. 1998. "Language Crossing and the Redefinition of Reality: Expanding the Agenda of Research on Code Switching." In *Code-Switching in Conversation: Language, Interaction and Identity,* ed. Peter Auer, 290–317. London: Routledge.

Sagoo, Bally. 2003. Personal interview conducted by author. Bangalore, 2 January.

Sharma, Ashwani. 1996. "Noisy Asians or 'Asian Noise'?" In Sharma, Hutnyk, and Sharma, *Disorienting Rhythms,* 32–57.

———. 2002. "South Asian Diaspora Music in Britain." *Salidaa.* South Asian Diaspora Literature and Arts Archive. 20 October 2005. www.salidaa.org.uk/salidaa/docrep/docs/sectionIntro/music/docm_render.html, accessed 8 August 2007.

Sharma, Sanjay, John Hutnyk, and Ashwani Sharma, eds. 1996. *Disorienting Rhythms: The Politics of the New Asian Dance Music.* London: Zed Books.

*Sikh Heritage in East Africa.* N.d. Part 3. www.sikh-heritage.co.uk/heritage/sikhhert%20EAfrica/sikhsEAfricapart3.htm, 4 October 2005; now available at www.sikh-heritage.co.uk/frame.htm, accessed 18 July 2007.

Solaar, M. C. 1994. "What Is Bhangra?" *Queer in Your Ear* 37. http://joeclark.org/QiYE37.html, accessed 15 July 2007.

Sukhbir. 2003. "Sukhbir Live." Etc Channel Punjabi. 13 July.

Tharoor, Shashi. 2004. "We're All Kenyans Here." *The Hindu.* Online edition of India's national newspaper. 7 November. www.hindu.com/mag/2004/11/07/stories/2004110700470300.htm, accessed 15 December 2005.

Vassanji, M. G. 1999. *The Gunny Sack.* New Delhi: Viking. "Aryan Invasion and Expansion in India." www.acns.com/~mm9n/hindu/ai/ai.htm, accessed 18 July 2007.

# 5

## "Hindu" Dance Groups and Indophilie in Senegal

*The Imagination of the Exotic Other*

Gwenda Vander Steene

At the beginning of my fieldwork period on dance in Senegal I was not very skilled in the Senegalese *sabar*[1] dances. However, I was always very proud to tell people I was a dancer as well. I didn't usually mention I practice *Bharata Natyam*, a South Indian dance style, as I thought people had probably never heard of such a thing as "Indian dance."[2] I was surprised to get enthusiastic reactions, and was even more astonished when some told me they also practiced "Hindu" dance (*dance indou-indo-hindou*)[3] in some of the numerous *dance indou* groups in Senegal. Not long after I started my quest for *dance indou* in Dakar, I learned there was a national federation (UNAIS, Union Nationale des Indouphiles au Senegal[4]), grouping over twenty associations of India-lovers throughout Senegal, organizing activities, *soirées indous* ("Hindu evenings"), and rehearsals.

Indophilie in Senegal (understood as the love for "Indian" music, dance, and films) seems to be more than a small, odd phenomenon. When turning on the radio, one is likely to come across one of the many Hindu programs broadcast almost every day on different radio stations. The anchormen often have their own association in the form of a fan club.

There is no Indian expatriate community in Senegal which can account for this Indophilie, as is the case in eastern Africa or the Caribbean.[5] Moreover, being a francophone country, one would presume Senegal lies out of the English influence sphere which is much stronger in Anglophone Africa. There has been very little research or even academic awareness of Indophilie and the import of Indian films in Africa. Furthermore, the little (recent) research devoted to Indophilie in Africa has all concentrated on Anglophone Africa.[6] In this article I want to fill this gap by looking at a francophone country without an Indian expatriate community.[7] By analyzing this Senegalese Indophilie we can learn it has its origin in the massive import and immense success of Bollywood films. Looking at Africa in general and Senegal in particular, it is interesting to investigate why people love these films and how this gave rise to Indophile associations imitating Bollywood song and dance. I deal with these questions with special reference to dance. Furthermore, I want to show how these *dance indous* have Senegalese roots, and how the *soirées indous* are in my view somehow similar to the *soirées sénégalaises*. As other essays in this volume indicate, imagination plays an important role—imagination as expressed through art, such as film (Jaspal Singh), music (Roy), or visual art (Rush). I want to complement their discussion of the imagined other with special reference to dance.

### Bollywood Films and African Audiences

#### Africa

In his article "Itineraries of Indian Cinema," Brian Larkin tries to answer the question why Indian films travel. He explains the popularity of this genre throughout the world (in "Third World" countries, with or without an Indian expatriate community, as well as in socialist countries such as Eastern Europe) because it offers a way of being modern that does not necessarily mean being Western (Larkin 2003: 172; 1997: 407). In northern Nigeria, where his own research is focused, it is also a way of distinguishing themselves from the south, which is much more oriented toward the West. Thus these transnational cultural flows become "a foil against which postcolonial identity can be fashioned, critiqued, and debated. They allow an alterity to Hollywood domination" (2003: 178). Following Larkin, this is not to say the story of Africans turning toward Bollywood films is a discourse of "local" resistance to "dominant" Western culture (1997: 408, 433).

Arabic and Bollywood films were first imported by Lebanese cinema owners in the 1950s, who thought Arabic films would become very popular in African Islamic countries (Larkin 2003: 181; 1997: 411).[8] Bollywood,

FIGURE 5.1. Group performance at a soirée indou, 24th of December, Médina

however, turned out to have a much bigger success. Lots of Hausa state "Indian culture" (at least how it is presented in the films) is "just like" Hausa culture (Larkin 2003: 183; 1997: 411, 433). In Senegal, the same explanation is heard. According to Larkin, the popularity of Indian films among Hausa rests, in part, on this dialectic of sameness ("just like'" and difference (2003: 183; 1997: 414). Characters in Indian films struggle over whether they should speak Hindi or borrow from English, whether they should marry the person they love or wed the person their parents choose, elements which are very relevant for Hausa viewers (1997: 410).[9]

### Senegal

Many elements pointed out for Nigeria by Larkin also hold true for Senegal. According to my research participants, the first Bollywood films appeared in Senegalese cinemas around the 1950s and were an immense success.[10] They soon became much more popular than Arabic films and were shown daily in most of the urban cinemas. Some research participants said this is because Arabic film is too "Western" or has fewer song-and-dance sequences which are typical for Bollywood. But why do Indian movies appeal to a Senegalese audience? Most Bollywood films are in Hindi, sometimes English, thus unintelligible for the Senegalese.[11] Why would people watch films about a culture so different from their own?[12] Why do they identify with Indians in particular? The following interview

abstract from an older Senegalese filmmaker and Indophile living in Paris
(Seydou)[13] is very revealing in this way:

> Seydou: . . . but what is also interesting is that the women from our country,
> many of them have never attended school, they managed to understand [em-
> phasis] those films, but really in an unbelievable [emphasis] manner. You put
> them a French, an American and an Indian film, they will not only choose
> the Indian film, but they will tell you the story from A to Z, and they have
> never been to school [claps his hands[14]], I find that incredible [emphasis]
> Gwenda: and why?
> S: yes and why, this brings us again, this brings us back [to an earlier point in
> our interview] to the question of approach (rapprochements culturels) of the
> two cultures, because it can only be this anyway, they can't read nor write,
> but those films, they understand the story. Those films talk to them as if
> they were in their own language, and in their own culture. To the contrary,
> if you bring them a French or American film, they will leave [the cinema],
> they won't even know what to tell you. It is therefore the culture which has
> permitted that approach and that understanding. That is really important.
> (Interview conducted 31 October 2004)

For him, as for many other Indophiles, Indian and Senegalese culture are
not that different at all, to the contrary.[15] Many say they love watching
Bollywood because it makes them think of their own "culture," country, or
customs. An expression which is often used to refer to this is "to find yourself in it" (s'y retrouver): "with films indous, you find yourself in Senegal
(vous vous retrouver ici au Sénégal), you find yourself'. This is the reason
why, according to Seydou, even illiterate people who cannot read the sub-
titles easily understand the story.

In this volume, Anjali Gera Roy poses a similar question related to
Bhangra: why did Bhangra hybridize with black, not white, music to reinvent itself? Whereas the phenomenon of Bhangra can, according to her,
be situated in border zones and has to be considered in the context of migration and suburban areas where "brown" and "black" mingle in a lower
working-class neighborhood, the situation in Senegal brings us to Indophiles' discourse of similarities.

Senegalese Indophiles have developed what I would call a discourse on
similarities. In *The Archaeology of Knowledge*, Foucault describes discourse as something which is context-specific (2003: 120). It is an individual or collective act, always related to an author. It should be located in its
spatio-temporal coordinates. Foucault states that discourse is everything
which is said about something, without implying whether it is "true" or
not (1984: 118). The group of statements heard from Indophiles on similarities between India and Senegal are context-specific and related to an
author. By calling the statements from Indophiles "a discourse" we do not
attach any judgments on whether the statements are true or not.

The similarities are perceived as a "cultural approach" between "Senegalese and Indian culture." Indophiles say they love "Indian culture" because it makes them think of their own. This discourse on similarities between Senegal and India can be brought together into different groups. Apart from similarities regarding food and clothing,[16] and the fact that many Indophiles said they love Bollywood because it's full of song and dance, I would like to focus on some constituent aspects of this discourse below.

## FAÇON DE VIVRE (WAY OF LIFE)

First of all there is what some research participants call *façon de vivre* (way of life). For this they often refer to the most popular Bollywood film ever: *Mère indienne* (*Mother India*, 1957).[17] The images of village life, horses and carts, women fetching water at the well or carrying fire wood on their heads "really make you think you are in Senegal." Some especially stressed similarities with the Fouta, a very rural area in northern Senegal, inhabited mostly by Fulani,[18] or with the Sereer, an ethnic group occupying mostly the coastal areas south of the Cap Vert peninsula (on which Dakar is situated). Some Indophiles linked the "animistic beliefs" of the Sereer or the Fulani with "animistic practices in Hinduism, such as the veneration of snakes or cows." Especially Indophiles from the older generation stress these aspects of the way of living and village activities. It makes them remember "the old days," "our own past."

## VALUES

Values which are, according to some Indophiles, highly regarded in Senegalese society can also be found in Bollywood films: such as respect for elders and marriage, piousness, and respect for women. The importance of family networks and living in an extended family is also mentioned as a strong similarity. The appreciation of values such as respect for elders or the extended family also relates to a preference for older films. More recent films are often criticized (especially by older Indophiles) for imitating Hollywood and for their "deteriorating" values. The fact that Senegalese appreciate this aspect of Bollywood shows how they actually would like to see themselves: it is a Senegalese ideal projected in Bollywood film.

## FULANI

In Indophile associations it is remarkable that many Indophiles are of Fulani origin, something which is stressed by many research participants as well. When asking why especially Fulani would be related to Indians, many Indophiles start talking about physical resemblance, an idea which is related to the "common origin" discourse and the idea of *peul indou* (see infra). Apart from physical resemblances, Indophiles explain the strong similarities by stressing that the similarities in values, clothing, or way of living are more prevalent when it comes to Fulani society. Some discussed this in the sense that there is a common cultural basis between Fulani and Indian culture. This brings us to the ideas on a common origin, something which is also developed by the participants of Senghor's research project on linguistic similarities between Senegal and South India (see infra). Some research participants said that the similarities between Africa and Asia can be explained by the fact that they once formed one continent and were not that remote as they are today.

Related to this discourse on common origin is the concept of *peul indou* ("Hindu Fulani") used by several (mostly Fulani) Indophiles to refer to the South Indian Tamil population. As the origin of Fulani is, according to Indophiles, to be found in India, the Tamil groups in India are said to be strongly related to the Fulani. Tamils (even called "black Indians," *les noirs indiens*) are referred to as the original inhabitants of India before the invasion of the (more pale skinned) Arians from the north. Although not stated by any Indophile, the fact that they use the term "black Indians" shows they make a link between their ideas about Arian invasion in India and their own colonial situation.

### LANGUAGE

According to Larkin, the argument that Hausa language and Hindi are similar is often used by people to stress the similarities between both cultures. The same holds true for Senegal. Wolof, Sereer, or Fulani are said to be "very similar" to Hindi. Some Indophiles even state they speak Hindi fluently. Indophile informants often mention the same words when asked for examples of similarities: *caabi* (key—Wolof) and *caabu* (Hindi), *asamaan* (heaven—Wolof and Hindi), *kaay* (come here—Wolof) and *aw* (Hindi). Sometimes the links were not that obvious, such as that between the Wolof word *jogal* (get up) and *uto* in Hindi. Linguists reinforced my inkling idea that most of these words are of Arabic origin (e.g., *asamaan*).[19] Why otherwise would Hausa *and* Wolof *and* Fulani *and* Sereer be similar to a language like Hindi? Wolof, Fulani, and Sereer are very mixed languages, with a strong Arabic influence of which people are often unaware. As mentioned earlier, the Indian film industry originated in Lahors, Pakistan, and the films were in Urdhu. This would explain similarities between Urdhu and Senegalese languages, as Urdhu has a strong Arabic influence.

Larkin's research among Hausa showed more or less the same discourses on similarities: visual (dress) and linguistic similarities, way of living (marriage celebrations, village life), and the importance of values such as family and kinship (1997: 412–13; 2003: 183). He also stresses the preference for older films: people say Indian films "have culture" in a way American films seem to lack it. Thus, the West is being defined as "other" whereas Indian culture is perceived as similar—similar because American films are different.

This discourse on similarities is, I feel, an expression of one of the central concerns of this collection of essays: the "hidden transcript" (as John Hawley calls it in the introduction) between two worlds which seem to have been involved in a process of globalization where the West is absent. The idea of a similar cultural basis and even of a common origin makes it necessary for us to accept that there are many strong (perceived or not) links between India and Africa. This imaginary bridge situated on the Indian Ocean has enabled a constant traffic of ideas, people and goods over the centuries. The fact that this global flow of ideas stands apart from the West is discussed in more detail further on in this essay.

## History of Indophilie in Senegal

### Indophilie

The first Bollywood film, *Mangala(an)*, came to Senegal in 1953 and, according to the first Indophile generation, created a furor. Before that one could only watch French, American, or Arabic films. Bollywood films became more and more popular and were imported massively in the 1970s. They soon outnumbered and surpassed Arabic films. All urban cinemas showed at least one Bollywood film every day. People often said that as a child they watched lots of Bollywood, whether they came to the cinema for the Bollywood film or for the Western or Chinese film shown afterward. Due to the arrival of TV and home videos, lots of cinemas are closed now, though the remaining ones still show Bollywood.

From the 1960s onward, Indophiles started organizing themselves. The first association, Les Amis de l'Inde (Friends of India), was established around 1966–68. Nowadays there are between twenty and thirty associations concentrating on Bollywood dance and music and spread all over Senegal in different cities. Dakar and Pikine have the largest amount of Indophile groups.[20] Contacts with the Indian embassy and the Ministry of Culture revealed the need for a federal organization covering all the different Indophile groups in Senegal. This is how the UNAIS emerged in 2003, as a first step toward a (future) Indian Cultural Centre.

In the 1960s–80s Bollywood apparently reached a wide audience, including many people who today could not be defined (or would not define themselves) as Indophiles. Today, the popularity of Bollywood films seems to be more restricted to a smaller group of people—people identifying themselves as Indophiles. However, I would not interpret this as a kind of "winding down" of the Indophile movement. I think one should make a clear distinction between the widespread popularity of Bollywood from the 1960s until the end of the 1980s on the one hand and the Indophile movement (with Bollywood dancing and *soirées*) on the other. The Indophile movement had its origin in the Bollywood popularity of the early days; it is a kind of spin-off of the Bollywood popularity and existed simultaneously with it for a long time. Nowadays the Indophile movement has continued, while the widespread popularity of Bollywood has declined.

Although the popularity of Bollywood is spread in many parts of Africa (East, South, and West), I have found no other example of this specific spin-off of Indophilie, namely the Indophile groups and dancing, as they are found in Senegal. Fuglesang and Larkin have confirmed to me that although Bollywood is popular in Kenya and Nigeria, respectively, they have found no Indophile associations or Bollywood dance groups. Other scholars have said they have not found any associations in Mali, Mauritania, or Guinea. The only other example of people imitating Bollywood dances in Africa (but in a completely different context) was mentioned by Casey in her dissertation on spirit possession among young girls in Kano, Nigeria (1997). However, this has nothing to do with Indophile associations, with people getting together to enjoy Bollywood music and dances.

### Leopold Sédar Senghor and the UCAD Project

From independence onward, Léopold Sédar Senghor, the first president, launched his theory of *négritude:* from now on everyone could be proud to be African and should be proud of his or her "own" culture.[21] The cultural politics of Senghor were therefore marked by a "back to our roots" movement and an intense promotion of "traditional culture." While this was the official road, the 1960s were also the period during which the Senegalese urban population was exposed to salsa, rock, pop, jazz, and Indian music. Especially salsa became extremely popular (see Shain 2002).[22]

Senghor was also a popular intellectual and poet who liked to theorize about the universality of humankind and the mixing and origin of cultures. His visit to Chennai (India) made him develop ideas about possible relations between (South) Indians (of Dravidian origin) and Africans. He was struck by the "physical resemblance" between the two groups and called the Dravidians "black Indians." He also noted linguistic similarities and started developing the idea of a common origin. On his return, he contacted the University Cheikh Anta Diop (UCAD) in Dakar and charged his Ministry of Culture to find him researchers who would work on the cultural and linguistic affiliations between India and Senegal. Three researchers set off for India, all carrying out comparative linguistic research between different local languages (Wolof, Fulani, and Sereer) and Tamil.[23]

The scholars indeed found "lots of affinities" regarding vocabulary and grammar. They reinforced the theory developed by intellectual Cheikh Anta Diop (who is also mentioned by Roy in this volume) on the Egyptian origin of most West Africans.[24] At that time Indian researchers had developed a similar idea of an Egyptian origin of Dravidians. The similarities cannot, however, account for a genetic affiliation. According to the scholars, more research is needed from other disciplines (history, anthropology, etc.) to prove this. Though it was Senghor's idea to develop this, and even to establish an Indo-African research institute at the UCAD, all this did not happen due to his departure in 1980, the year the research projects ended. Of course, Senghor's ideas about *négritude* and theorization on the origin of Africans have to be placed in their historical context. Until now there has been no continuation of Senghor's projects, even though they have stimulated academic exchanges between India and Senegal, which were continued under President Diouf.

The hypothesis that Dravidian languages on the one hand and Egyptian or Wolof on the other hand would be related is unique in the history of linguistics. According to linguist G. De Boel, a specialist in language relatedness, the hypothesis cannot be proven: "even if they would be related, the distance in time is too big to enable researchers to prove it" (personal communication, 5 October 2004). Similar words in different languages can be a coincidence, apart from the use of loanwords, which can also account for an impression of relatedness. Dravidian languages do not seem to be related to any other language group in the world. Arabic influence in Dravidian languages might occur, though much less than in Hindi.

### Links between Senghor and Indophilie

There is no link nor influence at all between the Bollywood-originated Indophilie and Senghor's project. First, Senghor's project encompassed Dravidian languages, not Hindi. As Bollywood films are in Hindi, there is a difference between the linguistic similarities mentioned by people watching these movies and the similarities pointed out in the research project. Hindi and Tamil are completely different languages, belonging to different (Indo-European and Dravidian, respectively) language groups. Furthermore, Senghor's project has never been popularized.

### Portrait of the Senegalese Indophile

### Gender

Most dancers at *soirées indous* are women. The few male dancers usually participate in duos and focus more on playback then on dancing. According to one Indophile, this is mainly because *danse indou* is more suitable for women. They are, according to her, also more capable of doing it. Apart from the dancers, most of the audience consists of women. However, we should not essentialize the view that the films are watched only by women: apart from women, *films indous* were also massively attended by schoolboys and schoolgirls. We could, however, say that they had a mostly female audience.

Some say that Bollywood films are mostly watched by a female audience because the themes (love and marriage) especially appeal to them. Others mentioned a more practical reason: men do not have as much time as women have. *Soirées indous* usually start very late, and for men it is therefore more difficult to attend as they have to get up early to work. According to them, the same reason accounts for the fact that the afternoon films were (and are) mostly attended by women, who would also have more time to go to the cinema daily. In Nigeria the situation is somewhat different. As they were living indoors, women were absent in the cinemas in the 1970s but gained access to Indian films through the rise of home videos. According to Larkin, Indian films have since then become identified as "women's films" because of their huge popularity among women (1997: 424).

Some Indophiles affirm there are also lots of male Indophiles, but they keep their passion more hidden, at least in the past. When some men were asked about their experience as male Indophiles, they said it was sometimes hard in the beginning, as men watching Bollywood were often criticized for being gay.[25] This criticism toward Indophile men has diminished, making it probably easier for them to openly manifest their love for Bollywood.

### Age

Earlier it was mentioned that age plays a role in the way people appreciate Bollywood. The older generation of Indophiles prefers older films such as *Devdaz* and *Mother India*. Among the younger generation, more recent films also seem to be popular. In general, we could say that many old films remain popular among young people, who watch old and modern, whereas the older generation sticks to old films. Several young dancers stressed that older films are particularly useful for dancing, as "you can put classical steps on modern music, but you can't put modern steps on old music."

An often-heard critique by older people is that recent films are too modern, too "Hollywood-like," a trend indicated by several older Indophiles as modernism (*le modernisme*). For them, the quality of classical music, dance, dress style, and scenery has deteriorated. One Indophile made a clear distinction between old films showing "traditional India" (*cosaan*, which can be translated as "tradition," "culture," "roots'") and modern films, showing "another, Western, culture." He criticized the Americans for having "destroyed" Indian culture, which is the reason why, according to him, Indians have "lost their roots."

Tremblay's article on the representation and reflection of self and society in Bollywood reveals that in the older films, tradition and modernity are presented as a dichotomy (1996: 304). This view corresponds very well with the ideas of the older generation of Indophiles: they also make a dichotomous distinction between older films (as more "traditional," "authentic") and modern ones (*le modernisme*). Tremblay states that during the last two decades, Bollywood films have offered an alternative view on modernity, an indigenous notion of modernity. They "examine the problems particular to Indian modernity" (Tremblay 1996: 305). Kaur also confirms this idea that whereas older Bollywood films represent India/tradition and the West/modernity in a simplistic, dichotomous way, recent films seem to have incorporated this "indigenous" notion of modernity (2002: 207). As the older generation has not yet been capable of incorporating this new attitude, the youth seems to be have developed a skillfulness to be able to deal with this "modernity." It should, however, be said that older films remain popular, especially for dancing.

The association of the West with a corrupt form of modernity ("Americans have destroyed Indian culture'" in which Indophiles do not want to engage is one indication that the global flows which are at stake here have nothing to do with (and are sometimes clearly distinguished from) the West. I later return to this issue as it is one of the central themes in this collection of essays.

### Intellectual versus Popular?

A university professor involved in the Senghor project commented:

> The *films indous, you don't need to think to understand the drama.* ( . . . ) It's always the same, some fights ( . . . ) This has defavored the appropriation, adoption of *films indous* in the city centre, and they stayed in the margins, in the urban margins. ( . . . ) Maybe it is related to class [*hesitates*]. But it's true that the tastes are not the same among people from the suburb and those who inhabit the [*hesitates*] regular quarters, the quarters of officials, the quarters of [*hesitates*] people who are well-off, bourgeois quarters. (21 April 2004; emphasis mine)

The fact that you don't need to think when watching Bollywood is something the Indophiles themselves will not like to hear. It is a commonly heard view, from an intellectual who wants to distance himself from "entertainment for the masses." He, as well as other intellectuals, makes a clear distinction between intellectuals (themselves) and (uneducated) Indophiles. Would there indeed be a distinction between intellectual and popular, or even between educated and Indophile? Although, indeed, many Indophiles are illiterate, most of them unable to speak French fluently, there are educated Indophiles as well.

Other studies on cross-cultural media reception elsewhere in the world reveal similar ideas. Straubhaar also talks about the "internationalisation of the bourgeoisie" (elites and upper-middle classes are more internationalized in their tastes) and concludes that there is a relation between "class" and the consumption of local (*telenovelas*) versus internationally oriented (U.S. imported) media in Latin America (1991a: 51; 1991b: 196–98). Abdazi's article on Bollywood popularity among the working-class people in Greece in the 1950s also mentions that middle-class and educated Greeks "looked westward for entertainment" and "did not look kindly on the Hindi movies and songs" (n.d.: 2, 4).

I would, however, not associate Indophilie exclusively with poverty and would not make a distinction between poor and rich Indophiles. As there are educated Indophiles, I also met several rich Indophiles. If one should make a distinction, it seems to me that the distinction between educated and popular is more appropriate. Bourdieu has demonstrated that there is indeed a relation between education and cultural capital (Bourdieu cited in Straubhaar 1991b: 198). One has to be aware, however, that in our case the distinction of intellectual versus popular reflects an intellectual point of view. Kaur (2002: 201) and Tremblay (1996: 303) also warn about this elitist-biased interpretation of Bollywood, placing the latter (as mass or low culture) in a subordinate position to art or high culture. I would suggest using care in making distinctions, especially that they not be represented as dichotomies in an essentialist way. The only term we should retain is "popular culture."

### Urban or Suburban Context?

In the quote mentioned above, the professor talks about the geographical difference between city center and suburb. Intellectuals inhabiting the central areas seem to be more oriented toward the West, whereas the suburbs go for Bollywood. Bollywood films are mostly shown in suburban cinemas, whereas the cinemas in the city center focus on French and American films. My research participants are a good sample of the whole Indophile community as far as residential patters are concerned. Most of the research participants live in popular quarters. Many of them live in Pikine or its annexes. Another important segment lives in popular quarters in central Dakar (Medina or Grand Dakar).

Pikine is indeed considered the center of Indophilie, a place where many Indophiles and dance groups are based and many *soirées indous* are organized. This relates to the moving of people from central Dakar to newly created suburbs such as Pikine and Guediawaye in the 1950s and

1960s. In that time, efforts had been made to modernize the popular quarters in central Dakar. The government stimulated people to move out of the crowded popular quarters such as Médina, Fas, and Colobane, and a lot of cinemas from central Dakar moved with them. The fact that only people who used to live in the popular quarters in central Dakar moved to Pikine could explain the Bollywood popularity in the new suburb.

The considerations made on Pikine would suggest Indophilie is a suburban phenomenon. However, it is not restricted only to suburban areas. Other popular quarters such as Médina, Colobane, or Grand Dakar also count many Indophiles. We could say that Indophilie is more prevalent in popular quarters, in central Dakar or suburbs, with Pikine being the biggest "center."

### Cultural Translation: *Dance Indou* Groups

The National Palace Museum in Taipei, Taiwan, displays a ceramic vase from the Ming Dynasty (fifteenth century). The belly of the vase shows a beautiful Arabic inscription. When trying to decipher the calligraphy, however, scholars noticed that the inscription made no sense at all. Even though it seemed perfect Arabic to an outsider, it does not mean anything, just aesthetically imitating Arabic calligraphy. This vase made me think about *danse indou* groups in Senegal: people imitate Bollywood song and dancing styles for the aesthetic pleasure of it. Of course, this cultural translation is much more than merely copying. The dances are re-created into another vital form, translated, reinterpreted. The *danse indou* groups form a good example of cultural translation of a danced form.[26]

### *Danse Indou*

It was a hot day in April when I set off for my first *danse indou* rehearsal. The group was called Chandini (Moonshine) and was based in Naari Tali in Grand Dakar. After sitting for a while watching children playing in a rather disorganized courtyard, someone put a cassette from *Kuch Kuch Hota Hai*[27] in the cassette player, and some girls started dancing to it. After the first group choreography by the younger girls, the director of the group put *Devdaz* in the cassette player. It was time for some solos and duos. *Devdaz* (1955) is an old film where dance is still mostly inspired by Indian classical dance forms—this was definitely a job for the more advanced dancers who had already acquired more technical skills.

### *Choreographing*

Most *indou* dancers choose a song and then start choreographing it. Nowadays, home videos are a welcome tool to help dancers with the learning. Sometimes they first look at the video, although this is not necessary:

they can also start choreographing without having seen the movie. The more acquainted you are with Bollywood dancing, the more you can leave the original filmic version behind and make your own choreographies. Those who have just started dancing *danse indou* usually make more use of the videos when choreographing. Only some very experienced dancers can just enter the scene during a *soirée indou* and start improvising without any choreography fixed beforehand. Apart from those few, improvisation is hardly done.

### Transcultural Transmission and Translation: Mixing toward a Third Dance

During our interview, Diadou put on the video of the *soirée indou* she organized Chez Marina in 2004. At a certain moment while she was dancing, Aziz entered the dancing circle. He put one knee on the ground, one hand in his hips and the other on his head, and moved his torso back and front in a short, rhythmic way. I had seen this step before at *soirées sénégalaises* or *sabars*, mostly performed by men. Diadou said she had also once made a "mixed" choreography on a small *soirée* organized by her dance group. She had taken a song from Omar Pene, a popular Senegalese *mbalax* singer,[28] and had made a "mixed" choreography, "resembling Indian steps" (*ressemblant à des pas indous*). I found it very much like a *mbalax*-disco-like kind of dancing. She told me someone else also once had made a "mixed choreography" on a song by Youssou N'Dour, which was also performed during a *soirée indou* (fieldnotes, 25 January 2005).

In the case of making *indou* choreographies on *mbalax* it should be said that "disco" Bollywood of course resembles other disco-influenced styles such as *mbalax* (which has Western-style drums and guitars), making it easier to "mix." Apart from making *danse indou* on *mbalax* music, Senegalese steps are incorporated in *danse indou*. This kind of mixing seems to be frequent in *danse indou*. Especially *sabar* (and *mbalax*) was used when mixing. Some Indophiles point out many similarities between Indian and Fulani and Wolof dance. When talking about *sabar*, for example, one referred to the typical play of eye movements (*ragaju*) and linked this to the way Indian actresses "play with their eyes." This would help Senegalese women to dance Bollywood. Indophile dancers try to "harmonize" Indian and Senegalese dance styles. This kind of mixing goes beyond incorporating *sabar* steps in an *indou* choreography: it actually tries to mix the steps into an integrated whole. This suggests that the discourse on similarities is not only "experienced" or "felt," but it is also actively *created* through dance, by working out movements which approach both dancing styles. Mixing is done because it enables Senegalese women to dance *danse indou* "without giving up their feeling of being Senegalese."

One Indophile talked about the marriage of two cultures throughout the dances (*le marriage de deux cultures à travers la danse*). This implies *indou* dancing is more than merely imitating Bollywood. Iain Chambers develops similar ideas on hybridity and the creation of a "third space" in his book *Migrancy, Culture, Identity* (1994). He explores the translation of one cultural form into another culture, which always, according to him, gives rise to hybridity. He disagrees with the idea that two "original" cultures (in an essentialist way) would merge to give a "third" (also essential) form.

Chambers also stresses the fact that cultural translation is never a one-way process: "in the ensuing dialog of difference ( . . . ) both of us emerge modified" (1994: 85). Similar ideas are addressed by Bastide, who therefore prefers to talk about "interpenetration" (*interpénétration*) or "intercrossing" (*entrecroisement*) instead of transculturation, as in those terms the dialogical process is implied (Bastide, cited in Décoret-Ahiha 2004: 14). In the case of *danse indou*, we could say that it is much like a one-way process. However, even though the Senegalese *danse indou* has not had direct impacts in India, the export of Bollywood films on the one hand and the worldwide dispersal of Indian dances on the other have had serious effects on practices in India.[29]

Décoret-Ahiha is, however, a little reluctant about the use of the term "crossing" (*métissage*) (2004: 281–82): "the notion of crossing ( . . . ) is embedded in the common idea that cultures are pure entities, homogenous, stable, separated from one another" (281). She follows Amselle, who prefers to use the electric metaphor of *branchement*. We could translate Amselle's term as "connection," although the English term is vaguer and does not have the specific association with electricity. Gruzinsky espresses similar concerns regarding the use of the terms "mix" and "hybridity":

> Perceived as the passage from the homogenous to the heterogenous, from the singular to the plural, from order to disorder, the idea of mix (*mélange*) carries connotations and presumptions which are to be avoided like the plague. The same holds true for the term hybridity (*hybridité*). (Gruzinsky, cited in Décoret-Ahiha 2004: 281)

The ideas developed by Chambers, Bastide, and Décoret-Ahiha remind us of two other prominent writers in the post-colonial landscape: Fernando-Ortiz and Bhabha. The first talked about transculturation, the second called it hybridity and the "third space." Transculturation was launched as a concept by Fernando-Ortiz in 1947 to describe the phenomenon of merging and converging culturalities. Transculturation occurs in any context that deals with more than one culturality. We could say that transcultural contact creates a third, hybrid space. In his reflections on hybridity and the "third space," Bhabha warns for an essentialist interpretation of two "original" forms merged into a hybrid "third":

> the act of cultural translation ( . . . ) denies the essentialism of a prior given original or originary culture ( . . . ), all forms of culture are continually in a process of hybridity. But for me the importance of hybridity is not to be able to trace two original moments from which the third emerges, rather hybridity to me is the "third space" which enables other positions to emerge. (Bhabha cited in Rutherford 1990: 211)

I agree we should be aware of too essentialist interpretations of culturalities as "pure, homogenous, stable." The use of the term "connection" would therefore seem a better solution, although the term is in my opinion less accurate than it's French counterpart of *branchement*. Hybridity does not necessarily reduce the complexity of intercultural relations, which are always interactional and dynamic. I would therefore not leave the term completely behind, nevertheless bearing in mind that we should not ascribe it any essentialist connotation.

I would conclude *danse indou* is not about trying to imitate as much as possible, but about making another vital hybrid with the material at your disposal, without leaving behind your own identity (of "feeling Senegalese" or of a dancer). In a similar way, Roy's essay in this collection discusses mixing and hybridity among black and (what she calls) brown music.

### Soirées indous

At least once a month or every two months a *soirée indou* is organized in Dakar. *Soirées indous* are often organized by radio anchormen of Indophile programs or by Indophile associations. Apart from the *soirées*, Indophiles also gather in the smaller *tours*. A *tour* is basically a "getting together" with friends, or if connected with a smaller or bigger association (local football club, dance or theatre group), it is an informal get-together of the people of the association. The people attending a *tour* contribute so that the costs for the food or drinks are shared.

*Soirées indous* usually start very late and always have a similar course: a few group choreographies alternated with solos and duos of old and modern Bollywood films. People sit in a circle or square around the dance space. A *soirée* is filmed and professionally mixed. The video is proudly kept afterward as a souvenir and shown to visitors. The presence of the camera is an important factor. Filming is not only to record the performance (the dances) but also to record the audience: who attended the *soirée*, who was wearing what and who gave how much to which dancer. The

FIGURE 5.2. Duet at the Miss Indou election, June 2005. Note the bank notes on the floor given to the dancers by the audience.

attention given to filming for hours before the performance starts, filming the arrival, and greeting the guests makes this clear.

*Soirées indous* are also occasions where lots of money is flowing. First of all, *soirées* always have guests of honor, *marraines*. They are not the sponsors of the whole evening but usually contribute in the costs. The guests of honor usually come very late, to be sure that everyone has already arrived and will see their arrival. They usually come in a whole delegation, accompanied by many friends. The delegation of guests of honor can easily be recognized by the large number of people arriving, their clothing (they are more dressed up than the rest of the audience), and the elaborate welcoming and greeting, with a lot of camera attention. A *soirée* is usually closed with a gift-giving "ceremony," where the organizers and the guests of honor give each other gifts, such as cloth, *pagnes* (wrap-arounds), or money.[30] Sometimes praise songs are sung for the guests of honor.

Apart from the guests of honor, people from the audience stand up to throw money at the dancers during the performances. Sometimes the money is put between the folds of the costume of the dancer. Also, often the people giving money kiss the dancer or dance along for a little bit, before returning slowly to their place, lingering before the camera. When a dancer has a lot of success, the dance floor might be strewn with notes. Giving money is not only a sign of appreciation. It is, first of all, reinforcing social relations. You give money only to the people you know. As a friend of a dancer you are always obliged to give to your dancing friend. Dancers or groups bring their fans and friends along to a soirée.[31]

Outward appearance (women with fancy dresses, expensive make-up, and lots of bank notes) seems to be important, as well as augmenting one's status within the group by showing off with the money you have. On one evening the guest of honor was a very rich Indophile, a trade woman, dressed in a boubou cocaïne, so called because of the extremely expensive cloth from which it is made. She was accompanied by her female géwél[32] (griotte), who sang her praises as she showed the crowd note after note that her patron gave—500,000 cfa (the equivalent of 760 euros or $915 USD)—to the organizer.

### Stress on Aesthetic Aspects

The Ming vase is a good example of cultural translation on a purely aesthetic level. Aesthetic pleasure seems to be an important aspect of danse indou and soirées indous. Much time and effort are spent on splendid costumes and make-up, not only by the dancers (who change costumes all the time) but also by the audience. Women will never go to a soirée indou without first spending a few hours in the beauty parlor, especially the guests of honor, who will arrive in the most expensive dresses and make-up. Many women present have burns from overbleaching their skin or from using bad bleaching products.[33] The body of the dancer also plays a role: preferably dancers should be young, pale, and with a perfect body.

Other evidence of the emphasis on aesthetics is the Miss Indou elections organized every year. In 2005 about two hundred people attended the soirée. Popular (Senegalese) artists performed a playback in between the Indophile dance choreographies and the miss parades. At the end, out of the eighteen young women one was chosen to be Miss Indou for one year. The young women reflect the Senegalese beauty ideal: very pale skin, slim, and young. The candidates don't have a very Indian look. They get on the catwalk dressed in fancy mini skirts and shiny tops. The only criteria for participating is being an Indophile. For this reason, the elections are controversial among Indophiles, with some complaining that there is nothing Indian about the Miss Indou elections.

### Similarities between Sabar and Soirées Indous

*Soirées indous* are typically Senegalese. They are not found in other surrounding countries, and I found that the concept of *soirées indous* is similar to the *soirées sénégalaises* which are now very popular in night-clubs and which are based on *sabar* parties. The concept of *sabar* parties or *soirées sénégalaises* is similar to that of *soirées indous*: people sit or stand in a circle or square around the dance space, which is occupied by mainly female individual dancers taking turns performing their dance steps (*sabar*) or Hindu choreographies. Individual success seems to be very important, as is also shown in the huge amount of money flowing. Skilled dancers usually receive money from the audience. It seems that during *soirées indous* even more money is flowing than during *soirées sénégalaises*.

Apart from this, a *soirée sénégalaise* is, like all *sabar* parties, mainly a woman's business. The dancers are mainly women, and the dance space becomes highly female gendered. First, there are only women in the circle around the dance space. The few men who are watching restrict themselves to the outer circles. Second, the performance becomes filled with female sexuality, as is evident in the dancer's clothes and sugges-tive movements. Thus, *sabar* parties (and *soirées sénégalaises*) are mainly by and for women and about female sexuality. These ideas of sexuality also relate to concepts about beauty and the ideal female body.

Indophilie is often regarded as women's business, with many more fe-male India-lovers than male ones. Most of the dancers and audience of *soirées indous* are women. Furthermore, ideas of female sensuality also prevail in *dance indous*, as has become evident in the use of disguise to ex-oticize oneself as a mysterious, sensual "other," in the practice of veiling and unveiling or in the yearly Miss Indou elections. An earlier reference has already been made to the importance attached to beauty, aesthetics, and bodily preferences in *dance indou*.

Let's make one final remark on women and traditional dress. Being a woman, I had been asked to wear traditional clothes (*yere wolof*) when I went to a *soirée sénégalaise*. When I asked why only women, and not men, had to dress traditionally, the response was that it "colors" and "decorates" the evening. This is something which comes from the *sabar parties*. And here also, as *sabar* must convey a "national unity" message (as it is being put forward as a "national" dance style), nationalism seems to be linked with gender: women in traditional dress are portrayed as bearers of the collective (national) identity. The aspect of women in tra-ditional dress in *soirées indous* (and Bollywood) has been discussed earlier.

## Different Postcolonial Answers Allowing for
## Different Cultural Identities

### Parallel Modernities

One video of a *soirée indou* showed a young man accompanying a dancer with a self-made cardboard *sitar*. He wore a dark green open jacket without sleeves and a small red scarf around his head, knotted to the side, which made him look a bit like Rambo. He held the *sitar* as if he was holding an electric guitar, banging his head and playing it full of passion and devotion as if he was a *grunge* band member.

This scene made me think about Larkin's reflections on *parallel modernities* (1997: 407–10, 434): "I use the term 'parallel modernities' to refer to the coexistence in space and time of multiple economic, religious, and cultural flows that are often subsumed within the term 'modernity'" (1997: 407). He makes a distinction between his ideas and the concept of *alternative modernities* applied by Appadurai (1991), who links it with increased deterritorialization of the world and the movement of people. According to Larkin, the concept of *parallel modernities* is not necessarily linked with nostalgic needs of expatriate communities for establishing contact with their homelands. It is not about imagining a partly invented native land but about imagining other cultures (as part of daily life). His point is that for the Hausa (especially the younger people) watching Bollywood is a way of being modern without being Western, without being criticized for being "Western decadent" (1997: 433; 2003: 172). Scheld (2003: 9–10) reinforces Larkin's ideas by arguing that modernities develop in tandem, not as "alternatives" to "dominant" discourses. Appadurai's term indeed implies an unequal relationship. A similar connotation is found in terms such as *sub*(under)-*altern*(other) or *post*(after)-coloniality: when trying to mind the trap of "mental colonialism,"[34] "postcolonial" scholars reinforce it by implying inequality in the language they use.

An idea which is definitely applicable to the Senegalese case is that Bollywood films offer Hausa viewers a third space, mediating between Hausa Islamic tradition and Western modernity, disrupting the dichotomies between "West" and non-"West" (Larkin 2003: 172; 1997: 414). We have already discussed Chambers' ideas on hybridity and the creation of a "third space" in transcultural translation of cultural forms. Chambers's conception of "third space" coincides with Larkin's ideas in the sense that it disrupts dichotomies and essentialist views on and between the two cultures involved.

Thus, Indian films are situated in a cultural space that stands outside binary distinctions between tradition and modernity, Africa and West, resistance and domination (Larkin 1997: 433). Earlier I discussed how Bollywood films from the first generation presented tradition and modernity as a dichotomy (see Tremblay 1996: 304; Kaur 2002: 207; Jaikumar 2003: 4–5). Tremblay states that during the last two decades, Bollywood films offer an alternative, indigenous notion of modernity (1996: 305).

According to Larkin, the Hausa engage in forms of tradition different from their own while at the same time conceiving of a modernity that comes without political and ideological significance of the "West" (2003: 176, 183). "Indian films work for Hausa because they rest on a dialectic of presence and absence culturally similar to Hausa society but at the same time reassuringly distant'" (188). This politics of absence and presence, desire and imagination, proximity and distance, difference and sameness, has been referred to earlier. In my opinion, it is also one of the constituting aspects of Senegalese Indophilie. Bollywood is "just like," but at the same time different, exotic. Maybe that is also why Arabic films have never been successful. They are not exotic enough.

### Similar Because the West Is Different

Moreover, the above considerations can also account for the reason why Bollywood might be conceived as "just like," explaining the discourse on similarities (see supra): Indian culture is similar because Western is different. Following Larkin (2000: 232) I would say that Hausa videos, like Bollywood, explore a similar way of being modern while criticizing Western patterns of consumption and materialism. Several elements from the interviews I conducted also point in this direction. Seydou (who has been cited earlier) even talks about the way of walking: the "Indian" and "Senegalese" way of walking would be very similar, contrary to the "Western" way of walking, which is very different. Earlier we have discussed other similarities between India and Senegal, perceived as similar and placed in contrast to the West, such as the importance of intense relations between members of an extended family. When asked his opinion about this idea of "similar *because* the West is different," Seydou says he definitely agrees, because, according to him, the West was more remote at the time when India and Africa formed one continent. This aspect of "the West is different" is a constituent aspect of the concept of parallel modernities.

I would like to relate this idea of *parallel modernities* to the theory of culture spheres developed by Pinxten (1994). Culture spheres are groups which are drawn toward each other due to a strong internal coherence, such as Western Europe, Japan and South East Asia, sub-Sahara Africa, India. But not only groups within one culture sphere experience similarities. Culture spheres situated in a *parallel modernity* (such as sub-Sahara Africa/Senegal and India) can also experience similarities, while maintaining differences because they belong to different culture spheres. This can be related to Larkin's "politics of *absence* and *presence*, difference and sameness," an idea which he develops from his *parallel modernities* concept. These similarities might be due to similar cultural intuitions[35] or similarities between culture spheres which might be drawn to each other because they are both more different from a third culture sphere (e.g., the West). To give an example from the cases: respect for elders or the importance of social networks might be shared cultural intuitions between Senegal and India. The concept of (shared or similar) cultural intuitions by different culture spheres can be placed in the light of the discourse on similarities between Senegal and India perceived by Senegalese Indophile informants.

### Orientalism and (Self-)Exoticization

One ballet and contemporary dancer who also did some *dance indu* used to dance with real snakes around his neck, as was obvious from a picture shown to me by his uncle. An Indophile mentioned another "very good dancer" who used snakes in her performances. Dancing with real snakes is not found in India.[36] This might suggest that dancing with snakes around your neck might be a Senegalese invention. It might have been inspired by statues or imagery of Siva, the lord of the dance, who wears snakes around his neck. However, it also makes one think about Mami Wata imagery, which is discussed by Rush in this volume. Although Mami Wata is not venerated in Senegal, her images might have circulated, or those of a nineteenth-century German snake charmer on which most of the Mami Wata imagery would be inspired (see also Rush 1999: 63).[37] But we can say for sure that dancing with snakes is an exoticization of Indian dance—the dancer being presented as an exotic "other."[38]

The imagination of an exotic other brings us to the concept of orientalism. Orientalism in dance has been studied mainly in Western belly dance (see Dox 1996, 2004, 2005; Sellers-Young 2004; Sellers-Young and Shay 2005). Western belly dance reinforces several ideas typical about the male, orientalist gaze, such as sensuality, the harem as a place of liberal sexuality, mystery, femininity. The image of the orient as a sensual and mysterious and innately feminine exotic other is perpetuated within transnational media (Bhabha 1994 and Savigliano 1995, cited in Sellers-Young 2004: 2). The image of the feminine exotic is also found in Bollywood films: not men but women are wearing traditional dress and are perceived on a transnational level as being associated with "Indianness" and also with exotic otherness.

*Dance indou* is all about orientalizing oneself in the guise of an imagined, mysterious other. Dancers disguise or exoticize themselves in a costume which is different from those found in their own culture (or at least perceived as different) and dance to "other" music from "other" films. Exoticism implies "creating power over the unknown in an act of indiscriminately combining fragments, crumbs of knowledge and fantasy" (Savigliano 1995: 169). This definitely holds true for *dance indou*: just as the Ghanaian artist Joseph Kossivi Ahiator mentioned by Rush often "visits" India in his head, none of the dancers has been to India (apart from a few very rich Indophiles). They combine their knowledge about India, or rather about the India shown in Bollywood, with fantasy and imagination. According to Barbara Sellers-Young, Western belly dance also imagined the other through film: the costumes used by Western belly dancers (two-piece costume, heels, and veil), as well as their dance styles, are more defined by Hollywood adaptations and images of Middle Eastern dancers (2004: 3–4, 6). In these examples, imagination has become a social practice, which Arjun Appadurai relates to recent globalization: "The world we live in today is characterized by a new role for the imagination in social life. The image, the imagined, the imaginary these are all terms that direct us to something critical and new in global processes: the imagination as a social practice" (1996: 31).

Savigliano refers to the impact of orientalist imagery on dancers as a form of auto- or self-exoticism (Sellers-Young 2004: 2). The self-exoticization of the Western belly dancer seems at first to disguise her Western identity in order to represent the East of the orientalist fantasy (Dox 2004: 10, 16). The audience completes the fantasy: "The deeper more personal meaning of that dance vocabulary to the dancer and related community is mediated by the relationship between dancer and the audience; and ultimately in their combined imagination within the moment of performance'" (Sellers-Young 2004: 9).

An important item for "disguising" oneself is the veil. Apart from being intensively used in Western belly dance, it is also used in *dance indou*. The veil is used as a mask, enabling the dancer to disguise herself as cultural other. In her guise as the other the dancer must remain inaccessible in order to sustain the fantasy's exoticism (Dox 2004: 20). The guise also gives the dancer a kind of legitimacy. Apart from the practice of veiling, the dancer often unveils herself throughout the dance. According to Dox, unveiling in Western belly dance relates to flirtation and sexual pleasure: "Western belly dancers' self-presentation as a forbidden cultural 'other' offers a protective shield unavailable to strippers, exotic dancers, or belly dancers in Middle Eastern countries" (2004: 20). Dox states that unveiling (at least the way it is done in Western belly dance) is only thinkable in the West, where overtly displaying (the beauty of) one's body is accepted.

Among Middle Eastern dancers, unveiling is not a common practice, and the way it is done shows it is definitely not associated with open display of the sensual body.[39] Western belly dance plays with veil and display. In *dance indou* the veil is used in a very similar way. Unveiling also stands for an open display of one's sensual and attractive body. As mentioned previously, the aesthetic (and the aesthetic of one's body) is a constituent aspect of *dance indou*.

Although orientalism and exoticism have been studied mostly within the context of belly dance, other dance practices incorporate orientalism, sometimes in different forms. Another form of self-orientalism is the Taiwanese modern dance's Eastern Body Aesthetics, which has now deteriorated due to an orientalist demand of international curators.[40] Orientalism in Taiwanese dance also recurred in the so-called *Minzu Wudao* of the Kuomintang government, which tried to capture an imagined Chinese identity ("swept out" on the mainland by the Communists) through dance (Chen 2004: 3).

It has become clear that *dance indou* can be placed in this context of orientalism and self-exoticization. However, just as in the Taiwanese case, it places orientalism in a wholly different light, as it is not about a colonizing West imagining a subaltern colonized other. (This use of orientalism, including colonial power relations, is also discussed in Jaspal Singh's essay in the present volume). It does not hold a negative judgment about the West "getting it all wrong," such as Western belly dancers trying to be Middle Eastern but actually being more Hollywood. As stated by Appadurai, imagination has become a social practice throughout the world due to new globalizing processes. It has become clear in the previous paragraph that veiling and unveiling as openly displaying one's sensuality is therefore not "Western." Trying to trace dichotomies between West and Other has become old-fashioned. Other processes are going on, such as Africans imagining exotic others in India or Taiwanese exoticizing themselves in order to meet the demands that international dance curators impose on them. This coincides with the creation of a "third space" mentioned by Larkin. Orientalism in *dance indou* is an outcome of transnational dynamics which stand outside the dichotomy of West and Other, and which therefore is part of the theory of *parallel modernity* and "third space."

### Conclusion

*Dance indou* is an adapted Bollywood dance, performed by mostly female dancers who have learned it from watching Bollywood films. As their knowledge of Indian culture and dance is very restricted (because it has been filtered through the films, the only source of information they have), people use their imagination to fill the gaps in their knowledge. The result is a very Senegalese phenomenon, Senegalese in dancing or dress styles, with examples of self-exoticization such as dancing with snakes or using veils. It can therefore be placed in an orientalist discourse, broadening the definition of orientalism toward a non-culture-specific concept (more than "the colonizing West [wrongly] imagining the colonized East"). The fact that *dance indou* is a typically Senegalese phenomenon has also become evident in the fact that it is found in Senegal only, and that the *soirées indous* are to some extend also similar to *soirées sénégalaises*.

In this essay I have tried to disentangle the reasons why Indophilie is more than a merely superficial phenomenon in Senegal. The discourse on similarities seems to be a key element in the popularity of Bollywood films and Indophilie: "Indian" culture is "just like" Senegalese. This even develops into theories of common origin and linguistic relatedness. This discourse can be linked to the concept of *parallel modernities* and (similar) culture spheres and cultural intuitions. It shows how India and Africa have developed global flows where "the other" is at the same time perceived as similar and imagined as an exotic other. Moreover, these flows, going south-south instead of the classical north-south globalization theories, stand out of the Western influence sphere. In this way, a parallel modernity or parallel globalization has been developed by two areas linked by the Indian Ocean. Whereas other essays in this volume have focused on the global flows within the areas directly surrounding this ocean, my attempt has been to show how this influence sphere extends beyond its actual borders into the domain of the imaginary. The remarks by Larkin on Hausa Indophilie as related to a discourse on absence and presence, similarity and difference, exoticness and sameness, have shown to be very useful in this discussion. More research should be dedicated to these transnational cultural flows standing outside the dichotomies of West and Other. The phenomena of cultural mixing, exoticism, and orientalism as described in this essay could shed a new light on global processes and on transnational and national identities.

**Notes**

1. *Sabar* is a Wolof rhythm, instrument, and dance style. Every wedding, name-giving ceremony or quarter party is livened up by a group of *sabar* drummers. Wolof refers to the language as well as the Wolof-speaking groups. Wolof is the mother tongue of 43 percent of Senegal's population. As almost 80 percent of the whole Senegalese population can understand and speak Wolof, it is used as a common language and is, after French, the second language.

2. I put this term in quotes as there is, of course, no such thing as "Indian dance" (there are many different styles and techniques), though the Senegalese use this generalizing term, just as "Indian film" is a generalization for the Hindi Bollywood films.

3. The term "Hindu" is a literal translation from the French term used in Senegal: *indou/hindou/indo*. The question why people talked about *films hindou* (thus referring to Hinduism, the religion) instead of *films indiens* (Indian films, a term used in Anglophone Africa), remains open. The issue is complicated, as the Senegalese are very aware of the fact that the first films have been produced in Lahors (Pakistan), the actors being all Muslims. I suppose this is due to a confusion between Hindu (the religion) and Hindi (the language), as several people stated to me they could speak *indou* (referring to the language but by mistake using the wrong term). One Indophile confirmed this when being asked about the term *indou*: "it's a way of talking ( . . . ) I think it's mainly due to those people who do not know the difference between *indou*, which refers to the religion, and Hindi, which refers to the language. It's because they don't know. But those who know, know this difference." I will keep the term *danse indou, film indou, soirée indou*.

4. National Union of Senegalese Indophiles.

5. It might also be that Bollywood is popular *because* there is no Indian expatriate community in Senegal, contrary to eastern Africa where Indian expatriates form a separate social group and are sometimes not very loved by the "indigenous" groups. This process would be similar to Mauritius, where English as the national language is popular *because* no one speaks it (e.g., it is not Creole). I am grateful to Burkhard Schnepel to point these things out to me.

6. Minou Fuglesang has worked on the popularity of Bollywood films among female Kenyan youth in her work *Veils and Videos* (1994: 7, 163–70, 302–3), while Heike Behrend has concentrated on the influence of Bollywood on Kenyan photography (1998). Brian Larkin (1997, 2000, 2003), Graham Furniss (2003), and Yusufu M. Adamu (2002) have written about the popularity and influence of Bollywood films on Hausa culture. Awam Amkpa (2004) has done research on the influence of Bollywood on Ghanaian cinema and religion, and Dana Rush (1999; see also her article in this volume) has researched the incorporation of imported Hindu chromolithographic imagery in Benin voodoo. Marloes Janson has also worked on the popularity of a Pakistani (Islamic) religious movement in the Gambia (2005). Little research has been done in the francophone parts of Africa such as Senegal. Suzanne Scheld came across Bollywood when looking at the *style indou* dress style in her dissertation on clothing consumption among youth in Dakar (2003). As a reply to my request placed on H-Net Africa and H-Net West-Africa, Allen Roberts from UCLA mentioned that Polly Nooter Roberts once filmed women and children imitating Bollywood dancing on a rooftop gathering in Dakar.

7. There are many issues I cannot address in one article. I can refer to my forthcoming article in *Sociologus* for more information on the dancing with snakes and the relation with the *dance indou* in Paris (see infra), and especially for a more elaborate discussion of the concept of orientalism and imagination.

8. In her article in the present volume, Dana Rush also mentions the process of incorporation of Indian imagery in West African voodoo started in the 1950s. This is remarkable, as the presence of Indian commodities in West Africa dates back to the fifteenth century (mainly Indian cloth traded by Portuguese), while the spread of images started in the late nineteenth century. Further on in her text, Rush says that Hindu films are "another likely source for Hindu imagery" used in voodoo. Does this

mean there would be a relation between the introduction of Bollywood and the incorporation of Indian imagery, which both have to be situated in the 1950s? According to Rush, there is a relationship between the introduction of Bollywood films and the incorporation of Indian lithographs into Vodun, as the first "proved" the importance of Indian gods (interpreted as Vodun gods) in Vodun practice (Dana Rush, personal communication).

9. Bollywood has also had a huge impact on local video and literature production in Nigeria. See Larkin (1997, 1998, 2003) for an elaborate discussion of this.

10. I have deliberately chosen to use the word "participant" instead of "informant," as the latter actually finds its origin in the judicial sphere (Leiris, cited in Jamin 1996: 38–39) and therefore suggests an unequal relationship. If Leiris already in the 1930s objected to the way ethnographic fieldwork during the Dakar-Djibouti expedition, led by Marcel Griaule, was conceived as "a protocol of inquiry just like those done by the police," using "judicial metaphors," I think nowadays the need to leave the term "informant" behind has become a necessity. We should look for less power-laden terms which suggest a rather equal relationship and which reflect the interactiveness of the research process. I find that "participant" is a more neutral term which does include the interactiveness of the process: everyone (including myself) has been a "participant" in the research we conducted together.

11. Although many films were subtitled in French by Egyptian agencies, it must be said that the majority of women (especially in the years 1950–1980) were illiterate.

12. It must be said, however, that in most Bollywood films, the narrative structure follows a prefixed pattern, and the story is usually not that difficult to follow even if one does not understand the dialogues (something which is also mentioned by Fuglesang 1994: 166–70). According to Larkin, the same reason accounts for the success of action films (1997: 435).

13. The names in this article are pseudonyms.

14. Clapping one's hands during a conversation is a way to emphasize one's statement.

15. Indophiles often talked about approaches between Senegalese and Indian culture.

16. The *style indou*, e.g., is a Senegalese mixed dress style combining "Senegalese" and "Indian" elements.

17. Larkin also mentioned this film being the most popular one in Hausa land (1997: 433). It is a film about a poor village woman who fights against a rich landowner who exploits the poor farmers. Mehboob Khan, the producer, was not formally associated with the Communist Party, though the fact that he used a hammer and sickle as the emblem for his production house, Mehboob Productions (http://www. upperstall.com/people/mehboob.html), might show his inclination toward communist ideology.

18. Fulani (Peul) are nomadic groups spread over different West African countries.

19. Larkin made the same remark (1997: 435). Fuglesang also mentioned that there are many Arabic loanwords in Swahili and Hindi, accounting for the linguistic similarities (1994: 303).

20. Pikine is a suburb created in the 1960s and 1970s as a solution for the ever-increasing immigration from rural areas to Dakar.

21. Though the concept of *négritude* was not invented by Senghor, he applied it to Senegalese politics.

22. Note that jazz, blues, and salsa did not sound that unfamiliar to the African ear. They carried the original African sound and rhythms with them and now "returned" in different variations (Shain 2002: 89, 91). In the case of Bollywood music, which is strongly influenced by north Indian Hindusthani music, one can say that this Arabic influence (present in Hindusthani music) also sounds familiar to Africans.

23. Tamil is a Dravidian language spoken in southern India.

24. Scholars continue to follow his footsteps, such as A. M. Lam at the Department of History at the University Cheikh Anta Diop (UCAD), who still theorizes and publishes on this subject.

25. The Wolof term for homosexual is *góorjigéen*, which literally means "man-woman," referring to someone who has a mix of male and female elements.

26. For a discussion of a "process of cultural translation" (a term applied by Larkin) in the context of the influence of Bollywood films on local literature production, see Larkin (2003: 184–88, 1997: 418–32).

27. *Something, Something Is Happening to My Heart*—a popular Bollywood film from 1998.

28. *Mbalax* is the popular Senegalese music mixing *sabar* drums with "Western" instruments such as guitar and keyboard.

29. See, e.g., O'Shea's article "At home in the World? The Bharata Natyam Dancer as Transnational Interpreter" (2003) on the popularity of this dance form on an international stage.

30. It made me think about gift-giving ceremonies I had seen at marriages.

31. I experienced this system of money giving: although many people said they really appreciated my dancing, I "earned" very little money on a *soirée*, and received it only from a few people I knew very well.

32. *Griots* (*géwél*) are singers, musicians who sing praises of the noble they accompany.

33. As mentioned above, pale skin is considered very beautiful. The use of products for bleaching the skin is, however, not always without risk.

34. See Pinxten 1994: 34.

35. For a discussion of this concept, see Pinxten 1994: 37–40.

36. There exists, however, a "snake dance" in Bharata Natyam and folk dance (e.g., Rajasthani Gypsy dance) where the dancer imitates the movement of the snake (Rajesh Karma, Bharata Natyam teacher at Kalaksetra Institute, Chennai, personal communication September 2004). This "snake dance" has been adopted in movies. The snake dancing indeed also made me think about *Nagin*, a Bollywood film from 1954 with Vyjantimala and Pradeep Kumar, which was (and still is ) also very popular in Senegal.

37. Mami Wata imagery might also have been inspired directly by Indian prints circulating via Indian merchants in West Africa. For more information about Mami Wata imagery, see Drewal (2002).

38. Dancing with snakes, as an exoticization of Indian dance, also occurred in Paris in the early twentieth century. The snakes were used during the *numéro hindou*, performed by Western dancers in the "music-halls," entertainment theatres such as the famous *Moulin Rouge*. See Décoret-Ahiha (2004: 128–46) for a discussion of this. I elaborate on this (in comparison with *danse indou* in Senegal) in my forthcoming article in *Sociologus*.

39. Dox mentions that higher-class performers in Egypt would not unveil unless the performance was intended as parody (2004: 22).

40. In Eastern Body Aesthetics, choreographers wanted to get away from a strictly Western-dominated ballet and contemporary dance vocabulary by incorporating, for example, *tai chi* (Chen 2004). Chen also points out that a space on the international stage means the need to self-orientalize. One can talk about a neo-colonial phenomenon in the world's art market where "Third World" arts are consumed by primarily "First World" audience (2004: 5).

## Works Cited

Adamu, Y. M. 2002. "Between the Word and the Screen: A Historical Perspective on the Hausa Literary Movement and the Home Video Invasion." *Journal of African Cultural Studies* 15.2: 203–13.

Amkpa, A. 2004. *Theatre and Postcolonial Desires.* London: Routledge.

Appadurai, A. 1991. "Global Ethnoscapes: Notes and Queries for a Transnational Anthropology." In *Recapturing Anthropology: Working in the Present,* ed. R. Fox, 191–210. Santa Fe, N.M.: SAR Press.

——. 1996. *Modernity at Large: Cultural Dimensions of Globalization.* Minneapolis: University of Minnesota Press.

Behrend, H. 1998. "Love à la Hollywood and Bombay in Kenyan Studio Photography." *Paideuma* 44: 139–53.

Bhabha, H. K. 1994. *Location of Culture.* London: Routledge.

Casey, C. 1997. *Medicines for Madness: Suffering, Disability and the Identification of Enemies in Northern Nigeria.* Ph.D. diss., University of California. Ann Arbor, Mich.: UMI, 1997.

Chambers, I. 1994. *Migrancy, Culture, Identity.* London: Routledge.

Chen, Y. 2004. "The Making of Taiwanese/Chinese/Eastern Identity on Taiwan's Dance Stage." Paper presented at the CORD/WDA/ICKL International Dance Conference, Taipei, Taiwan, 1–4 August 2004.

Decoret-Ahiha, A. 2004. *Les danses exotiques en France, 1880–1940.* Paris: Centre Nationale de la Danse.

Dox, D. 1996. "Thinking through Veils: Questions of Culture, Criticism and the Body." *Theatre Research International* 22.2: 150–61.

——. 2004. "Dancing Their Way out of Orientalism." Paper presented at the CORD/WDA/ICKL International Dance Conference, Taipei, Taiwan, 1–4 August 2004.

——. 2005. "Spirit from the Body: Belly Dance as a Spiritual Practice." In *Belly Dance: Orientalism, Transnationalism, and Harem Fantasy,* ed. A. Shay and B. Sellers-Young. Costa Mesa, Calif.: Mazda.

Drewal, H. J., ed. 2002. *Mami Wata.* Los Angeles: Fowler Museum of Cultural History, University of California, Los Angeles.

Foucault, M. 1984. "The Order of Discourse." In *Language and Politics,* ed. M. Shapiro, 108–38. New York: New York University Press.

——. 2003. *The Archaeology of Knowledge.* London: Routledge.

Friedman, K. E., and J. Friedman. 1995. "Global Complexity and the Simplicity of Everyday Life." In *Worlds Apart: Modernity through the Prism of the Local,* ed. D. Miller, 135–68.. Association of Social Anthropologists, Fourth Decennial Conference. London: Routledge.

Fuglesang, M. 1994. *Veils and Videos: Female Youth Culture on the Kenyan Coast.* Stockholm Studies in Social Anthropology, no. 32. Stockholm: Dept. of Social Anthropology, Stockholm University.

Furniss, G. 2003. "Hausa Popular Literature and Video Film: The Rapid Rise of Cultural Production in Times of Economic Decline." Working Papers no. 27 Institut für Ethnologie und Afrikastudien. Mainz, Germany: Dept. of Anthropology and African Studies.

Jaikumar, P. 2003. "Bollywood Spectaculars." *World Literature Today* 77.3/4: 24–30.

Jamin, Jean. 1996. *Michel Leiris. Mirroir de l'Afrique.* Paris: Editions Gallimard.

Janson, M. 2005. "Roaming About for God's Sake: The Upsurge of the Tabligh Jama'at in the Gambia." *Journal of Religion in Africa* 35.4: 450–81.

Kaur, R. 2002. "Viewing the West through Bollywood: A Celluloid Occident in the Making." *Contemporary South Asia* 11.2: 199–209.

Larkin, B. 1997. "Indian Films and Nigerian Lovers: Media and the Creation of Parallel Modernities." *Africa* 67.3: 406–40.

———. 1998. "Hausa Dramas and the Rise of Video Culture in Nigeria." In *Nigerian Video Films*, ed. J. Haynes, 209–41. Jos, Nigeria: Nigerian Film Corp.

———. 2000. "Hausa Dramas and the Rise of Video Culture in Nigeria." In *Nigerian Video Films*, rev. ed., ed. J. Haynes, 209–41. Athens, Ohio: Ohio University Center for International Studies.

———. 2003. "Itineraries of Indian Cinema: African Videos, Bollywood and Global Media." In *Multiculturalism, Postcoloniality, and Transnational Media*, ed. E. Shohat and R. Stam, 170–92. New Brunswick, N.J.: Rutgers University Press.

Ndiaye, M. 1980. "Comparative Studies in Dravidian and Pulaar Languages: A Possible Relationship." Ph.D. diss., University of Annamalai, India.

O'Shea, Janet. 2003. "At home in the World? The Bharata Natyam Dancer as Transnational Interpreter." *Drama Review* 47.1: 176–86.

Pinxten, R. 1994. *Culturen sterven langzaam: Over interculturele communicatie* [Cultures die slowly: On intercultural communication]. Antwerpen, Belgium: Houtekiet.

Rush, D. 1999. "Eternal Potential: Chromolithographs in *Vodunland.*" *African Arts* 32.4: 61–75.

Rutherford, J. 1990. "The Third Space: Interview with Homi Bhabha." *Identity: Community, Culture, Difference.* London: Lawrence and Wishart.

Savigliano, M. 1995. *Tango and the Political Economy of Passion.* Boulder, Colo.: Westview Press.

Scheld, S. 2003. "Clothes Talk: Youth Modernities and Commodity Consumption in Dakar, Senegal." Ph.D. diss., City University of New York.

Sellers-Young, B. 2004. "Whose Body Is This? Orientalism, Dance, and Women in Popular Culture." Paper presented at the CORD/WDA/ICKL International Dance Conference, Taipei, Taiwan, 1–4 August 2004.

Sellers-Young, B., and A. Shay. 2005. "Belly Dance: Orientalism–Self-Exoticism." In *Belly Dance: Orientalism, Transnationalism, and Harem Fantasy*, ed. A. Shay and B. Sellers-Young. Costa Mesa, Calif.: Mazda.

Shain, R. M. 2002. "Roots in Reverse: Cubanismo in Twentieth-Century Senegalese Music." *International Journal of African Historical Studies* 35.1: 83–101.

Straubhaar, J. D. 1991a. "Beyond Media Imperialism: Asymmetrical Interdependence and Cultural Proximity." *Critical Studies in Mass Communication* 8: 39–59.

———. 1991b. "The Reception of Telenovelas and Other Latin American Genres in the Regional Market: The Case of the Dominican Republic." *Studies in Latin American Popular Culture* 10: 191–206.

Tremblay, R. C. 1996. "Representation and Reflection of Self and Society in the Bombay Cinema." *Contemporary South Asia* 5.3: 303–14.

Vander Steene, G. Forthcoming. "Processes of Cultural Translation as a Postcolonial Dynamic in Senegalese Hindu Dances." *Sociologus.*

# 6

## The Idea of "India" in West African Vodun Art and Thought

Dana Rush

> . . . I grew up with two ideas of India. The first idea . . . was
> about the kind of country from which my ancestors had
> come. . . . There was a second India. It balanced the first.
> This second India was the India of the independence
> movement, the India of greatness. . . . This was the identity
> I took to India on my first visit in 1962. And when I got
> there, I found it had no meaning in India.
>
> —V. S. Naipaul, *India: A Million Mutinies Now*

There are many ideas of India.[1] As noted above by Trinidadian author
V. S. Naipaul, "India" does not always refer to the peninsula region of
South Asia, south of the Himalayas, between the Bay of Bengal and the Arabian Sea, where Hindus and others live and revere their gods. In west African Vodun art and thought, the idea of India is not simply one of geography
or theology.[2] Rather, "India" offers boundless aesthetic and spiritual opportunities in both time and space, going beyond the empirical known world
into the un-empirical, un-known world. Through an exploration of origins
and deployments of Indian imagery within contemporary Vodun art and
thought, outside influences emerge as constituent components therein,
whose origins have, at times, become lost in the process of creation. In this
analysis of the incorporation of Indian imagery into contemporary Vodun
art and thought, the present-day concept of globalism with its compelling

notions of international boundary-less-ness can be understood in a way which goes far beyond the visible, tangible, human domain into a world in which eternity and divine infinity are collapsed into the here and now.

Vodun arts document Vodun histories. For centuries, the coastline of Bénin Republic and Togo has acted as a vortex, incorporating items and ideas from across the sea into its littoral. This ongoing phenomenon has generated a fertile mosaic of international, transcontinental, and transoceanic peoples, histories, commodities, and spirits, made manifest in Vodun art and thought. The following chapter focuses upon a relatively contemporary aspect of this "vortextual phenomenon," that is, the incorporation of "India"—via chromolithographic imagery (mostly Hindu)—into the eternally organic religious system of Vodun. Although the idea of India in Vodun art and thought probably emerged no earlier than the late 1950s, it is the ancient, essentially elastic, conceptual system of Vodun which has allowed it to thrive on both sides of the Atlantic Ocean. The integration of Indian chromolithographs into Vodun epistemologies is exemplary of the overall incorporative sensibilities of Vodun art and thought.

### The Essential Sea

Coasts kept alive the dialectic between the
seen and the unseen . . . tangible horizons
making the unattainable attainable . . .
contract[ing] time as well as space.

—Paul Carter, "Dark with Excess of Bright: Mapping
the Coastlines of Knowledge"

In Vodun thought, India spirits are invariably from the sea, rendering "India" and the sea synonymous; they are both known yet unknowable, a paradox mediated through art. Because the sea is as deep as one's own imagination, and vice-versa, the breadth of India spirits, associated India arts, and India experiences is inexhaustible. The Atlantic coastline of Bénin Republic and Togo simultaneously effaces and defines the meeting of land and sea: that is where Africa and "India" merge. It is a place where awareness can be Janus-faced, and where space and time can and do alter. At the same time, this very coastline—liminal as it may be—is a gateway to centuries of intercontinental and transoceanic interactions and exchanges. This particular seaboard was a very real marketplace during the transatlantic slave trade (Law 1977, 1991; Lovejoy 1986; Manning 1982). As such, this coastline qualifies as a "diaspora space," a concept introduced by Avtar Brah as a meeting point of "economic, political, cultural, and psychic [spiritual] processes . . . where multiple subject positions are juxtaposed, contested, proclaimed, or disavowed, where the permitted and the prohibited perpetually interrogate, and where the accepted and the transgressive imperceptibly mingle" (1996: 208). The idea of "diaspora space" thus encapsulates the global position of "culture as a site of travel" (Clifford 1992). In effect, we confront along this west African seaboard two simultaneous processes in which the sea functions as both a passageway to vast cultural and spiritual potential and as an exceedingly lucrative portal to centuries of travel and commodities exchange. The idea of "India" in Vodun art and thought occupies its own "diaspora space."[3]

## Chromolithographs in Vodun

If images are invested with power, how then
are they made to work?

—David Freedberg, *The Power of Images*

Lithography, or the process of making prints from a metal plate or a flat surface of stone, was invented in 1796 by Aloys Senefelder of Prague, and color lithography was in use in Europe by the middle of the nineteenth century (Smith 1997: 6) In India, however, there was a long history of text printing before the advent and spread of lithographs. In 1556, the Portuguese intended to send the first printing press—via Goa, India—to missionaries in Abyssinia. However, the Abyssinian emperor changed his mind about welcoming missionaries; thus the press remained in Goa, where the first book was published on Indian soil in 1556 (Babb and Wadley 1995: 21). From that point on, printed texts were used extensively by missionaries to spread Christianity in India. Then, in the nineteenth century, print technology became a major factor in the transmission of Hindu and Muslim religious traditions through written text. Chromolithograph presses were operating in India by the late nineteenth century, and color prints began circulating throughout the subcontinent around the same time. Raja Ravi Varma (1848–1906), a south Indian portrait and landscape painter, is usually cited as the principal influence in the emergence of India's popular religious poster and calendar art. He not only painted popular portrayals of gods, goddesses, and legendary episodes, but he is also credited with setting up the first chromolithographic press in Bombay in 1891 (Inglis 1995: 58). In fact, before 1900 India had several chromolithographic presses, one of which is the press of Hem Chander Bhargava and Company in Chadni Chowk, Dehli, which has been continuously printing chromolithographs of religious subjects for over one hundred years (Babb and Wadley 1995: 22).

How and when did chromolithographs arrive in west Africa and become a part of the visual theology of Vodun? The potential for imported prints to have been seen in west Africa first existed shortly after the first color reproductions were executed in Bombay in 1891 (Inglis 1995:22). It is critical, however, to note that the presence of Indian commodities in west Africa dates back to the fifteenth century when Portuguese sea commanders and merchants of the British and Dutch East India Company began active participation in the trading and selling of Indian cloth between India and coastal west Africa (Eicher and Erekosima 1996). Consequently, the sea bordering this coast has been associated with foreign wealth and power since the fifteenth century. Then, the institution of colonial empires and increasing trade, connecting Africa with both the East and the West, brought about the quick spread of images that were incorporated into west African artistic and religious expression beginning as early as the late nineteenth century. Now, the contemporary appeal of Indian gods to west Africans has led to a burgeoning African market in Indian prints. According to Henry Drewal, around World War I, when Indian merchants set up firms along the west African coast, west African peoples began observing aspects of Hindu religious practice such as that of Gujeratis, devotees of Lakshmi, the Hindu goddess of wealth and patroness of merchants (1988b: 174–76).

Elaborately detailed Indian chromolithographs have been incorporated into the religious system of Vodun precisely because of their open-ended structures and richly suggestive imagery, which allow them to embody wildly diverse ideas, themes, beliefs, histories, and legends in Vodun art and thought. The prints both teach and serve as vehicles of divine worship; they suggest rules of conduct, recount legendary narratives, and act as objects of adoration. The specific animals, foods, drinks, jewelry, body markings, and accoutrements within these chromolithographs have become sacred to the Vodun spirits represented. Although, at some point, these images were newly seen, they have been approached in Vodun as something that was already known and understood; as something already familiar within the Vodun pantheon. These Indian gods have not been *combined with* local gods, but rather they *are* local gods.

Henry Drewal has documented the earliest evidence to date of the incorporation of a foreign printed image into a local religious vocabulary in west Africa. He has traced the history of the most popular representation of the water spirit-cum-seductress, known as Mami Wata, which was based on a late nineteenth-century chromolithograph of a snake charmer in a German circus from an original European painting (Drewal 1988a, 1988b, 1996; Salmons 1977). Dating from circa 1885, the chromolithograph was reprinted in large numbers in India and England and distributed widely in sub-Saharan west Africa. The edition that Drewal illustrates (1988b: 169, fig. 7) was printed in Bombay by the Shree Ram Calendar Company in 1955 to copy an earlier version provided by a trader in Kumasi, Ghana. During 1955–1956 twelve thousand copies (10 x 14") were sent to this trader and another trader in Kumasi (Drewal 1988b: 183, n. 6). The image has

FIGURE 6.1. Chromolithograph based on a late nineteenth-century painting of a snake charmer in a German circus, commonly known throughout West Africa as the water spirit Mami Wata. Lomé, Togo. October 1995. Photo: Dana Rush.

Figure 6.2. Indian and Christian prints at Asigamé market in Lomé, Togo. January 1999. Photo: Dana Rush.

since been reproduced *en masse* (figure 6.1) and has been found in the Dominican Republic and Haiti (Houlberg 1996) as well as in botánicas throughout the United States in the form of printed images, statues, candles, and pendants.[4]

Although by far the most popular chromolithograph, the image of the snake charmer is by no means the only print found in west African religious practice. Chromolithographs from an ancient Indian epic, the *Ramayana*, and other Hindu lore are available for purchase in local markets. There seems to be a quick turnover of the chromolithographs of Hindu gods at the market stands: as images are sold, new images are available. Some chromolithographs are wrinkled and slightly torn older images straight from India, while others are newly printed in and imported from Nigeria and England. There is a wide repertoire of chromolithographic imagery available including prints of Rama, Sita, Hanuman, Shiva, Datta-treya, Hare Krishnas, Shirdi Sai Baba, Buddha, Guru Nanak, and al-Buraq, as well as the Pope, Eve, Jesus Christ, the Virgin Mary, and various Christian saints (figure 6.2).[5] Other prints, available from Indian stores in the form of decorative promotional calendars, express a clear first-order advertising purpose within the Indian community. These same prints, however, have second- and third-order significances within Vodun artistic and spiritual sensibilities: the super-abundance of flowers, gold, jewels, coins, and other luxurious items surrounding the spiritually charged deities depicted in these prints function as links into particular Vodun sensibilities, especially those of Mami Wata, the Vodun of wealth and beauty who commands the sea and is known for her allure as a source of potential wealth, both religious and economic (figure 6.3).

Even though the exact arrival date of Indian chromolithographs along coastal west Africa is unknown, the images have become quite significant in contemporary Vodun practice. Though in demand, Indian prints are no longer as readily available for acquisition. Within view of the Atlantic coast, a particular market stand in the Asigamé Market in Lomé, Togo, was a "hot spot" for purchasing Indian prints in the 1990s (figure 6.4, and see figure 6.2). People used to travel there from the bordering countries of Bénin and Ghana to seek out India spirit prints from Mama Sikavi, the very discerning market woman who kept her stand full to overflowing with wide varieties of constantly changing images. She refused to sell these prints at a reasonable price, and some people would save money for up to a year just to purchase one—that is, to have access to "India" and the powers within. After working the same market stand for close to twenty years (early 1980s until 2004), Mama Sikavi is no longer selling prints.[6] However, a print seller around the corner continues to sell India prints, though his selection remains nowhere near as comprehensive as that of Mama Sikavi. Another likely source for Hindu imagery is the popular Hindu movie corpus shown throughout Africa.[7]

### The Use of Images

Most Vodun art forms are forever unfinished, and the seemingly static nature of a mass-produced image, such as a chromolithograph, is, indeed, misleading. Although a chromolithograph used in Vodun may appear "finished," it continues to change in terms of both form and meaning: it can expand in form from a two-dimensional image into three-dimensional spiritual and artistic presences in shrines, sculptures, and temple paintings; and a three-dimensional shrine can be represented by a chromolithograph as an ethereally collapsed ready-made two-dimensional shrine. Visual and spiritual saturation in an economical and portable equivalence is the appeal of the chromolithographic image in Vodun art and thought.

Chromolithographs in this "diaspora space" exist in an infinite aesthetic and spiritual synesthesia in which visual impact itself induces godly presence. For much Vodun art, "completion" is not the point. Hard as one tries, one will not find a positivist rationale behind the perpetually unfinished Vodun shrine, growing, changing, accumulating; continually transformed

जय श्री कृष्ण

est compliments from:

# STE. JUPITER ✳

### IMPORTS & EXPORTS

## B. P. 276, C/389 DANTOKPA

# COTONOU

Rep. DU BENIN     §★§     TEL: (229) 314755
FAX: (229) 314765

FIGURE 6.3. Calendar from Societé Jupiter of Cotonou, Bénin, featuring Indian deities that have adopted and adapted into Vodun spirits. Cotonou, Bénin. January 1994. Photo: Dana Rush.

Figure 6.4. Market stand at Asigamé market in Lomé, Togo, where chromolithographs of Hindu, Christian, and other imagery are sold. Koffi "Balbi" Gadoh points to a popular print depicting Hanuman. Lomé, Togo. February 1999. Photo: Dana Rush.

and transforming. Following the same line of thought, even if the outward form of a mass-produced chromolithograph seems complete, the name can change, the meaning can change, and the power residing within it can change depending on how it is used. A chromolithograph which appears ostensibly complete may, in fact, never be complete: not only its uses but its visual form when reproduced in temple paintings, shrines, and sculptures actualizes this eternal potential to adapt in response to any new problem or situation that arises needing spiritual guidance or intervention, or in acknowledgment of the changing demands and desires of the spirits.

Clearly, chromolithographs are outwardly mobile in that they are easily transported, copied, and reproduced. It is precisely this quality that allows for quick external proliferation. Equally important is the fact that chromolithographs are inwardly mobile: their inherent forms and meanings do not remain stationary and thus accumulate multiple readings. The same chromolithograph easily attracts a second and third audience and new range of interpretations and conventions beyond, for example, the first-order Hindu reading of the same image. Although various gods in separate Vodun compounds may be derivatives of the same Hindu image, they take on lives of their own. Similar images appear in different Vodun settings with different names. In most cases, the images are unrelated in any way except that they look alike. Arguments among Vodun priests and priestesses in different Vodun compounds ensue over "correct" appellation and use of images in religious practice, while the images in dispute are hardly, if ever, local in origin. Admittedly, there is overlap and grounds for potential confusion. However, what appears at first glance to be confusion can, in a "diaspora space," become multi-layered fusion.

### *Ramayana* Remix

The monkey-king, Hanuman, is a popular Indian hero who became a god in the ancient Hindu epic the *Ramayana*. Dedicated to Rama, the seventh incarnation of Vishnu, the epic narrates the trials and tribulations of Rama and his wife Sita as they go into exile, accompanied by Rama's brother Lakshmana. Sita is abducted by Ravanna, the demon-king of Lanka (now Sri Lanka), and is rescued by Hanuman, the faithful servant of Rama (Narayan 1972).

Attingali is a powerful witch-fighting Islamic Vodun concentrated in and around Abomey-Calavie, Bénin.[8] The strongest soldier in the Attingali pantheonis known as Foulani[9] Agbokanli, "Fulani cow-animal." An Attingali temple painting of Foulani Agbokanli (figure 6.5) resembles a chromolithograph from the *Ramayana*, illustrating a victorious Hanuman with a diminutive Rama and Lakshmana on his shoulders (figure 6.6). The demon king Ahiravana (Ravanna's son or, in some versions, his brother) is shown prostrate under Hanuman's foot as at the end of the *Ramayana* episode in the netherworld of Patala Loka (Lutgendorf 1995: 3–8). Yet, in Abomey-Calavie, the same small figures are known as Ablewa, or the "angels" of Foulani Agbokanli, who help him fight witchcraft. Another Foulani Agbokanli shrine, a five-minute walk away, displays the same Indian chromolithograph, but there Foulani Agbokanli has captured a second witch (figure 6.7). Thus, the chromolithographic image is ever-evolving. Although they look identical, there is no relationship between Foulani Agbokanli, the Fulani cow-animal, and Hanuman, the Indian monkey king.

An image photographed along the coast of Ghana, between Cape Coast and Accra, represents neither Hanuman nor Foulani Agbokanli, but a hero in a Fante belief system (figure 6.8).[10] The breadth of chromolithographic influence becomes even more evident in an Ibibio shrine sculpture likely found in a Kalahari Ijo shrine in the eastern Delta region of Nigeria. It dates from the last half of the nineteenth century. William Arnett proposes that the sculpture quite likely comes from a southern Ibibio group, such as Anang (illustrated in Arnett and Wittmer 1978).

### Hindu Images in Mami Wata Vodun

Along coastal Bénin and Togo, Mami Wata is much more than a single spirit: she is an entire pantheon. For any new problem or situation that arises needing spiritual intervention or guidance, a new Mami Wata spirit arises from the sea. Life's recently introduced or previously unfamiliar uncertainties (such as birth control, abortion, prostitution, and homosexuality, for example) often are embraced and made sense of through Hindu imagery used in Mami Wata religious practice.

The Mamisi (wives or devotees of Mami Wata) not only worship their own demanding spirits from the sea and new spirits addressing the needs of a quickly changing society, but they must also venerate the principal gods found in most Vodun houses such as Gu, Sakpata, Xeviosso, Tohosu, and Hohovi.[11] Mamisi have found an ingenious way to do so, with the aesthetic and spiritual flair that has come to be expected of Mami Wata. They have incorporated parts of the Hindu pantheon into the worship of these main gods who are represented by lavish Hindu chromolithographs reproduced on temple walls and placed in Mami Wata shrines.

Ghanaian artist Joseph Kossivi Ahiator is the most sought-after India spirit temple painter in Bénin, Togo, and Ghana. He consults his own array of chromolithographs when commissioned to paint Vodun temples and then elaborates the images based on his own dreams coupled with the dreams and desires of the temple owner. Ahiator is very connected to the

FIGURE 6.5.
Temple painting of Foulani
Agbokanli (Fulani cow-animal),
the ultimate witch-fighter in the
Attingali Vodun. Abomey-Calavie,
Bénin. December 1994.
Photo: Dana Rush.

FIGURE 6.6. Chromolithograph of
Hanuman, the Hindu monkey-
king, purchased from market
stand in Lomé, Togo. October
1995. Photo: Dana Rush.

FIGURE 6.7. Shrine painting of Foulani Agbokanli catching two witches, based on the chromolithograph of Hanuman. Abomey-Calavie, Bénin. December 1994. Photo: Dana Rush.

sea. He was born with India spirits and he visits "India" often; sometimes in his dreams, sometimes while at the beach. These travels thoroughly inform his art.[12] In a Vodun temple in Cotonou, Bénin, Ahiator has envisioned and executed representations of a particular set of spirits within the Mami Wata pantheon, which are recognizably derived from Hindu chromolithographs (figure 6.9). Ahiator has placed this particular set of spirits within the Mami Wata pantheon under the protective arch of the paired rainbow serpent Dan Aida Wedo, often associated with Mami Wata. Such conflation is based on the iridescent rainbow-like serpent, which encircles Mami Wata's neck and arches over her head in her most common depiction based on the snake charmer chromolithograph (figure 6.1). A discussion of some local-cum-India spirits illustrated in this large mural follows.

### Hanuman/Gniblin

Hanuman is often referred to as Gniblin in various Mami Wata Vodun in Bénin, Togo, and Ghana. Featured prominently in the center of the

FIGURE 6.8. Painting in a temple on the coast between Accra and Cape Coast, Ghana, based on the chromolithograph of Hanuman. January 1996. Photo: Dana Rush.

FIGURE 6.9. Right side of mural of Vodun spirits associated with Mami Wata and based on Hindu chromolithographs. Painted by Joseph Kossivi Ahiator. Cotonou, Bénin. February 1996. Photo: Dana Rush.

mural is a painting of the powerful half-animal, half-human super-being called Gniblin Egu, which can be translated as "cow-person" of Egu in Mina (left side of figure 6.9).[13] Gniblin is famous for his power of Egu, the Mina cognate of the Yoruba Ogun, and the Fon Gu, deities of iron, war, and technology. Gniblin Egu is credited with teaching iron technology to people. Hanuman is interpreted as bovine rather than simian, as is Foulani Agbokanli in Attingali. Although Gniblin Egu comes from the sea, Mami Wata adepts hold that he lives on the road and is associated with traffic accidents. He can travel anywhere, and his fiery tail is seen as he flies through the air. If he is angry, he can burn a whole city, and he can use his tail to beat witches.

In the *Ramayana*, Hanuman is revered as Prince Rama's loyal servant and protector who carries the essence of Rama (and sometimes Rama and Sita) with him wherever he goes. A popular chromolithograph (figure 6.10) shows Hanuman responding to the challenge that he does not have the power to do so. Hanuman has torn open his chest and to the bewilderment of his onlookers, reveals Rama and Sita within. Similarly, Gniblin Egu tore open his chest to demonstrate that he carries his deceased parents with him at all times, thus proving his eternal respect for them. Given

The Idea of "India" in West African    163

FIGURE 6.10. Chromolithograph of Hanuman, displayed in an Indian-owned fabric store. Cotonou, Bénin. March 1995. Photo: Dana Rush.

the importance of ancestral veneration among Fon and Mina peoples, Gniblin Egu is both a Vodun spirit and an ancestral shrine.

### Ganesh/Tohosu

To the right of Gniblin Egu is Tohosu Amlina (center of figure 6.9). Tohosu is the Fon Vodun of royalty, human deformations, lakes, and streams. Amlina means "strange" in Mina. The painting of Tohosu is based upon a chromolithograph of Ganesh, the elephant-headed, pot-bellied Hindu god of thresholds, beginnings, and wisdom who removes obstacles. This most popular of Hindu deities is pictured in the top left quadrant of a calendar from Societé Jupiter in figure 6.3. Although he has only one tusk, he has four arms in which he holds a shell, a discus, a club, and a water lily. His means of transportation is a rat, usually depicted in front of him. In Hindu belief, Ganesh is always called upon before the beginning of any new venture, from taking a trip to opening a business.

The image of Ganesh visually encapsulates the Fon spirit of Tohosu: royal (surrounded by wealth, corpulent from luxurious dining) and super-human (a human with an elephant's head and four arms). Although Ganesh is not known to be associated with lakes or streams, Mamisi often recognize the blue background of many Ganesh chromolithographs as representing a watery abode (cf. Drewal 1988b: 171). The chromolithograph reproduced in the upper left quadrant of the Societé Jupiter calendar has directly influenced the Mami Wata worship of Tohosu Amlina. A Mamisi with the spirit of Tohosu Amlina may never kill rats, for this creature, which is always depicted with Ganesh, has become sacred to the spirit's devotees. So, not only do Hindu chromolithographs suggest and reify characteristics already inherent in local gods, but they also introduce, influence, and change already established, albeit organic, religious practice attesting to the profundity of "visual piety" (cf. Morgan 1998).

### Shiva/Mami Dan

To the right of Tohosu in Ahiator's mural is Mami Dan,[14] also called Akpan, whose job is to clear the path for Mami Wata. Mami Dan was born with snakes draped around his neck and always appears that way. He is known to be old as the sea, and his job is to clear the path for Mami Wata. This depiction of Mami Dan comes directly from one of the best-known illustrations of Shiva, called Shiva-Dakshina-Murti or Mahayogi, one of the oldest gods of India (figure 6.11). In Brahamic theology, Shiva is the third member of the divine Trinity of Creator-Preserver-Destroyer, and although Shiva means "the friendly one," he is also the Lord of Destruction. Similarly, the Mina name Akpan means "the one with the bad temper."

The Indian chromolithograph shows Shiva as an ascetic in deep meditation atop the Himalayas. He is wearing a simple loincloth and is seated on a tiger skin, which Mamisi say is the panther who clears the path for Mami Dan and, in turn, Mami Wata. In northern India, Shiva always has a cobra around his neck and a trident, drum, and water jug nearby, all of which also surround Mami Dan in the Mami Wata temple painting.

FIGURE 6.11. Chromolithograph of Shiva purchased in Lomé, Togo. May 1995.
Photo: Dana Rush.

FIGURE 6.12. Painting of nineteen-headed Indian-Vodun god. Painted by Joseph Kossivi Ahiator (on left). Aflao, Ghana. January 2005. Photo: Dana Rush.

Mamisi call the trident *apia*, which is reproduced as a protective tattoo pattern and drawn on the earth with sacred powders. *Apia* tridents are also carried as ritual paraphernalia which, when not in active use, are stored in Mami Wata shrines.[15]

Hindu influence extends well into Nigeria and Togo. Joseph Nevadomsky photographed a chromolithograph of Shiva in a Mami Wata shrine in Benin City, Nigeria (Gore and Nevadomsky 1997: 63, figure 4). Other available prints, including those of the snake charmer, Dattatreya, and Jesus may have influenced a Benin City temple painting, also photographed by Nevadomsky, of a two-headed, double-haloed female Jesus with a snake around his/her waist held up in two of four arms. The foreheads of Jesus are graced with Indian *bindi* spots (Nevadomsky 1997: 58, figure 6).[16]

Two new Indian images have been reincorporated in Ahiator's India spirit Vodun corpus: a nineteen-headed Indian god known as the King of Mami Wata ( figure 6.12), as well as his wife, the nine-headed NaKrishna, based on Ravanna. Unfortunately, Ahiator does not remember the name of the nineteen-headed god, as it was first shown to him in 1977. In January 2005 he saw this image in his dreams; then he saw it while swimming in the ocean and was therefore compelled to paint it.[17]

The Idea of "India" in West African   167

RHADA

FIGURE 6.13. Bas-relief of Shiva (known here as Rhada) at entryway to the Vodun compound of Gilbert Attissou. Aneho, Togo. January 2000. Photo: Dana Rush.


### Aneho's "India"

Aneho, Togo, a coastal town known for its high concentration of Mami Wata devotees, also boasts a strong "diaspora space" of India. Upon entering the compound of a renowned Vodun priest, Gilbert Attissou, one is greeted by bas-reliefs of Shiva (figure 6.13) and Lakshmi flanking the other side of the doorway. Inside his compound, "India" becomes even more profound, and again Shiva prevails (figure 6.14). Through the doorway facing the compound is a shrine room called "India." From left to right on only one of the four fully decorated walls are Mami Wata, Lord Shiva, below is Lakshmi, and on the right is another Mami Wata with a

FIGURE 6.14. Shiva painting on outside of Gilbert Attissou's Vodun shrine room called "India." Aneho, Togo. January 2000. Photo: Dana Rush.

statue and chromolithograph of her three-headed husband Densu (from the Hindu Dattatreya) (figure 6.15). In this shrine room called "India," Attissou explained that the walls were blue because we were below the sea. Another doorway, which led further into an even more sacred space was brimming with more posters of Indian gods, perfumes, powders, alcohol, candles, statuettes, stuffed, plastic and ceramic animals, and other offerings (figure 6.16).

This shrine room—filled with mass-produced lithographs, plastic flowers, and dolls—may appear too obvious, repetitive, and artificial to be taken seriously. However, this imported object-filled site is actually subtle, and powerful within Vodun aesthetic sensibilities. The primary colors and glossy surfaces of things may seem gaudy, but in comparison to the vibrant color and noises of a west African market, these images and objects become pale, yet remain potent; they have power and presence, and most importantly, they work; they make things happen. Rather than "kitsch," these items are spiritual status symbols. This is religious imagery which has reached a high level of commodification, indeed, but on two very different levels: (1) it represents a considerable financial investment on the part of the devotee, and (2) it offers access to powers unattainable through

Figure 6.15. Painted temple wall in Gilbert Attissou's "India" shrine. Aneho, Togo. January 2000. Photo: Dana Rush.

FIGURE 6.16. Inner sanctuary of Gilbert Attissou's "India" shrine. Aneho, Togo. January 2000. Photo: Dana Rush.

any other means. This is a spiritual marketplace, and India spirits reflect the arbitrary nature of power and wealth.

In front of what appears to be a very typical Vodun shrine set-up, Attissou models his favorite Shiva cloth (figure 6.17). However, the shrine is dedicated to Nana-Yo, one of the many Vodun names for Shiva, and in front is a carved yoni receptacle, representing the female principal and origin of Hindu creation, placed here to receive Vodun offerings. Attissou holds Shiva's trident, which he found in an Indian boutique in Lomé, Togo, in the early 1960s. He says that he was always drawn to Indian gods and their power to control the sea. He bought whatever he could afford in these Indian boutiques and forged friendships with the Indian merchants.[18] During the 1960s, Attissou spent numerous hours at the seaboard where he would journey to "India" and find himself surrounded by beautiful things. He would spend months in "India," during a few hours at the beach. His family worried about his obsession with the sea and his curious behavior, so they brought him to a Christian Celeste church in order to exorcise these "demonic" spirits from his system. Christian Celeste, however, deemed these India spirits so powerful that they advised him to nurture them rather than eliminate them. Thus he began incorporating Indian items into his own Mami Wata worship.[19]

FIGURE 6.17. Gilbert Attissou wearing hand-painted Shiva cloth and holding a Shiva trident. He stands in front of his Shiva shrine. Aneho, Togo. January 2000. Photo: Dana Rush.

### Transatlantica: Chromolithograph as Crux

In conjunction with deep spiritual conviction, chromolithographs have been a central and critical feature in the maintenance and proliferation of African-derived religious systems throughout the Americas. The spread of chromolithographic imagery in African diasporic communities is commonly attributed to the stratagem of masking the identities of proscribed African deities. This explanation has proved limiting, and recent scholarship asserts more. In the case of Haiti's Vodun Sen Jak, represented by Catholic chromolithographs of St. James, Donald Cosentino writes that "chromolithographs constitute the single most important contemporary source for the elaboration of Ogou [Sen Jak's African counterpart] theology" (1995: 253).

More than simply a ubiquitous phenomenon in response to oppression and a means of problem solving under the difficult circumstances of enslavement, chromolithographs offered a mechanism for articulating deep-seated, centuries-strong African religious sensibilities. Chromolithographs represented, and continue to represent, Vodun's potential as a means of expression, assertion, creativity, and faith. They are adoptable and adaptable to all circumstances, from the worst to the best, on both sides of the Atlantic.

Within the conceptual "diaspora space" of "India" the late Haitian master assemblage artist Pierrot Barra (1942–1999)[20] incorporated chromolithographic imagery into his work. In figure 6.18, Barra honored Ezili Freda, famous in Haiti and throughout Haitian diasporas as "the goddess of love and luxury . . . a flirtatious Creole woman who adores fine clothes, jewels, perfumes, and lace" (Cosentino 1995: 240–41). She is represented by the Catholic chromolithograph of Mater Dolorosa, Our Lady of Sorrows ( figure 6.19), which graces the background of the piece. In the foreground, however, is another representation of Ezili Freda: a miniature statuette of clearly Indian origin, recognizable by the telltale Hindu *bindi* spot on her forehead. Hindu imagery may have played an even larger role in the artist's work. In his description of Barra's doll-assemblage-creation of the Vodou spirit Ti Jean Danto (with two extra legs and feet extending from her shoulders), Cosentino writes that the artist "has further reconfigured his doll to mirror lithographs of Shiva or Lakshmi, in whose many limbs Hindu worshippers recognize the polydexterity of their gods" (1998: 19, 53, plate 9).[21]

Other examples suggest that Eastern imagery seems to have a relevance and resonance in a large segment of African diaspora communities. The center of Haitian flag maker Clotaire Bazile's Petwo altar (illustrated in Cosentino 1998: 21) features a white ceramic figurine of a clearly Asian

FIGURE 6.18. Altar to Vodou spirit Ezili Freda, by late Haitian artist Pierrot Barra. The spirit is represented by both the catholic chromolithograph of the Mater Dolorosa (Our Lady of Sorrows) and a small ceramic statue of Indian origin. Port-au-Prince, Haiti. July 1997. Photo: Dana Rush.

god (probably Chinese), which fits—unquestionably—into the "diaspora space" of a Haitian shrine. A Gede shrine of *oungan* Saveur St. Cyr in Port-au-Prince, Haiti, has various statues of multilimbed Hindu deities, one of which (probably Lakshmi) St. Cyr identifies as the Virgin Mary.[22] Similarly, in his article on Catholic chromolithographs in Haitian Vodou, Michel Leiris describes Ezili as represented by an image of "Our Lady of Monserrate" which he correlates with what he witnessed a month earlier in a chapel near Carangaise, an area of Guadeloupe known for its Dravidian population. The chapel, which he reports is occasionally visited by Guadeloupeans of African descent, houses a statue which in Haitian Vodou would represent Ezili. In this Guadeloupean context, however, it represents Maryemen (or Madeyemin or Mayêmé or "Marie aimée"), a female Indian deity conflated here with the Virgin Mary. The white cloth that cloaks the figure, except for its face, hides four arms holding a sword, a gold disc, a branch, and a trident, all of which remind Leiris of the accoutrements found in Haitian shrines dedicated to Ezili (Leiris 1952: 206).

FIGURE 6.19. Chromolithograph of Mater Dolorosa, purchased in Chicago, 1993.
Photo: Dana Rush.

Although obscure, Leiris's observation is worth pondering. In this "diaspora space," the Catholic Virgin, the Hindu Lakshmi, and the Vodou Ezili become one and many; they blur from two to three dimensions and back, literally and conceptually.

This Indian-African phenomenon is in no way unidirectional. For some Afro-Trinidadian Indians in Brooklyn, for example, an image of Yemoja, the Yoruba goddess of the river Ogun, represented in a popular chromolithograph by a fair-skinned, long-haired, crowned female figure emerging from the water, can represent Lakshmi, the Hindu goddess of wealth and beauty.[23] In Trinidad, the Indian deity Kali can merge with Shango, the Yoruba god of thunder, lightning, and associated elements.[24] Statues and images of Indian gods are also found in botánicas in major U.S. cities.

The potential of Hindu chromolithographic imagery continues to be recognized as something already familiar within transatlantic Vodou. In her introduction to *Mama Lola: A Vodou Priestess in Brooklyn*, Karen McCarthy Brown recounts how she and a friend visited Mama Lola. Upon seeing—for the first time—Hindu chromolithographs of Krishna and Kali which Brown's friend had with her, the priestess cried, "Let me see . . . You gonna get me some for my altar?" (Brown 1991: 13). Mama Lola recognized instantly that there was a place for these richly suggestive images in her spiritual and religious sensibilities.

### Transatlantic Vortextual Momentum

Chromolithographs in the "diaspora space" of "India" do more than just echo an aesthetic precedent in a quickly changing world: they are, and always have been, essential to the process. The visual theology of chromolithographs in "India"—enhanced in its pervasiveness—reifies mass-production subsumed by inventiveness and faith. Take the truly authentic "aura" of God, multiply it in the Age of Mechanical Reproduction and find the omnipotence of Indian chromolithographs framed in a "diaspora space" Walter Benjamin never imagined (1968). Clearly, the integration of Indian images into Vodun epistemologies, in conjunction with deep spiritual conviction, attests to the ongoing, globally incorporative sensibilities of Vodun art and thought.

### Notes

1. Much of this research is based on a J. Paul Getty Postdoctoral Research Fellowship (1998–99). Thanks to Devi Chari, Elizabeth Corr, Philip Matesic, Stephanie Puccetti, and Kevin Solarte for their uproarious enthusiasm and support in my 2005 quest for a nineteen-headed Indian/Vodun spirit. In adoring memory of my grandmother, Nunu (1918–2005).

2. There are few words in the English language as charged with evocative power as the word "voodoo." The word "voodoo" derives from the west African religious system of Vodun and translates in the Fon language as "spirits." Although Vodun is one of the world's most misunderstood religions, it is, nonetheless, a legitimate and vital system of beliefs that originated in and around the country of Benin Republic and spread to the Caribbean and the Americas during the transatlantic slave trade. Note that I refer to the lowercased term "west Africa" to avoid any reference to colonial designations. That is, west Africa is not a country; it is meant to refer to a geographical region of the continent, which is clarified in the text.

3. This "diaspora space" of "India" is also deeply present in the African cultural imaginings of music (Roy), film (Singh), and dance (Vander Steene) found throughout this volume.

4. In the late 1990s I received a postcard from Senegal upon which was depicted a reverse glass painting by artist Mor Gueye based on this famous "Mami Wata" chromolithograph. Thus, this image is in circulation in Senegal and therefore supports Vander Steene's hypothesis that *dance indou* may have been influenced therein.

5. Chromolithographs from non-Indian cultures are also incorporated into Vodun shrines and temple paintings, but with nowhere near the frequency of Indian images (especially in Mami Wata). For example, I have documented Jesus, the Virgin Mary, and Pope John Paul II in a handful of Vodun temples. However, Christian persona are not regarded as nearly as powerful as those associated with India.

6. Personal communication, Market sellers at Asigamé Market, Lomé, Togo, January 2005.

7. In my quest to learn the origins of Hindu images I found in Vodun temples, I visited Hindu temples in Togo and Ghana, attended services, and talked to practitioners and priests. The walls of the Hindu temples were covered with a wide variety of Hindu chromolithographs, and large, active Hindu shrines were arranged with statues of the same Hindu gods. People attending the services—Togolese, Beninese, Ghanaians, and resident Indians—were devout and learned practitioners of Hinduism. The priests I spoke with concerning Hindu gods being incorporated into Vodun worship felt that the images were obtained through market stands and calendars and then shared among fellow Vodun adepts, which accounted for the "misinterpretation" of the gods. The priests seemed very certain that no one in any of their congregations was a Vodun adept.

8. Attingali originated in northern Ghana and spread to Nigeria. It is also known by abbreviated names such as Attinga and Tinga in Bénin, Alatinga (*al*=owner of, in Yoruba) and Tingare in Nigeria, and Tigare in Ghana. Although "Islamic Vodun" may seem to be a contradiction in terms, it is not. Vodun, as a religious system, incorporates and embraces foreign elements which appear, at first, antithetical in nature. Vodun thrives on apparent contradictions. Islam within the Attingali Vodun relates to its geographical origin in the predominantly Islamic northern Ghana. Within various Islamic Vodun (Attingali and Thron, for example), Islamic symbols (such as the crescent moon and star) are incorporated into their arts, and their practitioners observe holidays such as Ramadan and Tabaski, though the ceremonies are Vodun-ized in interpretation.

9. I am using the French spelling "Foulani" as it is painted on Vodun temples for this particular Vodun. Otherwise it is spelled "Fulani."

10. Another Ghanaian example of this image of Hanuman, the Indian monkey king, is illustrated in *Africa Explores* (Vogel 1991: 127).

11. See Blier (1995: 62) for a concise chart of principal Vodun.

12. Mr. Ahiator is a much sought after artist, especially by Mami Wata priests and priestesses. I have documented and written about his temple paintings along coastal Bénin, Togo, and Ghana. See Rush (forthcoming).

13. The relationship between Gniblin and Egu remains unclear. In *Cultures Vodun: Manifestations, Migrations, Métamorphoses*, Honorat Aguessy (n.d.: 58) in a list of Vodun from the Mono province in Bénin writes that Gniblin is the Vodun of the sacred forest. In "Les Pretres du dieu Nyigble dans la Forêt Sacrée de Bé," Abbé G. Kodjo Aziamble (1981) describes Nyigble (presumably just a different spelling of Gniblin) as the protector of the Sacred Forest of Bé and an important Vodun in the history of the quarter of Lomé called Bé. In *Voodoo*, Gert Chesi describes Gniblin as the most powerful fetish who came from Adja and rules over the holy forest (1980: 26). His symbol is a stone, but he has the shape of a panther.

14. Although this would appear to mean "the mother of Dan Aida Wedo," the term "Mami" is not gendered. Thus a spirit who is a "Mami" is a Mother, but is not necessarily female. Similarly, the suffix *si* (from *asi*) means "wife." Mamisi or Sakpatasi, although literally "wife of Mami" or "wife of Sakpata," refers to an adept of either gender.

15. This image of Shiva is the same image described by Vander Steene in her discussion of *dance indou* elsewhere in this collection.

16. Gert Chesi has photographed many Mami Wata shrines along southern Togo in which Hindu chromolithographs are found, but, unfortunately, he gives very little information concerning these images (Chesi 1979: 67–68, 85, 97–99, 159).

17. In January 2005, I commissioned the nineteen-headed King of Mami Wata mural painted on cloth for the exhibition *Sacred Waters: The Many Faces of Mami Wata and Other Afro-Atlantic Water Spirits* to open at the UCLA Fowler Museum of Cultural History in March 2008. This commission was based on a suggestion Mr. Ahiator had made to me in 1999 when I was working with him. Because he knew of my strong desire to learn about India Spirits, he suggested that he paint wall murals for me on cloth to hang in my bedroom so that I could study during my sleep. He feels that exhibition viewers can travel to "India" if they study his painting.

18. Indian art and artifacts, outside of the Vodun context, are primarily found within the Indian expatriate communities in large cities such at Lomé, Togo, and Cotonou, Bénin.

19. See *Voodoo* by Gert Chesi (1979) for an earlier photograph of Gilbert Attissou's "India" objects.

20. For Barra's obituary see Cosentino (1999.

21. A strong Indian presence in the Caribbean began after the abolition of slavery in 1838, when African slaves were replaced by indentured laborers mostly from India (Bettelheim and Nunley 1988: 120).

22. Personal communication, Eileen Moyer, July 1997.

23. Personal communication, John Peffer, August 1997.

24. Personal communication, Pamela Franco, April 1998.

**Works Cited**

Aguessy, Honorat. N.d. *Cultures Vodoun: Manifestations, Migrations, Métamorphoses (Afrique, Caraibes, Ameriques)*. Cotonou: Institut de Développement et d'Echanges Endogènes (IDEE).

Arnett, William, and Marcilene K. Wittmer. 1978. *Three Rivers of Nigeria*. Atlanta, Ga.: High Museum of Art.

Aziamblé, Abbé G. Kodjo. 1981. "Les Prêtres du dieu Nyigble dans la Forêt Sacrée de Bé." *Responsable de Culte en Mileu Traditionnel, La Voix de St. Gall* 38: 22–26.

Babb, L. A., and S. S. Wadley, eds. 1995. *Media and the Transformation of Religion in South Asia.* Philadelphia: University of Pennsylvania Press.

Benjamin, Walter. 1968. "The Work of Art in the Age of Mechanical Reproduction." *Illuminations.* New York: Harcourt, Brace and World.

Bettelheim, Judith, and John Nunley. 1988. *Caribbean Festival Arts.* Seattle: University of Washington Press.

Blier, Suzanne Preston. 1995. "Vodun: West African Roots of Vodou." In *Sacred Arts of Haitian Vodou,* ed. D. J. Cosentino, 60–87. Los Angeles: UCLA Fowler Museum of Cultural History.

Brah, Avtar. 1996. *Cartographies of Diaspora: Contesting Identities.* London: Routledge.

Brown, Karen McCarthy. 1991. *Mama Lola: A Vodou Priestess in Brooklyn.* Berkeley: University of California Press.

Carter, Paul. 1999. "Dark with Excess of Bright: Mapping the Coastlines of Knowledge." In *Mappings,* ed. Denis Cosgrove. London: Reaktion Books.

Chesi, Gert. 1980. *Voodoo: Africa's Secret Power.* Trans. Ernst Klambauer. Cape Town: C. Struik.

Clifford, James. 1992. "Traveling Cultures." In *Cultural Studies,* ed. L. Grossberg, C. Nelson, and P. Treichler. New York: Routledge.

Cosentino, Donald J. 1995. *Sacred Art of Haitian Vodou.* Los Angeles: UCLA Fowler Museum of Cultural History, 1995.

———. 1998. *Vodou Things: The Art of Pierrot Barra and Marie Cassaise.* Jackson: University Press of Mississippi.

———. 1999. "In Memoriam, Pierrot Barra, 1942–1999." *African Arts* 32.4 (Winter): 16–17.

Drewal, Henry J. 1988a. "Interpretation, Invention, and Re-presentation in the Worship of Mami Wata." In *Performance in Contemporary African Arts,* ed. Ruth M. Stone, 101–39. Bloomington: Folklore Institute, Indiana University.

———. 1988b. "Performing the Other: Mami Wata Worship in Africa." *Drama Review* 32.2: 160–85.

———. 1996. "Mami Wata Shrines: Exotica and the Constitution of Self." In *African Material Culture,* ed. Mary Jo Arnoldi, Christraud Geary, and Kris L. Hardin, 308–33. Bloomington: Indiana University Press.

Eicher, Joanne B., and Tonye V. Erokosima. 1996. "Indian Textiles in Kalabari Funerals." *Asian Art and Culture* 9.2: 68–79.

Freedberg, David. 1989. *The Power of Images: Studies in the History and Theory of Response.* Chicago: University of Chicago Press.

Gore, Charles, and Joseph Nevadomsky. 1997. "Practice and Agency in Mammy Wata Worship in Southern Nigeria." *African Arts* 30.2: 60–69, 95.

Houlberg, Marilyn. 1996. "Sirens and Snakes: Water Spirits in the Arts of Haitian Vodou." *African Arts* 29.2: 30–35, 101.

Inglis, Stephen R. 1995. "Suitable for Framing: The Work of a Modern Master." In *Media and the Transformation of Religion in South Asia,* ed. Lawrence A. Babb and Susan S. Wadley, 51–75. Philadelphia: University of Pennsylvania Press.

Law, Robin. 1977. *The Oyo Empire, c. 1600–c .1836: A West African Imperialism in the Era of the Atlantic Slave Trade.* Oxford: Calendon Press.

———. 1991. *The Slave Coast of West Africa, 1550–1750: The Impact of the Atlantic Slave Trade in an African Society.* Oxford: Calendon Press.

Leiris, Michel. 1952. "Notes sur l'usage de chromolithographies catholiques par les vodouisants d'Haiti." *Les Afro-Americains.* Dakar, Senegal: IFAN Museum.

Lovejoy, Paul E., ed. 1986. *Africans in Bondage: Studies in Slavery and the Slave Trade.* Madison: University of Wisconsin Press.

Lutgendorf, Philip. 1995. "Another Ravanna, Another Rama." Twelfth International Ramayana Conference, Leiden, Netherlands, 28–30 August.

Manning, Patrick. 1982. *Slavery, Colonialism, and Economic Growth in Dahomey, 1640.* Cambridge: Cambridge University Press.

Morgan, David. 1998. *Visual Piety: A History and Theory of Popular Religious Images.* Berkeley: University of California Press.

Naipaul, V. S. 1990. *India: A Million Mutinies Now.* New York: Viking Press.

Narayan, R. K. 1972. *The Ramayana.* New York: Penguin.

Nevadomsky, Joseph. 1997. "Contemporary Art and Artists in Benin City." *African Arts* 30.4: 54–63, 94.

Rush, Dana. Forthcoming. "Somewhere under Dan's Rainbow: Kossivi Ahiator's India Spirits in the Mami Wata Pantheon." *Sacred Waters: The Many Faces of Mami Wata and Other Afro-Atlantic Water Spirits.* Los Angeles: UCLA Fowler Museum of Cultural History.

Salmons, Jill. 1977. "Mammy Wata." *African Arts* 10.3: 8–15.

Smith, H. Daniel. 1997. "Introduction: The Impact of 'God Posters' on Hindus and Their Devotional Traditions." In *Changing Myths and Images: Twentieth-Century Popular Art in India,"* ed. G. J. Lawson, P. Pal, and H. D. Smith. Bloomington: Indiana University Art Museum.

Vogel, Susan. 1991. *Africa Explores: 20th Century African Art.* Munich, Germany: Prestel-Verlag for the Center for African Art (New York).

# 7

## Politics and Poetics of the Namesake:

Barlen Pyamootoo's *Bénarès*, Mauritius

Thangam Ravindranathan

*Oh! Mourir à Bénarès! Mourir au bord du Gange!*
—Pierre Loti, *L'Inde (sans les Anglais)*

*Où va la mémoire / quand nous perdons la mémoire?*
—Khal Torabully, *Appel d'Archipels (ou le livre des miroirs)*

### Introduction

"How would it make you feel to live somewhere and know there was somewhere else with the same name in a different country?" Such is the question posed by Barlen Pyamootoo's *Bénarès* (1999: 40).[1] And it is perhaps as much the question that disconcerts as the context in which it arises. This turn-of-the-century Mauritian novel spans but a few hours, the duration of a return journey. The latter half of the narrative features the homebound leg of the journey, as the protagonists drive from the capital Port Louis in the north of Mauritius to their native Bénarès in the far south. The women who are their companions for the night inquire about the place for which they are bound, feared for its remoteness, its rumored backwardness. In response the unnamed narrator and his friend evoke the derelict state of a village mourning its abandoned sugar mill; they speak of its former employees who have long left or still wander about idly; of playing football in grounds presided over by a grotesque chimney, sole vestige of the deceased mill. But as the titular destination approaches, this text of restrained melancholy charts a different sort of journey. "How would it make you feel to live somewhere and know there was somewhere else with the same name in a different country?" asks the narrator suddenly, unaccountably, to the women. So it is that the specter of the *other* Benares (the city in India and a place of pilgrimage for Hindus) irrupts onto the scene, and that a bound journey through a known landscape suddenly reveals an unsuspected element of unhomeliness. The structure of detour (via the other) resonates in interesting ways with Homi Bhabha's notion of how in modern time the past, present, and future continually haunt each other, instead of staying in their "proper places" (1994: 4). Indeed, the same could be said of modern spatiality. But there is a cryptic quality to Pyamootoo's evocation of Benares, which—within the fabric of a text that reads as explicitly *post-identitarian*—projects a reimagined horizon but seems to suspend closure of the questions thereby implicated. What I propose here is a layered, personal sort of interrogation of the context—historical (cultural) and literary—that is mobilized (even as it is silenced) by *Bénarès*. Only grudgingly does this narrative invite the recovery of a forgotten history; more urgently it seems to demand that one heed the irreducibility of the haunting: *How would it make you feel to live somewhere and know there was somewhere else with the same name in a different country?*

### Benares: Deconstructing Loss

The land where the Ganga does not flow is
likened in a hymn of the Kashi Khanda to
the sky without the sun, a home without a lamp,
a brahmin without the Vedas.

—Diana L. Eck, *Banares: City of Light*

The question, once posed, haunts the homebound journey, its careful, not to say somehow painful, unfolding structuring the economy of the prose. When prompted, the narrator describes the pilgrimage town on the banks of the Ganges, which he claims to have visited the previous August:

> Hindus believe they'll go to paradise if they die in Benares . . . [ . . . ] And that's how it's been for centuries,[ . . . ] lots of people head there as soon as they feel the first signs of death. They leave their homes and their families and embark on what are sometimes very long, arduous journeys just so they can die in Benares and be sure of going to paradise. (Pyamootoo 2004: 41)

The portrait of Benares drawn by the narrator is one that reduces it to its token features: burning *ghats*, moribund pilgrims, buses advertising the attractions of dying on holy banks. A long monologue further expounds on the theme of Benares as the final resting place to which Hindus from all parts flock in slow and miserable fashion (43–45). What emerges from these lines, and from all that concerns the *other* Benares in the book is upon first glance (and in almost caricatural fashion) its privileged *statu loci*, the special properties with which its banks are vested to deliver the pilgrim from the repeated cycle of births and deaths believed in the Hindu tradition to constitute earthly existence. In other words Benares is here referenced primarily as a symbolically charged site in a sacred geography.

Sanctity, in the context of nineteenth-century indentured labor, is, of course, precisely what was at stake for those who crossed the "black waters," left the shores of Hindu land, and believed that in doing so they surrendered their place in the karmic order and complex system of caste. Mauritian poet Khal Torabully evokes "the soul of the Hindu who left the Ganges [and who] was doomed to err perpetually, [ . . . ]cut from the cycle of reincarnation" (Carter and Torabully 2002: 164). Laurent Farrugia notes the "suicide by nostalgia" of certain coolies, who would let themselves die out of "a sense of guilt at having left the original homeland with its cosmogony, its sacred rules, the attachment to purity, the loss of one's place" (qtd. in Carter and Torabully 2002:161). Even a British colonial administrator writing in the latter half of the nineteenth century had described the Indian emigrant as forced to "wander through the ages a starving, suffering, malignant ghost, because his obsequies have not been duly performed" (Crooke 1817: 326). The sense of profanation attached to the crossing of the black waters has indeed come to be a recurrent motif in much of coolie (or "girmit") literature.[2] Its most recent avatar in Mauritian writing is in a historical novel by Natacha Appanah-Mouriquant, which traces the individual trajectories of a few characters as they undertake the voyage of disillusionment from India to Mauritius: "They said that those that crossed the *kala pani* [black waters] lost their caste. That they were damned for several generations and that they were reborn again and again without ever knowing peace. They said that beyond the kala pani there was only misfortune, the sulfur of hell and the cries of wandering souls" (Appanah-Mouriquant 2003: 12).[3] Among the episodes marking the sea voyage is the throwing off board of the corpses of Indian emigrants who die before arrival. The bodies are disposed of in the Indian Ocean after the improvisation of certain rituals by the surviving Indian passengers—chants that are largely opaque to the British passengers on the vessel, but which one of them nonetheless significantly links to the death rites conducted in Benares. In the pathos of this ceremony, where imitation verges on parody, an account is given of the gravest profanation entailed in the crossing of the black waters. In the impossibility of due cremation as per the proper Vedic prescriptions, the disposal of the bodies of the dead in unholy waters to the sound of amateur incantations offers a poignantly literalized staging of the ritual loss and destructuring entailed by the voyage.

Against such an alternative of eternal and distressed errancy, Benares—in India—comes to be invested with inflated symbolic value: the lost site of sanctity, it is the resting place which can no longer be sought, the object of an unending nostalgia. There is poignant numerical weight to such a loss: in the eleven years following the abolition of slavery in 1833, more than 83,000 Indian immigrants were brought to Mauritius to address the labor shortage (Macmillan 1914: 216). While each year saw a significant number of Indian laborers return to India, most earned a mere 5 rupees a month and could not afford the return fare (Manrakhan 1986: 12). Writing about the diaspora resulting from such "forced migrations," Makarand Paranjape describes the emigrants' inclination to sanctify the lost homeland:

> the laborers who were shipped out rarely had enough money to make the journey back to India; for most, it was a one-way ticket to another land. In other words, the distance, both physical, but more so psychological, was so vast, that the motherland remained frozen in the diasporic imagination as a sort of sacred site or symbol, almost like an idol of memory and imagination. (2001: 9)

Devarakshanam Govinden refers likewise, in another essay in this volume, to the constraint felt by Indians in South Africa to appeal to "the heritage of an 'ancient' civilization and culture," particularly in response to laws of segregation and to an identity imposed through terms (such as "Coolie") that were perceived as being derogatory. In the Mauritian "memory" of Benares, such nostalgia might also claim more literal, historically documented dimensions. Archival sources indeed indicate that a large number of Indian immigrants to Mauritius were from the Gangetic plains, where population pressures were severe in the late nineteenth century (Tinker 1986: 5).[4] It has also been recorded that recruiters frequently stationed themselves on roads leading to centers of pilgrimage, which might give us license to imagine that some Benares-bound pilgrims would have through an ironic set of circumstances found themselves headed for Mauritius (Carter and Torabully 2002: 24). This said, the districts surrounding Benares still rank below other areas—namely, the northern districts of Bihar and Bengal, the Madras presidency, or even, for a limited period (1834–65) the western coastal strip—in terms of recruitment of labor bound for Mauritius (Ly Tio Fane Pineo 1984: 98). In other words Benares can by no means be considered the place of provenance of a majority of Mauritian Indians. It is to be understood rather, and more interestingly, as a metonymically accredited signifier of origin, a hyperbolized reference in an imaginary and sacred geography.[5] Even the writings of Malcolm de Chazal, the most celebrated poet of Mauritius (incidentally of non-Indian descent), succumb to this curious metonymy whereby the holy Gangetic region unqualifiedly comes to stand in for the lost homeland; he is quoted as saying in 1970: "I am Western in my inheritance, my language, my way of eating and of expressing myself. But my soul is on the Ganges and in Benares, I breathe India" (Carter and Torabully 2002: 78). Now, there is a structural sense in which Benares would seem to lend itself particularly to such metonymization. As Diana Eck notes in her authoritative study *Benares: City of Light*, the city is described in Hindu scriptures as the still center that anchors space and time, the microcosm that contains all of the world, that grounds all that constitutes existence without ever participating in the ever-turning world of *saṃsāra* (1983: 23–24). Indeed the literature on Benares would seem to support this notion of a place of absolute wholeness, prior to history, the place of pure originariness so to speak, which, comprehensibly, in the context of an oft-traumatic history of migration, might become the object of a form of structural mourning.

All this provides a context to be kept in mind when considering the casting of Benares in a piece of contemporary Mauritian writing. Khal Torabully, in his reading of Pyamootoo's novel, appears most sensitive to the evocation of Benares as a signifier of ultimate loss, reading it in consonance with his own vision of a return to the motif of the sea voyage, the nodal moment of destructuring and regeneration of identity and a structuring metaphor in his poetics of "Coolitude" (Carter and Torabully 2002: 175; 14–15; 158).[6] Yet something altogether more ambiguous seems to emerge through Pyamootoo's prose, which in evoking Benares stops self-consciously short of gesturing toward loss, or at least complicates the reference to a lost sanctity. For Benares is evoked here as a dystopia, the stage for a grotesque spectacle of suffering, decay, and death: "You see them everywhere just waiting to die . . ." says the narrator, "[ . . . ]They're a little like the houses in Benares, exhausted by all they've been through, worn out by the heat and the monsoons, cracked . . . Not to mention the poverty they have to suffer and the injustices they have to endure at the hands of their fellow men—you should see how they're treated sometimes, like dogs squabbling over scraps who people kick or beat with sticks[ . . . ] And in fact it's thinking of their gods that gives them the strength to carry on living and keep going from one temple to the next and not let themselves drown when they bathe in the Ganges" (Pyamootoo 2004: 44–45). Immediately following this exchange Zelda (one of the women escorting the protagonists) discards a newly lit cigarette, referring by way of explanation to a sour taste in her mouth (45). The curious sense of community cemented between the passengers through the evocation of Benares is one that is born of a sense of horror.[7] But the empathy for the predicament of Benares pilgrims betrays another order of disquiet, which derives in part, no doubt, from the referential strain, so to speak, in the town's name (carried by another, otherwise dystopic place), but which also demands that one return to one of the metaphors at the heart of Benarsi sacredness. Diana Eck's study suggests that the town derives its sacredness precisely from its liminal status, for as a place, like certain others in the Hindu topography, Benares is a *tirtha*, or a place of "crossing"; a threshold, one might say, between this and the other worlds. Located at a river ford (where the old trade route through North India crossed the River Ganges) Benares is in the Hindu religious tradition "a spiritual ford [ . . . ] where one "crosses over" the river of *samsāra*—this round of repeated birth and death—to reach the "far shore" of liberation" (Eck 1983: 34). In other words Benares is not a final destination, nor in any "intrinsic" sense a sacred place; it is rather a port of embarkation, the shore from which the final journey (of *moksha*) is most safely, indeed most auspiciously, undertaken.

Might it be here that a certain uncanny poetics of homonymy in *Bénarès* finds its hidden (disavowed?) justification? For the Indians who emigrated to Mauritius also left a shore for another "far shore," and they too undertook a fearsome crossing of waters.[8] But where Benares pilgrims would have crossed the river of *samsāra* to reach *moksha*, Indian indentured laborers crossed waters considered profane toward a destination of which a large number were barely informed (Carter and Torabully 2002: 17–29). In Benares Shiva is said to whisper into the ears of the dying the *tāraka mantra* or "ferryboat mantra" that will safely carry them to the "far shore" (Eck 1983: 331–33). Indian emigrants, armed with no secret wisdom before boarding the vessels, traded *moksha* for loss of place and god. In a sense, then, a reference to Benares is a reference to the archetypal, absolute voyage and, in the context of Indian emigration, the voyage in whose stead countless other non-prescribed, unmapped voyages were made. The elusive exchange between Pyamootoo's protagonists addresses none of this directly. Yet it is precisely this entire paradigm (of sacredness, of loss of sanctity) that is at stake in the words exchanged. Or rather, the tragedy is dislodged from its most patent places: emptied of its substance, the promise of salvation represented by Benares is exposed to a more fundamental questioning than might have been permitted by a narrative of loss. Indeed, when Zelda reacts indignantly to the Hindu belief that all those (including criminals) who die in Benares will go to heaven, the narrator responds significantly with "It's only cruel if you believe in paradise" (Pyamootoo 2004: 42). Clearly, not just the sacred mandate of Benares but the very premises of (Hindu) sanctity are contested here, exposed as an

epistemological construct from which the deritualized/deritualizing up-
rootings of (labor) history have afforded an ambiguous emancipation, sacredness subjected, one might say, to an *ironic* reading. And so it is that
through a dismantling of the very semiology that gives the Hindu town its
sacred standing, and that might make it in the emigrant context an over-
significant object of ritual loss, *Bénarès* refuses the obvious objects of
mourning, deconstructing tragedy: "I tried to make her understand," says
the narrator, "that dying's not about paradise, it's not about anything at all,
but she didn't want to know" (42).

### Imagining the Namesake

New maps of the mind and memory have to
be reimagined from the ashes of history and
the wishes of people in power.

—Satendra Nandan, "The Adventure of Indenture"

The undermining of sanctity is taken a step further in the manner in
which the relationship between the namesakes is negotiated. The narrator's question about the *other* Benares opens a space wherein each of the
two places is affected with a disquieting element of alterity and the name
itself with irreparable ambivalence. Zelda's remarks betray the initial dis-
orientation provoked by the irruption of otherness. But the narrative goes
on to describe reactions elicited in the Indian Benares as well, thus playing on a mirror structure that doubles and ironizes on the motif of imagining the other. In the event the narrator is cast as a sort of messenger of otherness, he who imports it to each of the two worlds through the tense
conduit of a shared name. It is Zelda who insists: had the narrator told residents of the Indian Benares that in Mauritius too there was a place known
by that name? Somewhat tangentially the narrator responds: "Sometimes
[ . . . ] I wonder if I didn't go to Benares just for their sakes, so that one day
they can do the same journey themselves" (Pyamootoo 2004: 49). The
(startling) establishment of reciprocity, premised upon a reversal in the direction of the imagining, is given substance in the reactions of the
Benarsis:

> For one of them, it was like a blinding revelation when he found out, as if
> he'd personally discovered an unknown land. Every time we saw each other
> he'd tell me he'd never have thought it, that there could be another Bena-
> res, and it unnerved him, there being two places with the same name that
> are so far apart, so different, and he felt proud to live in one of them, maybe
> because it gave him the feeling of opening up to the world, of becoming
> part of some sort of network which must have seemed pretty vast and myste-
> rious, which he'd never suspected existed until then [ . . . ] There was

someone else who told me he'd been seeing double ever since. I suppose he meant feeling drunk or something like that. Whatever it was this whole thing seemed even stranger to him than paradise. (49–50)

The phrase "stranger . . . than paradise" interestingly exposes the way in which a subscription to the geographic or historical world rests on an effort of the imagination analogous to that involved in the adherence to religious or metaphysical belief. And within the logic of this imagination (of he who stays, so to speak) one is tempted to suggest that distance itself (asymptotically) merges with death, so that there is little to really distinguish the idea of a place that is far away from the mythicized notion of an afterlife. Or is it that the metaphysical utopia provides the only terms in which to imagine the elsewhere? In Pyamootoo's text the irony affecting the notion of paradise now extends to that of the elsewhere at large (and particularly the historically fraught elsewhere) and poses a fundamental question: what are the politics, the ethics, the poetics of imagining the other place?

A possible answer is provided by the Benarsi who, when informed of his town's African namesake, has "the feeling of opening up to the world, of becoming part of some sort of network" (Pyamootoo 2004: 49). The openness to the world and particularly the notion of a *network* in fact bear a marked affinity with the theorization of Francophone Caribbean identity in the 1990s by Martinican writer Edouard Glissant. Indeed one might expect Mauritian identity and memory to share some of the concerns that mark the Caribbean situation: colonialism and the slave trade, the highly problematic notion of origin, temporal discontinuities, spatial ruptures, hybridity, loss (Gallagher 2002: 1–13). In the wake of Négritude and its arguably conservative identity claims, Glissant's *Poetics of Relation* proposes an identity model that is plural, open, "archipelic" (as opposed to continental), ambiguous (as opposed to systemic) (1997: 89). This structure is itself closely based on Gilles Deleuze and Felix Guattari's concept of the *rhizome*, which unlike the root allows for a multiple, relational, and *processual* template for thinking identity. While Torabully was the first to spin a specifically Mauritian narrative out of such models of hybrid identity in his theorization of Coolitude, Pyamootoo's treatment of these questions is somewhat more qualified in its genuine unconcern for closure and in its assigning, in the task of imagining the Other and the elsewhere, of a paramount place to the role of *fiction*: "Sometimes I was bombarded with so many questions that I didn't know what answers to give anymore, it felt as if I'd said everything, so then I'd lie, I'd make up landscapes, I'd try to get their imaginations working too" (Pyamootoo 2004: 50). We might remember here the words of Zanzibar writer Abdulrazak Gurnah, mentioned in the introduction to this volume, which aptly describe the uncertain status of memory in a context (of historical interruption, dislocation) wherein recovery is also, necessarily, vitally invention: "Sometimes such gaps are filled in so convincingly that they become something "real" [ . . . ]; they develop their own logic and coherence. At first it might seem like this is a bit of a lie" (Nasta 2004: 353). In Pyamootoo's narrative reality is as if seamlessly extended by fiction, implying an uncanny space wherein imagination might meet, perhaps even be prolonged by, the imagination of the other. Besides, the vital mandate of fiction is exercised in *both* directions, for certain elements of the narration as well as a question from the narrator's friend when the women are out of earshot point to the likelihood that the visit to Benares in India was itself a fiction, invoked to claim the authority of the traveler, the license to improvise.[9]

The most strategic deferring to fiction, however, is seen in the refusal to provide a rationale behind the fact that the two places carry the same name. The question here is Mina's:

> "What I'd like is for someone to explain to me how come there are two Benareses." She stared at me and scratched her head, as if she was remembering a painful event that still upset her. She had a virginal expression, I mean an expression I didn't recognise on her, it was sad and fierce at the same time, like a wildcat that's been hurt, offended.
> [ . . . ] "It happened a long time ago, over two hundred years."
> "Yes, but how?" asked Mina impatiently.
> I looked away slightly and lied: "It's too long ago for anybody to remember properly," then I slumped down in my seat, I felt exhausted, drained and sad all of a sudden, like you do at the end of something." (Pyamootoo 2004: 51)

But "at the end of" what? Something important has indeed taken place in the space of this brief exchange, and which has to do with history, with contesting the prerogative of the linear narrative of history, the latter often critiqued as complicitous with European colonialism (Ashcroft, Griffiths, and Tiffin 1995: 355). Here by consigning the explanation for the shared name to "a long time ago," an era preceding and eluding memory, Pyamootoo's narrator resists the neat closure that historical rationality might provide, but without, for all that, offering in its place a recoupable counterhistory. Rather, it is the very *concept* of history, the assumed privilege of anteriority that finds itself reinterpreted, reappropriated—if that is indeed the term for something that seems to borrow the forms of a dispossession, a forgetting. If there is something like postcolonial allegory at work here, it is, then, in the specific sense in which Stephen Slemon discusses this modality, whereby "history as fixed monument [is refocused] into a concept of history as the creation of a discursive practice, and [thus opened] to the possibility of transformation" (Suk 2001: 6). In choosing not to supply a narrative that might gloss the name and thus iron out the "otherness" it carries, Pyamootoo's narrator refuses a "determinist view of history" (Slemon 1988: 159) that would necessarily establish a hierarchy between the namesakes. Instead, under the pretext of a disappeared, inaccessible past, the two Benareses are brought to coexist in a tense dis-inscribed space of imagining. In a sense, to refuse to ascribe anteriority to the Indian Benares is to leave otherness *unaccounted for* and to displace chronology onto spatiality (Gallagher 2002: 1–2).[10] Where history is left interrupted, suggested to be irrelevant, thinking, imagining, even a certain form of re-membering, of a "somewhere else" are made possible. Thus, the existence of the namesake, after at first being deemed somewhat scandalous, provides the fragile premises of a new way of seeing ("double"), indeed, inaugurating a singular poetics of homonymy. And this perhaps accounts the most plausibly for why an actual journey to the other Benares is not necessary, why, in other words, the lie is not really a lie: the very structure of Pyamootoo's narrative most eloquently performs the process of imagination—without appropriation—of the Other, whereby a homebound journey becomes a precarious approach to an elsewhere. When the protagonists finally arrive to behold the chimney of Bénarès, and Mina remarks: "It really looks like a monument to the dead [ . . . ] it sends shivers up my spine" (1999: 59),[11] there is a sense in which a momentary collapse has occurred between the destination and the *other* place through which symbolically it was reached, and the industrial ruin suddenly bears something of the Mahāshmashāna or the Great Cremation Ground, the more sinister name by which the Indian Benares is also known (Eck 1983: 32).

### Ambiguous Tragedies: The Road to Bénarès

the now smokeless funnel which sticks
a broken stump into the dirty July sky—
Bénarès, no more will the jaded urns
of your mouldy boilers pour the candy floss
and lollipop flavouring of roasted molasses
into the guzzle of the sugar-infested countryside.
("Andreanums," Régis Fanchette, 1972)

Indeed, "Bénarès," if in most ways a misnomer reminiscent of the incongruous names marking the Australian landscape (P. Carter 1989: 47), comes to share a dystopic quality with its Indian counterpart. On the road to Bénarès, the protagonists speak of its desolation since its sugar mill was closed thirty years earlier: "The owners thought there were too many mills for too small a cane crop" offers the driver Jimi, to explain the sudden shutdown that had left a whole village unemployed, "abandoned," "they said that some had to be shut to reduce their losses. Increase their profits, more like" (Pyamootoo 2004: 27, 29). A passage follows that describes the stilled temporality of Bénarès after the death of the sugar mill, that of "a whole village adrift," "counting the hours passing," waiting for promised re-employment that never quite materialized (28–29). Jimi also remembers the "good old days," "that feeling you always had of being one with the earth and the stones we heaped into piles and the cane we stripped and cut; that heady smell of wormwood which rose up every time it rained" (29). The idyllic portrait of labor on the sugar estate ironically revives a traditional theme in Mauritian Francophone literature: while Clément Charoux in his *Lettres* described the sugar factory as a "temple" and its chimney as a "belfry," a "symbol of faith and courage," Arthur Martial in 1929 wrote of the "immense sheets of glistening emerald" of the sugar cane fields that were the workers' "raison d'être," also hailing the Indian laborer as the "soul of the estate" (qtd. in Prosper 1978: 169–190).[12] Only in Pyamootoo's novel the idyll takes on dysphoric resonances, for it is evoked here in terms of a mourning, and that too an ambiguous mourning, if one remembers the history of exploitation and uprooting associated with the growth of the sugar industry in Mauritius. "[T]he owners weren't good to us," says Jimi; "[t]here were only three of them but it sounded like there was a hundred when they shouted their orders that stung like insults" (Pyamootoo 2004: 30). The tragedy of Bénarès, in its very over-determination, proves hard to locate: is it in the (mis-)naming of the estate after a faraway place of sanctity and death, is it in the migration of thousands of Indian laborers, is it the growth of the sugar industry or is it its decline, read in the death of this mill, that had for almost two hundred years sustained the livelihoods of a village?

In my journey with this text I too took the road to Bénarès and beheld "the now smokeless funnel" towering over ruins (Fanchette 1972). Nearby stands a small hut of a temple that had supposedly once served those who worked at the factory; through its locked windows one catches a glimpse of a terracotta floor, wooden benches, and idols with eyes burning bright, perplexed at having been abandoned. After the dismantling of the factory in 1968 the dwellings of workers all around were taken down too, and the workers moved to other places, some to the nearby village Chateau-Bénarès, a few to other African countries for employment.[13] So it is that the name Bénarès refers now only to the carcass of a mill and the fields of cane surrounding it.

What is the story of Bénarès? My investigation leads me to believe that it can hardly be told without invoking the entire history of "sweetness and power" in Mauritius.[14] In the latter half of the eighteenth century under the French East India Company an attempt was made to settle the Savane region in the south of Mauritius, which by then had become inhospitable land, a haven for runaway slaves left by the Dutch (Carter and La Hausse de Louvière 1997: 5). It was in this context, in 1772, that 1,250 (French) acres of land were obtained by two Frenchmen by the names of Jean-Baptiste Chevalier and Jean Law de Lauriston, both notable colonial administrators in India (Rouillard 1979: 367): Chevalier had in 1767 taken up the governorship of Chandernagor, while Lauriston was the king's governor in Pondicherry and president of all the upper and provincial councils established in India (Regnard, d'Unienville, et al. 1971: 1174). The name Bénarès appeared on the Mauritian map for the first time in 1779 (Rouillard 1979: 367), at which point the land had been mostly cleared of its trees and cultivation of coffee and other cash crops had started (Boodhoo 1991). Three years later a sugar mill was built, the first of its kind in the south of the island. Bénarès was indeed to become one of the most thriving sugar estates of Mauritius, producing up to 3,350 tons of sugar in a year (Macmillan 1914: 233). But in 1787, though the estate was starting to prosper, Chevalier and Lauriston sold their land, a decision that historian Guy Rouillard tentatively traces to the poor fortunes they made in India (1979: 368).

This is as much as is historically verifiable about the beginnings of Bénarès. The question of the name decidedly remains a matter for speculation—or fiction. Pyamootoo himself in a personal capacity confesses his suspicion that the two Frenchmen having known the Benares in India and what it represented gave its name to the southern coastal site in Mauritius in enlightened preparation for a quiet death.[15] However, one could reasonably wonder whether two men in their early forties and fifties and indeed at the height of their careers would really have been making such anticipatory arrangements for death.[16] Philippe Lenoir, writing about Bénarès, suggests in more general terms that it was a "nostalgia for the faraway India where they had lived many years" that led Chevalier and Lauriston to name their estate after India's holy city (n.d.: 1).[17] But, given the scarcity of documentation regarding the naming of Bénarès, one should perhaps more modestly settle for a geographic hypothesis: for Bénarès in Mauritius, situated between the mouths of two rivers, the St. Amand and the Dragon, in a sense reproduces the topography of its Indian counterpart, also known as Vārānasī, and whose etymology is traced in the Purānas to the two rivers that frame it, the Varanā (The Averter) and the Asi (The Sword) (Burren 1993: 165; Eck 1983: 26–27). In any case it would seem that the specific personal reasons for the choice of the name matter less than the broader paradigm it engages and the ironies it implies. For Bénarès was named thirty years before Mauritius was occupied by the British, and a good fifty-five years before the first Indian indentured laborers were officially introduced in the island. When in 1779 the name first appeared on the Mauritian map, the island was under French colonial rule, and labor was almost exclusively slave labor.[18] Thus, far from illustrating—and imprecise historicizing might indeed prompt such a retrospective illusion—a desire on the part of Indian immigrants to recreate in an unfamiliar setting landmarks of their spiritual geography,[19] "Bénarès" is an almost farcical reminder of who possessed the power to name and who didn't, the holiness of its name and romantic speculations concerning the naming only barely detracting from the violence of the "coercive spatialization known as colonization" (Gallagher 2002: 5). At this juncture, I would suggest that Pyamootoo's apparent reluctance to historicize is not (historically) irresponsible but, on the contrary, a commentary on the fact that the story of Bénarès can in no sense be comfortably reclaimed. The name, in fact, gestures neither toward forgotten ancestry nor to lost wholeness; rather it marks a site in a map of colonial itineraries: a name known through colonial presence in one land, usurped and repeated to mark a stake in a second, in a curiously un-self-conscious act of semiological possession.[20] Sentenced to a form of *migration*, the name reproduced in Mauritius bears perverse testimony, then, to an empire of unmoored signs. Is the silenced story of the crossing not told in the diacritical markers in the word "Bénarès," signs of the violence of *trans-lation*? These markers, and the inflections and resonances they force upon the name, are but another variant of the "scriptural wound" suffered by Indian patronyms as they were registered upon arrival (Carter and Torabully 2002: 160).

One can only imagine today how the ironies, the denatured Hindu resonances of the name, were experienced by the slaves—and then the indentured laborers—who worked at Bénarès. A textbook story of the estate is all that survives. In 1862 the old factory was torn down to make way for a modern one in close vicinity. In the late 1950s the annual yield peaked at 14,000 tons, a testimony indeed to advances in production technology, as well as improved organization of labor, optimization of handling and transportation costs, and so forth. This is the factory that was finally closed in 1968, also, interestingly, the year of Mauritian independence from British colonial rule. The death of Bénarès, an event related wistfully by Pyamootoo's narrator, is one among scores of tragedies that industrialization and the sugar trade have incurred over the years in Mauritius. The statistics speak for themselves: in 1860 there were more than 250 sugar mills on the island; by the end of the nineteenth century half of them had already been demolished; today there are a mere 11 surviving mills, of which a few are likely to be shut down in the coming years (Rouillard 1990: 34–35; Hazareesingh 1973: 58).[21] Chimneys like that of Bénarès dot the Mauritian landscape, tributes to as many ambiguous tragedies: for in terms of livelihoods these would appear to reveal the reverse side of the euphoric narrative of industrialization (as well as decolonization, one might say). In the name of "rationalization," the ironic title for this silenced narrative, operations involved in sugar production were, starting from the mid-nineteenth century, mechanized as well as centralized so that a larger area of cane could be cultivated for the smallest number of mills. The strategy paid off: in the year that Bénarès was shut down, national production of sugar had reached one of its all-time peaks of 700,000 tons, with a number of mills more than twenty times lower than the number functioning in 1862 when the (second) factory of Bénarès was built (Rouillard 1990: 34–35). The closing of Bénarès in 1968 was to mark the beginning of an ongoing move to restructure the Mauritian economy in light of pressures placed on the sugar industry due to World Trade Organization regulations and the imminent expiry of preferential agreements for export (principally, the Sugar Protocol signed with certain European countries in 1975 and the Special Preferential Sugar Agreement with the EU and ACP (African, Caribbean and Pacific Group of States) in 1995). Statistics indicate that in the year of the closing of Bénarès alone the sugar industry laid off 2,800 workers; since the year of Mauritian independence the sector has dispensed with no less than two thirds of its erstwhile employees.[22]

It is in this *post-industrial* time-space that Pyamootoo's *Bénarès* is set, and the world it frames is that of a sort of aftermath: unemployment, desolation, football amid the mill's ruins, gambling, prostitution . . . There is a sense, of course, in which this moment, beyond tragedy, where past icons of colonization and labor exploitation have been (or are still being) razed to the ground, is also one that allows the rebuilding/reimagining of a world. Perhaps this is how the evocation of the other Benares is best understood. Now with the view of the past getting cleared of its vestiges, and a certain narrative drawing to a close, might there not be time to rediscover the curious free play of abandoned (derationalized) signifiers, a sort of spatial poetry?

### Conclusion

At the end of my own investigation I am inclined to concede that Pyamootoo's version of memory—resolutely fictional, poetic, lacunary—might indeed be the most fitting ode to a fading story and to the perverse monument that survives it. In a recent conversation Pyamootoo spoke of the chimney that continues to stand over the ruins of the Bénarès sugar mill and that figures as an emblem of irony and desolation in his book. I was to learn on this occasion that the chimney, left intact to date in observance of national heritage laws, may soon be moved to another location (Bel-Ombre in the south west), where it is to stand at the entrance of a five-star hotel. The present owner of Bel-Air/Saint-Felix, the last group to administer the Bénarès mill before it was shut down, knew nothing of such a project. Perhaps I should have pressed Pyamootoo for more details, ascertained his sources, inquired further. But, in addition to not being convinced that I would have found textual evidence (this way or that), I am guilty of opting to defer to the truth of fiction, History's "other," so to speak.[23] Such a truth appropriately—if tragically—prolongs the uncertain gap-ridden story told here, and at the end of which the migration of a chimney gestures silently, *monumentally*, to what has passed. In the age of globalized trade regulations, of competition, falling prices and anticipated hardships for the export of Mauritian sugar, there is indeed today a deliberate move to shift labor and resources to more profitable sectors, such as tourism. We witness then, in a sense, in the (envisaged or imagined) transplantation of the Bénarès chimney, the concluding chapter of the vexed history of "sweetness and power," its unlikely eloquence matched perhaps only by that of another scrap of undocumented information I obtained while in Mauritius and which also features the migration of a piece of the deceased mill.[24] According to the management of the Bel-Air sugar estate, when in 1969 the Bénarès mill was dismantled, its machinery was sold to whomever was willing to purchase it. While significant units were sold to other Mauritian factories, the smaller vacuum pans were exported, via an agent, to India. I do not know where in India, and do not in any case wish for circles to be too neatly closed, but I am left wondering whether this dismembered posthumous journey was not a return of sorts, and whether it was not foretold in the ironies of a name.

### Notes

1. While I have chosen to preserve the diacritic markers in the book's original title as well as in the name of the Mauritian estate, all quotes unless indicated otherwise will be from Will Hobson's English translation of the book (Pyamootoo 2004).

2. For more on the notion of "kala pani" (black waters) and its presence as a leitmotiv in Indian immigrant literature, see Ravindra Jain's *Indian Communities Abroad, Themes and Literature* (1993); and also Vijay Mishra's *Rama's Banishment* (1979).

3. The translation is mine.

4. Indeed Bhojpuri speakers constitute the largest proportion of the Indian population in Mauritius even today.

5. One is, of course, reminded here of Salman Rushdie's words on the creation of "imaginary homelands," which lucidly envisage the displacements and inventive approximations (i.e., metonymic/metaphoric transpositions) involved in recreating the

lost space: "We will not be capable of reclaiming precisely the thing that was lost [ . . . ] We will, in short, create fictions, not actual cities or villages, but invisible ones, imaginary homelands, Indias of the mind" (1991).

6. Torabully's poetics of "Coolitude," as the term itself suggests, is modeled on Césaire's Négritude, while claiming the relationality and hybridity of Glissant's ulterior theorization of Caribbean identity. It takes as its central figure the "coolie," or Indian laborer, and seeks to recover the lost memory of the sea voyage and the survival of the fraught experience of indentured exile. For a more comprehensive discussion of the movement, see Carter and Torabully's *Coolitude* (2002: esp. ch. 5, "Some Theoretical Premises of Coolitude," 143–213).

7. Such a dystopic representation is reminiscent in a sense of certain older European accounts of Benares, where the sacred town is described for all its ghastly sights, its aggressive display of religious fervor and humiliations. See Mark Twain, for instance: "The town is a vast museum of idols—and all of them crude, misshapen, and ugly. They flock through one's dreams at night, a wild mob of nightmares" (qtd. in Eck 1983: 504). See also Eck's section titled "Seeing Banāras through Western Eyes" (8–19), as well as Pierre Loti's *L'Inde (Sans les Anglais),* where a spiritual journey toward Benares barely masks a subtext of distaste for the display of religious excesses and physical horrors.

8. Between 1834 and 1865 an average of 10,000 Indians (this average then fell to 1,500 until 1910) entered Mauritius, and today more than 60 percent of the population is of Indian descent. See *La Chambre d'Agriculture de L'Ile Maurice: 1853–53 (Livre d'Or).*

9. "'Why did you tell them that you'd been to Benares in India?' Mayi asked me.—'I don't know,' I answered. 'It just came out . . . Was that wrong?'—Mayi shrugged his shoulders and grimaced, but didn't say anything" (Pyamootoo 2004: 53). Other elements that reflexively point to the fictionality of the account of Benares include the choice of terms used by the narrator to describe his own narration: "in my mind's eye I saw" (48); "everything came back to me in the usual order" (49). In fact, the fiction threatens to lose its frontiers altogether at the end of the exchange with Zelda on the injustices of Benares wherein the narrator muses: "We were like two friends meeting up after a long separation, two travellers swapping stories from their wanderings, a few memories to enliven the late-night road. I thought to myself that stories must be what we travel for, to have something to tell the people we love" (45). Neither claim is really as sound as it would seem (travel nor friendship—for the characters are strangers to each other); moreover, the last sentence makes one wonder whether there is not a dialogue here with Sartre's *Nausea* (2004) where Roquentin concludes that adventures are impossible. Here though the possibility of stories is rehabilitated, it is in the intriguing form of self-(dis-)avowed fictions. Pyamootoo's second novel, *Le Tour de Babylone* (2002), also seems to valorize a fictional-autobiographical rapport with the elsewhere.

10. In an interesting variant of this transposition of temporality onto spatiality, Malcolm de Chazal in a 1976 article famously claimed on the basis of fauna, flora, etc., that Mauritius was geographically "coexistant" with India, having once been part of the subcontinent (Prosper 1978: 193).

11. Here I exceptionally depart from Hobson's translation ("It really is just like a war memorial") in order to preserve what would seem a crucial ambiguity in the term "monument aux morts" (page 91 of the original).

12. The translation is mine.

13. Information courtesy of Patrick Rowntree, management of Bel-Air sugar estate, Mauritius.

14. I borrow the expression "sweetness and power" from the title of a book by Sidney Mintz (1985), which retraces the history of the sugar trade, colonial settlement, and labor through the eighteenth and nineteenth centuries.

15. Conversations with the author, June 2004. Interestingly, Pyamootoo likes to associate with Benares its more euphoric name of Ānandavana or Forest of Bliss (Eck 1983: 29).

16. Lauriston was fifty-three, Chevalier ten years younger, when they acquired the land that was to become Bénarès (see Regnard, d'Unienville, et al. 1971: 1174; Deloche 2003: 5). Both had only very recently assumed their governorships in Chandernagore and Pondicherry, respectively. Chevalier did not die until 1789, and Lauriston in 1797, in other words well after selling the Bénarès estate (after which both had returned to France), so that whatever the intentions might have been, the place was not their last earthly abode, so to speak. Absurd reasoning of course, all of this, and which does not necessarily make Pyamootoo's fantasy any the less plausible.

17. Needless to say, "nostalgia" as a motive in a context so explicitly colonial is far from apolitical, testifying rather to the forced availability of signs that was the result of colonialism; see the subsequent discussion. The translation of Lenoir's words is mine.

18. While most slaves hailed from Africa, a handful, according to some historians, had been brought from French-held territories in India before 1833, and in particular from Pondichery. Thus in 1786 (unfortunately figures for earlier years are unavailable) the Bénarès sugar estate was described as comprising "154 good subjects, including 7 saws, a set of barrows, 6 squarers, 87 Indians, 30 mules, 35 bullocks, 12 carts, etc." (Rouillard 1979: 2; the translation is mine). This said, it is in fact difficult to obtain certain information about how significant a number of slaves from India there might have been. Manrakhan (1986), for example, writing about the French import of slaves to Mauritius, makes absolutely no mention of Indian slaves.

19. Of the few Indian names that can be found on a map of Mauritius today (and there are very few of them, given the limited agency of indentured laborers: Lalmitti, Coromandel, Gokulka, and Ganga Talao) and which can reasonably be supposed to have been given to places by Indian laborers who became landowners, Bénarès is thus the oldest, and the most accidental, not to say uncanny. (Information courtesy of historian Ivan Martial, Mauritius.)

20. See Paul Carter's *The Road to Botany Bay* (1989) for a remarkable analysis of naming as a tool of colonization and the notion of a "spatial history."

21. The latter piece of information was gathered at a presentation by the manager of Mon Désir Alma sugar mill in June 2004.

22. The total number of persons employed in the sugar industry in 2002 was 17,615. Excerpted from *A Survey of Employment Statistics*, Central Statistical Office.

23. Here I invert Suk's lucid formulation (see Suk 2001: 6).

24. This piece of information was obtained courtesy of Patrick Rowntree, management of Bel-Air Sugar Estate, Mauritius.

## Works Cited

Appanah-Mouriquant, Natacha. 2003. *Les Rochers de Poudre d'Or*. Paris: Gallimard.
Ashcroft, Bill, Gareth Griffiths, and Helen Tiffin. 1995. *The Post-Colonial Studies Reader*. London: Routledge.

Bhabha, Homi. 1994. *Location of Culture*. London: Routledge.

Boodhoo Raj. 1991. "Port Souillac: Le bicentenaire." *L'Express*, 23 April.

Burren, Breejan. 1993. *Randonnée au cœur de quelques localités mauriciennes (un sur-vol des noms et des attraits de lieux à l'île Maurice)*. Vacoas, Mauritius: Le Printemps.

Carter, Marina, and Philippe La Hausse de Louvière. 1997. *Souillac: Village Histo-rique et Cimetière Marin*, Port-Louis: Héritage.

Carter, Marina, and Khal Torabully. 2002. *Coolitude: An Anthology of the Indian Labour Diaspora*, London: Anthem Press.

Carter, Paul. 1989. *The Road to Botany Bay: An Exploration of Landscape and History*. London: Faber and Faber.

Crooke, William. 1817. *The North Western Provinces of India: Their History, Ethnol-ogy, and Administration*. London: Methuen.

Deloche, Jean. 2003. *Jean-Baptiste Chevalier (1729–1789): Le Dernier Champion de la Cause Française en Inde*. Paris: EFEO/Les Indes Savantes.

Eck, Diana L. 1983. *Banares: City of Light*. New Delhi: Penguin.

Fanchette, Régis. 1972. *Burntwood, Stardust and Shifting Sands*. Mauritius: self-published.

Gallagher, Mary. 2002. *Soundings in French Caribbean Writing since 1950: The Shock of Space and Time*. London: Oxford University Press.

Glissant, Edouard. 1997. *The Poetics of Relation*. Trans. Betsy Wing. Ann Arbor: Uni-versity of Michigan Press.

Hazareesingh, Koosoomsingh. 1973. *Histoire des Indiens à l'Ile Maurice/History of Indians in Mauritius*. Paris: Librairie d'Amérique et d'Orient.

Jain, Ravindra K. 1993. *Indian Communities Abroad: Themes and Literature*. New Delhi: Manohar.

Lenoir, Philippe. N.d. "Promenade Causerie de la Société de l'Histoire de l'Ile Mau-rice a La Savane, Bénarès et Quelques Vieilles Maisons Savanaises." Unpub-lished document, courtesy of Bel-Air Sugar Estate, Rivière des Anguilles, Mauritius.

*Livre d'Or*. 1953. Édité pour le centenaire de la Chambre d'Agriculture de l'Ile Mau-rice (1853–1953). Port Louis: Chambre d'Agriculture/General Printing and Stationery.

Loti, Pierre. 1910. *L'Inde (sans les Anglais)*. Paris: Calmann-Lévy.

Ly Tio Fane Pineo, Huguette. 1984. *Lured Away: The Life History of Indian Cane Workers in Mauritius*. Moka, Mauritius: Mahatma Gandhi Institute Press.

Macmillan, Allister, ed. 1914. *Mauritius Illustrated: Historical and Descriptive, Com-mercial and Industrial Facts, Figures and Resources*. Tahiti: Les Éditions du Pacifique.

Manrakhan, J. 1986. "Examination of Certain Aspects of the Slavery-Indenture Con-tinuum of Mauritius Including a Scenario that Never Was." In *Indian Labour Immigration: Papers Presented at the International Conference on Indian Labour Immigration 23–27 October 1984*, ed. U. Bissoondoyal and S. B. C. Servansing. Moka, Mauritius: Mahatma Gandhi Institute Press.

Mintz, Sidney W. 1985. *Sweetness and Power*. London: Penguin Books.

Mishra, Vijay, ed. 1979. *Rama's Banishment*. Auckland, New Zealand: Heinemann.

Nandan, Satendra. 2001. "The Adventure of Indenture: A Diasporic Identity." In *Diaspora: Theories, Histories, Texts*, ed. Makarand Paranjape. New Delhi: Indialog.

Nasta, Susheila, ed. 2004. *Writing across Worlds: Contemporary Writers Talk*. London: Routledge.

Paranjape, Makarand. 2001. "Displaced Relations: Diasporas, Empires, Homelands." In *Diaspora: Theories, Histories, Texts*, ed. Makarand Paranjape. New Delhi: Indialog.

Prosper, Jean-Georges. 1978. *Histoire de la Littérature Mauricienne de Langue Française*. Port Louis: Éditions de l'Océan Indien.

Pyamootoo, Barlen. 1999. *Bénarès*. Paris: Seuil.

———. 2002. *Le Tour de Babylone*, Paris: Seuil.

———. 2004. *Benares and in Babylon*. Trans. Will Hobson. Edinburgh, Scotland: Canongate.

Regnard, Noel, J. Raymond d'Unienville, et al., eds. 1971. *Dictionnaire de Biographie Mauricienne*. Port Louis, Mauritius: Escalpon.

Rouillard, Guy. 1979. *Histoire des Domaines Sucriers*. Les Pailles, Ile Maurice: Henry & Cie.

———. 1990. *Historique de la Canne à Sucre à l'Ile Maurice: 1639–1989*. Port Louis, Mauritius: Mauritius Chamber of Agriculture.

Rushdie, Salman. 1991. *Imaginary Homelands: Essays and Criticism, 1981–91*. London: Granta/Penguin.

Sartre, Jean-Paul. 2004. *Nausea*. London: Penguin.

Slemon, Stephen. 1988. "Post-Colonial Allegory and the Transformation of History." *Journal of Commonwealth Literature* 23.1: 157–68.

Suk, Jeannie. 2001. *Postcolonial Paradoxes in French Caribbean Writing: Césaire, Glissant, Condé*. Oxford: Clarendon Press.

Tinker, Hugh. 1986. "Continuity between Slavery and Indian Immigration?" *Indian Labour Immigration: Papers Presented at the International Conference on Indian Labour Immigration, 23–27 October 1984*, ed. U. Bissoondoyal and S. B. C. Servansing. Moka, Mauritius: Mahatma Gandhi Institute Press.

Torabully, Khal. 1987. *Appel d'Archipels (ou le livre des miroirs)*, Port-Louis: Pluralité-Babel.

# PART 2

# AFRICA IN INDIA

# 8

# Siddi as Mercenary or as African Success Story on the West Coast of India

Rahul C. Oka and Chapurukha M. Kusimba

## Introduction

In AD 1489, political control over the island of Janjira located off the west coast town of Danda-Rajpuri in India was captured from the local coastal polities and brought into the domains of the Ahmadnagar Sultanate in Central India. This feat was attributed to the Abyssinian slave elite group of the Daulatabad Sultanate and has been enshrined in multiple narratives by historians and contemporary residents of Janjira-Danda-Rajpuri (Chauhan 1995; Oka and Gogte 2004). The Abyssinians (henceforth Africans) were major power brokers in the Deccan polities (especially Ahmadnagar) and also controlled much of the sea lanes off Western India between AD 1400 and 1500. The subsequent development of Janjira remained obscure until the 1620s, when an African slave elite oligarchy, collectively known as the Siddi of Janjira, formally assumed command of the fortress and started playing a significant role in coastal and hinterland politics, eventually organizing as an independent state in the early eighteenth century (Ali 1996; Harris 1971, 1993).

Most studies on the Siddi community have focused on their military and elite past (Ali 1996; Banaji 1932; Chauhan 1995; Duff 1995; GBP 1833; Kincaid 1937; Parasnis 1987) or their present status as ethnic minorities in India (Basu 2000, 2001; COI 1931; Enthoven 1975; Kadetotad 1992; Palakshappa 1976; Roychoudhury 1957; Russell and Lal 1975; Sinha 1992; Trivedi 1961). While much work on the contemporary Siddi groups in India is highlighting the complex nature of African Indian societies today (see Basu 2000, Lodhi 1991, and Obeng this volume) for problems in ethnic studies on the Siddi, most historical studies rotate between three alternatives: a) seeing the Siddi of Janjira as unique slave-to-ruler African success stories (Ali 1996; Chauhan 1995; Harris 1971, 1993); b) analyzing the Siddi as enemies of the growing hinterland Maratha polity (Dighe 1944; Duff 1995; Gordon 2000; Parasnis 1987; Sardesai 1934–40; Sarkar 1973); or c) neglecting the significance of the coastal Siddi in medieval South Asian history (see Das Gupta 1967, 1979, 1987, 2001; Das Gupta and Pearson 1999; Fukazawa 1991; Kosambi 1985, 1996; Kulkarni et al. 1996; Moraes 1975; Pearson 1976, 1981, 1987, 1994, 1996, 1998). Recent studies on the rise of the African slave elite in South Asia suggest that the availability of local labor in South Asia allowed Africans to avoid Atlantic-style physical slavery and gain high posts in the hinterland and coastal polities (Jayasuriya and Pankhurst 2001; Pankhurst 2001).

We regard these interpretations as problematic. Many slave groups rose to elite positions as kings, kingmakers, and administrators in other areas of the Islamic world, so the rise of Siddi or African power in South Asia was not a unique event, nor was it a simple military success narrative of elite actions (Bacharach 1981; Crone 1980; Pipes 1981; Patterson 1982; Philipp and Haarmann 1998; Stillwell 2004; Toru and Philips 2000). Similarly, the relationship between the Siddi, Maratha, Europeans, and the hinterland Islamic polities was far more complex than the on-going feuds described by the historians of the Maratha polity (Ali 1996; Banaji 1932; Gordon 2000; G. Kulkarni 1982). The medieval historians' neglect of the Siddi as mere mercenaries is best summed up by the following description of the Janjira polity: "a small piratical maritime state tributary to the Mughals" (Richards 1993: 220). By Portuguese, Dutch, and English accounts, Siddi control over sea lanes and ports of Western India was a significant factor for both hinterland polities and European trading interests from the early sixteenth century CE onward (Ali 1996; Banaji 1932; Chauhan 1995; Correa-Afonso 1990; Danvers 1968; Foster 1906–1927; Gordon 2000). As with most historical processes, the development of Janjira and Siddi (African Indian) royalty is far more complex than the approach taken by the aforementioned alternatives.

In this essay we follow the argument first made by Helene Basu that the emergence of African slave elites in the Deccan or other areas of South

Asia was due to the supra-regional nexus between military slavery and Islamic polities (Basu 2001). We compare the relationship between slave elites and their masters across the Islamic world in an attempt to understand the motivations and means by which African slave elite groups gained power, first in hinterland India and then the western coast. We show within global, regional, and local political contexts how the naval specialists among the African slave elite groups of South Asia consolidated power along the west coast of India using multiple strategies and alliances between AD 1500 and 1700. This essay also shows that in an era long presumed to be dominated by European innovations, African subjugation and Asian despotic decline, the interactions between Africans and Asians and their control over their history and environment were far more significant than those between Europeans and Afrasians in the Indian Ocean.

### Slave Elites and Islam

In the context of trans-Atlantic slavery, the idea of a powerful slave elite group making high-level decisions, managing large armies, and acting as king-makers and kings seems unusual. However, there have been frequent episodes in history when enslaved individuals or groups of slaves have risen to positions of power in state administration (Tsugitaka 2000). Though slave elites have existed in Rome and China, it was in the Islamic world that the slave elite complexes, known as *mamluks*, *ghulams*, or *kuls*, became institutionalized parts of the administrative infrastructure (Bacharach 1981; Pipes 1981). A few examples include the Mamluk Sultanate in Egypt (AD 1250), the Slave Dynasty in Northern India during AD 1206–1290, and the Kano Mamluks in the Sokoto polity in West Africa in the nineteenth century (Naqvi 1987; Pankhurst 2001; Rabbat 2000; Stillwell 2000, 2003, 2004).

There were strict rules regarding slaves and slavery in the Islamic legal corpus. There were only two ways by which a person could be enslaved: as the offspring of a slave or as a war prisoner (Haarmann 1998; Tsugitaka 2000). Usually, enslaving fellow Muslims was forbidden, and these rules were "generally" followed though other practices, such as enslaving of Black Muslims (as lower-level Muslim or Kaffirs) or Muslim parents selling children into slavery, were also common (Pankhurst 2001). The Grand Wazir of Ahmadnagar, Malik Ambar, was sold into slavery by his parents in Harar (Ali 1996: 64, see also Seth 1957). In contrast to chattel slavery in the Americas, slaves in Muslim regions were free to marry and have families and hence generate actual and fictive kin groups. They were not forbidden from education and could rise to positions of power and trust within households and states (Stillwell 2000). A large corpus of scholarly work on the development of slave elite groups in Islamic polities seem to agree on five basic elements.

First, *the need for slave elites*: though descent in Islamic households was calculated through paternal line, there was no clear practice of primogeniture in the dominant elite ruling Turkish groups (Haarmann 1998; Naqvi 1972, 1987; Richards 1993). Hence the ruler had to treat all male members of the patrilineage as pretenders and rivals. This created a vacuum that had to be filled by trusted individuals with no other loyalties than to the ruler and his or her immediate family (Tolodano 1998, 2000).

Second, *generation of loyalties*: as slaves were educated and given positions of power, they were also bound to their masters by law and by obligation for kindnesses. Their loyalty, thus, was generated by law and by their defenselessness (lack of networks) outside their master's circle (Meillassoux 1991). The dependence of a slave's existence on that of the master has been a common argument in discussions of slavery and emergence of trust between slaves and their masters (Comaroff and Comaroff 1993; Meillassoux 1991; Miers and Kopytoff 1977; Patterson 1982). However, recent scholarship has problematized this idealized development of trust between master and slave and the slave's kinlessness as postulated by Africanists (see Tolodano 2000: 164). Comparative research among the *mamluks* in Egypt and Kano reveal a pragmatic process generating sustenance of power for both groups (Philipp 1998; Philips 2000; Stillwell 2003; Tolodano 1998). Slave elite groups had access to knowledge, and hence "social capital" and power comparable to the freeborn nobility. This knowledge was beyond the scope of free commoners. Hence, maintaining the system of elite slavery was favorable to the master and to the entrenched slave elites (Glassman 1991; Stillwell 2004). Trusted slaves were included in central circles of intrigue. Their opinions and advice were sought and they were often given jobs that would be dangerous in a non-slave's hands.

Third, *power over recruitment*: slaves were given command over other slaves and had the power to increase the ranks through purchase, inducement, or capture. This led to the formation of slave catchment and supply zones along ethnic lines, as slaves filled vacancies with enslaved individuals from their own former ethnic groups (Ali 1996; Allouche 1994; Chauhan 1995; Pearson 1976). This made it possible for the Circassian Mamluks of Egypt to keep the governing sultan and the oligarchic body Circassian Turk.

Fourth, *marital strategies*: the right to marry was also exercised along ethnic lines as marital relations were arranged within ethnic categories (Ali 1996, Philipp 1998). This combined with ethnic-based recruitment allowed the formation of complex slave elite oligarchies, bound to each other by marriage and fictive kinship, and with considerable say in the activities of their elite masters (Stillwell 2000).

The fifth and final point of similarity is *specialization in warfare:* the one activity with which slave elite oligarchies were trusted was the control over defense infrastructures (Crone 1980; Pipes 1981). As slaves were bound to their master, they were far less likely to follow the rivals into battle and would fight to the death to preserve their master's power. Hence, military slave elites were given charge of armies, elite guard units, and navies (Bacharach 1981; Pipes 1981; Prakash 1994, 1996, 1998). In time, slave elite groups were in positions of power all over the Islamic world. In fact, according to historian Dror Ze'evi: "in Islamdom such modes of government were ubiquitous, and dominant for many centuries. In the Mamluk and Ottoman cases the slaves themselves perpetuated the system and there were few serious attempts to replace it with a more 'natural system' such as bequeathing rule and power to progeny" (2000: 71).

### Africans in India and the Emergence of an African Slave Elite

Interactions between Africa and India have been recorded far back in prehistory. This was a bidirectional exchange of commodities, ideas, and peoples. Africa has provided commodities such as ivory, cat skins, rock crystals, and gold, and domesticates such as millet, sorghum, and teff, as well as traders, soldiers, and slaves to Asia since the early Bronze Age (Chaterji 1968; Gogte 2002, 2003; Kusimba 1999; Kusimba and Bronson 2000; Pankhurst 2001). The presence of Africans in South Asia was significant enough to have been rendered in the art of the Early Common Era as seen in the Ajanta paintings of western India (V. G. Gogte, personal communication). Africans have been settling on the west coast of India long before the emergence of military slave elite groups in hinterland India.

### Africans on the West Coast of India

The presence of Africans on the west coast of India predates the Turkish or Afghani invasions of North India and seems to be directly related to Indian Ocean trade. Based on emerging ethno-botanical evidence, the west coast of India shows the greatest influence of African domesticates in the form of millet (known as *ragi* or *nachani*) and the baobab tree (known locally as *gorakh chinch*). Both domesticates are heavily utilized in coastal cuisine and medicine and have become indicators of coastal influence and culture (Oka and Gogte 2004).

Surveys along the west coast of India have revealed a similar articulation between baobab trees and settlements. Baobabs older than 800 years have been recorded on the coast as well as dead baobabs dating back to the late first millennium, indicating that Africans were living on the coast, in their own or in larger assimilated settlements well before the early medieval period (Gogte 2003). In his travels along the west coast of India, Ibn Battuta (1304–1377) reported that the ship in which he sailed carried "fifty archers and fifty Abyssinian warriors who are the Lords of this Sea . . . whenever one of them is on a ship, the Hindu pirates and infidels avoid attacking it" (Jain 1990: 90). It stands to reason that specialists in naval matters would also settle along the coasts and near the ports that they policed. Battuta's report indicates that merchants and administrators heavily contracted Abyssinian warriors well before he made his journey; the reputation of Abyssinians as warriors also meant that they were present on the coast long enough to be entrenched in pirate lore and coastal memory by the mid-fourteenth century (Jain 1990).

The emergence of warfare and the Adal state in Ethiopia under Ahmed Gragn in the mid-sixteenth century created demographic upheaval in the Horn of Africa, and the number of Africans brought as slaves or fleeing the strife-torn areas increased significantly (Insoll 2003; Pankhurst 1994, 2001). They followed the normal trade routes, and many ended up on the west coast of India, where they were actively recruited by their fellow Africans and inducted into the slave elite much like the Mamluk (Pankhurst 2001). By all accounts, there were as many as 3,000–5,000 Africans resident in many ports along the coast, including Daman, Diu, Bassein, Danda-Rajpuri, Chaul, and Cochin. They adapted to life in South Asia and rapidly rose in local polities due to their naval, martial, and administrative skills (Pankhurst 2001).

As the migration of Africans to the coast from the hinterlands and the Indian Ocean areas intensified during 1450–1550, they increased their control over trade and territories on the northwest coast of India. Between 1500 and 1550, they controlled much of the naval territories in Gujarat and the northern Konkan coast of Maharashtra, in alliance with or as governors of the Gujarat or the Bahmani sultans (Ali 1996). In fact, given their control over the shipping and sea lanes, their rule was practically autonomous. Major ports such as Daman, Bassein, and Danda-Rajpuri along with their hinterland trade routes and agricultural production areas were under the control of Africans (Correa-Afonso 1990; G. Kulkarni 1982). They exacted revenues from the trade within their territories and from the port authorities of Surat, Chaul, or Cambay as payment for their protection (Banaji 1932). They were the main naval adversaries faced by the Portuguese during the first phase of the Portuguese incursions into India. It is precisely within this political context of intensifying African control over the northwest coast that we must place the establishment of the Janjira polity.

## Africans in the South Asian Hinterlands

Although the existence of slavery and African slaves in Asia pre-dates the Islamic period, the post–eighth-century trade boom resulted in increasing investment in the slave trade; as many as 10,000 slaves a year were being sent from Africa to Asia via the Red Sea (Insoll 2003; Lovejoy 1983). Many of these slaves were sold along the trade routes into India, and this process intensified with the establishment of Turkic Islamic rule in India from the eleventh century onward (Naqvi 1987).

Slaves (African, Indian, Armenian, Chinese) managed businesses, were given control over armies, land, or administration and were often influential in politics of the emerging Turkic sultanates of North India (Harris 1971). Although Islamic rule spread from the northern Delhi Sultanate to other parts of India, there was no major sustained consolidation of the eastern and southern territories into the Delhi Sultanate (Naqvi 1987). The period between the thirteenth and fifteenth centuries was a phase of regionalization in which breakaway Islamic polities arose and proclaimed their independence in southern (Bahmani Kingdoms) and eastern (Bengal Sultanate) India.[1]

In AD 1347, the governor of the Daulatabad Province, Hasan Bahman Shah, declared his independence from the Delhi Sultanate and established the Bahmani Kingdom (Fukazawa 1991). The cosmopolitan nature of the Bahmani Sultanate led many Africans to seek and find administrative and military careers in the south and the west right from the late fourteenth century. Many Africans were increasingly discriminated against in the northern Delhi Sultanate by the Turkish, Afghan, or Persian factions (Ali 1996; see Singh this volume for the development of these divisions lasting even into modern media representations of Africans in India). One result of this migration was the development of ethnic categories among the Muslim nobility in India similar to that followed by the Bahri and the Circassian Mamluk of Egypt and Syria (Athar 1985). This, however, is particular only to the development of ethnic categories among the African slave elites and not of all Africans in South Asia. According to English traveler and historian Robert Orme (1782, cited in Chauhan 1995: 19), the genesis of the African (Habshi) ethnic identity was a result of conscious decisions by the early slave elites of the Bahmani Sultanate. It is unlikely that the trajectory toward independent political existence was visualized and intended by the early slave elites. However, there appears to have been a conscious effort to create an African slave elite kin group based on ethnic and geographic origins—an African category was a survival tactic that provided a safety and opportunity network to all members of the group (Haarmann 1998). A caveat: African settlement and ethnogenesis in South

Asia as traders, soldiers, and slaves has been much more complex than Orme's suggestions or the case of the Mamluk of Egypt of the South Asian hinterland slave elites. Africans from many different areas in Africa came or were brought for different purposes and had different fortunes. Many slaves ran away from their masters and established maroon colonies foraging and practicing small-scale horticulture in the uplands in the Deccan (Lodhi 1991). Other groups lived in open communities along the coast and hinterland, either as slaves or manumitted soldiers, and indulged in trade, agriculture, administration, and military services (Obeng this volume). Hence, there are diverse narratives regarding the development of African communities in South Asia (Basu 2001).

Geographic and cultural origins were major factors in the determination of these categories. Though these ethnic categories were not absolute, they played a role in influencing postings, appointments, marriages, and movements of peoples from one polity to another. By the late fifteenth century, the category of Habash, Habsh, or Habshi had emerged as well as the respectable form used by African elite, "Siddi." Though most scholars see Siddi as a derogatory corruption of the term "Sayyad" used for Africans (Ali 1996; Chauhan 1995; Pankhurst 2001), the term might be a derivative of a more generic term referring to slave or slave elite of African origin: *Sudan* or *Sud*. This term was commonly used in Islamic polities and in India may have been transformed to Siddi (Allouche 1994).

The presence of Habshi or African power groups proved to be attractive factors for other Africans seeking employment, promotion, or escape from slavery. Perhaps owing to their skills in shipping, naval warfare, and trade as well as the known presence of African coastal settlements in Daman, Diu, Bassein, and Danda-Rajpuri, many Africans started migrating out of the hinterlands toward the west coast of India by the late sixteenth century (Chauhan 1995).

### Bahmani Decentralization and African Groups

During the emergence of the Bahmani polity, the sultans realized that they had inherited a well-established system of governance from the earlier Yadava rulers of Deogiri and the Silaharas of the coast (Fukazawa 1991; see also Kulkarni et al. 1996). This was similar to practices followed by the Fatimids, Ayubbids, and the Mamluk in Egypt as well as the Mughals in North India (Rabbat 2000; Richards 1993). They retained most of these infrastructures and incorporated some ideas from their own experiences in Turkish or Persian polities to the north and the west (Kulkarni et al. 1996).

The Bahmani sultans adopted the time-honored strategy of combining indirect rule and central control to administer the conquered periphery

(Kumar 1997; Subrahmanyam 1990). Conquered noblemen were offered the chance to rule as the sultan's vassals, collect tax, and pay tribute. Retention of the traditional elite class structure also ensured their loyalties to the sultan (Athar Ali 1985). The noblemen, in turn, provided military service for the sultan and had to submit to centrally appointed audits and checks by the sultan's officers (Fukazawa 1991). Pre-existing polities and their infrastructure were subsumed into a larger monarchial state through vassalage, tribute, and taxation (Stein 1980).

There were three types of politico-geographic divisions in all the Bahmani kingdoms: *parganas*, *qalahs/muamalas* and *muqasas*.[2] *Pargana* was a larger geographical division retained from pre-Bahmani times, nominally in the charge of a hereditary official called a *deshak* or *desai*, and consisted of 10–200 villages. The other two administrative units (*muqasa* and *qalah/ muamala*) were alternate means (introduced as Persian or Turkish innovations) of establishing some control over the governance of the *pargana*. *Muqasas* were fiefs or land grants given to high- or middle-ranking elite and were usually carved out of *parganas* but sometimes out of *qalahs*. Economically or militarily important regions (river confluences, valleys, ports, trade centers, frontier towns) were marked off into *qalahs* (military bases) and *muamalas* (economic centers), usually controlled from fortified hill forts, and were centrally administered by direct appointees of the sultan, namely the *havaldar* (*qalah* manager) and his deputies (Kosambi 1985; Kumar 1997).

It was common for one area to have all three types of administration (*pargana*, *muqasa*, and *qalah/muamala*) in operation at the same time. The three groups of elites had varying alliance to the center and served to check against hegemony from the center or rebellion from the periphery. Any act of rebellion against the center had to be agreed upon and supported by the administrators of the *paragana*, the *muqasa*, and the *qalah/ muamala*. The central administration system of the sultanates consisted of a) one or more *parganas* being assigned as fiefs to high-ranking bureaucrats; b) dividing part of one *pargana* into small fiefs (*muqasas*), each administered by medium-ranking nobles, and giving the rest to centrally appointed bureaucrats as *qalah/muamala*; and c) retaining the aforementioned *pargana* system but subjecting it to periodic audit.

Of these the first two were the most commonly used methods and were usually fought over by the elite lobbies closest to the sultan. Among the freeborn elites in the Bahmani Kingdom, the main lobbies were the Turkish, Indian Muslim, and Hindu nobility and among the slave elite were the Turk/Central Asian (Afaqi), African (Habshi), and Indian Muslim (Dakhni) (Ali 1996; Pankhurst 2001). As the nobility possessed their own armies, the hereditary rulers of the Bahmani Sultanate needed to counter any rebellion against the center by the nobles. Hence, the encouragement and development of military slavery led to the formation and ascension to power of the three slave elite oligarchies. As they owed their loyalties to the families at the center, they were frequently called upon to defend the royal family against rebellion or invasion (Basu 2001).

Fukazawa (1991) has proposed that political realities and increasing power of noblemen (hereditary rulers of fiefs or centrally appointed administrators) with their own standing armies made the Bahmani system subject to periodic destabilization and decentralization. This decentralization gave powerful noblemen the ability to rebel, negotiate for better terms of alliance, act independently, and still inherit a well-running administrative structure.[3] Thus the first split of the Bahmani Sultanate in the late fifteenth century created five independent sultanates that lasted for a period of 100–200 years. During AD 1400–1450, the Bahmani Kingdom expanded across most of central peninsular India but became decentralized as a result of the expansion (Kosambi 1996; Moraes 1975). In the latter fifteenth and early sixteenth centuries, it split into five kingdoms, Berar (AD 1510–1574), Bidar (AD 1504–1619), Ahmednagar (AD 1496–1636), Bijapur (AD 1489–1686) and Golconda (AD 1543–1687) (Ali 1996).

The last few years of the Bahmani Sultanate were characterized by power struggles between the three slave elite groups. The main struggle was between the Afaqi and Dakhni groups. Different groups allied themselves with different members of the ruling family. The Africans usually allied themselves with the Dakhni (Ali 1996).[4] Following the break-up of the Bahmani Sultanate between 1489 and 1543 CE, the African slave elite proved its loyalty to the Nizam of Ahmadnagar and grew to prominence in the Ahmadnagar Sultanate that controlled the north Konkan and bordered the Gujarat Sultanate to the northwest (Pankhurst 2001). Their coastal specialization as naval warriors, their lobbies in the central Ahmadnagar administration, and their knowledge of Indian Ocean trade allowed them to increase naval autonomy. The Ahmadnagar and Gujarat sultans recognized that naval power of the Africans protected the lucrative trade from the Konkan ports and encouraged their buildup of power (Basu 2001). The sixteenth century witnessed the rise of African administrators and noblemen in India to unprecedented levels as kingmakers in the Deccani sultanates, culminating in the rise of the greatest kingmaker of the sixteenth century, Malik Ambar (G. Kulkarni 1982; Seth 1957). During his tenure, the fleets of the Bijapur and Ahmadnagar Sultanates and the ports of Surat were under the command of the Naval Africans (Pankhurst 2001).

## Janjira, the West Coast, and the Deccan Hinterland

The areas immediately around Janjira and including Danda-Rajpuri remained under the Ahmadnagar Sultanate for the whole of the sixteenth
century. The territory was controlled as a *muamala* based at Chaul and
Danda-Rajpuri (both economically significant ports). The military administration center, the *qalah*, was based at the fortress of Rohira, and much of
the agricultural land and trade routes came under the *pargana* of Birwadi
(Fukazawa 1991). Political appointments in these polities were usually
given through nepotism and alliance networks (Allouche 1994). Appointments to the administration of the Danda-Rajpuri and Janjira were influenced by the elite at both the *muamala* of Danda-Rajpuri and by the African lobby at Ahmadnagar (Ali 1996). The result of this naval and political
power was a growing autonomy of African interests on the coast.

African claims to autonomy and control over the coastal provinces are
indicated in early Portuguese records (Correa-Afonso 1990; Subrahmanyam 1993). Their control over the northern Konkan and Gujarat trade and
shipping placed them at frequent odds with the Gujarat sultans. Though
they were paid for protection of trading vessels and routes, delays or differences over payments by the Gujaratis resulted in the Africans confiscating
ships or punitive attacks on merchants (Ali 1996). Mahmud Shah, the mi-
nor sultan of Gujarat, ceded Daman (AD 1558) and Bassein (AD 1534) to
the Portuguese to curb the rising power of the Africans over the coast
(Chauhan 1995; Pankhurst 2001).[5]

Since claims of autonomy have to be backed by actual control over territories, we view the gradual African takeover of Janjira in the sixteenth
century as the natural outcome of the African polity-building exercise
centered at Danda-Rajpuri. Though their navies were powerful, the land-
based armies of the other nobles or kings were a constant threat, and the
coastal ports that they controlled were at the mercy of these land forces
(Dighe 1944; Gordon 2000). The Africans needed a defensible base from
which they could protect their existing territories and settlements. The island of Janjira was ideal for this purpose. It protected the important port of
Danda-Rajpuri and provided a retreat if land-based oppositional armies
became too strong. The African elite of Danda-Rajpuri-Janjira used this
strategy frequently and to great effect against all their land-based enemies
(Banaji 1932).

The establishment of the Janjira fortress provided a base for African
ventures in Diu, Daman, and Bassein. Though their northern territories
around Gujarat were compromised by their wars with the Portuguese, the
Africans based at Janjira did not lose control over the surrounding territories and gained power due to immigration of naval specialists. As agents or

governors of the Ahmadnagar Sultanate, they derived political legitimacy through alliances in which they were rulers of the coastal waters and the immediate hinterlands (Pankhurst 2001).

With the fall of the ports of Daman in 1543 and Bassein in 1558 to the Portuguese, there was a huge influx of men with naval expertise into the Danda-Rajpuri/Janjira areas. Intermarriages and alliances between African noble families and their support from the African power groups of the hinterland resulted in the crystallization of a powerful African coastal slave elite parallel to that in the hinterland between AD 1560 and 1600 (Chauhan 1995). Though Danda-Rajpuri and Janjira was formally granted as a fiefdom carved from the *pargana* of Birwadi to Shah Tahir, a Persian noble of Ahmadnagar, the medium- and low-level administration of Janjira was in charge of the Africans under Siddi Yakut,[6] the conqueror of Janjira, even though the formal governor might not have been an African (Ali 1996; Basu 2001).

Even after Malik Ambar reclaimed the conquered territories of Danda-Rajpuri and Chaul from the Mughals in the early 1600s, the practice of retaining Mughal governors was continued at Danda-Rajpuri until AD 1618 (Ali 1996). This may have been due to the increased influence of the Mughals in central India and the alliance decisions of the African elite who recognized Mughal power. However, given the minimal non-African control over naval matters, the individual within the governor's post did not matter (see Behrens-Abouseif 1998). It was only after 1618 that the African elite were formally organized as rulers of Janjira, when Siddi Ambar Sanak was appointed as the admiral of the Janjira navy and hence the ruler of Janjira (Ali 1996). This period can also be seen as the emergence of the term "Siddi" as a political title of the coastal elite ruler of Janjira.

Notwithstanding their autonomy at sea and the impregnable fortress headquarters, the African rulers of the North Konkan and Janjira areas realized that political stability and alliances resulted in large revenue (Banaji 1932). Hence, they voluntarily maintained their titles as governors and slave-vassals of the Deccani sultans. In the initial period of emergence, they were vassals of the Nizamshahi Kingdom of Ahmadnagar, but they also maintained ties with the Bijapur polity (Pankhurst 2001). They constantly strengthened these alliances by gift exchange, favors, and marital relations with the strong lobby of African administrators and political kingmakers in the Ahmadnagar polity.

From the 1620s onward, many of the coastal African elite realized that though they were nominally vassals of the Deccani sultanates, they needed to form strong alliances with the Mughal Empire that had conquered Gujarat in 1578 CE and controlled the powerful ports of Gujarat and the north Konkan (Pearson 1976). Danda-Rajpuri and all areas north were conquered by the Mughals and ceded to the Bijapur Sultanate in 1636. Though the Mughals had an admiralty department and a small navy, they lacked the naval strength to police the coast and sub-contracted the Africans of Janjira to do so (Prakash 1979: 45). They also recognized the skills of Africans in warfare and naval matters, with the result that the number of Africans serving in the Mughal administration at high ranks increased exponentially between 1578 and 1627 CE (Athar Ali 1985).

The Africans were also quick to recognize that the political stability of Gujarat and the northern Konkan meant increased trade revenue and protection monies. They sought recognition for their control over Janjira by acting as vassals of the Mughals. In return, they were recognized as *Mir-I-Bahr* (admirals of the sea) and were also allotted 300,000 rupees per annum as payment for port and trade protection by the merchant guild of Gujarat (Athar Ali 1985; Banaji 1932). Hence the chief of the African oligarchy at Janjira was the admiral of both the Mughal fleet and the Janjira fleet. The strategy of securing legitimacy from the Mughals was employed by Africans and other emergent polities in India well into the eighteenth and nineteenth centuries (Gordon 2000).

In keeping with their autonomy, the alliance with the Mughals in Gujarat was uneasy, as it was with the former sultans. If the protection payment was delayed, the Africans confiscated trading vessels belonging to the Gujarati merchants or attacked the ports (Banaji 1932). Just as Bahadur Shah and Mahmud Shah allied with the Portuguese to control the rising influence of the Africans over naval matters in the sixteenth century, the Mughals tried to counter the rising African power by giving permission to the Dutch for building factories and presenting a naval challenge to the Africans (Richards 1993). The African rulers of Janjira sought political legitimacy from both the Bijapur and Mughal states but also realized that their naval power was challenged by the European trading companies and the Arab pirates. Hence, they entered into alliances with both the English and the Portuguese in the seventeenth century and used these alliances to great effect to engage the Mughals and the newly emergent Maratha polity (Chauhan 1995).

After AD 1618, the African slave elites were in political and economic control of the coast and the administration of Janjira. However, this was not the beginning of a hereditary kingship or independence of the Janjira polity. Leadership positions among the Africans followed "corporate" structure that marked slave elite oligarchies of the Islamic world, such as the Egyptian Mamluks. The aristocratic constitution of the African elite rulers of Janjira was based on a central body of administrators or warriors ranked in order of experience and seniority (Chauhan 1995). The leader, known as the *wazir* within African ranks, was usually the first officer of the

**Table 8.1. Timeline of the Main Interactions between Hinterland North, Central, and Coastal India from the Thirteenth to the Eighteenth Centuries**

| Year/Period | Events |
|---|---|
| AD 1300–1400 | • Free and enslaved Africans arrive through Indian Ocean trade<br>• African lobbies in administration and military increase and play a significant role in the rise of Bengal Sultanate<br>• Africans maritime and naval specialists settlements emerge on the west coast south of Gujarat, around Chaul, Danda-Rajpuri, mainland of Janjira |
| AD 1347 | • The Bahmani Kingdom is established<br>• Africans immigrants first appear in Eastern and Central India |
| AD 1450–1490 | • The Bahmani Kingdom is decentralized, increasing Africans' role in the kingdom as powerbrokers<br>• The Bahmani Kingdom expands toward the west coast of India<br>• The African naval power reigns supreme on the coast<br>• Hinterland Africans return to coast in large numbers following their waning of power brokerage in Bengal |
| AD 1489 | • Yakut Khan Habshi/Siddi acquired Janjita as a principality of Daulatabad ruled by Ahmad Nizamshah<br>• The breakaway Bijapur Sultanate is established by Sultan Adilshah |
| AD 1496 | • Ahmad Nizamshah establishes Ahmadnagar Sultanate and gains Danda-Rajpuri and much of the southern Konkan coast<br>• Africans gain power in the sultanate |
| AD 1500–1550 | • African consolidate their stranglehold over Janjira and the immediate hinterland and develop a powerful naval force which exercised control over Danda-Rajpuri, Janjira, Bassein, and Daman<br>• The Portuguese arrive at the northern Konkan coast<br>• The wars of Ahmed Gragn in Ethiopia increase the number of enslaved Africans on the west coast of India |
| AD 1543 | • Gujarat Ruler Mahmud Shah cedes Daman to Portuguese |
| AD 1558 | • Gujarat Ruler Mahmud Shah cedes Bassein to Portuguese |
| AD 1550–1600 | • Janjira emerges as the base for African polity, revenue is collected from most of northern and southern Konkan, rise |

**Table 8.1.** *(Continued)*

| Year/Period | Events |
|---|---|
| | of Malik Ambar (the Great Siddi) provides considerable legitimacy to independent activities of the Africans of Janjira |
| AD 1600–1610 | • Northern Konkan passes nominally into Mughal hands, but Malik Ambar and the African navy protect their control over the coast and sea lanes<br>• The British and Dutch East India Companies arrive<br>• The emergence of factories at Surat |
| AD 1618 | • Siddi Ambar Sanak is appointed as the first governor of Janjira<br>• Danda-Rajpuri is returned to the Ahmadnagar Sultanate |
| AD 1620–1657 | • The first peak of African power at Janjira<br>• Old Alliances with the Gujarat Sultan are transferred to the Mughals<br>• The "Siddi" becomes distinguished as title of elite from Janjira<br>• African rulers of Janjira accept legitimacy from both the Mughals and the Ahmadnagar and Bijapur Sultanates |
| AD 1636 | • Mughals re-conquer Ahmadnagar and cede northern Konkan and Janjira to the Bijapur Sultanate<br>• Africans consolidate power in both Bijapur and Mughal polities |
| AD 1650–1680 | • The Maratha polity emerges under Shivaji forcing Africans to temporarily withdraw to the Janjira fort<br>• Maratha and Janjira vie for control of Danda-Rajpuri and surrounding areas; both sides make effective use of the British, Dutch, and Portuguese against each other |
| AD 1680–1720 | • The second peak of African power at Janjira<br>• Death of Shivaji<br>• Mughal invasion of the Deccan and remnant Bahmani kingdoms of Bijapur, Golconda, and Golconda<br>• Renewal and strengthening of alliances between Africans and the Mughals and increased activity of African control over the coast<br>• The British and the Maratha under the Angre clan emerge as competing sea powers |
| AD 1720–1770 | • The Mughals decline and the emergence of the Peshwa Pune Polity as the dominant power<br>• Marathas under the Angre clan seize control of the sea<br>• African control over the coast declines |

fleet. Upon the death or removal of the *wazir*, the second officer of the fleet, not the son of the *wazir*, would succeed. This practice was legitimated by the sultan of Ahmadnagar until 1636, the Bijapuri Sultanate until the 1660s, and then the Mughal emperor (see Table 8.1).

The oligarchic council of the Siddi maintained strict control over the activities of the *wazir*. Banaji (1932: 40–51) discusses a power struggle over succession that took place in 1676. Siddi Sambal, the commander of both fleets and the *wazir* of Janjira, was accused of embezzlement of the community's funds. The community decreed his removal and legitimated this action as a decree from the Mughal emperor Aurangzeb. The newly appointed *wazir*, Siddi Kasim, had to fight Siddi Sambal and enforce the council's and hence the emperor's decree. The factions, intrigues, and infighting seen in the Egyptian Mamluk oligarchies were also common among the Siddi for similar reasons and were usually quelled when the majority of the council gathered behind a chosen leader and exerted military and diplomatic efforts on his behalf (Chauhan 1995).

Between 1630 and 1707, the Africans of Janjira, as staunch allies of the Bijapur sultans and the Mughal emperors Shah Jahan and Aurangzeb, were at the apex of their naval power and were treated with respect by the Europeans and other emergent Indian coastal polities such as the Marathas. The strength of their navy increased from 10,000 in the 1670s to more than 40,000 in 1689 (Banaji 1932: 48). According to historian Stewart Gordon, in the seventeenth century "the strongest actual power on the Konkan coast was not [the] well known European trading nations but the Sidis of Janjira, [ . . . ] who held sea forts and some nearby land possessions, and maintained an extensive navy to protect its merchant shipping" (2000:64).

### Comparing and Contrasting the Development of Slave Elites: Mamluks and Siddi

By the end of the seventeenth century, the Siddi of Janjira had developed a system of rule akin to that established by the Egyptian Mamluk, though their rule extended mainly to the coast hinterland off the island of Janjira (Ali 1996; Basu 2001; Dighe 1944). Like the Mamluk who derived their authority from the Caliphates and the Padishah in Istanbul, the Siddi derived legitimacy as admirals of the Deccan or Mughal polities (Allouche 1983; Chauhan 1995). Lastly, like the Mamluk, the Siddi never became popular among the local peoples of the Konkan. As major slave traders, the Siddi raided extensively in non-Islamic territories. According to British reports, they were also known for acts of extreme cruelty during their raiding and pillaging efforts (GBP 1833). The northern coast of Kurla and Mazgaon near the island of Bombay was frequently pillaged and locals carried off into slavery, and these events have been described as scenes of "plunder, outrages and insolent captures" (Banaji 1932: 33). During the frequent and forced use of Bombay harbor by the Siddi fleet, "many of the Siddi men took up abode in the town and committed such atrocities on the Hindu inhabitants that many of them were forced to leave town" (28).

Besides slavery and cruelty, the Siddi had taxation and revenue policies that differed from surrounding agrarian-based kingdoms or states (Fukazawa 1991). The land-poor Siddi polity had to raise money to pay for an increasing navy and constant battles with the Europeans, pirates, or coastal polities. Given their clashes over payment with the Gujarat polities, they had frequent cash flow problems (Banaji 1932). Maintaining a land revenue system assessed in grain was counter-productive for the Siddi (Chauhan 1995). Hence, they taxed means of transportation (bullock carts), retail and wholesale businesses (shops, banks, warehouses), and other cash- or export-based agricultural ventures such as orchards (cashew, betel nut, coconut, and mango) (Chauhan 1995). This placed an undue pressure on merchants who found business untenable in many parts of the Siddi polity (Oka and Gogte 2004).

In defense of Siddi policies, one might note that taxation and revenue decisions by elite rarely meet full approval from the populace and are generally criticized by contemporary observers (Sardesai 1934–40; see critiques of Mamluk policies in Allouche 1994; Haarmann 1998). Regarding their reputation for cruelty, the Siddi were no more or less cruel than any other contemporary ruler in South Asia or the Middle East (see Allouche 1983; Richards 1993). Like the Mamluk, due to their unpopular economic policies, their long reputation for ferocity, and possibly their strict ethnic difference and distance from the ruled population, the Siddi were especially singled out for hatred by their subjects—in particular, by the Hindus.[7] However, there are a few significant differences between the Siddi of Janjira and the other slave elite groups. Unlike the Mamluks of Egypt, Kano, or the Ottoman, the Siddi were relegated to the coastal strips, though undefeated at sea battles. They never controlled large territories in the hinterland (Dighe 1944). Another point of difference was the failed attempts for hereditary succession among the other Mamluk groups, while the Siddi polity of Janjira eventually became an independent and ultimately a hereditary monarchy. And last, the Mamluk oligarchs retained de facto power over land and resources in Egypt even under the Ottoman and were regaining visible power until the Napoleonic conquest while the Siddi lost naval power to the British between 1750 and 1800 and thus lost control of most of their land holdings expect Janjira and Danda-Rajpuri (Ali 1996; Basu 2001; Philipp 1998).

### From Slave Elites to Coastal Rulers

The reasons behind the different trajectory taken by the Siddi from other Mamluk or slave elite groups lie within the changing political landscapes in hinterland and coastal western India between 1650 and 1750 CE. As allies or vassals of the Islamic Ahmadnagar, Bijapur, or Mughal polities, the Siddi were legitimate rulers of the coast. However, from the 1650s, a non-Islamic polity, the Maratha, was engaged in a political and military struggle with the Bijapur and the Mughal states (Gordon 2000). The leader of the Marathas, Shivaji Bhonsale, considered the Konkan part of his polity and also realized the value of trade revenue and control over sea lanes (Sardesai 1934–40; Chauhan 1995). This brought the Marathas into direct conflict with the Siddi and the European powers. The period from 1657 until 1700 is marked by regular skirmishes between the Marathas and the Siddi. The narrative of the battles is almost clichéd: the Marathas prevailed upon the land, and the Siddi had naval superiority and easily defeated the nascent Maratha navy time and again (Ali 1996; Banaji 1932; Basu 2001). Shivaji and his son Sambhaji frequently conquered Danda-Rajpuri, driving the Siddi back to the sea or the island of Janjira, but they never managed to take Janjira (Dighe 1944).

Both groups used the Mughal alliance as well as the three European powers as leverage in their tussle (G. Kulkarni 1982). Though the British would have preferred to stay out of the coastal power struggle, they could not check the Siddi on the sea or the Marathas on land and needed to maintain neutrality on both accounts (Basu 2001). Their naval strength was not sufficient to prevent the Siddi from wintering their fleet in Bombay as and when they pleased. The Siddi were quite adept at using their naval alliance and their positions vis-à-vis the Mughal emperor to play the British against the Portuguese against the Marathas. The seventeenth century is usually seen as a century of European naval domination of the Indian Ocean, though trade remained in Afrasian hands (Das Gupta 1979, 1987, 2001; Kosambi 1996; Lombard and Aubin 2000; Pearson 1976, 1987, 1998; Subrahmanyam 1990, 1993). However, the seventeenth century on the northwest coast of India saw rising African domination as Portuguese power waned and the British and Dutch remained trading powers with little sustainable capacity for long-term naval warfare (Banaji 1932; Gordon 2000).

But, in spite of their sea power, the Siddi, due to lack of ethnic numbers and unpopularity among their own subjects, could not build a strong land army and were limited to sea-based attacks and raids. Hence, unlike the Mamluk, they could not conquer large territories on their own (Ali 1996). Furthermore, constant battles with the Marathas created an attrition effect in which the navy as the source of Siddi power was also the drain for constant expenditure of cash and resources and the justification for increased taxation and raiding of the coastal peoples (Banaji 1932).

Despite these problems, the Siddi elite transformed the nature of their political structure from a slave elite oligarchy to an independent monarchy: vassals but no longer as slave elite of the Mughal Empire. This was due to the power vacuum left behind by the collapse of the Mughal Empire between AD 1707 and 1730 (Richards 1993). The Marathas frustrated Aurangzeb attempts to conquer the Deccan and consolidate the Mughal Empire (Richards 1993). The death of Aurangzeb in 1707 left a collapsed infrastructure in the hinterland, the empire heavily decentralized, and the Siddi without a land-based suzerain or ally (Chauhan 1995). In the entire previous history of Janjira, there had always been a hinterland Islamic polity to which the Siddi pledged allegiance—Ahmadnagar, Bijapur, and Mughal. The emerging Maratha Hindu polity was not an acceptable alternative, and there was no Islamic group in the hinterland or the coast that could legitimately stake claim to the Mughal or the Deccani polities (Fukazawa 1991).

It was in this rapid restructuring of the political landscapes of Western India that the Siddi elites formally reinvented their former roles as independent princes. As the period between 1730 and 1818 saw a gradual British takeover of Western India, the Siddi used their century-old alliances with the British in Bombay to keep Janjira from the Angre Marathas. They also entered shifting alliances with the Peshwa Maratha Polity to protect their land holdings and strengthened their fleet using British alliances between 1700 and 1750. In the 1750s, they actually attacked and took over Surat for a few years (Harris 1993). Their growing power was viewed with concern by the British, who were increasing their control over the Surat trade and eying the production hinterland of Gujarat and Bombay (Nightingale 1970; Oka et al. forthcoming). The Siddi navy at Surat was attacked and defeated by the British in 1759, and the protection of Surat was handed over to the British navy after two hundred years of African control. This meant the loss of the 300,000 rupee yearly revenue that had been due the Siddi as Mir I Bahr during this time period. The decline in revenue led to further decline in the navy, which led to further losses against both the British and the emerging Maratha navy of the Angres (Ali 1996; Dighe 1944).

Between 1760 and 1800, the Janjira navy was no longer the dominant force on the western coast of India, and the Siddi began to depend on the British, who recognized the state of Janjira as a British protectorate in 1834 (Ali 1996). Merchants left Janjira to go to Bombay or Cochin, and the administrative infrastructure of Janjira begin to collapse (Chauhan 1995; Oka and Gogte 2004). On grounds of inefficient administration, Janjira was eventually subsumed into the growing British Empire in 1879 as a Princely State of India, with hereditary monarchs carrying the title of "Siddi" instead of the corporate elite slave *wazir* of the Deccani of the Mughal fleet (Chauhan 1995). In contemporary India, the Siddi elites of Janjira maintain their noble titles but, with the removal of the Purses due the Princely States, have taken part in the contemporary Indian business and political world. There is, however, a strict division between the Siddi elites still regarded as nobility and those classified as Siddi among the National Tribes of India. The transitions of past glory affected only the elite in the post-colonial period; the story of the Siddi non-elite is beyond the scope of this essay, but suffice to say that the common African warriors and denizens of the Janjira state found their way into other settlements along the coast and have developed their own ethnic pathways, distinct from the Siddi elites (Basu 2000, Enthoven 1975; Kadetotad 1992, Sinha 1992; see also Obeng this volume).

## Conclusions

We have attempted to show that the polity of Janjira had developed as 1) a result of African military slave specialization in naval matters and the evolution of alliances with hinterland polities (Ahmadnagar, Bijapur, and Mughal) which needed policing of trade routes; 2) a subset of the African slave elite oligarchy and their power struggles in the hinterland Bahmani between AD 1347 and 1496 and thence the Ahmadnagar sultanates between AD 1496 and 1636); and, 3) ultimately, part of parallel but non-linked development of slave elite groups common in Islamic polities across the world.

In this context, the characterizations of the African elites in South Asian history as mercenaries or as success stories fail to explain and underscore the complexity of African presence, settlement, and impact on South Asia socio-cultural landscapes. In both the Egyptian Mamluks and the African slave elites in South Asia, the development of slave elite groups was common in the Islamic world and encouraged by both slaves elites and their masters to propagate the power of the entrenched elite and to create a group of trusted lieutenants and captains loyal only to their owners, enabling slaves to access power, knowledge, and wealth beyond the scope of free-born commoners. Slave elite groups that gained power sustained their political, economic, and social positions through multiple alliances and leveling mechanisms that legitimated their power from above and within their communities. Slave elite groups were built as summarizing ethnic categories and maintained through marital alliances and fictive kinship groups. Due to their dynamic nature, slave groups were usually maintained as corporate oligarchies rather than hereditary network systems.

Despite these similarities across the global Islamic world, there are also differences in the development of slave elite groups. These differences are a function of regional and local histories of slave groups causing and reacting to events in their political environments. While the Mamluk power underwent a withdrawal from visible control between AD 1517 and 1750 due to the Ottoman conquest, the Siddi utilized the power vacuum following the decline of their suzerains, the Mughals, to forge new ties with the British and restructure their own place and maintain their control over Janjira in late eighteenth- and nineteenth-century South Asia as an independent monarchy. The emergence of Janjira and the Siddi nobility also underscores the marginality and frequent powerlessness of Europeans in Asian affairs during the so-called Age of European Discovery, AD 1500–1700. The Siddi curbed the European political domination of the northern Konkan and Gujarat coasts through their naval prowess between 1500 and 1750, similar to means used by African and Asian merchants to counter European attempts for trade control: specialization of strengths and alliances that played off one group against another.

While Siddi studies are becoming popular among Asianists, Africanists, and Diaspora researchers, much work remains to be done on the emergence of African–South Asian ethnicity during their development as slave elites and settlements as slaves, traders, nobility, and royalty. Since Africans from all over Africa were represented in this development, it would be fruitful to consider (after Basu 2001 and Obeng in this volume) how group formation processes and narratives emerged and how they were operationalized; how power structures evolved among Africans on the coast and in the hinterland; and what were the underlying mosaics and interactions behind the diverse nature of African settlement in South Asia: from the foraging maroon settlements to the powerful polity of Janjira, all placed under the rubric of one catch-all term—"Siddi."

The Indian Ocean interaction complex has been described by many as the center of the world's economy, particularly before AD 1500 (Abu-Lughod 1989; Chaudhuri 1985, 1990; Frank 1998; Pearson 1998). However, for many scholars and for the general public, the post-1500 world can be described thus: "the early 16th century, when Europeans began to divide the world into huge empires, opened up a new era in international trade" (Lye 2000: 42; see also Diamond 1997). Hence, post-1500 Afrasian interactions were largely shaped by European interests and actions to corner trade and polity in Africa and Asia. Furthermore, this period is seen as the emergence of a globalization scheme in which trading elites of Europe manipulated the Afrasian peripheries. Based on our ongoing research in East Africa and India, we find this view to be misleading and simplistic, as it ignores the facts that until 1750 Afrasian merchants dominated trade;

African and Asian mariners dominated much of the Oceanic routes between East Africa and West India; and European colonization of Afrasia was limited to coastal entrepôts, and their domination of the hinterlands did not begin in earnest until AD 1757 (Das Gupta 2001; Gordon 2000). In this chapter, we underscore both the depth and significance of African settlers and navies on the West Coast of India in the years AD 1500–1750. This development was due to the entrenchment of Africans in South Asian political and social life since the early thirteenth century AD and was a part of a larger process seen in and specific to the Islamic world. We place the emergence of the coastal Siddi state of Janjira in a political world where African slave elites in India used their connections among South Asian political elite to control the trade routes and the coastal littoral of the northwest coast of India. In this world, European influence was limited by a lack of trade control, the presence of powerful land-based policies in the hinterland, and the growth of Asian and African navies.

### Notes

1. Though African slave administrators had been active in the Delhi Sultanate following the Slave Dynasty and the Khiljis (e.g., Malik Kafur, Jalaluddin Yakut), it was in Bengal that they achieved full administrative status and elevated themselves to the positions of sultans in the late fifteenth century (Ali 1996). Following their expulsion from Bengal in AD 1493, many Africans migrated southward and to the west in response to the high demand for their military skills and political and economic acumen in the five Bahmani sultanates as well as the Gujarat Sultanate of Bahadur Shah.

2. This summary of Bahmani administration is from Hiroshi Fukazawa (1991): *Local Administration of the Adilshahi Sultanate* (1489–1686).

3. Fukazawa traces the origins of the five Sultanates and latter polities such as the Maratha polity under Shivaji Bhosale (in the mid-seventeenth century) to this tendency for decentralization.

4. Both Habshi and Dakhni groups were Sunni Muslims as opposed to the Shia Afaqi. Also, being African and indigenous, these two groups were viewed as cultural inferiors by the Shia Persian/Turkic Afaqi, giving them cause to unite (Pankhurst 2001).

5. The Portuguese won Bassein and Daman, only after considerable fighting, and had to face constant attacks from the African navies into the late seventeenth and eighteenth centuries (Chauhan 1995). Furthermore, this probably resulted in an influx of Africans into the Danda-Rajpuri area and helped in the consolidation of African power at Janjira thereafter.

6. The actual takeover of Janjira has two variations (Chauhan 1995). One version suggests that, led by their leaders from further up the coast, they tricked the Koli ( fishermen) owners of the island and smuggled their men onto the island hidden in crates. This variation of the Trojan horse has the African mercenaries emerging from their crates at night, taking the fishermen by surprise, and thus capturing the island. The other myth involves the ruler of Ahmadnagar, Sultan Ahmad Nizam Shah, who gave the island and the governorship of the surrounding territory to his African general Yakut (Yakut Khan Habshi/Siddi Yakut), as reward for his personal achievement in capturing Janjira. This feat involved Yakut and his African soldiers swimming

across the channel from Danda-Rajpuri by night with their swords or knives in their teeth and taking the island's inhabitants by surprise.

7. One story states that the Africans consulted a Hindu astrologer, Ganesh Daivadnya Joshi, for setting the time and day for the construction of the fort at Janjira after the invasion. The astrologer was absent when they came, and his daughter, who was also an accomplished albeit naïve astrologer, gave them the most propitious time for their construction. She asserted that if they started construction on the stipulated time and day, not only would the building be successful, but they would never be driven out of Janjira by any opposing hostile force. Her father, upon hearing this lamented: "Oh what have you done? This [time] is [extremely auspicious] and the fort will remain invincible for hundreds of years. We are Brahmins and the butchers should not be told where the cow is" (Chauhan 1995: 22–23).

## Works Cited

Abu-Lughod, Janet L. 1989. *Before European Hegemony: The World System A.D. 1250–1350*. New York: Oxford University Press.

Ali, Shanti Sadiq. 1996. *African Dispersal in the Deccan: From Medieval to Modern Times*. London: Sangam Books.

Allouche, Adel. 1983. *The Origins and Development of the Ottoman-Safavid Conflict (906–962/1500–1555)*. Berlin: Klaus Schwarz Verlag.

———. 1994. *Mamluk Economics: A Study and Translation of Al-Maqrizi's Ighathah*. Salt Lake City: University of Utah Press, 1994.

Athar Ali, M. 1985. *The Apparatus of Empire :Awards of Ranks, Offices, and Titles to the Mughal Nobility, 1574–1658*. New York: Oxford University Press, 1985.

Bacharach, Jere L. 1981. "African Military Slaves in the Medieval Middle East: The Cases of Iraq (869–955) and Egypt (868–1171)." *International Journal of Middle East Studies* 13: 471–95.

Banaji, D. R. 1932. *Bombay and the Sidis*. Bombay: University of Bombay.

Basu, Helene. 2000. "Theatre of Memory: Performances of Ritual Kinship of the African Diaspora in Sind/Pakistan." In *Culture, Creation and Procreation in South Asia*, ed. Aparna Rao and Monika Boeck, 243–70. Oxford: Berghahn.

———. 2001. "Slave, Soldier, Trader, Fakir: Fragments of African Histories in Gujarat." In *The African Diaspora in the Indian Ocean*, ed. Shihan de Silva Jayasuriya and Richard Pankhurst. Trenton, N.J.: Red Sea Press.

Behrens-Abouseif, Doris. 1998. "Patterns of Urban Patronage in Cairo." In Philipp and Haarmann, *Mamluks in Egyptian Politics and Society*, 224–34. Cambridge: Cambridge University Press.

Chaterji, S. K. 1968. *India and Ethiopia from the Seventh Century BC*. Calcutta: Asiatic Society, 1968.

Chaudhuri, K. N. 1985. *Trade and Civilization in the Indian Ocean: An Economic History from the Rise of Islam to 1750*. Cambridge: Cambridge University Press.

———. 1990. *Asia before Europe: Economy and Civilization of the Indian Ocean from the Rise of Islam to 1750*. Cambridge: Cambridge University Press.

Chauhan, R. S. S. 1995. *Africans in India: From Slavery to Royalty*. New Delhi: Asian.

COI. 1931. "Census of India, Bombay Presidency." Bombay: Government Central Press, Government of India.

Comaroff, Jean, and John Comaroff, eds. 1993. *Modernity and Its Malcontents*. Chicago: University of Chicago Press.

Correa-Afonso, John. 1990. *Intrepid Itinerant: Manuel Godinho and His Journey from India to Portugal in 1663.* Bombay: Oxford University Press.

Crone, Patricia. 1980. *Slaves on Horses.* Cambridge: Cambridge University Press.

Danvers, Frederic Charles, ed. 1968. *Letters Received by the East India Company from Its Servants in the East.* 6 vols. Amsterdam: N. Israel.

Das Gupta, Ashin. 1967. "Trade and Politics in 18th Century India." In *Islam and the Trade of Asia,* ed. D. S. Richards, 37–62. Oxford: Bruno Cassirer; Philadelphia:, University of Pennsylvania Press.

———. 1979. *Indian Merchants and the Decline of Surat: c. 1700–1750.* Beiträge zur Südasienforschung; no. 40. Wiesbaden, Germany: Steiner.

———. 1987. "Introduction II: The Story." In *India and the Indian Ocean,* ed. Ashin Das Gupta and M. N. Pearson, 25–45. Oxford: Oxford University Press.

———. 2001. *The World of the Indian Ocean Merchant, 1500–1800: Collected Essays of Ashin Das Gupta.* Comp. Uma Das Gupta. New Delhi: Oxford University Press.

Das Gupta, Ashin, and M. N. Pearson, eds. 1999. *India and the Indian Ocean, 1500–1800.* Delhi: Oxford University Press.

Diamond, Jared. 1997. *Guns, Germs and Steel: The Fates of Human Societies.* New York, W.W. Norton.

Dighe, V. G. 1944. *Peshwa Bajirao I and the Maratha Expansion.* Bombay: Karnatak.

Duff, James Grant. 1995. *History of the Mahrattas.* 3 vols. New Delhi: D. K.

Enthoven, R. E. 1975. *The Tribes and Castes of Bombay.* Vol. 3. New Delhi: Cosmo.

Foster, William, ed. 1906–1927. *The English Factories in India.* 13 vols. Oxford: Clarendon Press.

Frank, Andre-Gunder. 1998. *Reorient: Global Economy in the Asian Age.* Berkeley: University of California Press.

Fukazawa, Hiroshi. 1991. *The Medieval Deccan: Peasants, Social Systems and States, Sixteenth to Eighteenth Centuries.* Delhi: Oxford University Press.

GBP. 1833. "Gazeteer of Bombay Presidency." Bombay: India Office, 1833.

Glassman, Jonathon. 1991. "The Bondsman's New Clothes: The Contradictory Consciousness of Slave Resistance on the Swahili Coast." *Journal of African History* 32: 277–312.

Gogte, V. 2002. "Ancient Maritime Trade in the Indian Ocean; Evaluation by Scientific Studies of Pottery." *Man and Environment* 27, no. 1: 57–68.

———. 2003. "The Archaeology of Maritime Trade at Chaul, Western Coast of India." *Man and Environment* 28.1: 67–74.

Gordon, Stewart. 2000. *The Marathas: 1600–1818.* Ed. Gordon Johnson. 2nd ed. New Cambridge History of India series. New Delhi: Cambridge University Press.

Haarmann, Ulrich. 1998. "Joseph's Law: The Careers and Activities of Mamluk Descendants before the Ottoman Conquest of Egypt." In Philipp and Haarmann, *Mamluks in Egyptian Politics and Society,* 55–86.

Harris, Joseph E. 1971. *The African Presence in Asia: Consequences of the East African Slave Trade.* Evanston, Ill.: Northwestern University Press.

———. 1993. "Africans in Asian History." In *Global Dimensions of the African Diaspora,* ed. Joseph E. Harris, 325–38. Washington D.C.: Howard University Press.

Insoll, Timothy. 2003. *The Archaeology of Islam in Sub-Saharan Africa.* Cambridge: Cambridge University Press.

Jain, V. K. 1990. *Trade and Traders in Western India.* New Delhi: Munshiram Manoharlal.

Jayasuriya, S., and Richard Pankhurst. 2001. "On the African Diaspora in the Indian Ocean." In *The African Diaspora in the Indian Ocean,* ed. S. Jayasuriya and Richard Pankhurst, 7–18. Trenton, N.J.: Africa World Press.

Kadetotad, N. K. 1992. "Siddi." In *People of India: Karnataka,* ed. K. S. Singh, 1291–96. New Delhi: Anthropological Survey of India.

Kincaid, Dennis. 1937. *The Grand Rebel: An Impression of Shivaji, the Founder of the Maratha Empire.* New Delhi: Low Cost.

Kosambi, Meera. 1985. "Commerce, Conquest and the Colonial City: The Role of Locational Factors in the Rise of Bombay." *Economic and Political Weekly* 20.1: 32–37.

——. 1996. "The Konkan Ports and European Dominance: An Urban Perspective." In Kulkarni, Nayeem, and de Souza, *Medieval Deccan History,* 104–7.

Kulkarni, A. R., M. A. Nayeem, and T. R. de Souza, eds. 1996. *Medieval Deccan History: Commemoration Volume in Honour of Purushottam Mahadeo Joshi.* Bombay: Popular Prakashan.

Kulkarni, G. T. 1982. "The Mughal Struggle for Occupation of the Talkonkan." In *Studies in Shivaji and His Times,* ed. B. R. Kamble, 57–59. Kolhapur, India: Shivaji University.

Kumar, D. 1997. "The State and Private Property: Some Considerations." In Kulkarni, Nayeem, and de Souza, *Mediaeval Deccan History.* Bombay: Popular Prakashan.

Kusimba, C. M. 1999. *Rise and Fall of Swahili States.* Walnut Creek, Calif.: Altamira Press.

Kusimba, C. M., and B. Bronson. 2000. "What Does Africa Mean to You?" *In the Field,* March–April.

Levtzion, Nehemia, and Randall Pouwells, eds. 2000. *History of Islam in Africa.* Cambridge: Basil Blackwell.

Lodhi, A. 1991. "African Settlements in India." *Nordic Journal of African Studies* 1.1: 83–87.

Lombard, Denys, and Jean Aubin, eds. 2000. *Asian Merchants and Businessmen in the Indian Ocean and the China Sea.* Oxford: Oxford University Press.

Lovejoy, Paul. 1983. *Transformations in Slavery: A History of Slavery in Africa.* Cambridge: Cambridge University Press.

——, ed. 2003. *Slavery on the Frontiers of Islam.* Princeton, N.J.: Marcus Wiener.

Lye, Keith. 2000. "Trade and Commerce" In *Philips Concise World Atlas,* 42–43. London: George Philip.

Meillassoux, Claude. 1991. *The Anthropology of Slavery: The Womb and Iron and Gold.* Chicago: University of Chicago Press.

Miers, Suzanne, and Igor Kopytoff. 1977. "African "Slavery as an Institution of Marginality." In *Slavery in Africa,* ed. Suzanne Miers and Igor Kopytoff, 3–81. Madison: University of Wisconsin Press.

Moraes, G. M. 1975. "Political Relations of the Nizam Shahis of Ahmadnagar with the Portuguese." In *Aspects of Deccan History,* ed. Vasant Kumar Bava, 30–31. Hyderabad, India: Institute of Asian Studies.

Naqvi, H. K. 1972. *Urbanization and Urban Centres under the Great Mughals: 1556–1707.* Vol. 1. Shimla, India: Indian Institute of Advanced Study.

——. 1987. *Agricultural, Industrial and Urban Dynamism under the Sultans of Delhi, 1206–1555.* New Delhi: Munshiram Manoharlal.

Nightingale, Pamela. 1970. *Trade and Empire in Western India, 1784–1806.* Cambridge: Cambridge University Press.

Oka, Rahul, and Vishwas Gogte. 2004. "Ethno-archaeological Survey of Murud-Janjira." In *Chaul Notes.* Pune, India: Deccan College Post-Graduate and Research Institute.

Oka, Rahul, C. M. Kusimba, and P. F. Thorbahn. Forthcoming. "Gujarat Cotton and East African Ivory: The Role of The Indian Subcontinent in the Development of the Ivory Trade of East Africa." In *Prehistoric and Prohistoric Interactions in Tsavo, Kenya,* ed. C. M. Kusimba. Chicago: Fieldiana Press.

Palakshappa, T. C. 1976. *The Siddis of North Kanara.* New Delhi: Sterling.

Pankhurst, Richard. 1994. *The Ethiopians: A History.* Peoples of Africa series, ed. Parker Shipton. Oxford: Blackwell.

———. 2001. "The Ethiopian Diaspora to India: The Role of the Habshis and Sidis from Medieval Times to the End of the Eighteenth Century." In Jayasuriya and Pankhurst, *African Diaspora in the Indian Ocean,* 189–222. Trenton, N.J.: Africa World Press.

Parasnis, D. B. 1987. "History of the Siddis of Janjira." *Bharat Varsha.* New Delhi: Popular Prakashan.

Patterson, Orlando. 1982. *Slavery and Social Death: A Comparative Perspective.* Cambridge, Mass.: Harvard University Press.

Pearson, Michael Naylor. 1976. *Merchants and Rulers in Gujarat: The Response to the Portuguese in the Sixteenth Century.* Berkeley: University of California Press.

———. 1981. *Coastal Western India: Studies from the Portuguese Records.* XCHR Studies series, no. 2. New Delhi: Concept.

———. 1987. "India and the Indian Ocean in the Sixteenth Century." In *India and the Indian Ocean.,* ed. Ashin Das Gupta and M. N. Pearson, 71–93. Calcutta: Oxford University Press, 1987.

———. 1994. *Pious Passengers: The Hajj in Earlier Times.* London: Hurst.

———. 1996. *Pilgrimage to Mecca: The Indian Experience, 1500–1800.* Princeton, N.J.: Marcus Wiener.

———. 1998. *Port Cities and Intruders: The Swahili Coast, India, and Portugal in the Early Modern Era.* Baltimore: Johns Hopkins University Press.

Philipp, Thomas. 1998. "Personal Loyalty and Political Power of the Mamluks in the Eighteenth Century." In Philipp and Haarmann, *Mamluks in Egyptian Politics and Society,* 118–27.

Philipp, Thomas, and Ulrich Haarmann, eds. 1998. *The Mamluks in Egyptian Politics and Society.* Cambridge Studies in Islamic Civilization. Cambridge: Cambridge University Press.

Philips, John Edward. 2000. "The Persistence of Slave Officials in the Sokoto Caliphate." In Toru and Philips, *Slave Elites in the Middle East and Africa,* 215–34. London: Paul Kegan.

Pipes, Daniel. 1981. *Slave Soldiers and Islam.* New Haven, Conn.: Yale University Press.

Prakash, Om. 1979. "Asian Trade and European Impact: A Study of the Trade from Bengal, 1630–1720." In *The Age of Partnership: Europeans in Asia before the Dominion,* ed. B. B. Kling and M. N. Pearson, 43–70. Honolulu: University of Hawaii Press.

———, ed. 1994. *Precious Metals and Commerce: The Dutch East India Company in the Indian Ocean Trade.* Aldershot, UK: Variorum.

———. 1996. "The Dutch Factory at Vengurla in the Seventeenth Century." In Kulkarni, Nayeem, and de Souza, *Medieval Deccan History*, 185–91. Bombay: Popular Prakashan.

———. 1998. *European Commercial Enterprise in Pre-colonial India*. Cambridge: Cambridge University Press.

Rabbat, Nasser. 2000. "The Changing Concept of *Mamluk* in the Mamluk Sultanate in Egypt and Syria." In Toru and Philips, *Slave Elites in the Middle East and Africa*, 81–98.

Richards, John F. 1993. *The Mughal Empire*. New Cambridge History of India series. Cambridge: Cambridge University Press.

Roychoudhury, D. 1957. "Anthropometry of Siddhis, the Negroid Population of North Kanara, India." *Bulletin of the Department of Anthropology, Government of India* 6.1: 53–66.

Russell, R. V., and Hira Lal. 1975. *The Tribes and Castes of the Central Provinces of India*. New Delhi: Cosmo.

Sardesai, G. S. 1934–40. *Peshwa Daftar*. Vishrambaug Wada Archives, Pune, India.

Sarkar, J. N. 1973. *Shivaji and His Times*. New Delhi.

Seth, D. R. 1957. "Life and Times of Malik Ambar." *Indian Culture* 31: 142.

Sinha, N. K. 1992. "Siddi." In *People of India: Daman and Diu*, ed. K. S. Singh. Bombay: Anthropological Survey of India.

Stein, Burton. 1980. *Peasant State and Society in Medieval South India*. Delhi: Oxford University Press.

Stillwell, Sean. 2000. "The Power of Knowledge and the Knowledge of Power: Kinship, Community and Royal Slavery in Pre-Colonial Kano, 1807–1903." In Toru and Philips, *Slave Elites in the Middle East and Africa*, 117–58.

———. 2003. "The Development of *Mamluk* Slavery in the Sokoto Caliphate." In Lovejoy, *Slavery of the Frontiers of Islam*, 87–110.

———. 2004. *Paradoxes of Power: The Kano "Mamluks" and the Male Royal Slavery in the Sokoto Caliphate, 1804–1903*. Social History of Africa series. Portsmouth, N.H.: Heinemann.

Subrahmanyam, Sanjay. 1990. *The Political Economy of Commerce: Southern India, 1500–1650*. Cambridge: Cambridge University Press.

———. 1993. *The Portuguese Empire in Asia, 1500–1700: A Political and Economic History*. London: Longman.

Tolodano, Ehud. 1998. *Slavery and Abolition in the Ottoman Middle East*. Seattle: University of Washington Press.

———. 2000. "The Concept of Slavery in Ottoman and Other Muslim Societies: Dichotomy or Continuum." In Toru and Philips, *Slave Elites in the Middle East and Africa*, 159–76.

Toru, Miura, and John Edward Philips. 2000. *Slave Elites in the Middle East and Africa*. London: Paul Kegan.

Trivedi, R. K. 1961. *Siddi: A Negroid Tribe of Gujarat*. Vol. 5:B(1), *Ethnographic Series*. New Delhi: Census of India, 1961.

Tsugitaka, Sato. 2000. "Slave Elites in Islamic History." In Toru and Philips, *Slave Elites in the Middle East and Africa*, 1–12.

Ze'evi, Dror. 2000. "My Slave, My Son, My Lord: Slavery, Family and State in the Islamic Middle East." In Toru and Philips, *Slave Elites in the Middle East and Africa*, 71–80.

# 9

# Religion and Empire

*Belief and Identity among African Indians of*
*Karnataka, South India*

Pashington Obeng

## Introduction

African Asians' historic presence, their religio-political, cultural, and
military contributions, and their changing roles during the rise, expansion, and fall of Indian empires and dynasties from medieval times to the
present day, is an under-researched subject. Much of the scholarship on
Indian medieval and modern imperial history scarcely discusses the significant issue of African Indians' restructuring alliances, redefining themselves and contributing to the development of Indian kingdoms. The literature addressing the medieval and modern dynasties and empires of the
Indian subcontinent tends to highlight religious, political, and military
powers exercised by Bahmanis, Vijayanagars, Mughals, Reddis, Marathas,
Bijapuris, Portuguese, and the British (Banaji 1932; Chanana 1960; Eaton
1978; Gordon 1993; Richards 1993). Such historiography of empires and
religions in India has, at times, focused on architectural styles and on the
expansion of agrarian and commercial societies but has not provided
much analysis of "political forms" (Stein 1989: xii). For instance, the Mughal Empire of the 1600s was noted for its opulence and "high culture"

(Richards 1993: 1). Consequently, the focus of such literature has been individual rulers and their military, political, and religious institutions. Such works discuss the ideologies that undergirded the different religious and political structures, internal and external alliances, and individuals and groups that opposed the imperial systems.

Those who lived under the different empires have often been cast in binary relations: either as people who only responded to the structures and ideologies of imperial forces or as people who rebelled against imperial rule. The few scholars who have called attention to the economic and political history of African Indians often stress heroic individuals such as Malik Amber (Banaji 1932; Harris 1971; Khalidi 1989; Chauhan 1995).

The above works overlook the sovereign agencies of ordinary people and their religious and cultural energy, especially of minorities such as African Indians. The other shortcoming of the above approach is that it does not address either African Indians as important actors or how they contributed to the complex and plural religious landscape of India. For instance, the literature on the Karnataka African Indians categorizes them as Muslims, Christians, and Hindus (Harris 1971; Pinto 1992; Chauhan 1995), thus defining them with reference to the features and symbols of the "great" religions of the imperial regimes in India. The above categorization overlooks ways in which African Indians have appropriated local practices into their own versions of religiosity as they practiced faiths of their choice. Available literature on African Asians has often addressed their origins, settlements, and the military and political prominence of a few among them (Harris 1971; Irwin 1977; Khalidi 1989; Chauhan 1995). The economic and social plight of African Indians has also been discussed (Rao 1973; D. K. Bhattacharya 1970; Lobo 1984). However, prevalent theories of marginalization at times downplay the creative and responsible political action of the African Indians. Other aspects of African Indians that have been researched are their retention of African linguistic and cultural elements (Freeman-Grenville 1988; Gupta 1991). And finally, in addition to the above studies, Alpers (1997) argues that scholars need to research the contributions African Asians have made to shape the history, politics, and cultures of their host communities. Because there is no focused study on African Indian identity formation and their religious and cultural contributions in the Indian subcontinent since the medieval period, this essay seeks to address that neglect.

The chapter therefore goes further to provide insight into how ordinary or "folk" African Indians employ their beliefs and practices to reinforce and reproduce boundaries based on status in such a highly stratified society. In the process, they sometimes develop and promote new identities and a consciousness outside of the modern imperial religious, caste, and class structures. In the context of imperial religion and politics African Indians formed and negotiated their own private and public spaces within the larger structure of Indian society. They were, and still are, actors in their own right within their realms. African Indians have over the past four hundred years played many roles in the Indian subcontinent.

This essay examines how African Indians of Karnataka in south India, like their forbearers, have been forging relationships, redefining themselves, and articulating their agency by drawing on both Indian and African religious and cultural resources. The African Indians among whom my research was done in 1998, 1999, and 2001 live in Haliyal, Yellapur, Hubli, Mundgod, and Sirsi taluks (subdistricts) in the Karnataka State of south India. The Karnataka African Indians are a part of African Asians who are also found on the west coast of India in Gujarat, Diu, and Maharashtra (Khalidi 1989; Ali 1996; Lobo 1984).

Among Karnataka African Indians are found the following: Muslims who trace their history in India to the Bijapur kingdom founded in 1490, when the Omani Arab slave traders sold their forebears to serve as dock workers, domestics, and guards of Muslim leaders; Christians who trace their roots to Goa (the Estado da India), which was ruled by the Portuguese; and Hindus whose ancestors were sold by Arabs, Indian merchants, and Portuguese to Havik Brahmins (Hindus) "in exchange for local products" (Palakshappa 1976: 11). Harris (1971) points out that the forebears of present-day African Indians voluntarily or forcibly emigrated at different times across the Sahara, the Mediterranean and Red Seas, and the Indian Ocean from Ethiopia (Abyssinia), Sudan, Somalia, and the Swahili coast of East Africa.

Since the above historic movements of peoples from Africa to India, other diasporic and continental Africans have been visiting India. In Karnataka where the African Indians live mostly in areas away from towns and cities, there is not much interaction between them and recent African immigrants.

This study is based on historical accounts of Indian medieval and contemporary regimes, recent anthropological works, and ethnographic data I have been collecting since the summer of 1998. The chapter draws on the pioneering historical works of Joseph Harris (1971), Eaton (1978), Richards (1993), Pinto (1992), and Chauhan (1995). Khalidi's (1989) insightful discussion of African Indians (Habshis) in the Deccan and Ruth Simms Hamilton's (1990) seminal work on creating a paradigm for studying diasporic Africans have also shaped this article.

This essay seeks to contribute to diaspora studies by highlighting the nature and process of contributions, the shifting alliances, and the relationships diasporic Africans have formed to assert political action in the Indian subcontinent. The chapter begins with a brief history of African Indian involvement in a series of imperial regimes in India and then focuses on how contemporary Karnataka African Indians deploy their history, culture, and religion in redefining themselves.

The essay helps clarify and develop a conceptual framework for understanding the geo-social, economic, cultural, and religious displacements experienced by individuals and groups based on race, color, class, religion, and gender (Hamilton 1990). The religious experience and cultural practices of African Indians provide a context for understanding ways in which religion and culture become a contested locus for creating and recreating a "counterhegemonic world view" (Basu and Werbner 1998: 117) and generating new meaning systems for themselves and for other Indians. They have depended on their faith and other cultural resources to endure, to resist, to struggle for freedom, and to order their lives.

The history of the African Indians since medieval times shows that in spite of the fact that they have always been regarded as foreigners (Eaton1978; Harris 1975; Lobo 1984) and a minority (numerically and sometimes marginalized), they have adjusted to India by playing critical roles as military leaders, regents, rulers, and domestics and have contributed to the polities of their communities. As Chauhan points out, African Indian services were used "for imperial expansion or for development and growth of kingdoms" (1995: 240). Some of the military commanders, foot soldiers, administrators, domestics, and servants who played considerable roles in India from the fourteenth century until India became independent of British rule were Africans, also referred to as Abyssinians, Habshis, or Siddis (Khalidi 1989; Harris 1971; Ali 1996; Palakshappa 1976). In addition to tapping the African Indians for their military skills, imperial powers have exploited this people for cheap labor (Ali 1996; Pinto 1992).

The focus on ordinary African Indians is crucial because it helps us appreciate how both present-day African Asians and their forebears have evolved strategies to live and function in India. The cultural and religious strategies deployed by African Indians to define themselves are simultaneously used for exposing structures and symbols of domination and subordination. For instance, as some of them venerate their ancestors and others worship Ellama, a south Indian goddess (who is independent of the Brahminical Hindu deities), African Indians draw attention to social and religious systems that subjugate Indians. By so doing, African Indians utilize religious and cultural elements for reinventing avenues for transformative power relations. African Indian life ways reveal "subtle peculiarities" (Cohen 1976: 15) in, specifically, how they express themselves in their religion—which are mechanisms for developing boundaries and styles of interaction and communication within their groupings. Though they belong to the larger Indian linguistic and cultural clusters of Karnataka, African Indians through symbolic activities articulate "subcultures" or alternative cultures.

In sum, the essay shows that African Indians are not passive victims of their geo-social and religious displacements but that they have actively drawn on their religious and cultural resources to endure and resist their exploitation. They have struggled for the freedom to create their personal and collective sovereignty. By so doing, African Indians have generated religious, cultural, and political action in Karnataka. They have adjusted to both premodern and modern Indian imperial conditions by developing practices within Indian and African symbols to reinforce their distinctiveness. The following sections highlight the varying ways in which African Indians have retained and reworked aspects of their identities to articulate their religious and political action under the contemporary complex structures and symbols of the Indian state power.

### A Brief History of the African Presence in India

As early as in the thirteenth century, Queen Raziya, the sovereign of the sultanate of Delhi, befriended an enslaved African (Habshi) slave named Jalal-ud-din Yaqut. She later appointed Yaqut to the post of royal stable master. During the late 1400s Africans in "northern India, Bengal, organized and asserted considerable political power" (Harris 1971: 79). Rukn-ud-din Barbak, king of Bengal (1459–1474), is said to have been the first Indian king to promote many previously enslaved Africans to high rank. It is estimated that he had 8,000 African slave-soldiers in his army. When Habesh Khan, king of Bengal, became dictatorial, Sidi Badr, an African guardsman, seized the throne in 1490. Badr ruled for more than three years, under the title of Shams-ud-din Abu Nasr Muzaffar Shah. He had an army of 30,000 of which 5,000 were Africans (Abyssinians) of Ethiopian descent. When he was murdered in 1493, the Africans in high posts were dismissed and expelled from the kingdom. This marked the end of the African dynasty in Bengal (Majumdar 1960: 345–46).

The second half of the seventeenth century was marked by interimperial conflicts. For instance, there were "conflicts between the Mughals and the Marathas, and between both of them and the English, the Portuguese, and the Dutch, the last three of whom were competing for political and economic spheres of influence in western India as well as in East Africa" (Harris 1971: 84). In 1665 the Portuguese lost "Bombay to the British government, which in 1668 transferred it to the East India

Company; Janjira then became vital to the company as a base for protecting its maritime vessels" (84).

### African Indian Imperial Rule of Janjira

The island of Janjira is located off the west coast of India about forty-five miles south of Bombay (Mumbai). By 1872 it is estimated that it had a population of 1,700, of whom 258 were Africans. Most of the Africans were "relatives of the *nawab* (king); they were the principal landowners and civil servants and constituted the largest Muslim group on the island. Other religious groups included Hindus, Jews and Christians" (Harris 1971: 80). Until the British took over the island in 1879, a council of African nobles chose the *nawab*, who was the head of state and religion (Islam). Some descendants of the *nawab* are reported to still hold prestigious positions in and outside of India (Robbins and McLeod 2006). The British negotiated a treaty of alliance and friendship with the Africans of Janjira in 1733.

In the 1800s the influence of the Janjira Africans declined as Britain's political and economic stakes in India rose. Britain "could not allow even the more powerful European countries to interfere; without a doubt, Sidi influence had to be eliminated" (Harris 1971: 85–86). According to the British, the Africans were using Janjira, a Portuguese property, to launch attacks into British territories, especially Bombay (Thekkedath 1988; Gordon 1993; Richards 1993). The British divided India into administrative presidencies to consolidate their position in India. Today the African Indians' power and influence remain insignificant in India.

### Peoples and Polities of the Deccan

It was during the 1300s that the first Muslim invasions of Maharashtra and other parts of the Deccan took place under the leadership of Ala-ud-Din Khilji, a "rebel nephew of the sultan of Delhi" (Gordon 1993: 13). The invasion fostered religious and political turmoil in the Deccan. Ali (1996) also points out that from the beginning of the Bahmani empire (1347–1489) in the Deccan, Africans (Habshis/Abyssinians) served as mercenaries (*jangju*) fighting for or against various political and military powers. Later when there were struggles between the Dakhani (Muslim old-comers) and the Afagis (the Muslim newcomers), the Africans were found to have forged alliances with the Dakhanis, who were Sunnis, against the Afagis, who were Shias from Iran and Iraq (Sherwani and Soshi 1973).

After settling in the Deccan, Africans incorporated some local practices into their expression of Sunni Islam. For instance, the veneration of local Islamic saints was combined with their own use of charms and amulets (*ta'wiz*). This combination was widely practiced by the Dakhanis. Among the saints that were and are still venerated by the Africans of the Haliyal, Mundgod, Yellapur, and Sirsi taluks of Karnataka is the founder of the Qadiri Sufi order, 'Abd al-Qadir Jilani (d. 1166) of Baghdad, also called Mahbub al-Subhani. Other practices that the Africans embraced were *sama'* (sufi mystical music) and *rags* (modes of classical Indian music) (Eaton 1978). The Africans adopted the Sufi practice of dancing in spiritual ecstasy.

Among the pre-Islamic dynasties in the Deccan, the Hindu dynasties featured Brahmins who performed official rituals to "ensure not just fertility but the continued proper ordering of the entire cosmos" (Gordon 1993: 17). However, between the fourteenth and nineteenth centuries, the "Maratha" identity in the Deccan came to consist of different castes— Kunbi, Lohar, Sutar, Bhandari, Dhangars (shepherds), etc. Martial skills later became a new yardstick for redrawing caste categories. The ordinary people were distinguished from warrior families by the rights and awards the latter received because of war services. Brahmins became less dominant in the Deccan around this period. Given their military prowess, courage, and strength, some of the Africans between the fourteenth and nineteenth centuries, though male slaves (*gulams*), rose to positions of power. For instance, toward the end of the fourteenth century, Malik Sarwar, an African eunuch who gained his freedom from the Delhi sultans, founded the Shargis Dynasty (1394–1479) of Jaunpur, which is now part of present-day Uttar Pradesh (Khalidi 1989; Harris 1971).

As new class cleavages were being formed between the fifteenth and sixteenth centuries, a popular brand of Hindu, *bhakti*, was propagated by peripatetic Hindus. This form of faith spread outside the kingly courts and "Brahmin-controlled temples" (Gordon 1993: 18). *Bhakti*, in the Deccan, was a new Hindu devotional movement which originated in the mid-tenth century in the Tamil country of south India, as a reaction to the rigidly formal Vedic Hindu practices.

It is important at this stage to provide some broad features of the Hindu caste system and to emphasize that since not all the African Indians were or are Hindus, they have defined themselves in ways other than with reference to the Hindu caste logic. The Hindu system divides people into four major social classes or varnas: the priestly class and intellectuals are the Brahmins; the Kshatriyas are the rulers and warriors; the Vaishiyas are agriculturalists, salespeople, and merchants; and the Shudras are servants and laborers. The varnas have specific rules about jobs, diet, and marriage partners. Outside of these broad classes are the Untouchables, also called Harijans (God's people) or Dalits (the oppressed). Since there are many jati subcastes within each social class, Hinduism ends up having many subgroups. In bhakti, however, followers were free to use their vernacular in worship and relax the caste rules and the strictures of prohibitions about pollution.

This religious atmosphere encouraged Muslims and Hindus to seek commonalties in expressing their devotion (Gordon 1993: 18). Hindus were at times found worshipping at the tombs of Muslim saints (*dargahs*), and some Hindus embraced the Muslim tenet of brotherhood which implicitly challenged the caste logic (20).

### African Involvement in Deccan Political History

The new class and caste cleavages and the religious and political fluidity of the period fostered the inclusion of Africans who had either been brought to India to fight for their slave-masters or voluntarily entered the Deccan (Harris 1971; Khalidi 1989; Gordon 1993; Pinto 1992). For instance, Africans played important roles in the Bijapur kingdom which was founded in 1490, but by 1686 it had been annexed by the Mughals.

Under the attack of the Mughals in 1678, the African leader Siddi Masud was called upon to help defend the Bijapur kingdom. Africans were not only fighters. Some were architects and builders. An African named Yaqut Dabuli, for instance, was commissioned by Muhammad Shah (1627–1656) to decorate the "great mihrab in the Jami Masjid." Dabuli's name was inscribed in the Jumma mosque. The inscription read "Yaqut Dabuli was servant and slave of Mahmoo Shah, whose shadow may God protect, A.D. 1635" (Ali 1996: 137). Thus besides the recognition they received for their military skills, African Indians shaped Indian religious culture as artisans. Before the decline in their socio-economic and political importance in India, African Indians demonstrated their ability to mobilize human and other resources to assert their influence under different regimes.

It is not surprising that African leader Malik Amber, born in Ethiopia in 1550, enslaved by the Arabs and sold in Baghdad, would, upon his arrival in the Deccan, rise to power as *wazir* (regent-minister) and defeat the great Mughal forces in 1601 at Berar (Khalidi 1989; Ali 1996). It was under Amber that the Nizam Shahi kingdom of Ahmednagar was galvanized and aimed at expelling the Mughals from the Deccan. He recruited Marathas and Africans and gave them guerrilla training which they deployed in fighting off most of their attackers including the Mughals (Ali 1996: 2).

In addition to their asserting themselves by their martial skills, African Indians restructured alliances among themselves. For instance, whenever any of them came into power, they recruited other Africans to fill key administrative and military positions. When Malik Amber rose to power, he appointed African guards, had Africans in his administration, and established diplomatic ties with the Africans of Janjira. Amber relied on those Africans as "his naval squadron" (Harris 1971: 123), although there were other coastal Indians whose services he could have used. In 1583 the African Sunni Muslim Dilawar became regent after he had served as a bodyguard. In his new role as regent he immediately dismissed all the nearly six thousand Shia Muslim soldiers and replaced them with African Sunni Muslims. He thus marshaled religious identity and racial filiation to forge new political alliances. Also, as Amber and others were regrouping and empowering people of their own race, they were redrawing the boundaries of Indian religion and culture by engaging and challenging the religio-political and cultural structures and ideologies of the time. The African Indians were creating and recreating their religious, racial, and cultural sovereignties.

By selecting Africans rather than other Indians, Amber, Dilawar, Randaula Khan, and others like them were articulating their self-conscious outsider identities and were redefining their identities in India. Africans in power were restating and reaffirming the unbroken bond of their African-ness. Also, as they were repositioning their African alliances they were creating pan-African military and political communities to override their primordial ethnic particularities. In addition to the Africans who arrived in India as a result of the Arab slave trade, there were others who were forcibly taken to India during the European slave trade.

### African Indians under European Empires

The number of Africans who migrated to India on their own combined with those enslaved, at any one time, was small, but their arrival was fairly continuous under the Portuguese until about 1740, when Portuguese maritime dominance was seriously challenged by the French and British (Harris 1971; Chauhan 1995). Beginning in about 1530 the Portuguese exercised political and economic control over parts of the west coast of India, especially the Konkan coast, which was also the destination of many African slaves who were imported from East Africa (Pinto 1992; Khalidi 1989; Alpers 1967). The enslaved Africans were generally used by the Portuguese in business, on farms, in domestic positions, and in other menial jobs in Goa, which became Portugal's headquarters for its East African and Asian colonies (Harris 1971:81; Pinto 1992: 48). The enslaved African women were used as servants and mistresses, the men as laborers, craftsmen, sailors, and soldiers—especially the warriors as infantry. Catholic monks even had Africans slaves in their monasteries. Jesuit priests who had African servants used these enslaved Africans for cleaning, housekeeping, and cooking at the Jesuit centers. In Goa the retinue of Africans who accompanied the Portuguese became a status symbol: luxury and prestige.

Chauhan points out that under the Portuguese some of the baptized enslaved Africans fled to other states where rulers were Muslims (1995: 231). Such Muslim leaders used male slaves in their armies. Among those who escaped from their slave masters were some who switched religious affiliation. Consequently, some Christians, while serving Muslim rulers, practiced Islam.

By the nineteenth century European slave masters included the British, the Dutch, the Danes, and the Portuguese. The British, like the other European powers, sought to centralize political and economic power by putting resources into the hands of the English and a few Indian officers. The British Act V of 1843 served as the basis of the Penal Code of 1860 that banned the slave trade in British India. The Portuguese Crown also eventually issued a decree that abolished slavery and sought to accord full "rights" to the enslaved people. British rule in India continued until 1947, when India gained its independence. By the end of the slave trade, the African Indians who had served as sailors, soldiers, rulers, and domestics had suffered collective and individual decline in fortune and status (Palakshappa 1976; Eaton 1978; Ali 1996). That decline in their power and status in the Deccan plateau, coupled with their search for jobs and new places to settle, prompted or caused African Indians to disperse into the Karnataka forest areas of the Western Ghats and other parts of south India.

### Contemporary Caste, Class, and Status-Conscious Imperialism

The independence of India in 1947 did not end the patterns of patronage, individual assertion, and political positioning of groups, nor did it usher in total freedom for the African Indians. African Indians live under the age-long Brahminical Hindu caste and other hierarchically structured systems of India that have survived the rise and fall of the various dynasties. Most of present-day Karnataka African Indians are part of the underclass as regards their socio-economic status in India. Caste dominance and other forms of status consciousness legitimized by religion, custom, and pedigree are still powerful forces that shape people's social interaction and status. For instance, Thekkedath points out that although the Havik Brahmins of northern Karnataka may be only 10 percent of the population, they and the Lingayats and the Reddis have over the years been the priests, merchants, landholders, and administrators in the area. As landowners, some of them still have "slaves and servants who cultivate their lands" (Thekkedath 1988: 279).

About 80 percent of the African Indians are agricultural laborers or gatherers of areca nuts and honey. Some of them supplement their seasonal agricultural labor with hunting, tailoring, and fishing. There are others who serve as domestics at Brahmin households and in convents in the Karwar district. Those who cultivate lands on which they have lived for over thirty to forty years are not necessarily the landholders (Prasad 1991; Palakshappa 1976). They are therefore called "encroachers," so they could at any time be dispossessed of those pieces of land by the state government or any of the legally recognized landholders.

The different forms of labor control under local politicians and landholders have accentuated the level of poverty and lowered the social status of the African Indians. Under such economic and social marginalization, some African Indians are forced to give their whole household or their children in debt bondage. Debt bondage, which is perpetuated from one generation to the next, is another disempowering system that operates today in Karnataka. Widespread debt bondage is practiced in impoverished drought-prone areas and among poverty-stricken peoples of Karnataka. Besides the economic and political exploitation suffered by the African Indians, the way in which governmental agencies—and even some scholars—categorize them further obscures and marginalizes the African Indians. These African Asians bear Hindu, Muslim, and Portuguese names, and because of such names, bureaucrats and intellectuals have grouped them in with "different religious groups, thus obliterating their social cultural or ethnic identity" (Prasad 1991: 215). As a result of collapsing their identities into religious groups, Prasad contends, the African Indians of Karnataka have not been recognized as a "Scheduled Tribe" (ST) to make them eligible for some state and national government social assistance (215).

### Identity Restructuring and Religion

The Karnataka African Indians, like their forebears, have developed strategies for adjusting and contributing to the religions and cultures of India. Since Palakshappa (1976), Chauhan (1995), and Ali (1996) tend to describe African Indians by collapsing their socio-cultural, ethnic, and religious identities under Christianity, Islam, and Hinduism, it is necessary to examine briefly how these diasporic Africans practice some of their faiths.

For instance, though the Karnataka African Indians are known by the nomenclature Siddi, some of the Hindus and Muslims among them view their identities through caste and class logic, thus reproducing and reinforcing aspects of the boundaries and stratification in their society.

Hindus in Bilki and Yellapur regard themselves as superior to other castes such as the Bandhis and Namadaris (hunting and pastoral castes) in Karnataka (Chauhan 1995). Chauhan points out that some African Indians avoid eating with the Bandhis and Namadaris, although the latter groups would invite the African Indians to their homes (241).

As the Muslims among the African Indians relate to the larger society and within their race, some of them trace their roots to prominent African personalities such as Hazrat Bilal, an Ethiopian (Abyssinian) disciple of the Prophet Muhammad (Basu and Werbner 1998). It is believed that Bilal was the first to recite the Islamic call to prayer (Palakshappa 1976; Trivedi 1969). In the towns of Kendalgeri and Gunjavatti (during personal communications in 1998 and 1999), some African Indians stressed that their communities consist of the descendants of the Sunni "apical ancestors" (Basu and Werbner 1998: 119), Husein and Sayyid. These African Indians are in effect claiming descent from the Prophet Muhammad through his daughter Fatimah. That pedigree accords them prestige in their communities. Also, as Sayyid Sab Siddï, a thirty-four-year-old Muslim farmer from Kirvatti indicated, he and the others with the Sayyid pedigree have also inherited some blessings and skills. He is considered the best farmer in his community, and he attributes this talent to the *baraka* (charisma, blessing, and power) which he inherited (119). Since they claim descent from such prestigious Muslim ancestors, although they are considered and treated as underclass by Indian society, they perceive themselves as a people with royal and prominent ancestry. When status difference and religious rank are stressed among African Indians and in their relations with the larger society, we observe that the principles by which the Muslims organize and perceive themselves are internal to Islam rather than to the Hindu caste system. As Pandian argues, much scholarship on the Indian subcontinent often erroneously depicts Muslims and other non-Hindus as organizing their lives within the Hindu ethos and social order (1987: 142).

Among the African Indian Catholics of Mainelli and Ugenigeri, there is a sense that their form of Christianity—headed by nuns, priests, bishops, and, finally, the pope—is more established and respectable than the Pentecostal (also called "Blessings") churches that have recently been founded in their communities. The Pentecostal churches are often led by non-clergy evangelists who have not received any theological education. Those leaders legitimize their role by arguing that they have been called by the Holy Spirit to found and lead their congregations.

There are times when African Indians regardless of their religious affiliation get together to celebrate Muharram (Muslim), Holi (Hindu), and Christmas (Christian) festivals. For instance, in 1999 during the celebration of Muharram in Kirvattii and Gunjavatti, non-Muslim African Indians joined in the dance and music. According to Ganappa Subha Siddi, a Hindu, "We are all Siddis and this is our music and it is our dance. We use them to worship God" (personal communication). This is an example of how the African Indians consider themselves as people with the same heritage of music and dance in worship, regardless of class and religious differences.

Within the Yellapur, Haliyal, and Mundgod taluks especially in Bilki, Kuchagaon, and Kirwatti, there are African Indians who practice "folk religions" (Obeng 2000). Apart from those who employ herbal medicine to cure diseases, there are also among them "god-men/women" who are consulted by other African Indians and even by non-African Indians. In addition to what I observed in Mainelli from an informant (personal interview in August 1998) about his belief in the efficacy of "folk medicine," I learned from the project director of the Siddi Development Program, North Kanara, that he witnessed a healing event in Gutti administered by "a Siddi god-man." Some of these religious specialists employ divination and herbal medicines to heal their clients. The African Indians, like other forest dwellers in south India, use folk medicine to relieve and cure diseases (Singh et al. 1998). As they deploy their *materia medica* of folk medicine, the African Indians create and recreate a therapeutic culture that may borrow from other therapies but is free of the control of the larger society. Their medicine people are highly respected, so the therapy is drawn upon to provide space in which African Indians generate life, dignity, and personal and social worth for themselves. The medicine women and men among the African Indians fuse religious symbolism with herbology to heal various diseases.

Though African Indians are not original to north Karnataka (Uttara Kannada), their encyclopedic knowledge of plant and animal life in their forest environment as passed on from generation to generation is attested to by Palakshappa (1976), Lobo (1984), and Bhandary et al. (1995). They live among other marginalized communities such as the Gowlis, but the African Indians are said to be the only group to have identified and utilized medicinal plants such as birth control or anti-fertility herbs (*arecaceae*) and herbs for managing diabetes (*apocynaceae*) (157). Their forest habitat is central to herbal medicine. Bustin, a seventy-year-old traditional midwife, utilizes flowers, leaves, and roots to help both African Indian and non-African Indian women in labor. Her knowledge of herbs and her skill as a midwife enable her to render service to her own people and to others beyond her racial group.

### Ancestral Veneration

The role of ancestors among the African Indians has been described by Palakshappa (1976), Chauhan (1995), Lobo (1984), and Ali (1996). But

Palakshappa's assertion that African Indians "worship the spirits of their dead parents" (1976: 72) needs to be revised. Ancestral veneration should be understood from the practitioner's viewpoint. For the African Indians, ancestral veneration underscores their belief that their dead take an active role in the lives of the living. Whereas other people in Karnataka—especially the Hindus—according to Palakshappa (76), do everything to prevent the spirits of the dead from taking residence in their house, the African Indians welcome their dead home. In the larger Indian society, especially where there is Hindu influence, the family is considered polluted upon the death of a relative until *sraddha* (final funeral) rites are performed. When non-African Indian Hindus offer rice balls (*pinda*) to the dead, they do so to help reconstitute the body of the dead for the next world/life of spirits (*preta-loka*). In the case of African Indians, their ancestral veneration, *hiriyaru*, does not send the dead away. When they feed the dead and offer incense, the spirit of the dead is being reintegrated into the family. The other point worthy of note is that while the coconut used in the ritual is supposed to represent the Hindu deity Balidevaru for other Hindus, the African Indians use it to symbolize their ancestors.

African Indians interpret inexplicable misfortunes as a sign that the ancestors have been offended and are therefore punishing the living. Household shrines for ancestors are kept by African Indians of all religious traditions. In Kirvatti and Kendelgari Muslim household ancestral shrines contain unhusked coconuts placed on little pedestals. The pedestals, according to Rahman Saab, a thirty-year-old agricultural laborer of Kirvatti, are for his dead parents to sit on. Ancestral veneration is mainly a family affair. Generally, all of one's ancestors are venerated together (or "at once") annually by living family members. The dates and time during which an individual ancestor might be offered food and remembered would be set by the family head. Those individual remembrances tend to be held on the third and twelfth anniversaries of a relative's death (Prasad 1991: 231). While ancestral veneration articulates the family's gratitude to the dead and its desire for ancestral services and protection in coming years, it also enables the living to renew relations with the dead and among themselves. If any family member misses an anniversary celebration of the death of an elder, that person is expected to find another time to participate in it before the end of the year (Palakshappa 1976).

Ancestral veneration is used to affirm individuals' beliefs that their families consist of a long line of people who, when born into a family, remain part of it for all time. Therefore, no one among them will get lost. For instance, I learned from Suleman Sab Patil of Mainelli that he and his family had to propitiate their family Hindu deity before he could go to the mosque to get married. During my interview with Sab Patil's family they stressed that even though they are Muslims, they inherited Laxmi (the Hindu deity) from their ancestors and were thus bound by duty to offer food and incense to the deity. More importantly, as RajaSab Patil (father of the groom) pointed out, his grandparents used to live near Belgaum where they found an icon of Laxmi that had been abandoned. According to RajaSab Patil, ever since his grandparents provided a home for the deity, she had protected them in many ways. Whenever they forgot to feed the deity, some misfortune befell their family. RajaSab Patil recalled how his wife almost became blind sometime ago when they neglected to feed the deity. Thus when they worshipped Laxmi at home on 5 April 2000, before they went to the mosque for the Muslim rite of marriage, they were simultaneously honoring their ancestors who first found the goddess and passed her on to the present generation. Ancestral veneration also refocuses the religious and social centrality of the family unit, as in Africa.

In different parts of traditional Africa the family unit embraces the dead and the living (Ephirim-Donkor 1997; Sarpong 1974; Opoku 1978; Olupona 1991). There the ancestors are custodians of morality and the land. Kinship obligations do not end at death since the dead live on among the living community, discharging their obligations. When family members feed the ancestors, the dead are enabled to continue their services to the living as they did when they were alive. Ancestral veneration is thus employed by the African Indians to uphold the values of family responsibility and accountability towards both the living and the dead. For instance, when Kumar of Haliyal indicated that he received inspiration and curative information from his ancestor, he was underscoring the importance of ancestral involvement in the lives of the living. By providing for one another they also maintain patterns and attitudes that sustain a balance in their personal and social lives. As with some people in Africa, the African Indians of Karnataka believe that ancestors have an unlimited mobility and "cannot be confined to palpable objects of the environment" (Opoku 1978: 54). The ancestors, according to the Patil family of Mainelli, have power to protect, guide, and bless the living, and that is one of the reasons they continue to feed the Hindu deity they inherited from their forebears. Ancestral veneration (*hiriyaru*) is another context in which African Indians re-narrate their personal, family, and collective histories within south Indian religion and culture.

### Women, Religion, and Resistance in Contemporary India

Apart from ancestral veneration, some African Indians are devotees of goddesses including Ellama and Devi. Devi, for instance, is a goddess who bestows freedom to worshippers. She frees people from fear, suffering, and evil (Flood 1996; Klostermaier 1994). Since the worship of Ellama raises religious, social, and economic issues for the African Indians, we briefly touch on the importance of this deity in the lives of devotees in Gullapur, Bilki, and Mainelli.

Some African Indians in Mainelli, Bilki, Dharwar, Belgaum, and Gullapur worship Ellama (Ellaiyamman) (Obeng 2002: 168). The principal shrine of Ellama in northern Karnataka (Uttara Kannada) is on the Saundatti hill in Belgaum. Ellama is the mother goddess who has retained her independence from the Vedic deities (Sontheimer 1993). Although she is sometimes considered the wife of the sage Jamadagni and thus equivalent to Renuka, Ellama is a goddess who does not submit to the Brahminical hierarchy (Sontheimer 1993; Clarke 1996). Ellama is a south Indian deity "not coopted by the caste Hindu religious iconographic and mythological imagination"(Clarke 1996: 71). Clarke's research on Ellama in Tamil Nadu revealed that, like her shrines in Karnataka, Ellama is situated at the outskirts of villages because she is a boundary goddess (71).

Laxmi Ganappa Siddi, an African Indian woman religious specialist in Gullapur, is a devotee of Ellama. A healer, she has clients who come from within and outside of Gullapur. Since Gullapur's location on the main road between the major town of Yellapur and the city of Ankola makes it easily accessible to travelers, Laxmi Siddi's fame has spread outside her immediate community. Laxmi Siddi employs spirit possession during which she heals many diseases including mental illness and infertility. She became a devotee after she was healed of an illness that almost paralyzed her (personal interview in May 2000). She has set up her own Ellama shrine at her house. When the Gullapur community heard about it, according to her, some of the African Indian and non-African men objected to her having a shrine for Ellama. Laxmi Siddi stated, "some said a woman should not establish a shrine, and I said to them, 'Ellama instructed me, so I have done it'" (personal interview, May 2000). In a patriarchal community, where the Hindu caste system is pronounced, Laxmi Siddi asserted her social, religious, and economic right to serve Ellama. Since she has clients who pay her for services, she was not going to allow anyone to put a squeeze on her source of income or curtail her determination to be a religious specialist.

Ellama devotees such as Laxmi Siddi, Sarah Anton of Mainelli, and Ganappathi Siddi of Bilki wander villages, begging for alms in the name of Ellama on Tuesdays and Fridays and during Hindu festivals. When these African Indians walk the villages, they embody Ellama, and so people who give alms to them are in effect giving to the deity. Those who give the alms ask Ellama through the devotees to grant them all kinds of blessings. According to Laxmi Siddi, the donors often receive the blessings they ask for. As Basu and Werbner point out, unlike Brahminical Hinduism in which gifts from worshippers may be imbued with the negative spirit of the giver and can thus render the priests inauspicious, African Indian devotees of Ellama transform the gifts by the logic of "situational inversion of hierarchy" (1998: 135). Instead of the giving and receiving devaluing the giver, as is the case in the asymmetrical relations between the "holy and pure" Hindu priest and the "impure" worshipper, the African Indian practice confronts and subverts that hierarchy of moral and spiritual uprightness. Alms given to Ellama's African Indian religious specialists or devotees provide alternative values for structuring relations. At the same time, they enable clients and religious specialists the latitude to experience a sense of equality. Apart from the direct benefits that come to Laxmi Siddi and others like her, "the purpose of the dedication to the goddess is to counter the individual's or the family's misfortune" (Assayag 1967: 363).

According to Laxmi Siddi in Gullapur and Sarah Anton of Mainelli, since they became Ellama devotees, many misfortunes that might have befallen them were averted. Also, the goddess will fulfill all her obligations as long as the devotee honors her or his side of the obligation by leading an exemplary life, described by Assayag as "the devotee's good behaviour" (1967: 263). Devotion to Ellama thus accords Laxmi and others social recognition and moral and spiritual power. Devotion to Ellama, according to Assayag, enables the worshipper to ward off all malevolent forces and to reorient the planetary influences on . . . one's fate" (263). Within the community's cosmology, Laxmi Siddi's devotion also has cosmic significance. Ellama is the goddess whose worship allows the African Indian devotees to resist Hindu caste domination and the socio-economic barriers that the powerful set up to exploit the underclass.

For example, on 2 October 1999, the African Indian women of Mainelli teamed up with the Gowlis of Siddligundhi and put on a demonstration, blocking traffic to protest the opening of liquor stores in their villages. The demonstrating women were led by Surekha Siddi, a religious specialist and a devotee of Ellama. She inspired the other women to follow her in resisting the ways in which alcohol was being used by the rich and the powerful to destroy their families. The police were brought in by the rich businessmen who ran the liquor stores in the African Indian communities. As a result of the demonstration, all the unlicensed liquor stores were closed down. The goal of the women was to eradicate drinking, especially in their communities. Surekha Siddi and the other women contended that if they succeeded in eradicating or minimizing drunkenness, their men would save money for the education of their children and for the general development of their people.

The women of Mainclli and Siddligundi timed their demonstration to the celebration of coincide with Mahatma Gandhi's birthday, which fell on 2 October. According to Surekha Siddi, a national day in honor of Gandhi was chosen because Gandhi spoke against alcoholism. Thus as the women were honoring Gandhi, they were simultaneously deploying the occasion to articulate their sense of power and, more importantly, to criticize the men whose alcoholism aided the exploitation of their people. The African Indian women's objective in October 1999 was to put an end to the suffering they experienced at the hands of the liquor storeowners.

The liquor storeowners are among the present-day Indians who exert political and financial control over the underclass. Yet the marginalized group of women in these two villages of Karnataka were also negotiating their identities and reorienting themselves and their men, the targets of the liquor storeowners. Surekha's leadership, furthermore, is an example of how an underclass woman, a devotee of Ellama, is able to embody and deploy religious power for political action (Obeng 2002: 170). Surekha Siddi, who carries Ellama's basket representing the universe (Assayag 1967: 367) to beg for alms and who speaks for the goddess of emancipation, was a symbol of liberation for the other women. Surekha Siddi and the other women have drawn on their cultural and religious resources to endure, resist oppression, and struggle to create their own personal and collective resistance. Although some of the women were Christians, Muslims, and devotees of other deities, their loyalty to Surekha was an expression of their determination to seek the power needed to confront and correct the abusive power of the liquor store owners (Obeng 2002: 171). By worshipping Ellama (the deity who protects people against all forms of domination), the African Indians and the Gowlis were articulating another way by which they were reconfiguring their religious lifeways and their identities and simultaneously contributing to the religious, cultural, and political landscapes of India. The women's local political action condenses and formulates a counter hegemonic stance to address their local and societal exploitation. Though localized, such a political resistance created a national event that acted as a context for negotiating and mediating their local concerns.

In pre-independence imperial periods African Indians restructured their alliances along religious, racial, and military lines. However, in contemporary times socio-economic status and cultural alienation have become additional factors that they mobilize to protest their marginalized conditions.

### Conclusion

This chapter has tried to show ways in which African Indians, called "Siddis" or "Habshis," have actively constructed their multidimensional identities and their religious and cultural practices within differing Indian religious and political power structures. I have focused on the intriguing dialogue of African Indians' historical forms and individual and corporate power for fashioning and using socio-political, religious, and military strategies to respond to India's religious socio-economic systems. From medieval times to the present, African Indians have lived and adjusted under different dynastic and imperial systems. During those regimes African Indians have created and preserved aspects of their culture, religion, and identities. At some times they asserted their influence in the military, social, and political spheres by stressing their racial identity. On other occasions they contributed their services as agricultural laborers, basket weavers, domestics, drivers, and social workers. All this human activity has taken place within state and national boundaries, where there have been both overt and unstated ways of ordering social relations and of putting people into groups and subgroups. African Indians have further utilized their patterns of social interaction both to challenge dominant systems and to replicate aspects of the social and religious ranking in India in ways that meet their own needs. Within caste and class structures reminiscent of imperial regimes, African Indians have created avenues of minority national identities to assert, reassert, and deploy their own agency. This essay provides a guidepost and a conceptual framework for further research into the counter-hegemonic positioning of "ordinary" diasporic Africans and alliances that can be forged on a regional, national, and global scale. Further, it will help scholars to explore the global implications of the diversity within diasporic African identity, the patterns and processes of networks of relations, and the limitations and flexibility of diasporic political action.

## Note

This article is a revised version of my paper "Empires and Religion: African Indians of South India," which I presented at the New England/Maritimes region of the AAR/SBL held at Brown University, Providence, R.I., on 14 April 1999. I wish to thank Amy Catlin, Susan Schomburg, Chambers Moore, Sabrin Beg, and Anne R. Heskel for their comments on an earlier draft.

## Works Cited

Ali, S. S. 1996. *African Dispersal in the Deccan: From Medieval to Modern Time*. London: Sangam Books.

Alpers, Edward A. 1967. *The East African Slave Trade*. Nairobi: Historical Association of Tanzania.

———. 1997. "The African Diaspora in the Northwestern Indian Ocean: Reconsideration of an Old Problem, New Directions for Research." *Comparative Studies of South Asia, Africa and the Middle East* 17.2: 61–81.

Assayag, J. 1967. "Women-Goddess, Women Distress Yellama Goddess Devotees in South India (Karnataka)." *Man in India* 69.4: 359–73.

Banaji, D. R. 1932. *Bombay and the Siddis*. Bombay: Macmillan.

Basu, Helene, and Pnina Werbner. 1998. *Embodying Charisma: Modernity, Locality and the Performance of Emotion in Sufi Cults*. London: Routledge.

Bhandary, M. J., et al. 1995. "Medical Ethnobotany of the Siddis of Uttara Kannada District, Karnataka, India." *Journal of Ethnopharmacology* 47: 149–58.

Bhattacharya, D. K. 1968. "Siddis of Rajkot." *Hindustan Times Weekly*, 16 June 1968, 7, 1A.

——. 1969. "Anthropometry of a Negro Tribe in India: The Siddis of Gujarat." *Zinruigaku Zassi: Journal of the Anthropological Society of Nippon*, 77.5–6: 30–43.

——. 1970. "Indians of African Origin," *Cahiers d'Etudes Africaines*, 10/40: 579–82.

Bhattacharya, Pratibha. 1970. "Siddis of Gujarat." *Times Weekly* (Bombay), 20 June 1970, 4.

Chanana, Dev Raj. 1960. *Slavery in Ancient India*. New Delhi: People's Pub. House.

Chauhan, R. R. S. 1995. *Africans in Indian: From Slavery to Royalty*. New Delhi: Asian Publication Service.

Clarke, Sathianathan. 1996. "Re-Viewing the Religion of the Paraiyars: Ellaiyamman as an Iconic Symbol of Collective Resistance and Emanicipatory Mythography." In *Re-Visioning India's Religious Traditions: Essays in Honour of Eric Lott*, ed. David C. Scott and Israel Selvanayagam. Delhi: United Theological College.

Cohen, Abner. 1976. *Two Dimensional Man: An Essay on the Anthropology of Power and Symbolism in Complex Society*. Berkeley: University of California Press.

Eaton, Richard Maxwell. 1978. *Sufis of Bijapur, 1300–1700: Social Roles of Sufis in Medieval India*. Princeton, N.J.: Princeton University Press.

Ephirim-Donkor, A. 1997. *African Spirituality: On Becoming Ancestors*. Trenton, N.J.: Africa World Press.

Flood, Gavin. 1996. *An Introduction to Hinduism*. New York: Cambridge University Press.

Freeman-Grenville, G. S. P. 1988. *The Swahili Coast, 2nd to 19th Centuries: Islam, Christianity, and Commerce in Eastern Africa*. London: Variorum Reprints.

Gordon, Stewart. 1993. *The New Cambridge History of India: The Marathas, 1600–1818*. Cambridge: Cambridge University Press.

Gupta, A., ed. 1991. *Minorities on India's West Coast: History and Society*. Delhi: Kalinga.

Hamilton, Ruth Simms, ed. 1990. *Creating a Paradigm and Research Agenda for Comparative Studies of the Worldwide Dispersion of African Peoples*. East Lansing: Michigan State University.

Harris, Joseph E., ed. 1971. *The African Presence in Asia: Consequences of the East African Slave Trade*. Evanston, Ill.: Northwestern University Press.

—— 1975. "The Black Peoples of Asia," In *World Encyclopedia of Black Peoples*, 264–72. St. Clair Shores, Mich.: Scholarly Press.

Irwin, Graham W. 1977. *Africans Abroad: A Documentary History of the Black Diaspora in Asia, Latin America, and the Caribbean during the Age of Slavery*. New York: Columbia University Press.

Khalidi, O. 1989. "African Diaspora in India: The Case of the Habashis of the Dakan." *Islamic Culture* 63.1–2: 85–107.

Klostermaier, Klaus K. 1994. *A Survey of Hinduism.* 2d ed. Albany: State University of New York Press.

Lobo, Cyprian. 1984. *Siddis in Karnataka.* Bangalore: Centre for Non-Formal and Continuing Education.

Majumdar, R. C. 1960. *The History and Culture of the Indian People: The Delhi Sultanate.* Bombay: Macmillan.

Obeng, Pashington. 2000. "Survival Strategies of African Indians of Karnataka, South India." *Princeton Seminary InSpire* 4.4: 21–23.

———. 2002. "Womanist Survival Strategies and Globalization." In *Black Women, Globalization, and Economic Justice,* ed. Filomena Steady. Rochester, Vt.: Schneckman Books.

Olupona, J. K., ed. 1991. *African Traditional Religion in Contemporary Society.* New York: Paragon House.

Opoku, K. A. 1978. *West African Traditional Religion.* Jurong, Singapore: F. E. P. International.

Palakshappa, T. C. 1976. *The Siddhis of Karnataka.* New Delhi: Sterling.

Pandian, Jacob. 1987. *Caste, Nationalism and Ethnicity: An Interpretation of Tamil Culture, History and Social Order.* Bombay: Popular Prakashan.

Pinto, Jeanette. 1992. *Slavery in Portuguese India, 1510–1842.* Bombay: Himalaya.

Prasad, Kiran Kamal. 1991. "The Identity of Siddis in Karnataka." In *Relevance of Anthropology: The Indian Scenario,* ed. B. G. Halbar and C. G. Hussain Khan. Jaipur: Rawat.

Rao, Vasant D. 1973. "The Habashis: India's Unknown Africans." *Africa Report* 18.5: 35–38.

Richards, John F. 1993. *The New Cambridge History of India: The Mughal Empire.* New York: Cambridge University Press.

Robbins, Kenneth X., and McLeod, John, eds. 2006. *African Elites in India: Habshi Amarat.* Ahmedabad, India: Mapin.

Sarpong, P. 1974. *Ghana in Retrospect.* Tema, Ghana: Ghana Pub.

Sherwani, H. K., and P. M. Joshi, eds. 1973. *History of Medieval Deccan (1295–1724.* Vol. 1: *Mainly Political and Military Aspects.* Chanchalguda, Hyderabad, India: Government of Andhra Pradesh.

Singh, A. K., et al. 1998. *Forest and Tribals in India.* New Delhi: Classical Pub.

Sontheimer, Gunther-Dietz. 1993. *Pastoral Deities in Western India.* Trans. A. Feldhaus. New Delhi: Oxford University Press.

Stein, Burton. 1989. *The New Cambridge History of India: Vijayanagara.* New York: Cambridge University Press.

Thekkedath, Joseph. 1988. *History of Christianity in India.* Vol. 2: *From the Middle of the Sixteenth Century to the End of the Seventeenth Century.* Bangalore: Church History Association of India.

Trivedi, R. K. 1969. "Siddi: A Negro Tribe of Gujarat." *Census of India 1961.* vol. 5, pt. 4–B, no. 1. Delhi: Navajivan Press.

# 10

## Marriage and Identity among the Sidis of Janjira and Sachin

John McLeod

What is Africa in India? A constituent (and a product) of a cosmopolitan Indian Ocean cultural world? An African-Indian diasporic community? Independent communities of Sidis,[1] or Indians who happen to be of African descent? Or perhaps all of these, or none of them? With the recent spurt in interest in Africans in India and around the Indian Ocean (de Silva Jayasuriya and Pankhurst 2003; Catlin-Jairazbhoy and Alpers 2003; Robbins and McLeod 2006), scholars have begun to try to answer this question. For example, in this volume Pashington Obeng argues in favor of a distinct cultural identity, crafted by Sidis for themselves in their resistance against forces of domination around them, while Gwyn Campbell rejects the whole notion of a cohesive African diaspora in the Indian Ocean.

The core of Obeng's argument is the existence among one group of Sidis of syncretistic religious beliefs and practices; but such blends of folk beliefs and the "great tradition" forms of Islam, Hinduism, and Christianity are found all over India and are not distinctively African-Indian, any more than the folk beliefs themselves. Campbell, meanwhile, bases his conclusions on a "generally agreed" checklist of the characteristics of a diaspora; this check-list, however, is so restrictive that it would probably exclude even the original diaspora, the Jews of the Hellenistic world, and in any case it is not binding on scholars.

A better understanding of Africa in India begins with the realization that any identity is membership in an imagined community (Anderson 1991: 6). If Indians of African ancestry consider themselves to have a distinct identity, then they are a community. Dispensing with Campbell's checklist, with its assumption that a true diaspora retains a relatively "pure" identity traceable back to its homeland and a perpetual sense of exile, and rejecting his contention that anything less exhaustive "renders meaningless the concept of diaspora" (Campbell, this volume), it may be further suggested that if these African-Indians regard their African origin as a central part of that identity, then they are a diasporic community. Scholars, activists, and some Sidis are trying to build just an imagined community in the minds of all Indians of African origin (Camara 2003: 111). At the moment, however, there is no African-Indian diasporic community, as the great majority of Sidis lack a sense of shared identity, much less the knowledge that their ancestors came from Africa.

That being said, there is at least one group of African-Indians who identify themselves as a distinct community with origins in Africa, although they are so few in number that it may be more correct to regard them as an extended family than a community. These are the Sidis who until 1948 ruled the kingdoms of Janjira and Sachin on the west coast of India. The preservation of their identity is an exception to Campbell's dictum that "The history of Africans in India is overwhelmingly one of integration, in which they have shed their African identity and adopted a local Asian identity" (Campbell, this volume). It equally departs from the pattern noted by Richard Eaton with regard to the African elite military slaves of the Deccan (peninsular India), to whom the Sidis of Janjira and Sachin trace their origins. "By the eighteenth century," Eaton writes, "Habshis [literally Abyssinians, but more often Africans in general] had disappeared as a distinct Deccani group and military caste" (Eaton 2006: 60). He suggests three major reasons for this: the paucity of African females in the Deccan, which meant that Habshi men usually married local women, so that their descendants were progressively absorbed into the local population; the end of the importation of Africans into India as elite military and administrative slaves; and the nature of elite slavery in India, which allowed a single individual to go from being a kinless alien to a native householder, and to all intents and purposes a free man (60).

The Sidis of Janjira and Sachin, however, retained an identity which, though created in India and supplemented with additional Indian identities, was rooted in their African origin. The process is observable in their marriage patterns, the subject of this chapter. At the beginning of the twenty-first century, these Sidis are simultaneously a segment of the African diaspora and members of what can only be described as a cosmopolitan elite whose heritage goes back to not only Africa but also Afghanistan, Central Asia, Iran, and India itself.

Marriage patterns in the Janjira and Sachin families show similarities to Hindu royal marriages in colonial India, as well as differences (McLeod 1986). They also echo some of Theodore P. Wright's findings on marriages among royal and non-royal elite Muslim families of South Asia but diverge from the observations made by Francis Taft Plunkett on the Hindu Rajput royal families of Rajasthan (Wright 1991, 1994; Plunkett 1972). Despite the fact that they were ruled by related families, the histories of Janjira and Sachin meant that the two states were structured somewhat differently, which in turn affected marriage patterns (at least until the late nineteenth century). This essay therefore examines marriages first in Janjira, then Sachin, and finally offers some observations about the patterns and what they tell us about the identities of the two modern Sidi royal families. The data on which the chapter is based are drawn from the author's genealogical research on Indian princely families (see McLeod 2006a, 2006c). They are admittedly incomplete, but they provide enough information to support some tentative conclusions.

## Janjira

Janjira state lay on the Arabian Sea, about forty miles south of Bombay (Mumbai). It had an area of 326 square miles and a population, in 1941, of 103,557. The heart of the state, and its capital until 1904, was the great fortified island of Janjira (this name comes from the Arabic word for island). During the wars with the Marathas in the seventeenth and eighteenth centuries, the Sidis were sometimes temporarily driven from all of their mainland possessions, but they retained the island through seven Maratha sieges between 1659 and 1760 (Jasdanwalla 2006; McLeod 2006b).

Traditional marriage patterns among the Sidis of Janjira reflect the history and political structure of the state. The island of Janjira came under the rule of the sultan of Ahmadnagar in the late fifteenth century. A hundred years later, the African Malik Ambar became master of the Ahmadnagar sultanate (Eaton 2006). Perhaps because of the strategic importance of Janjira, Malik Ambar apparently decided that the island fortress should be governed by fellow Africans, and in 1618 he appointed an African named Sidi Surur as commandant of Janjira.[2] From then on, Malik Ambar consistently appointed Africans to command Janjira, Sidi Yaqut I in

1620, and Sidi Ambar the Little in 1621. During the command of Sidi Ambar the Little (1621–42), the administration of the Ahmadnagar sultanate broke down under the pressure of constant war with the Mughal emperors Jahangir and Shah Jahan. Janjira became effectively independent, to the point that in the mid-1620s Sidi Ambar the Little successfully defied Malik Ambar's attempt to replace him with a new commandant, Habash Khan (who was apparently also an African). Sidi Ambar the Little is accordingly considered to have been the first *nawab*, or monarch, of the princely state of Janjira.

The early African commandants were presumably accompanied to Janjira by their families, friends, soldiers, and subordinates, many of whom would themselves have been Africans. At any rate, by the mid-seventeenth century, there was a sizeable African community living within Janjira fort, alongside the Hindu Koli fisherfolk who had inhabited the island since time immemorial. These Sidi *sardars*, or chiefs, formed the aristocracy of Janjira. The recruitment of Sidis to Janjira during the seventeenth and eighteenth centuries has yet to be studied. The first generation of sardars, men such as Sidi Surur, Sidi Yaqut I, and Sidi Ambar the Little, were almost certainly from the same background as Malik Ambar himself: freeborn in non-Muslim communities in eastern Africa, enslaved and converted to Islam, sold in India for service as elite military slaves, and rising from subalternity to high rank and power through ability and good luck (Eaton 2006: 47–54; Oka and Kusimba this volume).

It is not clear whether subsequent additions to the community came directly from Africa, or whether they were members of the wider African-Indian elite who settled at Janjira as opportunities narrowed in other parts of India. Quite possibly both mechanisms operated. The Mughal conquests of the Deccan sultanates of Ahmadnagar in 1636 and Bijapur in 1686 brought many Sidi nobles into the service of the Mughal emperors (Robbins and McLeod 2006: 40, 164), but others may well have settled in Janjira. At the same time, the name of one nineteenth-century sardar, Sidi Husain Jabarti, to be discussed shortly, indicates an origin in Muslim Ethiopia. Ethiopian Christians variously use the word "Jabarti" to refer to Muslims living in the mainly Christian plateau of Ethiopia and Eritrea, to all Ethiopian Muslims, or to all Muslims. More correctly, it means an inhabitant of the Muslim region of Jabart (Jabara), or Zayla and Ifat, and this is the sense in which Muslims use the word (Ullendorf 1965). In either case, if Sidi Husain Jabarti's ancestors were Ethiopian Muslims, then they must have come to India as free people, since Muslims are barred from enslaving their coreligionists.

By whatever means they came to India, as they refashioned themselves into rulers, the Sidis became a community. All were Muslims, whether by birth or by conversion subsequent to enslavement. Like other African elite military slaves, they would have originated in different parts of Africa and thus lacked a common language. From the time of their arrival in India, however, they would quickly have learned Urdu, the colloquial language of many Indian Muslims, in which they spoke to their masters, their men, and each other, and to this day Urdu is the mother tongue of the Sidis of Janjira. Some Janjira Sidis also learned Persian, which until the nineteenth century was the formal language of government and diplomacy in much of India, or the Marathi and Konkani of their non-Sidi subjects. The possibility of the Janjira Sidis going back to Africa was remote, and it is most unlikely that any sardars would have wanted to return to their birthplaces, given the high status they had achieved in India. Campbell has said that educated, cultivated, and literate, or politically powerful, African-Indians "without exception expressed a local rather than 'African' identity" (Campbell this volume). This is not wholly true, as the Sidis of Janjira have remained aware of their African ancestry. Thus, Janjira state was often called Habsan, a derivative of the Persian and Urdu word *habshi*, "Abyssinian" (which, even to those who could not precisely identify it with the modern country of Ethiopia, was known to be in eastern Africa), and one of the most common rupee coins issued by the Sidis of Janjira was known as the *habshi nishani rupaya*, "the rupee marked by the Abyssinians" (Bhandare 2006: 199–200). In their forewords to a recent book on African elites in India, members of the Janjira and Sachin families stressed their African origins (Sachin 2006: 7; Janjira 2006: 8).

United by religion, language, their African ancestry, and their elite status in their new Indian homeland, the Sidi sardars of Janjira became a closed group. By the beginning of the nineteenth century, outside recruitment had ceased, and the community was replenished exclusively by birth. According to a census taken in 1901, Sidis numbered 240 out of the Janjira fort's total population of 1,620 (*Imperial Gazetteer* 1908–9: 14:59, 61).

It appears that the position of nawab of Janjira was initially hereditary, as the first nawab Sidi Ambar the Little seems to have been succeeded by his son Sidi Yusuf in 1642 and then his grandson Sidi Fateh in 1648 (although, according to the seventeenth-century historian Khafi Khan, Sidi Fateh was not only not Sidi Yusuf's son, he was not even a Sidi at all, but a Pashtun or Pathan from Afghanistan). By the mid-seventeenth century, however, the Sidi sardars had become powerful enough to challenge Sidi Fateh for control of Janjira. For some time Sidi Fateh held the upper hand, which he maintained by executing about fifty sardars. Then, in 1667 (or 1670, according to another account), three leading sardars deposed him and chose one of their number, Sidi Khairiyat, to rule in his stead. For the next 140 years, the nawabs of Janjira were merely first among their equals, the Sidi sardars. The sardars had—and often used—the power to remove the ruling nawab from office and to elect a successor when the nawab died or was deposed. An indication of the relative importance of the nawab and the sardars may be seen in the fact that the first treaty between Janjira and the British East India Company, concluded in 1733, was signed by seven Sidi sardars but not by the nawab (the treaty and list of signatories are in Aitchison 1929: 8:89–92). This was because an agreement entered into by the sardars was considered binding on the Sidis of Janjira, with or without the involvement of the nawab.

Then, in 1804 (or 1803), the sardars chose one Sidi Ibrahim II as nawab. Sidi Ibrahim had already served one term as nawab; his first reign had ended when he was deposed and imprisoned by a sardar named Sidi Jam-rud. Now, he refused to accept the election unless the sardars consented to make the office of nawab hereditary in his family. The chiefs apparently accepted this condition, and since Sidi Ibrahim II the title of nawab of Janjira has descended in an unbroken line from father to son through six generations to the present. Nevertheless, it will be seen that as late as 1879 the sardars claimed the right to make and unmake nawabs.

The historic relationship between the nawabs of Janjira and the Sidi sardars is significant in a consideration of marriage patterns. Given that for almost a century and a half the nawab was merely one among many sardars, and that any sardar could theoretically become nawab, marriage patterns for the nawabs and their families were inseparable from those of the sardars as a whole. The data are incomplete, but it appears that the sardars were endogamous—that is to say, the sons and daughters of sardars married the daughters and sons of other sardars.[3] For example, Sidi Jauhar, a sardar who was nawab from 1784 to 1789, was married to the daughter of his predecessor Sidi Abd ul-Rahim (reigned 1772–84). This pattern seems to have held for several generations after the institution of hereditary succession in 1804, as the first three wives of Sidi Ibrahim II's grandson Nawab Sidi Ibrahim III (reigned 1848–79) were all apparently the daughters of Sidi sardars: Sharifa Bibi, Fatima Bibi I, and Fatima Bibi II.

Despite these family ties, however, Sidi Ibrahim III was keen to assert himself over the sardars. In a pattern common in princely India in the nineteenth century (Ramusack 2004: 111–14), he sought to reduce the power of his nobles and filled many administrative posts with educated Hindus rather than with the old Sidi aristocracy. This naturally embittered the sardars. So did the nawab's relationship with a woman named Saidabai, the daughter of a Maniyar or bangle-seller. The Maniyars are Muslims of low status and today rank as an Other Backward Caste in Maharashtra. Sidi Ibrahim claimed that he had legally married Saidabai, whom he renamed Zainab Begam, and her son Sidi Mohammad (b 1853, d 1920) was his favorite child. There were even indications that Sidi Ibra-him intended to name Sidi Mohammad as his heir-apparent. This was of particular concern to supporters of his Sidi wife Fatima Bibi II, whose own son Sidi Ahmad (b 1862, d 1922) was of pure Sidi descent. One thing led to another, and in 1869 Fatima Bibi II was murdered by supporters of Zainab Begam.

Marriage patterns in the Janjira royal family had now led to violence, but Nawab Sidi Ibrahim apparently took no action against the murderers. The following year, he went to Bombay to meet Queen Victoria's second son, the duke of Edinburgh, who was visiting India. During his absence, the murdered Fatima Bibi's father Sidi Husain Jabarti led a revolt of the sardars, who seized control of Janjira fort, proclaimed the deposition of Sidi Ibrahim, and installed the young Sidi Ahmad as nawab. This marked a reversion to the practice of the seventeenth and eighteenth centuries, when the sardars could make and unmake nawabs. The British, who in 1834 had established themselves as the overlords of Janjira, however, felt that the old ways were no longer suitable and forcibly reinstated Sidi Ibra-him as nawab; the sardars finally acquiesced in this in 1873 (National Ar-chives of India, Foreign Department Proceedings, Political B, March 1874, nos. 79–82).

The sardars asserted themselves for the last time after Sidi Ibrahim died in 1879. The disagreements as to whether the late nawab had ever actually married Zainab Begam meant that it was uncertain whether her son Sidi Mohammad was legitimate or not. On the other hand, there were no such questions about the next son, Sidi Ahmad, whose mother was the Sidi Fatima Bibi II. Sidi Ahmad had been the sardars' choice as nawab in 1870, and one would assume that the nobles would again support him in prefer-ence to the elder—but only half-Sidi—Sidi Mohammad. Instead, this time, the sardars elected Sidi Mohammad, perhaps merely in an attempt to assert their old rights. The British, however, rejected the election, osten-sibly at least on the grounds of Sidi Mohammad's questionable legitimacy, and placed Sidi Ahmad on the throne of Janjira; he reigned from 1879 to 1922 (National Archives of India, Foreign Department Proceedings, Politi-cal A, May 1879, nos. 158–64, and Political A, August 1879, nos. 67–86).

By this time, the separation between Indian princes and their nobles was moving to a new level, with princes forming part of an All-India community in which monarchs from different parts of the subcontinent had more in common with each other than they did with the nobles in their own states. One aspect of this was education. From the 1870s, the Chiefs' Schools brought together young members of royal families. Sidi Ahmad was no exception—he was the first member of the Janjira family to attend the oldest Chiefs' School, Rajkumar College at Rajkot in

Gujarat (Ramusack 2004: 111; N. Khan 1898), where he studied alongside Hindu and Muslim princes from across western India.

Another aspect of this growing Indian princely identity was in the choice of marriage partners. Historically, most princely families—Hindu or Muslim—had married within a relatively small circle. Partners typically belonged to the same community, so that Rajputs married Rajputs, Marathas married Marathas, Pathans married Pathans, and so on; and while marriage alliances between two princely families did occur, a prince was just as likely to take a wife from a noble family of his own state belonging to his community as he was to marry the daughter of another prince (Plunkett 1972: 67, 79). The endogamous marriages of the Sidis of Janjira were historically of this pattern. In the late nineteenth century, however, princely families increasingly intermarried with other princely families, even if they came from different communities and a considerable distance, to the exclusion of marriages with their own nobles. This clearly reflects a growing sense that a royal family's community—from which marriage partners should be selected—was South Asian royalty as a whole rather than the local nobility.[4] (At this stage religion was still a consideration, although the process continued to the point that in the twentieth century, one Hindu prince saw his eldest son marry a Muslim princess and his second son a Buddhist princess.) In 1882, Sidi Ahmad became the first recorded nawab of Janjira to marry a wife belonging to another princely family.

It is notoriously impossible to offer a precise figure for the number of princely and chiefly states in India. Taking only those whose rulers were recognized by the governments of India and Pakistan after independence, however, there were a total of 39 Muslim states in the Subcontinent. Eight of these (all now in Pakistan) were ruled by Baloch, Burusha, or Brahoi families, and 3 small states in Gujarat were ruled by descendants of Hindu converts to Islam. The remaining 28 comprised the two Sidi states of Janjira and Sachin, 20 states ruled by Pathans, and 6 by Mughals. (Mughal in this case refers to a Turkic origin in modern Uzbekistan and not necessarily to kinship with the imperial Mughal dynasty.)

Given the preponderance of Pathans among the Muslim royal families of India, it is not surprising that Sidi Ahmad's non-Sidi bride came from a Pathan family. Her name was Ahmad Bibi, and her father was Nawab Abd ul-Khair Khan of Savanur, a small state near the center of what is now Karnataka. In the seventeenth century, the ancestors of its nawabs held high office under the sultans of Bijapur; on the Mughal conquest of Bijapur in 1686, a member of the family submitted to the emperor Aurangzeb and received a grant of land that became the Savanur state (Chitnis 2000).

However, Ahmad Bibi died childless after just three years of marriage. At the suggestion of Lord Reay, the British governor of Bombay, Sidi Ahmad in 1887 married a lady of rather unexpected antecedents. This was Nazli Rafia Begam, both of whose parents came from the distinguished Tyabji (Tayyibji) family of Bombay (National Archives of India, Foreign and Political Department Proceedings, 286–P/1928; Wright 1976). The Tyabjis belonged to an Ismaili sect from Gujarat known as the Sulaimani Bohras and were well known for their "progressiveness" (they ceased to practice female seclusion in the 1890s) and community leadership; Nazli Rafia Begam's maternal great uncle Badr ud-Din Tyabji was the first Indian admitted to the bar, a distinguished judge, and the president of the 1887 session of the Indian National Congress. The Congress poetess Sarojini Naidu later wrote a poem in Nazli Rafia Begam's honor (McLeod 2006b: 194). It may seem odd that a British governor would encourage a young prince to marry a woman from such a family, but Lord Reay was known for his own liberalism, and in any case the marriage took place before Congress clashed with the British. Reay probably hoped that the marriage would help spread the Tyabjis' progressive sentiments in what was then perceived as the backward state of Janjira. The fact that the Tyabjis are Shias, while the Janjira family are Sunni, may also make the marriage seem odd. As Wright notes, however, marriages between elite Sunnis and Shias were more common in the past than might be expected (Wright 1994: 143 n. 45). Moreover, the Janjira Sidis show some Shia traits; for example, the ritual center of Janjira fort is a shrine containing relics of the Holy Family (the Prophet, Fatima, Ali, Hasan, and Husain), whose veneration is typically Shia.

Unfortunately, this marriage too was childless. In 1913, in order to secure the succession, Sidi Ahmad took another wife, Kulsum Begam, thirty-five years his junior (National Archives of India, Foreign Department Proceedings, Internal B, April 1913, nos. 267–68). Perhaps because his ventures into matrimony with wives from non-traditional backgrounds had been unsuccessful, Sidi Ahmad now reverted to the ways of his ancestors, as Kulsum Begam was a Sidi, the daughter of a sardar named Sidi Husain, who was distantly related to the nawab. The following year, Kulsum Begam bore Sidi Ahmad his only child, Sidi Mohammad (b 1914, d 1972), who in 1922 succeeded his father on the throne of Janjira.

The new nawab, now Sidi Mohammad III (reigned 1922–72), was raised to consider himself a member of the wider princely fraternity. Like his father, he attended Rajkumar College and from there he went on to Deccan College in Pune. In 1933 he married his only wife, in a choice that further reflected the notion of a Muslim princely community. This was Rabia Sultan Jahan Begam, whose father was Mohammad Iftikhar Ali Khan, nawab of the princely state of Jaora on the border between the present states of Madhya Pradesh and Rajasthan (*List of Ruling Princes* 1941: 11; Luard

1908: 182–88). The ruling family of Jaora is descended from a Pathan named Abd ul-Ghafur Khan, a military commander in the service of the Maratha maharajas of Indore. At the outbreak of the Third Anglo-Maratha War in 1817, Abd ul-Ghafur Khan submitted to the British, who in reward recognized him as sovereign nawab of Jaora. Until 1933, the royal family of Jaora had generally intermarried with other Pathan families, so the marriage of Sidi Mohammad III and Rabia Sultan Jahan Begam represented a new departure for both dynasties.

Fourteen years after this marriage, British rule ended with the independence of India and Pakistan. In 1948–49, the Indian states were merged and integrated into the new India (Menon 1956). Their rulers remained a distinct class in the eyes of the law until 1971, when the Constitution (26th Amendment) Act deleted the constitutional provisions that had guaranteed their personal rights, privileges, and dignities and the payment of their privy purses and had provided for presidential recognition of rulers (Mankekar 1974). The end of the existence of the states meant that there was no longer any political reason for princely families to conclude marriage alliances, and the abolition of the last vestiges of rulership in 1971 meant that the princely families ceased to form a community except insofar as they shared a common history. Meanwhile, many members of princely families left their ancestral homes for larger cities, where they were often integrated into upper-class urban society. At the same time, "love matches" became increasingly common in some circles in India, including princely families.

The result of all of this is that while many princely families have continued their traditional marriage practices over the last half century, many others have intermarried with the wider upper classes of India. Thus, one Hindu maharani is married to a leading industrialist. A Muslim nawab and a member of a Hindu princely family are each married to Bollywood actresses (in both cases, their children have followed their mothers into film). Other members of princely families have taken spouses from military or professional backgrounds. Marriages between members of different religions occur with some frequency, and in an increasing number of marriages, one of the partners is a non-Indian.

These patterns also apply to the last two generations of the Janjira family. Nawab Sidi Mohammad III and Rabia Sultan Begam had four daughters and one son. The second daughter never married, but the others wed diverse husbands. The eldest, Fatma Begam (b 1934), married Adamji Jasdanwalla, member of a family of Dawudi Bohras originally from Jasdan in Gujarat, but prominent in trade and industry in Bombay family for many years; the Dawudi Bohras are an Ismaili sect, who like the Sulaimani Bohras (including the Tyabjis) were historically merchants in Gujarat. The third daughter, Mumtaz Jahan Begam (b 1939), married Salim Ahmad Khan, a Pathan from western Uttar Pradesh; his father was a police commissioner, but the family are first and foremost land-owners. The fourth, Qamr uz-Zaman Begam (b 1943), married a fellow Sidi, her distant cousin Sidi Zaher, a member of the Sachin royal family. Sidi Mohammad III's only son, the present nawab Sidi Shah Mahmud (b 1952; reigned 1972–), married Kishwar Monim Begam, of a Muslim family of tea planters from Jalpaiguri in northern West Bengal (her family owns several estates, and her father is on the board of a leading tea company in Calcutta).

At the moment, three of Sidi Mohammad III's grandchildren are married. Fatma Begam's son Arshad Jasdanwalla (b 1970) is married to Shireen, the daughter of a Parsi construction engineer who belongs to the Parsi priestly class and is trained as a priest. Mumtaz Jahan Begam's daughter Sahar Khan (b 1971) is married to Noman Mughal, a Pakistani living in Dubai, whose name points to a Mughal origin. And Nawab Sidi Shah Mahmud's elder daughter Tazeen Jahan Begam (b 1978) is married to Shaad Khan, a physician who practices in Mauritius (incidentally taking the Sidis to another region of the Indian Ocean world).

## Sachin

The other modern Sidi state, Sachin, was founded by the son of an eighteenth-century nawab of Janjira (McLeod 2006c). Its ruling family might therefore have been expected to follow the same marriage patterns as that of Janjira. In fact, the circumstances under which Sachin was established represented a rejection of the idea that the nawab was merely one among the Sidi sardars, and instead postulated him as having an inherited royal status that set him at the top of society. For this reason, Sachin—unlike Janjira—did not have a community of Sidi nobles, and its nawabs apparently began marrying non-Sidi wives earlier than their kinsmen in Janjira.

What occurred is this. On the death of Nawab Abd ul-Rahim of Janjira in 1784, a sardar (who happened to be his son-in-law), Sidi Jauhar, became nawab. Abd ul-Rahim's eldest son Balu Miyan challenged the new ruler's right to the throne, claiming that as the late nawab's eldest son he himself was the rightful sovereign of Janjira. This implied a belief in succession by primogeniture and a repudiation of the notion that any Sidi sardar could become nawab. When his challenge was unsuccessful, Balu Miyan fled to Pune and sought the help of the Peshwa, the principal ruler of the Marathas. The Peshwa saw an opportunity to achieve his ancestors' long-cherished hope of acquiring the island fortress of Janjira. At the suggestion of his (temporary) British allies, the Peshwa entered into an agreement with Balu Miyan by which the would-be nawab was recognized as the lawful ruler of Janjira and immediately ceded to the Peshwa all his rights over his ancestral kingdom. In return, the Peshwa undertook to compensate Balu Miyan with lands in Gujarat that yielded a revenue equal in value to that of Janjira. The idea was that this would give the Peshwa legal title to Janjira. He could then drive Sidi Jauhar from the island as a usurper and annex Janjira to his own dominions.

In the event, Balu Miyan got the better of the arrangement. The Peshwa was never able to take Janjira, but he did give Balu Miyan the lands in Gujarat which became Sachin state. Sachin lay near the city of Surat. It had an area of 49 square miles and, in 1941, a population of 26,231. Not surprisingly, Balu Miyan had no desire to surround himself with a body of sardars. As a result, the only Sidis in Sachin were his direct descendants.

The origins of the earlier queens of Sachin are unknown, although the names of Maryam Bi (wife of Balu Miyan's son Sidi Ibrahim I, reigned 1802–53) and Saheb un-Nisa Begam (wife of Sidi Ibrahim II, reigned 1868–73) may suggest Mughal or Pathan antecedents. The picture becomes clearer in the latter part of the nineteenth century, as an All-India princely community began to form. Like their contemporary Sidi Ahmad of Janjira, Nawab Sidi Abd ul-Qadir of Sachin (b 1864/6, d 1896; reigned 1873–87) and his brother Sidi Nasrullah (d 1924) attended Rajkumar College at Rajkot. They and their two sisters, however, made marriages that apparently reflect links with the wider South Asian Muslim aristocracy rather than with princely families specifically: Sidi Abd ul-Qadir's wife was Mehr un-Nisa Begam, possibly another Mughal or Pathan; Sidi Nasrullah's wife Rabia Sultan was the daughter of Sir M. A. Nakuda; and Karim un-Nisa and Vazir un-Nisa both married men of the Edrus family, whose members have been prominent as Sufi scholars in Yemen, India, Indonesia, and Malaysia since the fifteenth century (Löfgren 1965).

Nawab Sidi Abd ul-Qadir's sons' marriages suggest simultaneous membership in the Sidi community, a princely community, and an upper-class Muslim community. The eldest son, Nawab Sidi Ibrahim III (b 1886, d 1930; reigned 1887–1930), married four wives. Fatima Sultan Jahan was a Sidi and his own first cousin, the daughter of his uncle Sidi Nasrullah. Mehr un-Nisa Begam came from the princely state of Radhanpur in north Gujarat; the Radhanpur nawabs belong to the Babi family of Pathans, who held high rank under the Mughal emperors and ruled five states into the twentieth century (*Cutch, Palanpur* 1880: 322–28). Fakhr un-Nisa Begam belonged to the Beg family, prominent Muslims from the Maratha state of Baroda, and was related to Sidi Ibrahim III on his mother's side; judging by their name, the Begs were probably of Mughal origin. Iqbal Jahan Begam was the daughter of a widow of Nawab Jafar Ali Khan of Cambay, a princely state in Gujarat whose Mughal rulers had served the shahs of Iran before settling in India (*Rewa Kantha* 1880: 220–333).[5] Before marrying Sidi Ibrahim, Iqbal Jahan Begam had been the wife of Abd ul-Razzaq, son of a sometime sheriff of Bombay named Hajji Suleman Abd ul-Wahed (National Archives of India, Foreign and Political Department, Internal Proceedings, B, March 1919, nos. 66–67).

Nawab Sidi Ibrahim III's brother Sidi Ahmad (b 1889, d ?) sought his fortune in Hyderabad, the most important princely state in India. Like many African-Indians, he entered the Hyderabad army (Khalidi 2006). Unlike these humbler soldiers, he was an officer, and became second in command of one of the state military units. As was common with senior officers, Sidi Ahmad was absorbed into the Muslim nobility of Hyderabad; he married Laiq un-Nisa Begam, daughter of a noble named Nawab Mumtaz Yar ud-Daula. Their sons' marriages reflect the same simultaneous membership in princely and broader aristocratic communities: Mustafa Khan married Mumtaz, daughter of Sir Shahnawaz Bhutto (Wright 1994: 135), one of the greatest landlords of Sindh (and father and grandfather of Pakistani prime ministers), while Imtiyaz Khan married Sartaj Jahan Begam, daughter of Nawab Abd ul-Majid Khan of Savanur and a distant kinswoman of Ahmad Bibi, the Savanur lady who married Nawab Sidi Ahmad of Janjira.

The five sons and one daughter of Nawab Sidi Ibrahim III made a total of ten marriages, all of them either with princely families, or with nobles from Muslim princely states. Four of the ten marriages were with members of the ruling family of Loharu, a state in Haryana: the eldest son Nawab Sidi Haidar (b 1909, d 1970; reigned 1930–70) married as his first wife Arjumand Bano Begam, daughter of Nawab Aiz ud-Din Khan Ahmad of Loharu, and then her first cousin Alima Sultan; the third son Sidi Salim (b 1913, d 1975) married as his second wife Alima Sultan's sister Abida Sultan; and the daughter Roshanara Begam married Arjumand Bano Begam's brother Salah ud-Din Ahmad Khan. The Loharu family is Mughal, descended from an eighteenth-century immigrant from Bukhara in Uzbekistan; in 1806 Ahmad Bakhsh Khan, son of the immigrant, received the territory of Loharu from the raja of Alwar in Rajasthan in recognition of his role in negotiations with the British. Loharu is only eighty miles from Delhi, and in the nineteenth century the family made marriages that tied it to the Mughal imperial family and to the great poet Mirza Ghalib (*Loharu State* 1916; Wright 1994: 137–38).

The other marriages of Sidi Ibrahim III's children were as follows. After his two Loharu wives, Nawab Sidi Haidar married Manzar Sultan and then Khurshid Zaman Begam, who by their names may also have been Mughals. Sidi Ibrahim III's second son, Nawab Sidi Surur (b 1911, d 1990; reigned 1970–90), married one wife, Habiba Sultan Begam, daughter of Sardar Nishat Mohammad Khan, a Pathan who was one of the leading nobles of the princely state of Bhopal in Madhya Pradesh (S. Khan 2000). Like the Sidi sardars of Janjira, the Pathan sardars of Bhopal traditionally intermarried with their nawabs (Sultaan 2004). The third son, Sidi Salim, who as noted above married Abida Sultan of Loharu, had taken as his first wife a lady named Rukhia Sultan. She came from the princely state of Cambay but was apparently unrelated to its nawab. Her father was named Aga Saheb, which suggests that she belonged to an Iranian family known to have lived in Cambay.

Sidi Ibrahim III's two remaining sons each married one wife: Sidi Abd ul-Qadir (b 1926, d 1994) married his first cousin Mihr un-Nisa Begam, who came from his mother's Beg family in Baroda. Sidi Yaqut (b 1928, d 1980) made a marriage into a ruling family, to Khushhal Sultan, daughter of the chief of the tiny state of Bantwa, which like Radhanpur was ruled by the Babi family of Pathans.

The next generation saw the first marriage recorded between the Janjira and Sachin families, when in 1974 Sidi Zaher, son of Sidi Salim of Sachin, married Qamr uz-Zaman Sultan, daughter of Nawab Sidi Mohammad III of Janjira. Sidi Zaher's first cousin Nawab Sidi Nasrullah (b 1933, d 2006; reigned 1990–2006) was a physician and the son and successor of Nawab Sidi Surur. His wife, Shams un-Nisa Begam, belongs to a noble Pathan family from Nipani in Karnataka. His three children are all married: the present nawab, Sidi Reza (b 1961; reigned 2006–), to Fatima Sultan Jahan, whose father is a Hyderabad noble named Nawab Ghulam Mohammad Omar Khan of Walia Estate; the daughter Farah Sultan (b 1963), to Mohammad Adil; and the younger son, Sidi Faisal (b 1965), to Bilqis Jahan, daughter of two Pathan nobles from Bhopal, Mohammad Iqbal Khan and Surur Jahan. At least on the basis of these marriages, the Sachin family appear in recent generations to have maintained more conservative marriage patterns than their kinsmen in Janjira.

### Conclusions

The accompanying table summarizes marriages in the Janjira and Sachin families over the last 150 years. It is arranged according to the birth dates of the Janjira and Sachin partners; the remaining columns indicate the backgrounds of the fathers of the Janjira and Sachin partners' spouses. "Urban nobility" indicates a partner from the urban upper classes, whether

Table 10.1. Marriages in the Janjira and Sachin Families

| Birth date: | Janjira: Wives from: | Husbands from: | Sachin: Wives from: | Husbands from: |
|---|---|---|---|---|
| 1820–1850 | 3 Sidi, sardar<br>1 Maniyar, commoner | | | |
| 1850–1880 | 1 Pathan, prince<br>1 (Muslim), urban nobility<br>1 Sidi, sardar | | 1 Mughal or Pathan (?)<br>1 (Muslim), urban nobility | 2 (Muslim), urban nobility |
| 1880–1905 | | | 1 Sidi, princely family<br>1 Pathan, prince<br>1 Mughal, rural nobility<br>1 Mughal, prince (?)<br>1 (Muslim), rural nobility | 1 Sidi, prince |
| 1905–1930 | 1 Pathan, prince | | 3 Mughal, prince<br>2 Mughal (?)<br>1 Pathan, rural nobility<br>3 (Muslim), rural nobility<br>2 Pathan, prince | 1 Mughal, prince |
| 1930–1955 | 1 (Muslim), rural nobility | 1 (Muslim), urban nobility<br>1 Pathan, rural nobility<br>1 Sidi, princely family | 1 Pathan, rural nobility<br>1 Sidi, princely family | |
| 1955–1980 | 1 Parsi, urban nobility | 1 Mughal, urban nobility<br>1 (Muslim), urban nobility | 1 (Muslim), rural nobility<br>1 Pathan, rural nobility | 1 (Muslim), rural nobility |

commercial, industrial, or religious; "rural nobility" means a partner from a rural landowning background or the nobility of a princely state (the distinction between the two is sometimes subjective).

On the basis of these data, which are admittedly limited, some conclusions may be offered. Despite the estrangement between the nawabs and their sardars (which took place gradually in Janjira during the first three-quarters of the nineteenth century and immediately in Sachin following the exclusion of Balu Miyan from the Janjira throne in 1784), the two royal families have always been conscious of their identity as Sidis. From the beginning, the word "Sidi" has been an element of their names, and as noted above they have always been aware of their African ancestry. Historically, the Janjira and Sachin Sidis had no sense of identity with other Sidi communities in India, although that is changing: in 2000, the late nawab of Sachin participated in the Rajpipla conference which first brought together Sidis and scholars (Catlin-Jairazbhoy and Alpers 2003: 3), and two members of the Janjira family attended the 2006 Goa conference, where they were the center of attention for scholars and Sidis alike.

Not surprisingly, the Sidis' sense of themselves as a diasporic African community in India has been reflected in their marriages. Until the latter part of the nineteenth century, the Janjira family apparently intermarried exclusively with Sidi sardars, and the last such marriage took place as recently as 1913. There were no sardars in Sachin, but members of that family have married into both their own house and (in 1974) the Janjira house.

At the same time, from the 1870s, the Sidis of Janjira and Sachin shared in the growing consciousness that Indian princely families, of whatever background, formed another distinct community. This may be seen in the marriages concluded by persons born between 1850 (the generation in which this consciousness first became clear) and 1930 (the last generation to reach adulthood before the end of princely rule). The partners have been identified with certainty in twenty-three of these marriages, and eleven of the partners were from princely families elsewhere in India. This is fully in keeping with patterns observed in other Indian princely families. Nevertheless, these marriages with princely families were never to the exclusion of marriages with Sidis, indicating that the princely identity supplemented (or complemented) the Sidi identity in both families but did not supersede it. Meanwhile, marriages with the urban elite, rural landowning families, and nobles from other princely states show the existence of a third identity, that of the upper class Muslim.

Since the end of the princely states in 1948–1949, the Sachin family has maintained traditional marriage patterns, even though the fact that the late nawab was a physician might suggest an identification with the urban professional classes. The members of the Janjira family, on the other hand, have married into a range of princely, industrial or professional, and rural noble families. This is a pattern observed in other princely families as well. The best way to look at the three identities revealed in marriage patterns may be as a series of circles: the small Sidi circle overlapping two larger circles, princely India and the Muslim upper classes of South Asia, which themselves overlap.

And so in the Janjira and Sachin families, the Africans who attained power in the Deccan in the seventeenth century have preserved a distinct identity down to the present, through which they may be considered an African-Indian diasporic community (even if they do not meet all of Campbell's requirements). At the same time, their integration into the princely Indian and upper-class Muslim communities make them in one sense Indians who happen to be of African descent (alongside marriage partners of other non-Indian ancestries) and also a constituent of the cosmopolitan Indian Ocean cultural world which produced them in the first place.

### Notes

An earlier version of this paper was delivered at the International Conference on the African Diaspora in Asia in Goa in January 2006. I must acknowledge the assistance of Ms Faaeza Jasdanwalla and Professor Theodore P. Wright Jr. in the preparation of this paper. Ms Jasdanwalla, His late Highness Nawab Sidi Mohammad Surur Khan of Sachin, His late Highness Nawab Dr Sidi Mohammad Nasrullah Khan of Sachin, and Rev. Lawrence M. Ober, SJ, supplied information on the genealogies of the Janjira and Sachin families.

1. Sidi, probably derived from the Arabic *sayyidi,* "my master," is a common name for Indians of African ancestry. It takes various forms in different Indian languages, such as Siddi or Sidhi. The group studied in this essay, the aristocracy of Janjira and Sachin, have always written their name as Sidi (in Arabic, Persian, Urdu, and English), and this spelling is accordingly followed here.

2. The first commandant appointed by the sultan of Ahmadnagar after he acquired Janjira in the late fifteenth century was also an African, Sidi Yaqut. This has led to the claim that Janjira was continuously under Sidi rule from the fifteenth century until 1948. Actually, it does not appear that any Sidis served as commandants for over a hundred years after Sidi Yaqut, until the appointment of Sidi Surur in 1618.

3. Given this, it is not surprising that the Sidis of Janjira never followed the marriage patterns noted by Plunkett among the Rajput royal families of Rajasthan, where although sons of rulers took both royal and non-royal wives, "the daughters of ruling houses were invariably married to ruling princes or their heirs" (Plunkett 1972: 67). Wright comments that elite Muslims in South Asia do not necessarily follow the supposed Muslim preference for marrying their own first cousins (Wright 1994: 131). This seems to be equally true of traditional marriages among the Sidis of Janjira, with the qualification that the small size of the Sidi sardar community meant that even if they were not first cousins, husbands and wives must often have been close relatives.

4. This new sense of an All-India princely community has not previously been noted, but my extensive research into marriage patterns seems to confirm its existence. Both Plunkett (1972: 68, 71), and Wright (1994: 131), comment on the central role of royal or elite marriages in cementing alliances. The precise nature of these alliances with regard to princely marriages of the nineteenth and twentieth

centuries requires further examination. I offer some speculations in McLeod (1986: 189).

5. Jafar Ali Khan of Cambay (b 1846/8, d 1915) apparently left at least two widows, Khurshid Jahan Begam (granddaughter of a sometime Iranian consul in India) and Sikandar Jahan Begam; it is unclear which of them was the mother of Iqbal Jahan Begam.

## Works Cited

*Unpublished*

National Archives of India, Foreign Department Proceedings
National Archives of India, Foreign and Political Department files


*Published*

Aitchison, C. U. 1929–1933. *A Collection of Treaties, Engagements, and Sanads Relating to India and Neighbouring Countries.* 14 vols. Calcutta: Government of India Central Publication Branch.
Anderson, Benedict. 1991. *Imagined Communities: Reflections on the Origin and Spread of Nationalism.* London: Verso.
Bhandare, Shailendra. 2006. "The Coins of the Sidis of Janjira." In Robbins and McLeod, *African Elites in India,* 198–209.
Camara, Charles. 2003. "The Siddis of Uttara Kannada: History, Identity and Change among African Descendants in Contemporary Karnataka." In Catlin-Jairazbhoy and Alpers, *Sidis and Scholars,* 100–114.
Catlin-Jairazbhoy, Amy, and Edward A. Alpers, editors. 2003. *Sidis and Scholars: Essays on African Indians.* Noida, India: Rainbow.
Chitnis, K. N. 2000. *The Nawabs of Savanur.* New Delhi: Atlantic.
*Cutch, Palanpur, and Mahi Kantha (Gazetteer of the Bombay Presidency, vol. 5).* 1880. Bombay: Government Central Press.
Eaton, Richard M. 2006. "Malik Ambar and Elite Slavery in the Deccan, 1400–1650." In Robbins and McLeod, *African Elites in India,* 45–67.
*Imperial Gazetteer of India.* 1908–9. 26 vols. Oxford: Clarendon Press.
Janjira, Nawabzadi Fatma Begum A. Jasdanwalla of. 2006. Foreword to Robbins and McLeod, *African Elites in India.*
Jasdanwalla, Faaeza. 2006. "The Sidi Kingdom of Janjira: The African Legacy." In Robbins and McLeod, *African Elites in India,* 177–83.
Jayasuriya, Shihan de Silva, and Richard Pankhurst, eds. 2003. *The African Diaspora in the Indian Ocean.* Trenton, N.J.: Africa World Press.
Khalidi, Omar. 2006. "The Habshis of Hyderabad." In Robbins and McLeod, *African Elites in India,* 245–259.
Khan, Nawabzada Nasrullah. 1898. *The Ruling Chiefs of Western India and the Rajkumar College.* Bombay: Thacker.
Khan, Shaharyar M. 2000. *The Begums of Bhopal: A History of the Princely State of Bhopal.* London: I.B. Tauris.
*List of Ruling Princes, Chiefs and Leading Personages in the Kolhapur and Deccan States.* 1941. Delhi: Manager of Publications.
Löfgren, O. 1965. "Aydarus." *Encyclopaedia of Islam.* 2nd ed. 11 vols. + supplements. 1:780–82. Leiden, Netherlands: Brill.

Loharu State (Punjab State Gazetteers, vol. 2). 1916. Lahore: Superintendent of Government Printing.

Luard, C. Eckford. 1908. Western States (Malwa) Gazetteer (Central India State Gazetteers Series, vol. 5). Bombay: British India Press.

Mankekar, D. R. 1974. Accession to Extinction: The Story of Indian Princes. New Delhi: Vikas.

McLeod, John. 1986. "Towards the Analysis of Hindu Princely Genealogy in the British Period, 1850–1950." South Asia Research 6.2: 181–93.

———. 2006a. "Genealogy of the Nawabs of Janjira." In Robbins and McLeod, African Elites in India, 213–15.

———. 2006b."The Later History of Janjira." In Robbins and McLeod, African Elites in India, 188–98.

———. 2006c. "The Nawabs of Sachin." In Robbins and McLeod, African Elites in India, 219–33.

Menon, V. P. 1956. The Story of the Integration of the Indian States. New York: Macmillan.

Plunkett, Frances Taft. 1972. "Royal Marriages in Rajasthan." Contributions to Indian Sociology, n.s., 7: 64–80.

Ramusack, Barbara. 2004. The Indian Princes and Their States. New Cambridge History of India series, vol. III.6. Cambridge: Cambridge University Press.

Rewa Kantha, Narukot, Cambay, and Surat States (Gazetteer of the Bombay Presidency, vol. 6). 1880. Bombay: Government Central Press.

Robbins, Kenneth X., and John McLeod, eds. 2006. African Elites in India: Habshi Amarat. Ahmedabad, India: Mapin.

Sachin, His Highness Nawab Dr. Sidi N. Khan, Nawab of. 2006. Foreword to Robbins and McLeod, African Elites in India, 7.

Sultaan, Abida. 2004. Memoirs of a Rebel Princess. Karachi, Pakistan: Oxford University Press.

Ullendorf, E. 1965. "Djabart." The Encyclopaedia of Islam. 2nd ed. 11 vols. + supplements. 2:355 Leiden, Netherlands: Brill.

Wright, Theodore P., Jr. 1976. "Muslim Kinship and Modernization: The Tyabji Clan of Bombay." In Family Kinship and Marriage among Muslims in India, ed. Imtiaz Ahmad. New Delhi: Manohar Book Service.

———. 1991. "Muslim Politics in South Asia: Who You Are and Who You Marry." The 1991 Aziz Ahmad Lecture, Centre for South Asian Studies, University of Toronto.

———. 1994. "Can There Be a Melting Pot in Pakistan? Interprovincial Marriage and National Integration." Contemporary South Asia 3.2: 131–44.

# 11

## African Indians in Bollywood

*Kamal Amrohi's* Razia Sultan

Jaspal Singh

Contradicting *historical* evidence, colonial and post-colonial texts often (mis)represent the past by configuring it through contemporary *hybridized and fractured* eyes, resulting in a skewed viewpoint that not only dilutes our perception of the present but, perhaps more importantly, mitigates our understanding of the past, which may lead to a dangerously totalizing Eurocentric and Westernized world-view. This essay examines Kamal Amrohi's *Razia Sultan* and his depiction of India's pre-colonial blacks only in modern, racialized terms, resulting in (mis)representation of the Africans in modern India. Therefore, Amrohi's attempt compromises the motion picture's value as an empowering tool for *inferiorized*, racialized, and gendered Africans in India and those who wish to understand their rich history and continued struggles in a post-colonial world. In fact, it was an important but failed attempt to inform on and clarify a significant period in India's (pre-colonial) history. How this happened is a remarkable story in the development of a colonialist world view requiring an understanding of the historical events which preceded them. Why is it that in spite of anti-colonial and nationalist struggles to free Indians from the shackles of colonialist mentality, it is virtually impossible to escape the binarist logic and ideology imposed by European colonialism? My reading tries to re-instate the marginalized and feminized Africans as well as Indian woman-hood into India's history by correcting (mis)interpretations of both the historical Jalal-ud-din Yakut, an African slave who achieved a high status in the Delhi Sultanate in thirteenth-century India, and Razia Sultan, the Indian Empress of Turkish origin, who ruled Delhi and in whose court Yakut gained further eminence; it also, however, tries to uncovers the internalization of European colonialist biases in Amrohi's depiction of pre-modern subjects, leading, in part to the negation of the powerful presence of Africans in India, but more importantly perhaps, this essay attempts to uncover the insidious nature of Eurocentricism and its extensive influences in silencing or repressing powerful histories.

Despite attempts to portray a strong pre-modern African warrior and a powerful Indian Empress of Delhi, *Razia Sultan* (1983) remains a commercial and artistic failure, due, in part, to the use of highbrow Urdu in its dialogue and to the excruciatingly slow narrative structure. For my purposes, however, its more significant failure as a post-colonial text must be attributed to the director's portrayals of African and Indian protagonists as modern caricatures, thereby eliding parallel universalism and competing cosmopolitanisms and unwittingly and tragically becoming complicit with a dominating world-view.

In the title roles are Hema Malini as the Indian empress of Turkish origin and Dharmendra as the Abyssinian slave/warrior, Yakut. Amrohi's depiction of Razia Sultan's love for her black slave and their eventual marriage yielded mixed reviews among Indian audiences. Some reviewers call it the most underrated film of its time, while others praise Amrohi's attempt at putting Razia back into popular culture, as most Indians seem to have forgotten the first and only empress of Delhi. The synopsis provided on Indiaplaza.com for this movie is typical of its flavor when it was first released:

> *Razia Sultan*, a celluloid marvel, depicts the pulsating tale of stormy love, un-flinching loyalty and sacrifice unfolded from the leaves of History. It is the story of the tempestuous love between a bewitching beauty, Razia, the Queen Empress of India and a lowly Abyssinian slave, Yaqub. Razia staked and lost everything—her honor, kingdom and life—for her love but she did not allow the powerful proud Turks, affronted by her love of a slave, to trample and break her sacrament of love for a slave. She laid down her life to keep the flames of her love ablaze and high and became immortalized in the hearts of her subjects as a symbol of the highest, the noblest and the most sacred love.
>
> With the passage of time, however, she was branded a vain sinful lover and it was not until the 20th century that a creative and sensitive artist Kamal Am-rohi got her to the silver screen with all her glory and honor and restored her

rightful place in History in the form of his most loving creation—RAZIA SULTAN—an unforgettable and memorable marvel and extravaganza.

Thus, even in Bollywood (India's Bombay film industry) cinema, the space provided for the African diaspora in India, which could have been a groundbreaking occurrence, managed to trivialize and eroticize its contribution to Indian social and cultural lives. Although history attempts to acknowledge Africans' contributions to India, however nominal, in the popular imagination, a warrior such as Yakut, who attained a high-ranking position in the Delhi Sultanate, is seen as only a "lowly Abyssinian slave."[1] Such sentiments can be attributed to the virtual non-existence of positive representations of Africans in popular Indian or Western culture.

When I researched Africans in India, the only images are of poor Siddhis, who continue to use traditional African musical instruments and folk dances during national holidays and festivals. The only filmic representation of a black African reaching a high position in the navy or army is that of Yakut in Amrohi's film. Yet, this film too manages to misrepresent the early powerful African presence in India due to post-colonial India's internalizations of colonialist binary logic and assumptions. Indians in India perpetuated binarisms and exclusions through nationalism and ideas of belonging to the nation defined in opposition to Englishness.

Constructions of otherness vary in colonialist texts. In his essay "The Economy of Manichean Allegory," for example, Abdul JanMohamed discusses two categories of colonialist, literary otherness: imaginary (emotive) literature and symbolic (reflexive) literature. In the imaginary construction, reality is defined by colonialists who ignore the perspective of the very people being observed. In short, reality is not what is real to both the observer and the observed, but only what is real to the former, who defines materiality solely from his or her perspective:

> The "imaginary" representation of indigenous people tends to coalesce the signifier and the signified. In describing the attributes or actions of the native, issues such as intention, causality, extenuating circumstances, and so forth, are completely ignored; in the "imaginary" colonialist realm, to say "native" is to say "evil" and to evoke immediately the economy of the Manichean allegory. (JanMohamed 1995: 18)

As JanMohamed goes on to note, this "imaginary" definition of the *other* is little more than a "narcissistic" projection of the colonizer's negative self-image that totally negates the inherent attributes, beliefs, customs, and consciousness of a "degraded and inhuman" *native* beneath subjectivity. To be reflexive and to write within the symbolic realm, colonialist writers must practice the impossible task of negating their "very own be-ing"; otherwise, such "literature merely affirms its own Eurocentric assumptions; instead of actually depicting the outer limits of 'civilization,' it simply codifies and preservers the structures of its own mentality" (Jan-Mohamed 1995: 20). While JanMohamed's discussion concerns itself with colonialists' representation of the colonized through the "economy of the Manichean allegory," my purpose in bringing it up here is to show that the colonized imbibed such Manichaeism through colonial education.

During British colonialism in India, "imaginary" representations of the other were imposed and taught to Indians. In reading colonialist literature, then, we must uncover how colonized people internalized myths and constructions of their own inferiority as real. JanMohamed explains that in the fetishization of the other, "all the evil characteristics and habits with which the colonialist endows the native are thereby not presented as products of social and cultural difference but as characteristics inherent in the race—in the 'blood'—of the native" (1995: 21). As Ashcroft, Griffith, and Tiffin note, "The 'difference' of the post-colonial subject by which s/he can be 'othered' is felt directly and immediately in the way in which the superficial difference of the body and voice (skin colour, eye shape, hair texture, body shape, language, dialect or accent) are read as indelible signs of the 'natural' inferiority of their possessors" (321). It is impossible to "abolish" dualism, to "transcend oppositions," so a post-colonial artist can "exist beyond contradictions" (Dash 1995: 333). Post-colonial artists, who create in order to establish a "dialogic relation with colonialist fiction [in order to] attempt to negate the prior European negation of the colonized cultures and its adoption and creative modification of Western languages and artistic forms in conjunction with indigenous languages and form" (JanMohamed 1995: 23), often fail. This failure is due to the postcolonial artists' orientalization of themselves. I how that in spite of Amrohi's best intention and attempt at recovery and syncretism as a "Third World" artist, he failed because he could not completely negate "prior European negation of the colonized cultures," particularly the African diaspora in India. The tragedy of rewriting history through "contesting discourses" of "inclusion and exclusions," of black and white, is that "the spirit of resistance itself is caught in the disempowering binarism of imperial history" (Walcott 1995: 370–74).

### History of Africans in India

I uncovered two books while researching the Indian diaspora at the University of KwaZulu-Natal in Durban, South Africa, in 2005: R. R. S.

Chauhan's *Africans in India: From Slavery to Royalty* (1995) and Shanti Sadiq Ali's *The African Dispersal in the Deccan: From Medieval to Modern Times* (1995). Since then, I found a few other volumes. Although the African diaspora in the Americas and the Caribbean is well recorded, little is known about the history of black Africans in India.[2]

Countless Africans were brought to the Konkani Coast by Arab slave traders in the first century AD. Many became rulers in fifteenth-century Bengal, while others rose to prominence in military and governmental circles during the Mughul and British rules.[3] Many, however, remained slaves.[4]

In contemporary India, notes Chauhan, Africans have continued to maintain "their indigenous customs, traditions, identity and the way of life despite settling in India for several centuries" (1995: 1).

In direct contrast to Chauhan's study, Ali suggests that "in India, a relatively liberal society absorbed foreigners in their midst, providing the means of facilitating inter-marriage between the Africans and the local people" (1995: 4). She attributes inter-marriage to "racial and cultural identity being blurred over the centuries" (5).

In Hyderabad, the Siddhis continue to uphold distinct cultural characteristics, such as "musical instruments, folk songs, dances," but after 1948, when the nizam was removed from power, their social and economic status rapidly declined, and now they live in abject poverty. In Karnataka, there are Christians, Hindus, and Muslim Africans, who have "adopted the local language and customs but have retained a distinct identity" (Ali 1995: 3). They too live in relative poverty.[5] "Estimated population [of Siddis] range from 14,000 to 30,000" (Campbell this volume).

Although these texts record a large presence of Africans holding positions of power in the Indian royal courts, "not only in armies and navies but also in civil administration" (Chauhan 1995: 23), many were either retained as slaves (*ghulam*) or mercenary warriors (*jangju*) in various courts.[6] It is here that the history of Africans in India—who held positions of power in the Indian royal courts—and Amrohi's enterprise converge with my research.

### Historical Razia Sultan and Jalal-ud-din Yakut

Iltutmish, father of Razia Sultan, himself a former slave of Turkish origins, rose to the level of sultan and ruled Delhi (which included Punjab—namely, Sursuti, Bhatinda, and Kuhram, including Lahore) in AD 1210. By AD 1228, Iltutmish had "solved the problem of territorial integration under a single command, and when he died in AD 1236. . . . his greatest achievement was the initiation of a dynastic monarchy, and in utilizing it in welding the loosely conquered territories into a political unity" (Majumdar 1957: 135). He achieved the right to a crown, the Caliph's investiture, which he received in AD 1229, and became Delhi's first king.

After the death of the crown prince Nasir-ud-din (Mahmud) in AD 1229, Iltutmish nominated his daughter Razia over his sons as his successor. Her intelligence and abilities to rule were considered more than adequate, and Razia's nomination was fairly well received. Her father had left her in charge of the government during his frequent campaign absences, and she carried out her duties well. Just before his death, Iltutmish intimated his intention of making Razia his successor to his son, Firuz, in the hope of putting things in order. He was aware of his son's jealousy of Razia, but at any event, in spite of pre-planning, on the night of his father's death, Firuz proclaimed himself king (Majumdar 1957: 136).

The governors of Multan, Lahore, Hansi, Budaun, and Awadh marched toward Delhi to end this "turncoat" rule; Firuz met the rebels head-on, but even his own army revolted against him. Quickly, Razia maneuvered the populace against Firuz and, upon his returned, imprisoned him. Army officers immediately proclaimed Razia's accession to the throne. Firuz died in prison after a misrule of seven short months. The queen was equal to the task of defeating all oppositions, particularly insurgent governors displeased with her methods. Her reign of three years forms "a brief interlude in a decade of oligarchic misrule increased by factiousness" (Majumdar 1957: 137):

> History describes her as a young woman with kingly demeanor.
> She discarded female attire, rode out in public, and held court; she selected for high office men of her own choice and, deliberately, not always from among Iltutmish's freedmen who came to be known as "the forty." Among these new appointees was the Abyssinian Jalal-ud-din Yaqut whose promotion to the post of *Amir-I-Akhur* (Master of the Stables), a sinecure carrying more prestige than power, was obviously calculated to counter the Forty's monopolistic control of all such offices.

The Forty attempted many coups to depose Razia, but with bravery and foresight she managed to quell them. However, when Malik Altuniya, the governor of Bhatinda, rebelled against her, Razia, unmindful of the heat and the "inconvenience of the month of *Ramazan*," marched out for battle, but the rebels in her own army rose against her, killed Yaqut, and threw her in prison in Bhatinda fort (Majumdar 1957: 138). Iltutmish's third son Bahram was quickly proclaimed the successor. Altuniya, who was guarding Razia, aligned himself with her, and after she agreed to marry him, marched to Delhi to regain her power.

However, the mercenary troops, "recruited mostly from the Khokar tribe, proved no match for the regulars of the Delhi government, and they were easily repulsed" (Majumdar 1957: 138). When Razia fled from the pursuing army, her mercenaries deserted her at Kaithal, where she was murdered by Hindu robbers while resting.

Despite conflicts and detractors envious of her rule and their alliance, Yakut's and Razia's relationship was accepted and honored, in part, due to their both being Muslims. And although there appears no historical evidence that they married, they were, nevertheless, powerful, respected figures in Indian history.

Yet, in Amrohi's cinematic *mis*representation, they are cast, respectively, as a caricature of a Western-style African slave and an emotionally weak, contemporary Indian woman. How did it come to this? How could the historical record be so blatantly bastardized as to embrace an Indian in sporadic blackface and a weak-willed Indian woman as protagonists in a film that so patently misrepresents their roles as strong, historical characters? Why and when did such historical intermingling and rich synthesis of African and India culture become repressed, leading to repression, regression, and distortion?

### The Evolution of Otherness: From Religious Differentiation to Racialized Subjugation

From the days of the Greek and Roman Empires, subjugation and control has been a multifaceted enterprise composed of self-referencing religious components. Conquest and control of natural resources, usurpation of political power, as well as the exploitation and management of wealth all required military, organizational, and moral structures that both promoted and justified empire. In medieval Europe, justification derived from religious imperatives reinforced by a supposed, providential superiority over conquered *others* requiring conversion or deserving of deracination.

To be sure, however, *otherness* did not originate in medieval Europe. Ania Loomba notes Greeks and Romans created "abiding templates for subsequent European images of 'barbarians' and outsiders" (Loomba 1998: 105–6). As she points out, otherness was merely "re-configured" by medieval and early modern Europeans at a time when "Christianity became the prism through which all knowledge of the world was refracted" (105). Citing Samuel Chew, Loomba adds: "[I]n medieval and early modern Europe, Christian identities were constructed in opposition to Islam, Judaism or heathenism (which loosely incorporated all other religions, nature worship, paganism and animism). Above all, it was Islam that functioned as the predominant binary opposite of and threat to Christianity" (106).

Loomba also notes in *Shakespeare, Race, and Colonialism*, "The religious underpinning of 'race' stretched back to the Crusades" (2002: 25). Religious otherness, however, would be supplanted by more obvious, racial markers between Europeans and the Muslim world. Indeed, as Loomba clarifies, the racialization of *otherness* began taking root as *blackness* came to signify dark, Arab peoples, and, eventually, the terms "Turks" or "Moors" would be blurred and blended to reflect these physically recognizable differences between Europeans and their defined *others*. Loomba continues:

> The term "Moors" at first referred to Arab Muslims, and although not all Muslims were dark skinned (and travelogues as well as literary texts abound with references to white Moors) over time, Moors came overwhelmingly to be associated with blackness as is evident from the term "blackamoors" (Loomba 1998: 106)

In my research, I found pre-modern European sensibilities were more threatened by Muslim religious expansionism than by racialized otherness. It was only over time that blackness, once exclusive to Islam—the religious other of Christian Europe—evolved to incorporate all non-white races. According to Loomba, "Greek and Roman literatures, Christian religions thought, as well as medieval writings, were influenced in their views of cultural, ethnic, and linguistic difference. These views have been shaped by various histories of contact and conflict, the most important of which were the Greek and Roman interactions with the people they conquered, the Crusades, as well as the interactions between Jews, Muslim, and Christians within Europe, especially Iberia" (2002: 6). In the early modern European history, the worst conflict between the Christians and their others had to do with religion, asserts Loomba (2).

> In medieval culture (and earlier in Greek and Roman traditions) blackness was a symbol for a variety of differences. . . . The devil, the Saracens, and other enemies of Christianity were represented as black; so were the Jews, allies of the feared Mongol emperors, or the Turks. Blackness represents danger, and becomes a way of signifying what lies outside familiar or approved social, political, religious, and sexual structures. The stages of the early modern period were rife with images of black people as lewd, unprincipled, and evil, ugly and repulsive. (2002: 36)

And although the word "Moor" increasingly became associated with blackness, it first indicated those who belonged to "'Mahomet's sect'" (Loomba 2002: 46). Medieval and early modern Europe did not develop a biological understanding of race, even though the term was deployed to denote religious and linguistic others (38). Pre-modern religious blackness was socially constructed while early modern and modern racial blackness is constructed as biological, which became even more complex as Europe encountered its others in the New World. Pre-modern and early modern notions of blackness suggest one could convert to Christianity and remove this blackness to an extent, but racialized blackness could never be washed away as it was "genetically distinct" (26). Thus it is only in the modern period that racialization of skin color difference defined in biological terms of blackness—"what is outside reflects what is inside"—that racial difference became essentialized and biologized.

British colonial education imposed ideas of blackness and racial inferiority on the Indians, and it is this notion of the racialized and biologized other on which Amrohi reflects in his attempt to portray a thirteenth-century high-ranking African warrior in his film *Razia Sultan* (1983). Amrohi is a representative of the colonial hybrid who, in spite of anti-colonial struggles and nationalism, becomes complicit with colonial ideology and is unable to escape imposed binary logic.

### Kamal Amrohi's *Razia Sultan:* A Modern Misinterpretation of Historical Reality

Kamal Amrohi's *Razia Sultan* was a commercial and artistic failure. Ultimately, the failure of this film is multifold: the principal reason, however, is the imposition of a colonialist historical perspective that alters the historical evidence, compromises and negates the meaning of the African diaspora in India, and perpetuates the myth of African inferiority. However, to support this argument, I suggest the onus rests on Amrohi's modern sensibilities as well as post-colonial India's misreading of *Razia Sultan*. Ultimately, however, it the hegemony of European ideology and the construction of Africa as backward and barbaric that contribute to the repression of the rich history of Africans, not only in India but in the world.

Many, such as Modisane or Césaire, re-read Shakespeare's *The Tempest* in modern terms, suggests Loomba; some see it as a mis-reading. But for George Lamming, the Caribbean writer, there is no other way. As Lamming suggests, if his reading of *The Tempest* as a play that celebrates Caliban was a mistake, it was a "mistake, lived and felt by millions of men like me" (Loomba 2002: 5). Films like *Razia Sultan* "have spoken about race to an audience whose lives have been, and continue to be, enormously affected by the racial question" (5). Can we re-read *Razia Sultan* as a celebration of Yakut?

If one re-reads for empowerment, that effort has to be lauded, but when misreadings denigrating racialized others continue, it is our job as post-colonial critics to right the wrong because, ultimately, such views of blackness inform the social, political, and economic imperatives of European colonialism and neocolonialism and, equally important, the postcolonial societies that inherit their world-view.[7] Perhaps not surprisingly then, and despite its pre-modern setting, Kamal Amrohi's *Razia Sultan* reflects this modern concept of blackness in terms of racialized otherness and is received as such.[8] Let us examine the film.

*Razia Sultan* revolves around Razia Sultan, the Turkish Indian Empress of Delhi; her father, Sultan Iltutmish, emperor of Delhi; Shah Turkaan, the sultan's wife; Firuz, her son; Jalal-ud-din Yakut, the Abyssinian slave and warrior, and Amir Altunia, the amir of Bhatinda. Yakut is a mercenary warrior, a *Jhangju* at the Delhi courts, while Razia, a princess, is being trained by Yakut in warfare.

Here is a short synopsis of the film: As Razia trains as a warrior with Yakut, they fall in love. Shah Turkaan, the sultan's wife, is jealous of Razia and plots against her. Sultan Iltutmish asks to see Razia perform; pleased at her expertise, he releases Yakut from slavery and promotes him to chief of stables. Iltutmish proclaims Razia his successor; however, her brother proclaims himself sultan at his father's death. Yakut, who was given charge of the sultan's will, has it etched on his body; he, along with Razia, mobilizes the Delhi population and reclaims the throne for her. In the meantime, many suitors ask for Razia's hand in marriage, but she chooses Yakut. Her choice is met with resistance due to their racial differences, but ultimately love prevails and they get married. After a few years, the neighboring governors, led by Amir Altunia, revolt against her. Razia and Yakut fight bravely, but Yakut is injured. As the film ends, Yakut and Razia ride away into the sunset.

The film opens with a shot of Yakut's dark, shirtless torso—which foreshadows the importance of skin color—as Razia rides up to him. As she dismounts, Yakut kneels down to lend her a hand. Razia's training as a warrior by Yakut is trivialized when she falls into his arms while dismounting, the narrative going into slow motion as they gaze into each other's eyes. Dhramendra's wooly wig caricatures blackness, as does the painted-on skin color.

When Iltutmish entrusts Yakut with his will, naming Razia his successor, Yakut asks his maid, Laila, to etch the words with a knife on his body. At his impassioned pleading, Iltutmish brands his seal on Yakut's bleeding chest. Thus, on the body of the black slave is inscribed the last will and testament of Iltutmish. His black body becomes the site of loyalty. The visual representation disavows the importance of Yakut's warrior-like demeanor and stance, and Yakut's historical significance is minimized. Amrohi's romanticizing of Yakut's inscripted body is rendered in orientalist (Edward Said) terms. When Yakut's dark and inscribed naked torso is exhibited around the city in order to mobilize the Delhi public, a noble and eminent African warrior becomes an object—a spectacle—of someone else's power.

When Malik Ikhtiar-ud-din Altuniya, the governor of Bhatinda, proposes marriage to her, Razia—knowing Yakut's prowess in swordsmanship—declares her intention to marry the victor in a sword-fighting contest. Yakut at first refuses; he doesn't wish Razia to face dishonor and shame. He declares that her shame will be wrapped in the shroud of dishonor throughout eternity if he wins and marries her, thus refusing to participate. This portrayal of Yakut as cowed and thankful to his masters, more in line with portrayals of black slaves in American films, demonstrates a humility that undermines the self-respect of an eminent warrior.

Amrohi's modern sensibilities see the union of Razia and Yakut in racialized terms. When Yakut wins Razia's hand in marriage by wining the contest, Prime Minister Amir Balbal finds the union of a Turk with an African disgusting. He states that the hot *White* blood of the Turkish Amirs will boil with rage if the "moon of their chastity is *blackened*" by the blood of a *Habishi*, even though Balbal is reminded by the senior minister that calling Yakut without his proper title is an offense. His titles, the senior minister declares, are more important than his race.

Just as the idea of class as rooted in biological differences prevails, racialization of Yakut in terms of his dark body and blood ensues in this film. As Yakut and Razia are both Muslim, the idea of the religious otherness as blackness, as in Shakespeare's *Othello*, is absent from the film as well as from history. In spite of Yakut's titles and his status, the officials reiterate that the white blood of the Turks must not be tarnished by the black blood of a slave, a *Habishi*. Here again, the specter of "blackness" as racialized is raised in biological terms in pre-modern India. Thus, modern notions of race permeate Amrohi's sensibilities, reflecting the character and plot development of *Razia Sultan*.

A long drawn-out dramatic and emotional scene unfolds between Yakut and Razia at their eventual wedding.[9] Finally, after the courtship drama, when she announces her decision to abdicate the throne at the Dewaan-e-Aam, a public arena—after a reign of three years and eight months by taking off her crown and taking up her veil again—in order to marry Yakut, her subjects are distraught. The senior minister proclaims his sorrow and support of Razia by lamenting—"let her go! Since their white Turkish blood cannot be contaminated by the *Habishi's* black blood! Let her go! What if she sees his humanity and loves him as a human!" The idea of his humanity and the specter of black blood as compared to the purity of white Turkish blood appear to mimic European construction. Finally, when Altuniya rebels against Delhi, Razia is overpowered but is rescued by Yakut at the last minute. Her character throughout the film is one of emotional and sexual weakness, and the idea of giving up everything for love is rendered entirely in modern romantic terms.

As the wounded Yakut rides with Razia into the sunset, a voice from heaven proclaims—"come to the world in the sky. Stars, obey God's order! I am decorating another world for you by Khuda's order. The sacrificed love drenched in blood is coming to my protection! This world is unfit for you!"

Finally, the world is declared unfit for racial mixing, although, as I suggest above, the fear of miscegenation and race mixing in terms of black and white began with European colonial expansion. Pre-modern India's racial intermixing and religious tolerance prove that the film's phobias are indeed modern. Communalism and genocide due to race and religious differences were not endemic in pre-modern India as they became in the post-colonial nation.

The failure of this movie to become a space for empowerment, both for the African diaspora in India as well as the Indian woman, rests upon questions of race, gender, sexuality, and miscegenation due to British colonial ideology. Women, even if they are sultans, cannot transgress racial and gender boundaries. As a postcolonial reading of a pre-colonial story, the film is also weak for failing to showcase any domestic scenes. In terms of race and gender the narrative is therefore unable to normalize intercultural marriages; blacks, no matter what levels of government they ascend to *Othello*-like, cannot transgress racial boundaries. Amrohi's modern sensibilities are clearly detected and underpin the plot structure and character development throughout the film. He posits romantic love between two people of African and Turkish descent in terms of black and white and depicts the opposition to the liaisons in purely racial terms. While history shows Africans ascending to the role of rulers, which assumes hierarchies in terms of class as well as rich syncretic histories, Amrohi's modern sensibilities rewrite history in essentialized and racialized notions. That miscegenation raised its ugly head in India during late British rule and is still with the post-colonial nation is particularly underlined by this movie.

*Razia Sultan* could have become a site for negotiations for gender identity representation and construction, and it could also have empowered the African diaspora in India by showing Africa's contribution to Indian social and cultural development. However, that did not occur, and as the resolution of the film shows, the time is not yet ripe for racial pluralism in any form in a country divided not only by class, religious, and caste divisions, but also, and more importantly, by a "globalization" with its totalizing logic of capitalism and of Euro-American imperialism. Thus this film sunk with barely a ripple in post-colonial India, and, sadly, Amrohi's attempt at rescuing the parallel discourse of the powerful pre-colonial African presence in Indian is rendered moot.

## Conclusion

For this film to be truly empowering, Amrohi could have portrayed more faithfully and accurately the historical reality of the lives of both Yakut and Razia. That Yakut rose to the rank of not only the head of the stables but also the chief of the army is indicative of the status achieved by many Africans in India. The reality of Razia's strength and power, where she continued to fight back despite Yakut's death, when she managed to marry her captor, Altuniya, and marched toward Delhi to recapture her throne from her brother, should have been part of the film for it to be a truly empowering paradigm for women. That she was killed in the context of a battle, where she was indeed an awesome fighter, would have added to the ethos of the queen as powerful, thus rendering Yakut's role in her court significant.

Ultimately, contemporary rewriting of history in *Razia Sultan* proves that "the trace of European expansionism continues to exit in the bodies and minds of the rest of the world"; and many post-colonial and hybrid artists, in their attempts to "write back" (Rabasa 1995: 358) and reclaim history, are not successful. The story remains a significant element in Indian history; to turn it into a modern soap opera is to undermine its significance and devalue its lessons. For a truly empowering interpretation of this film, both for the African diaspora in India and for Indian women, then, the historical reality plus the modern and post-modern sensibilities of the filmmaker need to be incorporated in the criticism. As there are not too many texts that showcase the contributions of Africans in India, the importance of this film should not be negated. This post-colonial reading attempts to uncover modernist assumptions by correcting the (mis)representation of Jalal Udin Yakut, the *Habishi* high-ranking government official of the Delhi Sultanate, and of Razia Sultan, the able and shrewd ruler of Delhi in thirteenth-century India, by situating the film within the historical and contemporary realities of the presence of the African diaspora in India.

In this discussion then, my attempt at revising history has been twofold. First I have attempted to correct Amrohi's misrepresentation, in modern and racialized terms, of the pre-modern African diaspora in India. When scholars envision the history of Africans in the diasporas, they typically focus on the Africans' presence in the "new world" and see them from the dominant viewpoint. Since little is known about pre-modern Africans in

India, they too become modern caricatures. However, while many Africans *were* taken as slaves by Arab traders to India, and while many were retained as slaves or mercenary warriors in various courts, their contribution to pre-modern India is immeasurable in many ways. The Indian rulers valued their contributions highly. What is known and recorded shows that they rose to high ranks in the military and governmental circles as well as in civil administrations; in fact, many rose to become rulers themselves in various states. This history should be readily available for the oppressed and disenfranchised African diaspora in India so that the contributions of their ancestors to the nation can be validated and acknowledged.

Second, recovering the history of African success in India would demonstrate that systems of cultural and economic exchange existed historically and that the non-Eurocentric cosmopolitan world of the Indian Ocean produced (and continues to produce) cultural fusion and hybridity long before those terms became fashionable in the colonial and postcolonial world views. As Dana Rush rightly points out regarding diasporas, in her chapter in this volume, "what appears at first glance to be confusion can, in a 'diaspora space,' become multi-layered fusion." It is this fusion which "attests to the ongoing, globally incorporate sensibilities" that we must recover in order to position the non-Western cultures with their parallel discourses as global partners and players so that alliances that have been forged "on a regional, national, and global scale" can be uncovered for "diasporic [and transnational] political action" (Obeng, this volume). Such political actions will uncover and validate the non-Eurocentric cosmopolitanisms and parallel universalisms, hopefully equalizing and balancing Euro-America's rampant neo-colonialist globalism and expansionisms, and leading to a more equitable economic and cultural future.

### Notes

1. Black Africans were referred to variously as Siddis, Habishis, Caffres, etc. While the Marathi documents describe them as "Shamal," which translates to "black face," Portuguese and English spell them variously as "Seede, Siddhis, Siddie, Siddee, Siddy, Sidi, Sidy, Seedee, Scidee, Scidy, Seydee, Sciddee, Abexin, Abeixm, Habshis, Abyssinians, Caffre, Caffree, Kaphirs, Kafra, Mullatoes, etc." (Chauhan 1995: 132).

Ali indicates the term "Abyssinians" is used for slaves taken from Ethiopia, while slaves called "Zanj," "who provide the vast majority of Mesopotamian slaves. . . . between AD 1000 and 1498," were from East Africa, whereas in medieval Gujurat, most slaves came from the present day Tanzania. The Portuguese brought slaves to India from Mozambique. The term "Habshi" refers to slaves from the Red Sea region, while Siddhi refers to slaves from the southern region of Arabia (Ali 1995: 2).

2. As a child raised by a traditional Indian family in Burma, I've heard the word "Habishi" used as a "cuss" word. Remarkably, despite my childhood in Burma and fifteen years spent living in India, I'd never heard of any African Indians. Indeed, I first heard of India's Siddhis in 1989 while attending a lecture sponsored by the Ethnomu-

sicology Department at the University of California, Los Angeles, finding their connections to Africa and African music intriguing.

3. For more information on African Indians historic presence in India, please see Pashington Obeng's "Religion and Empire: Belief and Identity among African Indians of Karnataka, South India," in this volume.

4. For a more detailed account of the slave trade and the presence of Africans in India, please see Gwyn Campbell's "Slave Trades and Indian Ocean World," in this volume.

5. In contemporary India, Siddhis are predominantly Muslims, typically farmers in Gujarat, Daman and Diu, Maharashtra, Karnataka, Andhra Pradesh, among other cities, and designated Scheduled Tribe members.

6. The Portuguese and French also bought slaves from East Africa as well as from agents in Goa. Ali also cites various historical texts regarding the presence of Abyssinian colonies in India, such as Rajpuri, along the western coast of India and from Cape Comorin upward in the very early Christian era. When the "Negro" dynasty in Bengal ended in 1493, according to Ali, "thousands of Africans expelled from the kingdom" were turned back from "Delhi and Jaunpur, and finally drifted to Gurjarat and the Deccan, where there was a considerable Negro population." In 1490 AD, the fort of Janjira came under direct Abyssinian rule when it was "lost" to them by a trick played by the Abyssinian on the local Koli chief. Janjira is the fortified island, which was the "focal point where the Africans emerged as a political force . . . is located between Kolaba and Ratnagiri in western Maharastra" (Ali 1995: 3–33).

Chauhan shows the history of Janjira and the importance of the African presence in India by indicating that the Abyssinians held on to the fort with their military might and great fighting prowess. The Danda-Rajpuri area—the town and the fortress—formed the administrative headquarters of the land possession of the Siddhis. "During the rule of the Siddhis, the passage from Rajpuri to the castle was defended by artillery thereby making the entry of any intruder almost impossible" (Chauhan 1995: 125–87).

Alphonso de Albuquerque, the first Portuguese governor of Goa, in a letter dated 1 January 1514 addressed to the King of the Portuguese, described Danda as "a good place and the chief port for the Caracks all to come to it, and has a very small island on which the Moors have a beautiful fortress, very full of trees and many tanks of water. . . . It seems to me, sir, that we ought to take it" (Ali 1995: 2).

7. Slowly, almost imperceptibly, religious justification gave way to a self-serving and equally devaluating racial hierarchy premised on the supremacy of whites and the subjugation of non-white *others*, but, as with previous ecumenical arguments, always under the guise of civilizing native populations.

8. Set in thirteenth-century India, Amrohi's text posited otherness in racialized terms as opposed to Shakespeare's *Othello*. For example, the imagery of hell and the devil—associated with non-Christians, and "the barbary horse" (111. iii.201) are used, so when Othello is termed an old ram about to "tup a white ewe" (i. ii. 88–89), the popular notion of Muslims or moors as lascivious and corrupting whiteness is due to Othello's religious otherness. See Shakespeare, *Othello* (1974: 1198–1248.

9. When the senior prime minister confronts Razia on her marriage decision, she declares that she will abdicate her throne for love. When the prime minister demands from Yakut his life as a sacrifice, Yakut extends his sword to him. Instead, the prime minister asks him to leave the city. Yakut leaves a note with Laila, stating that he does not wish even his corpse to blemish the pure Turkish soil. Razia, who

follows him, finds a dehydrated and disoriented, albeit adamant, Yakut. At his refusal to return, she assaults him with her sword and turns to leave. At the last minute, she rushes back as he collapses, entreating him once more to return when he gives in.

## Works Cited

Ali, Shanti Sadiq. 1995. *The African Dispersal in the Deccan: From Medieval to Modern Times.* New Delhi: Orient Longman.

Ashcroft, Bill, Garreth Griffith, and Helen Tiffin, eds. 1995. *The Postcolonial Studies Reader.* New York: Routledge.

Chauhan, R. R. S. 1995. *Africans in India: From Slavery to Royalty.* New Delhi: Asian Publishing Services.

Chew, Samuel. 1937. *The Crescent and the Rose: Islam and England During the Renaissance.* Reprint, New York: Oxford University Press.

Dash, Michael. 1995. "In Search of the Lost Body: Redefining the Subject in Caribbean Literature." In Ashcroft, Griffith, and Tiffin, *Postcolonial Studies Reader,* 332–35.

JanMohamed, Abdul R. 1995. "The Economy of Manichean Allegory." In Ashcroft, Griffith, and Tiffin, *Postcolonial Studies Reader,* 18–23.

Loomba, Ania. 1998. *Colonialism/Postcolonialism.* London: Routledge.

———. 2002. *Shakespeare, Race, and Colonialism.* London: Oxford University Press.

Majumdar, R. C. 1957. *The History and Culture of the Indian People: The Struggle for Empire.* Vol. 5. Bombay: Bharatiya Vidhya Bhavan.

Rabasa, Jose. 1995. "Allegories of Atlas," In Ashcroft, Griffith, and Tiffin, *Postcolonial Studies Reader,* 358–64.

Rashidi, Runoko, and Ivan Van Sertima. 1985. *African Presence in Early Asia.* New Brunswick, N.J.: Transaction.

*Razia Sultan.* 1983. Dir. Kamal Amrohi. Rajdhani Films, India.

Shakespeare, William. *Othello.* 1974. In *The Riverside Shakespeare,* 1198–1248. Ed. G. Blakemore Evans. Boston: Houghton Mifflin.

Walcott, Derek. 1995. "The Muse of History." In Ashcroft, Griffith, and Tiffin, *Postcolonial Studies Reader,* 370–74.

# CONTRIBUTORS

**Gwyn Campbell** is Professor of History at McGill University and a Canada Research Chair in Indian Ocean World History. Born in Madagascar, he served as an academic consultant for the South African government in the first phase of inter-governmental meetings leading to the 1997 formation of an Indian Ocean regional association. His publications include *An Economic History of Imperial Madagascar, 1750–1895: The Rise and Fall of an Island Empire* and (as editor) *Abolition and Its Aftermath in Indian Ocean Africa and Asia.*

**Devarakshanam Govinden** is Research Fellow in the Faculty of Education at the University of KwaZulu-Natal. She has written on Gcina Mhlophe, and others.

**John C. Hawley** is Professor of English and Chair of Department at Santa Clara University. He is author of *Amitav Ghosh: An Introduction* and editor or co-editor of eleven books, including *Encyclopedia of Postcolonial Studies* and *The Postcolonial and the Global* (with Revathi Krishnaswamy). He is Associate Editor of the *South Asian Review.*

**Chapurukha M. Kusimba** is Curator of African Archaeology and Ethnology at the Field Museum and Adjunct Associate Professor at Northwestern University and the University of Illinois at Chicago. He is author of *The Rise and Fall of the Swahili States; East African Archaeology: Foragers, Potters, Smiths, and Traders* (with Sibel B. Kusimba); *Unwrapping Textile Traditions of Madagascar;* and *James W. Vanstone: A Legend in Arctic and Museum Anthropology* (with Charles Stanish).

**John McLeod** is Associate Professor of History at the University of Louisville and Honorary Rajvansi Genealogist of the Rajvara Heritage Institution at Rajkuman College, Rajkot. He is author of *Sovereignty, Power, Control: Politics in the States of Western India, 1916–1947* and *The History of India,* and editor (with Kenneth X. Robbins) of *African Elites in India.*

**Savita Nair** is Assistant Professor of History and of Asian Studies at Furman University. She is revising her manuscript "Gujarat, East Africa, and the Indian Diaspora," on early twentieth-century Gujarti merchant family migrations, as part of a project that expands the historical geography of South Asia and makes migrants central rather than marginal to history writing.

**Pashington Obeng** is Assistant Professor of Religion at Wellesley College. He is author of *Asante Catholicism: Religious and Cultural Reproduction among* *the Akan of Ghana* and *Asante Women Dancers: Architects of Power Realignment in Corpus Christi.*

**Rahul C. Oka** is Visiting Assistant Professor at the Department of Anthropology, University of Notre Dame Du Lac.

**Thangam Ravindranathan** is Assistant Professor of French Studies at Brown University.

**Anjali Gera Roy** is Professor in the Department of Humanities and Social Sciences at the Indian Institute of Technology, Kharagpur. Her books include *Three Great African Novelists; Wole Soyinka: An Anthology of Recent Criticism; Rohinton Mistry: An Anthology of Recent Criticism;* and *Partitioned Lives: Narratives of Home, Displacement and Resettlement.*

**Dana Rush** is Assistant Professor of African and African Diaspora Art History at the University of Illinois at Urbana-Champaign.

**Jaspal Singh** is Assistant Professor of English at Northern Michigan University.

**Gwenda Vander Steene** is a doctoral candidate in the Department of Comparative Sciences of Culture at Ghent University.

# INDEX

Page numbers in italics indicate illustrations.